F-111 AARDVARK

F-111 AARDVARK

Peter E. Davies and
Anthony M. Thornborough

First published in 1997 by
The Crowood Press Ltd
Ramsbury, Marlborough
Wiltshire SN8 2HR

© Peter E. Davies and Anthony M. Thornborough 1997

All rights reserved. No part of this publication may be reproduced or transmitted in any form or by any means, electronic or mechanical, including photocopy, recording, or any information storage and retrieval system, without permission in writing from the publishers.

British Library Cataloguing-in-Publication Data
A catalogue record for this book is available from the British Library.

ISBN 1 86126 079 2

Photograph previous page: two F-111Gs from the Buccaneers on the wing in 1992. The smart overall 'Gunship Grey' was first introduced at Cannon AFB, while USAFE examples retained their black, tan and greens. Cannon's long-spanned 'Gs were replaced by AMP'ed F-111Es from March 1993, and fifteen of the 'Golf' models were acquired by the RAAF. Courtesy of Craig Brown.

Typefaces used: Goudy (*text*),
Cheltenham (*headings*).

Typeset and designed by
D & N Publishing
Membury Business Park, Lambourn Woodlands
Hungerford, Berkshire.

Printed and bound in Great Britain by Butler & Tanner Ltd, Frome.

Acknowledgements

Seldom are aviation historians so privileged as to be given so much assistance by those intimately involved in a combat aircraft's operational genesis. To these crews and many others who helped us compile this book, and to many organizations involved over the years, we extend our heartfelt thanks:

Dennis Allen; The American Legion Association; Aeronautical Systems Division, USAF; Col Rob Balph; Col Thomas B. Barnes (Ret); Capt Dev Basudev; Kearney S. Bothwell; British Aerospace plc; Capt Craig 'Quizmo' Brown; Joseph B. Brown Jr; Maj Richard 'Downtown' Brown (Ret); Tony Cassanova; Maj James R. Chamberlain (Ret); Richard Colley; Roger Crysliver; Lt Col Lee P. Dodd Jr (Ret); 1Lt Bernadette J. Dozier; Lesley (née) Fisher; Don Flamm; Col Tom Germscheid (Ret); Michael Gibson; 'Chip' Glissom; Win Godwin; Karen Hagar; Roger Holman; Les Holland; Hughes Aircraft, Radars & Missiles; Capt Lewis Brad Insley (Ret); Capt Tom 'TJ' Johnson; Lt Col Jon Jordan; Maj George Kelman; Donald J. Laing; Col Ken Law; 1Lt Sonia E. Leach; Lockheed-Martin Tactical Aircraft Systems; Lois Lovisolo; Capt Greg Lowrimore; Capt Jim 'Scurvy' McIrvin; Maj Casey Mahon; Frank A. Markut; Col Richard M. Matteis (Ret); Col Roger J. Mathiasen (Ret); Dave Menard; Mike Moore; Northrop-Grumman Corporation; Wg Cdr Kym 'Koz' Osley, RAAF; Richard L. Palmay; Kenneth L. Perkins; Roger E. Peterson; Col David H. Reiner (Ret); David Robinson; Robert M. Robinson; Air Vice Marshal David N. Rogers, RAAF DCAS; Capt Chris Ross; Capt Frank Rossi; Maj James E. Rotramel (Ret); Chris M. Reed; Ed Rossman; Col Tom Runge; Lt Col Terry Simpson; Col David Skakal; Col Tony Sobol; Capt Greg Stevens; Texas Instruments Inc; United States Air Force; US Air Force Association; 'Aardvark Annie' and Mike Wate; Col Robert Wendrock; Lt Col Chuck West (Ret); Lt Col Roger F. Wickert; Col Chris Wright (Ret).

Contents

Acknowledgements		4
Glossary		6
Foreword: Dick 'Downtown' Brown		9
Preface		12
1	McNAMARA'S 'FLYING EDSEL'	13
2	MISSILEERS	27
3	ACES	35
4	BULLET BOMBERS	57
5	ECHOES AT UPPER HEYFORD	75
6	HIGH PLAINS DELTAS	95
7	THE SOUND OF FREEDOM	109
8	DESERT PIGS: *DESERT SHIELD* and *DESERT STORM*	125
9	BUCKSHOTS AND FALCONS	141
10	LAST OF THE RED-HOT PORCINES	153
Appendix I	USAF F-111 Operational Variant Main Differences	160
Appendix II	F-111 Production	163
Appendix III	USAF F-111 Units and Codes	183
Notes		186
Index		189

Glossary

A/A	Air-to-Air	APN	Airborne, radar, navigational aid	CNN	Cable News Network company
AAA	Anti-Aircraft Artillery				
AAR	Air-to-Air Refuelling	APQ	Airborne, radar, special purpose	CO	Commanding Officer
AB	Air Base			CPM	Combat Profile Mission
A/B	Afterburner	ARCP	Aerial Refuelling Control Point	CRS	rf-spectrum counter-measures receiving set
AC	Aircraft Commander				
ACC	Air Combat Command	ARS	Attack Radar Set	CW	Composite Wing
ACLS	Automatic Carrier Landing System	ASD	USAF Aeronautical Systems Division (Wright-Patterson AFB, Ohio)	CWIP	Colossal Weight Improvement Program
ADI	Attitude Director Indicator			DBT	Dual Bombing Timer
				DCC	Digital Computer Complex or Dedicated Crew Chief
ADTC	Armament Development Test Center (Eglin AFB, Florida)	ASP	Armament Select Panel		
		ASQ	Airborne, special type, combination of purposes	DDD	Detail Data Display
AEW	Airborne Early Warning	ATC	Air Traffic Control	DDI	Data Display Indicator
AF	Air Force	AUP	RAAF Avionics Update Programme	Det	Detachment
AFB	Air Force Base			DEWS	Defensive Electronic Warfare Systems
AFLC	Air Force Logistics Command	AVVI	Altitude/Vertical Velocity Indicator		
				DFC	Distinguished Flying Cross
AFFTC	Air Force Flight Test Center (Edwards AFB, California)	AWACS	Airborne Warning and Control System		
				DMZ	Demilitarized Zone
		BCU	Ballistics Computer Unit	DT&E	Development Test and Evaluation
AFSATCOM	Air Force Satellite Communications	BDA	Bomb Damage Assessment		
				DTM	Data Transfer Module
AFV	Armoured Fighting Vehicle	BDU	Bomb, Dummy Unit	EAM	Emergency Action Message
		BG	Bomb Group		
AGL	Above Ground Level	BRU	Bomb Release Unit	ECM	Electronic Counter-measures
AGM	Air-to-Ground Missile	BMS	Bomb (Medium) Squadron		
AIM	Air Intercept Missile			ECRS	Electronic Combat Range Squadron
AIR	Air Inflatable Retard	BW(M)	Bomb Wing, Medium		
ALE	Airborne, counter-measures, dispenser	CAP	Combat Air Patrol	ECS	Electronic Combat Squadron or Environmental Control System
		CARA	Combined Radar Altimeter		
ALQ	Airborne, counter-measures, special purpose				
		CAS	Close Air Support	ECW	Electronic Combat Wing
		CBU	Cluster Bomb Unit	EGT	Exhaust Gas Temperature
AMARC	Aircraft Material and Reclamation Center (Davis-Monthan AFB, Arizona)	CCIP	Continuously Computed Impact Point	EGUA	RAF Upper Heyford, Oxfordshire, England
		CCTS	Combat Crew Training Squadron	EGUL	RAF Lakenheath, Suffolk, England
AMI	Airspeed Mach Indicator	CFIT	Controlled Flight Into Terrain	EWO	Emergency War Order or Electronic Warfare Officer
AMP	Avionics Modernization Program				
		CMDS	Countermeasures Dispensing Set	FADF	Fleet Air Defense Fighter
AMRAAM	Advanced Medium-Range Air-to-Air Missile				
		CMRS	Cryogenic counter-measures receiver set	FCF	Functional Check-Flight
AMU	Aircraft Maintenance Unit			FOD	Foreign Object Damage
		CIA	Central Intelligence Agency	FOT&E	Follow-on Test and Evaluation
ANG	Air National Guard				
A/NTDS	Aerial/Naval Tactical Data-Link	CNI	Communication Navigation Identification	FS	Fighter Squadron or Federal Standards
AOA	Angle of Attack			FW	Fighter Wing

FWIC	Fighter Weapons Instructor Course	LED	Light Emitting Diode display	R&R	Rest and Recuperation
FWW	Fighter Weapons Wing	LGB	Laser Guided Bomb	RBS	Radar Bomb Scoring
FY	Fiscal Year	LLEP	Low Level Entry Point	RCS	Radar Cross-Section
G	Gravity	LOX	Liquid Oxygen	RDT&E	Research, Development, Test and Evaluation
GAC	Grumman Aircraft Corporation	LRU	Line Replaceable Unit	rf	Radio frequency
GBU	Guided Bomb Unit	MCO	Mission/Missile Control Officer	RHAWS	Radar Homing and Warning System
GCI	Ground Control Intercept	MEA	Minimum En-route Altitude	RLG	Ring Laser Gyro
GD	General Dynamics Corporation	MIA	Missing In Action	RP	Route Pack
GDFW	General Dynamics, Fort Worth Division	MiG	Mikoyan-Guryevich (Soviet-built fighter)	RSP	Radarscope Photography
				RTAB	Royal Thai Air Base
GE(USA)	General Electric Company, USA	MIL	Military (thrust, or SPEC/specification)	RTT	Realistic Training Target
				RTU	Replacement Training Unit
GFAD	Government Flight Acceptance Department	MFD	Multi-Function Display	RZIP	Rendezvous Initial Point
		MLG	Main Landing Gears	SA	Situational Awareness
GNC	General Navigation Computer	MMH/FH	Maintenance Manhours per Flight Hour	SAC	Strategic Air Command
				SAM	Surface-to-Air Missile
GPS	Global Positioning System, Navstar	MRC	Major Regional Conflict	SCP	Set Clearance Plane
		MSD	Multi-Sensor Display	SEAD	Suppression of Enemy Air Defences
HARM	High-speed Anti-Radiation Missile	MTBF	Mean Time Between Failure	SIOP	Single Integrated Operations Plan
HAS	Hardened Aircraft Shelter	MUO	Mountain Home AFB, Idaho	SIP	Structural Integrity Program/Systems Improvement Program
HF	High frequency				
HSD	Horizontal Situation Display	MX	Mission Specialists		
		NASA	National Aeronautics and Space Administration	SIS	Stall Inhibitor System
HSI	Horizontal Situation Indicator	NATF	Naval Air Test Field	SMALC	Sacramento Air Logistics Center (McClellan AFB, California)
HUD	Head-Up Display	NATO	North Atlantic Treaty Organization		
IBM	International Business Machines	NCU	Navigation Computer Unit	SMDC	Shielded Mild Detonating Cord
IFF	Identification Friend or Foe	NDDP	Navigation Data Display Panel	SOR	Specific Operational Requirement
IFR	Instrument Flight Rules	NDU	Navigation Display Unit	Sqn	Squadron
IMC	Instrument Meteorological Conditions/Capable	NLG	Nose Landing Gear	SRAM	Short Range Attack Missile
		NORAD	North American Air Defense		
IMU	Inertial Measurement Unit			STRC	Strategic Training Route Complex
		NOTAMs	Notices to airmen		
INS	Inertial Navigation Set	NVA	North Vietnamese people's Army	Stan/Eval	Standardization and Evaluation
IOC	Initial Operational Capability				
		OAALC	Oklahoma City Air Logistics Center (Tinker AFB, Oklahoma)	STU	Signal Transfer Unit
IOT&E	Initial Operational Test Evaluation			SUAWACS	Soviet AWACS
IP	Identification or Initial Point			SUU	Suspension Underwing Unit
		OAP	Offset Aimpoint		
IR	Instrument Route	OBC	Optical Bar Camera	SW	RAAF Strike Wing
JSS	Jamming Sub-System	OC	Officer Commanding	SWIP	Super Weight Improvement Program
KCVF	Cannon AFB, New Mexico	ODS	Optical Display Sight		
		ORI	Operational Readiness Inspection	TAB-V	Theater Air Base–Vulnerability (shelter)
KIA	Killed In Action				
kT	Kilotons yield	OT&E	Operational Test and Evaluation	TAC	Tactical Air Command
LADD	Low Angle Drogued Delivery			TACAIR	Tactical Air power
		PDM	Programmed Depot Maintenance	TAM	Tactical Air Meet
LARA	Low Altitude Radar Altimeter			TAWC	Tactical Air Warfare Center (Eglin AFB, Florida)
		POW	Prisoner Of War		
LCOS	Lead Computing Optical Sight	PPI	Plan Position Indicator		
		RAF	Royal Air Force (base)	TCTO	Time Compliance Technical Order
LDGP	Low Drag General Purpose	RAAF	Royal Australian Air Force (base)		
				TDY	Temporary Duty

GLOSSARY

TEOC	Technical Objective Camera	TTC	Technical Training Center	V/HUD	Vertical Display Indicator/Head-Up Display
TES	Test and Evaluation Squadron	TTG	Time To Go	VID	Virtual Image Display
TFR	Terrain Following Radar	TTT	Time To Target	VMC	Visual Meterological Conditions
TFS	Tactical Fighter Squadron	TTW	Tactical Training Wing	VR	Visual Route
TFTS	Tactical Fighter Training Squadron	TTWS	Terminal Threat Warning System	VSD	Vertical Situation Display
TFW	Tactical Fighter Wing	TW	Test Wing	VTAS	Visual Target Acquisition System
TFW(P)	Tactical Fighter Wing (Provisional)	UK	United Kingdom of Britain and Northern Ireland	WCP	Weapons Control Panel
TFX/-N	Tactical Fighter Experimental/-Navy			WCTB	Wing Carry-Through Box
		USAF	United States Air Force	WDC	Weapons Delivery Computer
TID	Tactical Information Display	USAFE	United States Air Forces Europe	Wizzo	*see* WSO
				WSO	Weapons Systems Officer
TIT	Turbine Inlet Temperature	USMC	United States Marine Corps	WTD	Weapons and Tactics Deployment
TJS	Tactical Jamming System				
TO	Technical Order	USN	United States Navy	WWMCCS	Worldwide Military Command & Control System
TOT	Time Over Target	VFX	Navy Fighter Experimental		
TRAM	Target Recognition Attack Multisensor	V-G	Variable Geometry	Z	Zulu or GMT

Foreword

The Navy EA-6B completed one more trip of its electronic jamming orbit as the pilot glanced at the brightly lit city in the distance. The night sky had begun to fill with anti-aircraft artillery tracers and surface-to-air missiles. It would be a rough night for the aircraft and their crews that were about to fly into that barrage of hot, deadly metal. Suddenly the night erupted into a bright orange flash. 'The first bombs', thought the pilot as his aircraft clock caught his eye. Precisely 0000 Zulu! Just as the Air Force officer had briefed on the aircraft carrier earlier that night. 'No wonder he gave us a "hack time" during the brief', the pilot recalled to his crew members. *Whispering Death* had struck a blow for freedom and was about to change aviation history forever.

As I sat among friends at the final F-111 farewell and reunion in July 1996 I found myself contemplating my nearly seventeen years in the Tactical Air Command's version of the F-111. Having the second highest total time in the F-111 (4,550 hours) and the most F-111 Instructor Pilot time ever (3,454 hours) it seemed that I had personally flown with many of the hundreds of people who had come to bid this mighty warrior goodbye. My mind wandered back to the first week of October 1974 when it all began. I had just received a telephone call from my wife. She told me that my squadron commander had called and said my next flying assignment and orders had arrived. It was an F-111 to Korat, Thailand by way of training at Nellis AFB. I thought to myself, 'What is an F-111 and what can it do?' My wife asked me the same question. I had no way of knowing then, so many years ago, that I would fly and come to admire one of the greatest fighting machines in history – the F-111 Aardvark.

'What is an F-111 and what can it do?' Not really a fighter but only a bomber! One of the many questions that beset the F-111 for nearly its entire life. The Aardvark – *Whispering Death* as it was called by the North Viet Namese – maybe the most misunderstood and unappreciated of all tactical aircraft; yet one of the most lethal. However, time has a way of vindicating cloudy issues. Finally on 14–15 April 1986, during *El Dorado Canyon*, the raid on Libya, this great aircraft took its long-due place in aviation history by projecting the tactical might of America in a retaliatory strike against the tyranny of terrorism. When it came time to call on a weapons system to champion America's resolve and the pursuit of freedom for all people, the choice was clear and undisputed – the F-111. There obviously was not another aircraft in the world that could have accomplished such a long and demanding mission! True, the raid on Libya could have been accomplished in part by a few other aircraft – well, at least they could have found the assigned targets and dropped their bombs (the Air Force, at that time, had several modern and more sophisticated aircraft than the F-111). One critical detail was that none of them could have flown the attack from England, in the middle of the night, flown a two-hour night low-level at 200ft [60m] and 570–640kt [1,060–1,190kph] from Sicily and back on internal fuel only, and against such formidable target defences. The F-111 and its people had been ready (they had always been – waiting to be called off the bench). As one Air Force General spoke summarizing the event, 'The raid on Libya may be spoken of by historians as on a level equivalent to the Doolittle Raid during World War II'. It was the longest projection of tactical airpower in the history of modern aviation. What once was the 'step child' of the tactical fighter community had transfigured itself, before the eyes of the skeptics, into an aircraft commanding awe and respect. The adversary had always known this (ask the North Vietnamese or the Soviets) it simply took the others all those years to figure out what we in the F-111 community had known all along! The mission commander of the raid stated later, 'This historic mission doesn't mean we are any better than anyone else. It just means we now have bragging rights'.

Shortly after *El Dorado Canyon* numerous people from all over the world, civilian and military, began to show up at RAF Lakenheath to view this once perceived lumbering, impotent and mysterious dragon now made alive (it was never dead or impotent – only in the minds of the uninformed). Immediately the question changed from 'What is an F-111 and what can it do' to 'I did not know you guys could do that – wow!' Tactical aviation's opinion of the F-111 had made a leap into a new dimension never to return again.

The F-111 was to go on in *Desert Storm* in 1990–91 and lead the Alliance forces in battle and again prove its unmatched record as the premiere low-level attack aircraft in the world.

I have deliberately not mentioned Viet Nam and the Aardvark's role there (a notable one, however). That conflict was near the F-111's inception and was nearly its undoing (through no fault of its own) while the raid on Libya was its crowning moment and revelation of the F-111's true capability to the military world.

Suddenly I heard my name called and I drifted back from the past to the present. Now some 32 years later after its birth, those who flew and maintained the Aardvark had gathered to bid one last farewell to a genuine and faithful friend – retired maybe prematurely but nonetheless retired.

One of the former F-111 wing commanders in a closing speech, at the farewell and reunion, accurately stated, 'The F-111 is simply just a machine. It is the people who have flown and maintained her who determine what she is and how she will be remembered'. As I studied the hundreds of people, who had gathered from near and far for this last tribute to the F-111, I could not help being astonished by the quality of the men and women with whom I had the privilege to serve and fly with for all those years. It was also a time of remembrance of the many faces of friends who were no longer with us. They had given the supreme sacrifice of their lives in defence of our nation.

If you are reading this foreword you are either an aviation enthusiast or simply curious. You now hold in your hand an extraordinary book written by Peter Davies and Tony Thornborough, who may be the ultimate historical authorities on the F-111. *Aardvark F-111* is a brilliant and unequalled labour of love and dedication. These authors have devoted numerous hours to meticulous detail and research that had produced the most accurate, credibly written and photographed, historical account fitting one of the greatest combat aircraft in the annuals of aviation history!

To Peter and Tony – I take the liberty in speaking for the entire F-111 community – we extend our deeply felt and profound thanks and appreciation for your efforts.

To my friends and fellow warrior-fighter Pilots and WSOs (Weapons Systems Officers) I offer my most sincere gratitude for the honour and privilege of serving, leading and flying with such a peerless and extraordinary group of people. And, to the men and women who made it happen on the ground – without you, none of this could have happened.

Finally to the F-111 Aardvark, we who have flown you say to a cherished and reliable friend, farewell and thanks for bringing us safely home in peace and war. You will lie in our hearts forever – may you now find the honour you have so long deserved!

God bless all,

Dick 'Downtown' Brown
F-111 Fighter Pilot 1974–1990

November 1996

Squadron and Campaign Patches

Preface

F-111 was a far-sighted concept; a harbinger of many new technologies which were revolutionary in their own right. Inevitably, these presented many development problems given the enormous challenge of combining them in a tactical-sized attack aircraft, and it was only through the dogged perseverance of the engineers and flight crews that the F-111 matured into such a remarkable weapons system. That it was overshadowed by bad press and a popular misconception of its true abilities really did not matter much in the end: the enemy respected the units flying the aircraft and were always extremely wary of them. That underlying acquiescence of the military effectiveness of the 'F-111 Program' was really the greatest accolade the aircraft and her crews could receive.

Amongst the many 'firsts' pioneered by the F-111 were the variable-geometry 'swing-wings', swept forward for slow approaches and maximum cruise economy and swept back for high-speed, 'glassy smooth' low-level flight. Then there was the escape 'module', which created something akin to a 'shirtsleeve environment' with full harness movement for the crew, and which avoided the horror of flailing injuries during ejection at high-speed. Stuffed inside the airframe was a fully integrated avionics suite which coupled attack and terrain-monitoring radars, instruments, computers, electronic penetration aids and stability-augmented flight controls for global navigation and precision strike in poor weather and by night. And the ensemble was pushed by an altogether new powerplant concept combining a five-zone augmented-thrust turbofan engine qualified to go supersonic at sea-level, fed by a variable spike inlet system (three firsts-in-one). There were a host of other 'firsts' which are also aired in this book. Crews praised its unique characteristics: a hitherto unprecedented operational independence from tankers and other support aircraft, a hefty warload of up to nine tons, and a low-level night-time penetration capability.

Things still did go wrong. Firstly, it took several years to resolve fully some structural issues (most of which were related to flaws in quality control at the sub-contractor level rather than anything inherent in its design). And maximum military (dry) engine thrust also remained slightly short even with the ultimate F-111F variant, which incidentally closed-out the run with 562 aircraft in November 1976. But the aircraft just kept getting better and better as the 'hiccups' were cured, and it was continually adapted during numerous updates and conversion programmes to keep it at the 'leading edge'.

By the mid-1980s these updates included laser and infra-red optronics so that the crews could see at night to deliver PGMs (Precision Guided Munitions), some of them supersonically. Ravens – known to their crews as Spark'Varks – were adapted with three tons of additional electronics to provide dedicated support-jamming, mostly to protect fighters of a less capable pedigree than the Aardvark. Reconnaissance, anti-shipping and counter-terrorist operations also entered into its repertoire. To cap it all, an American AMP (Avionics Modernization Program) and Australian AUP (Avionics Update Programme) was incorporated into much of the force beginning in the late 1980s to ensure its viability well into the next century.

Sadly for many, in the aftermath of renewed East-West relations, a new generation of 'bean counters' in charge of the purse strings showed a pronounced preference for the 'two wings of F-16s for the same Operations & Maintenance price of one F-111 wing', and with massively shrinking defence budgets to balance, the sophisticated F-111's days rapidly became numbered. Only following the unparalleled success of the Aardvark and Spark'Vark during the Gulf War – when the F-111F alone notched-up some 40 per cent of targets claimed as destroyed while representing a mere 7 per cent of USAF tactical air power – were these definitive models grudgingly afforded a little reprieve. However, the bulk of the force bowed out from service in 1992–93, and consequently AMP and the digital models' Pacer Strike update efforts were curtailed prematurely. The last of the F-111Fs flew to the 'boneyard' on Monday 29 July 1996; and it was only during that farewell weekend, 'The Last Hurrah', that the nickname Aardvark finally became official.

At the time of writing, the last of the Spark'Varks are also drawing-down, leaving just forty 'Pigs' (the more down-to-earth Antipodean nickname for the Aardvark) congregated at RAAF 'Super Pen' Amberley, near Brisbane. Australia has kept its faith with the aircraft and intends to continue operating the 'Pig' until the F-111 nears its sixth decade of service. Occasionally, they make visits to the US and Europe; so, if in the coming years you hear the 'The Sound of Freedom' and witness the unmistakable shape of the 'Vark in the skies darting above you, you can be certain it has Kangaroos painted on its flanks.

To close, the Aardvark aviators' enthusiasm for their remarkable steed is completely sincere, reflecting a real underlying confidence in the aircraft and its capabilities, particularly survivability. This, doubtless, in turn added to its operational prowess over the years, as crews continually 'pushed the edge'. Aardvark aviators undertook terrifying combat assignments, yet by far the majority of them lived to help further fine-tune the aircraft and many ultimately stayed with the machine as long as they possibly could: true testimony to a 20th-Century Aeroclassic.

**Peter E. Davies and
Anthony M. Thornborough**
November 1996

CHAPTER ONE

McNamara's 'Flying Edsel'

The F-111 and the ill-fated Ford Edsel were both products of Robert McNamara. Both products fell short of Mr McNamara's goals: the Edsel didn't sell and the F-111 was found to be unable to satisfy all of the Air Force and Navy requirements. In the pre-deployment days at Nellis, Dennis Graham found an Edsel which was in a poor state of repair and bought it just to get the distinctive grill from it. We hung the grill in the squadron lounge at Nellis and all had a big laugh every time we saw it. Col Dethman directed us to get rid of the grill; instead, Dennis Graham had it packed up and sent along to Takhli. The Thais are big on making nice wood carvings from teak wood. We purchased a 3ft-long set of wooden pilot's wings, mounted the grill in the center and mounted the combination in the pilot's lounge at Takhli. Seeing that helped to relieve the frustration and tensions of our situation!

Col Richard Matteis, on the inaugural 1968 combat deployment.

The Defence of Camelot

John F. Kennedy became the thirty-fifth and youngest-ever President of the United States on 20 January 1961. He took over from Gen 'Ike' Eisenhower, then the oldest incumbent, who had presided over an era in which US defence technology experienced spiralling levels of achievement – and cost. The legacy of air power's decisive roles in WWII and Korea had left a huge and somewhat inefficient, self-serving Pentagon superstructure in place, and a tradition whereby each of the proudly independent armed services made its own deals with suppliers for the equipment it required. Kennedy wanted American power projection abroad to increase markedly, but he also wanted to give taxpayers the impression that costs were being held down through improved efficiency. His advisors told him this could best be done by applying business management practices to the defence bureaucracy, and Kennedy's choice of Defense Secretary reflected this view. Robert S. McNamara, ex-Harvard Business School, ex-Ford Motor Company Vice-President was selected to impose cost efficiency upon the military.

Central to Kennedy's global defence strategy in 1961 was a significant increase in deployable tactical airpower. It was thought that this could be achieved with two new aircraft types; a light attacker (which eventually emerged as the LTV A-7 Corsair II), and a larger, long-ranging strike fighter, later to be called TFX (Tactical Fighter, Experimental). McNamara's observation of the McDonnell F-4 Phantom's development persuaded him that a versatile design such as that could be adapted for both Navy and Air Force needs, saving huge sums in the process.[1] His concept of 'commonality' began to take root and McNamara quickly envisaged larger applications. He studied the USAF's own new tactical fighter requirement alongside another major proposal, the US Navy's cancelled long-range Fleet Air Defense Fighter (FADF). This all-weather carrier-borne interceptor had been intended to loiter on Fleet Combat Air Patrol (CAP) carrying a large load of heavy missiles with a much longer range than the F-4 Phantom's AIM-7 Sparrows. Rather than high-speed or fighter-type manoeuvrability, FADF required a complex radar and missile control system and a fuel load sufficient to carry up to six Bendix AAM-N-10 Eagle missiles (forerunner of the Phoenix and weighing up to 1,000lb/450kg each) to a loiter station at the outer perimeter of a Naval Task Group's air defence circle. From there the aircraft was supposed to take out multiple threats approaching at any altitude at ranges of up to 130 miles (210km).[2]

The USAF's requirement, leading to TFX, was rather more complex. It had first taken shape in June 1960 as Specific Operational Requirement (SOR) 183. Its immediate purpose was to replace TAC's main fighter-bomber, the F-105 Thunderchief. Only 833 of these fast but rather primitive fighters, whose design role was nuclear strike, had been produced in Republic's 'Thunder Factory'. The F-105 mission was used as the baseline for SOR 183, but the new aircraft was expected to show better low-speed handling and a far shorter take-off run. A Thunderchief needed SAC-type 10,000ft (3,050m) runways and it used to be said that the fighter (and its F-84F predecessor) had a dirt-sniffer built into its nose-wheel so that it would not leave the ground until it picked up the scent of the earth at the end of the runway. Designing a relatively large airframe which would reach at least Mach 2.5, 'behave' at low speeds and land or take off in half the distance of an F-105 was a challenging task. Fortunately, NASA had a solution which was to provide the trademark for TFX: 'swing-wing'.

American research into variable-sweep wings began in America with the Bell X-5, a copy of a war booty Messerschmitt P1101 prototype, which flew in June, 1951. A year later the Grumman XF10F-1 Jaguar took to the air. Both used a system of translating rollers and rails so that the wing root moved fore and aft as the wing swept, in order to preserve the aerodynamic centre. This hydraulic or electric apparatus was prohibitively heavy and complex, but the two aircraft did show that variable sweep could work. John Stack, Assistant Director at NASA's Langley Research Center had developed in 1958 an arrangement originated in Britain whereby the wing roots 'swung' around a fixed pivot situated outboard of the aircraft centreline.[3] That way, less of the wing needed to swing and the inboard 'glove' area, into which the swinging portion folded, was an important lifting surface. Stack's tests affirmed the cg (centre of gravity) stability could be maintained in this very simple way with virtually no weight penalty. His findings were passed to the Commander of TAC (Tactical Air Command), General Frank Everest, who moved quickly to sell the idea of variable sweep to decision-makers in the Air Force and industry. It was thereby incorporated into SOR 183. Stack predicted that improvements in high-lift devices (wing slats and flaps) would improve short-field performance still further, giving the variable geometry aircraft the range and warload of a bomber with wings at mid-sweep, Mach 2.5 fighter performance with wings swept back, and docile short landings and take-offs with the wings spread.

As a further aid to long-range endurance Stack and Everest explored the idea of using a fuel-miserly turbofan in place of a conventional turbojet engine. Developed mainly in the UK for the commercial aviation market, the turbofan passes a proportion of the air from the compressor straight through the engine without entering the combustion process. This makes the engine more efficient than a pure jet, although normally at the cost of less peak thrust. But if a turbofan was equipped with an afterburner it could offer a useful military performance envelope, though this had not yet been done by 1960. Equally forward-looking were the two men's discussions of modular avionics to simplify maintenance and the use of new materials such as titanium in the primary structure. SOR 183 reflected their deliberations with its ambitious aims of Mach 0.92 at sea level for low-level strike/interdiction, Mach 2.5 for high-altitude interception, trans-Atlantic (3,000nm/5,600km) unrefuelled ferry range and the ability to operate from short (3,000ft/900m) unprepared airfields. Everest then insisted on Mach 1.2 as the low-level 'dash' speed, an extra demand which had important consequences. Both SOR 183 and the USN's replacement for FADF were extremely advanced concepts, including much unexplored technology, but in comparing them McNamara looked for 'commonality'. He defined the common features in terms of 'mission areas' which applied to both USN and USAF; air defence, strike, Close Air Support (CAS), etc. Increasingly, SOR 183 seemed to offer a basis for an adaptable shared design. Dr Harold Brown, his Director of Defense Research, was asked to examine the possibilities that a common SOR 183-based design, with a good measure of recognition of USN aims too, was indeed feasible – to the amazement of both armed services, and the Navy in particular. Admittedly, for carrier use, variable sweep was seen as a means of reducing landing speeds and improving take-off weights and performance on the catapult, neither of which were very strong points for the F-4 Phantom. Long range, space for heavy radar and missiles and good fuel economy were also thought to be achievable for Navy purposes. However, the Navy had its own ideas for a new fighter and plenty of helpful input from Grumman and Hughes to help define its goals.

In mid-February 1961, less than a month after entering the job, McNamara insisted that the USAF and USN should re-work their requirements around a mutually agreed design package. To McNamara the prospect of a 2,000-plus production run for the Navy, Air Force and Marines, with perhaps another 1,500 for export seemed to vindicate his policies. However, sensing hostility from the armed services he took the even more extreme step of removing procurement of new equipment from their direct control and setting up independent procurement agencies which were partly manned by cost-conscious civilians. His concept of overall programme management also embraced the establishment of Air Force Systems Command to control the development of new aircraft types. Traditional links between generals or admirals and their suppliers were therefore severed in the interests of competition and the elimination of wasteful duplication.[4]

Check that instruction sheet! The F-111's escape capsules were built by McDonnell Douglas and shipped to a final assembly line at GD Fort Worth for completion. Lockheed-Martin

TFX Competition

Predictably, both armed services resisted McNamara's instructions and continued to pursue their own design objectives in their 'commonality' meetings. By September 1961, McNamara lost patience and decided to impose an SOR 183-based project. This proved particularly disadvantageous to the USN as Everest's Mach 1.2 goal implied a much stronger, heavier airframe to withstand the stresses of supersonic flight at low level. FADF had needed only Mach 0.92 at sea level and a commensurately lighter airframe. Requests for Proposals for TFX were issued to the aviation industry on 1 October 1961, and by December McNamara's thirty-six man evaluation team had six responses on which to base their decision. All were basically similar, with passing external resemblance to today's F-111, but, unsurprisingly in view of SOR 183's extreme demands, none was selected.[5] Boeing's brochure seemed most attractive but it depended on the untried GE MF295 engine rather than a military version of Pratt & Whitney's JTF-10 turbofan (known as the TF30 in service) which featured in both the Republic and General Dynamics/Grumman submissions. (Grumman had been invited to team with GD in order to promote a USN-oriented design incorporating the Hughes radar and missile system.[6]) Boeing's Model 818 was favourite through three more rounds of the competition, in which it met an increasing number of SOR 183 criteria. Like the GD/Grumman proposal, which also met most of the requirements, it had two side-by-side seats, fitting a Navy need for a wide-nosed fuselage with a large radar dish instead of the tandem seats strongly favoured by the USAF. Twin TF30 engines, which Boeing finally accepted, were fed by dorsal intakes. GD put their intakes under the wing glove in their final submission, though most early drawings showed side-mounted semi-circular intakes with large, movable 'spikes'. Both companies opted for similar wing-gloves with an all-moving stabilator, mid-mounted on the rear fuselage and large enough to overcome the airflow disturbance caused by the thick glove. Boeing favoured a long-travel, high flotation main undercarriage whereas GD/Grumman went for a unique, wider, high flotation unit with massive semi-balloon tyres for rough-field work. It looked more suitable for a road-levelling machine than a supersonic jet.

The TF30-P-1 engine which powered early F-111As and the first five F-111Bs. The large three-stage fan (left) fronts an engine core whose final low-pressure stage is to the left of the engineer in the light-coloured shirt. The rear half of the unit is the long afterburner section. P&WA United Technologies

Despite general support from the USAF for the Boeing 818, McNamara reversed the selection board's choice of that design and told the Department of Defense on 24 November 1962 to announce GD/Grumman the winners. The resultant outcry included threats of legal action and accusations of fraud, leading to a Senate Committee hearing in 1963. McNamara, forced to defend his choice as a witness, conceded that the Boeing 818 won on price, range, loiter time and low-altitude handling. He defended GD's TFX on its longer fatigue life, better supersonic dash, internal ECM (Electronic Countermeasures) and, above all, commonality. Whereas GD proposed an airframe with 'a very high degree of identical structure for the Air Force and Navy versions, Boeing is, in effect, proposing two different airplanes'. Although McNamara won the day it was an inauspicious start to a major programme.

F-111A

General Dynamics signed the 'largest single airplane contract that has ever been awarded', with Grumman in charge of the USN version's (TFX-N) design.[7] All funds for 'start-up' were from the USAF, with the USN later to pay for the radar and missile systems development for their aircraft. The USAF designation F-111A followed the USAF version of the Phantom (originally F-110A) and was thought to be the last in the Century Series of fighters before McNamara introduced a new system of nomenclature.[8] Although they had won the contract against all predictions GD's problems were only just beginning. The extraordinary challenges of the new design were to require a number of technological breakthroughs at a time when most designers would have been delighted with only one. Apart from its revolutionary swing-wing the F-111 was to have the world's first afterburning turbofan and the first rough-field landing gear on a supersonic fighter. Also, it introduced automatic terrain-following radar for low-altitude day and night interdiction as well as a unique escape system.[9] Early design models included separation of the entire nose just forward of the intakes but the ejectable portion was progressively reduced to a capsule including the cockpit and relevant post-ejection support gear.

The sleek, simple lines of the F-111A, complicated only by the early 'quarter moon' air intakes with their translating cowls. Lockheed-Martin

Early RDT&E F-111As in maximum (72.5°) sweep configuration over west Texas, June, 1967. Tail number 63-9771 later tested an extended tail-cone body as a base drag reduction device. Both aircraft later served as ground instructional airframes. Lockheed-Martin

Escape Module

BACKGROUND Designed by McDonnell Douglas, the module was one of the least problematic innovations in the F-111, although its use involved an extremely complex automatic sequence of events. In keeping with GD's claim that the F-111 was the 'world's most tested aircraft', development capsules were subjected to 24,300 pyrotechnic firings (23,800 more than the Mercury space capsule). The parachute system was effectively demonstrated in April, 1967, and the full capsule system was proven on Holloman AFB's missile development test track that October. Aircraft No. 12 (63-9777) was the first to be fitted with the capsule, in May 1966. Earlier F-111As had standard Douglas Escapac seats as interim equipment.

AIRCREW PROVISION The F-111's crew were freed of the usual complex parachute harness and confining ejection seats. The 'chutes were in the capsule, not the seats. Although the manufacturers boasted that the cockpit provided a 'shirtsleeve environment', normal USAF dress rules applied, but without the need for the confining survival/immersion suit (which was stowed by the crew, when overwater operations were envisaged). The capsule contained generous supplies of survival gear (ranging from medical necessaries to such items as a fishing line and hook), and gave plenty of space for stowage of maps and other essentials.

OPERATION If 'punching out' was the final solution, either crewman could pull one of the yellow ejection handles situated each side of the central console. Ejection was possible at all speeds and altitudes, though a 50kt (90kph) forward speed was normally considered necessary for 'zero zero' bale-outs. If at low altitude, crews were briefed to perform a 'zoom-up manoeuvre' if possible, to bring the nose above the horizon to aid the upward trajectory of the module. Crews were also encouraged to trade speed for height whenever they could, as the chances of a successful ejection diminished marginally at altitudes below 2,000ft (600m) AGL. As for speed, the fastest successful ejection achieved by the USAF was from a rolling F-111D at Mach 2.0, a speed at which serious injury would have been almost certain in standard seats.

When the handle was pulled an initiation system was fired, consisting of shielded mild detonating cord (SMDC) in a complex series of one-way explosive 'transfer connections' to ensure proper sequencing of the ejection process. SMDC detonations operated guillotines which severed control cables, antenna leads and LOX lines (a gaseous oxygen supply was triggered), while at the same time the crew's inertia-reel harnesses were tightened. Barely 0.3 seconds from initiation an extremely powerful centrally-located Rocket Power Inc. motor blasted the capsule clear of the F-111, as a flexible linear-shaped charge detonated to cut the capsule free of the fuselage and let loose the stabilization 'brake chute'. It was obviously vital for the capsule to avoid tumbling or inversion, particularly for ejections in attitudes other than straight-and-level, and this was controlled by two rocket nozzles which corrected the capsule's trajectory automatically. To ensure that this balancing act worked correctly the aircrew pair had to be of similar weight. Document TO 1-1B-40 specified crew weight limits: crews plus paraphernalia were not to exceed 430lb (195kg), and the difference in their body weight was not to exceed 65lb (20kg), to ensure safe module operation.

During this complicated firework display a radio beacon was activated while a chaff dispenser 'marked' the ejection point for the radars of potential rescuers; a facility which could be cancelled in hostile airspace. In high-altitude ejections the system would wait until the capsule had fallen to around 15,000ft (4,600m), when a barostatic lock initiator released a catapult to deploy the main recovery parachute. (Until recent times three 'chutes were used, but a tendency to tear coupled with increased capsule weight caused their ultimate replacement by a single Kevlar canopy.) A further burst of pyrotechnics activated a UHF antenna and released compressed air into an inflatable 'mattress' attached beneath the capsule. This in turn deflated through blow-out plugs on landing, which was never a gentle affair. Increasingly weighty cockpit equipment in later F-111s made the impact rather more jarring than the aircrew would have expected in a normal parachute landing. Despite the straight-back-against the seat back routine, injuries occurred, particularly among taller aircrew for whom the seat's pitch-angle was harder to adapt to.

McDonnell Douglas designed the capsule to survive water landings too. Yellow handles on the canopy's central roof beam released the main recovery parachute and inflated a series of flotation airbags which righted an upturned capsule and then kept it at a stable attitude in the water. Capsule deployment from a ditched aircraft was also possible. If a leak developed the two control columns magically doubled as bilge pumps when moved fore and aft!

The capsule has a safety record comparable to standard ejection methods and it has preserved aircrew in some unusual circumstances. In one instance a capsule rolled down a mountainside in Nevada but survived, as did its occupants. The elaborate SMDC network and other 'pyros' were replaced at each Programmed Depot Maintenance (PDM) 'overhaul', standardized at four-year intervals.

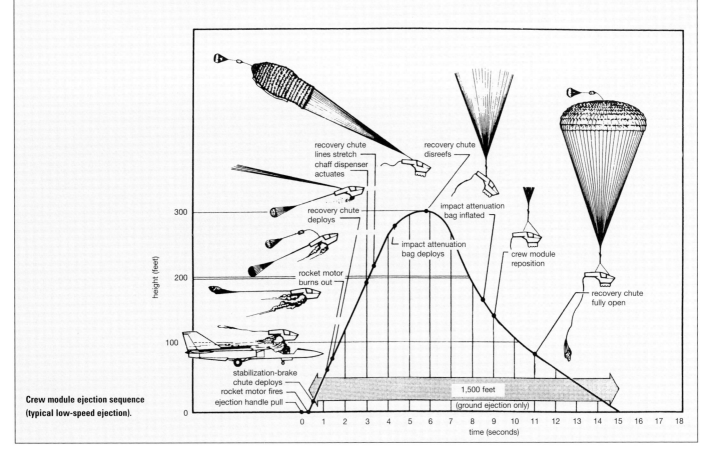

Crew module ejection sequence (typical low-speed ejection).

(Above) **In bare metal finish, the Number Four aircraft flight-tests Phoenix missile aerodynamic shapes for the F-111B programme. It was one of the busiest RDT&E airframes.** Lockheed-Martin

(Below) **A deluge of twenty-four Mk 82 LDGP bombs leaves the four multiple ejection racks (MERs) on 63-9772, which is also equipped with cameras at five points beneath the wing-tips and fuselage to record weapons separation.** Lockheed-Martin

F-111A 63-9772 (A1-07) seen again with Mk/B43 nuclear shapes on its four swivelling pylons. Lockheed-Martin

GD could at least rely on established technology for the F-111's attack radar. General Electric's AN/APQ-113 drew upon development work for the Navy's A-5 Vigilante and A-6 Intruder, as well as for the B-58 bomber, in providing a ground-mapping and target acquisition system for the new aircraft.[10] An entirely new pulse-Doppler set was needed for the F-111B. However, the automatic terrain-following radar was a new and separate installation which would allow the USAF version to follow the contours of the earth at pre-set altitudes as low as 200ft (60m). British research for the TSR-2 low-level strike aircraft provided some data, so did work at Cornell Laboratories, but it fell to Texas Instruments to develop this unique system for the F-111.

(Right)
The F-111As in the foreground became the Harvest Reaper aircraft, the first to be sent to Vietnam, and A1-40 (66-0022) was the first F-111A combat loss. Its Wing Carry Through Box is visible (lower right) with wing pivots at each end. Lockheed-Martin

Terrain-following Radar Systems

PHILOSOPHY OF TFR In the days before Stealth technology became available, terrain-following flight below the enemy's defensive radar umbrella – which guided flak, fighters and SAMs – offered the only realistic means of entering hostile airspace, hitting the target and coming back alive. Texas Instruments evolved the TFR system for several aircraft in the 1960s, but the F-111 was the first to adopt it as a 'hands-off' system that could be linked to the aircraft's autopilot controls.

MINIMUM EN-ROUTE ALTITUDE In understanding how Terrain-Following Radar (or TF'ing) flight was accomplished, it is important to appreciate that there were a multiplex of radars, computers and allied displays, and above all else a well-coordinated crew, all working in concert to ensure safety. It was not just a 'switch on and go' affair. This package, and related procedures, remained fairly constant throughout the aircraft's tenure with the USAF and RAAF, and later changes in systems nomenclature largely reflected reliability improvements.

The first thing crews did to help with safety happened on the ground. During Mission Planning, when crews plotted their flight plans on the 'bumpies' (contour maps), they would note the highest terrain obstacle within 5nm (9km) of the planned route – the course line – to the target and back. To this a safety margin would be added, later standardized at 1,000ft (300m) AGL (Above Ground Level) during peacetime training, and this became the Minimum En-route Altitude (MEA) for the mission. In combat, the MEA was usually around 500–700ft (150–210m) AGL and the value changed as the segment of the route progressed, so that combat routes had segmented MEAs. Pilots could 'crank' the altitude(s) into their AVVI (Altitude/Vertical Velocity Indicator), their right-hand tape instrument, and during subsequent 'let downs' and 'fly-ups' they would use this marker as a handy reference. Autopilot override was then required to actually reinitiate TFR flight.

LARA AND TFR RADARS The primary sensors engaged in automatic TF'ing flight comprised two 'bug eye' radars located behind the big radome, the AN/APQ-110 TFRs (Terrain-Following Radars), and a skin-flush, ventral nose barrel mounted Honeywell AN/APN-167 LARA (Low-Altitude Radar Altimeter) multiplex. With terrain-following activated, one of the two TFRs would scan ahead of the aircraft between a minimum of 1,250ft (380m) and as far as 5 miles (8km) along its velocity vector. It would search for terrain obstacles, and send commensurate pull-up and nose-over commands to the autopilot, to keep the aircraft automatically flying above the hard ground beneath. The other scanner was there as back-up, working in a ground-mapping mode out to between 5 and 15 miles (8 and 24km), and would take over if a failure occurred. Internal systems checks were accomplished automatically at 0.7 sec intervals. The LARA multiplex looked straight down to measure height up to 5,000ft (1520m) AGL, and was effective at bank angles of up to 45 degree and 20 degree pitch. If the aircraft went below 68 per cent (later 83 per cent) of the set TFR altitude – the SCP (Set Clearance Plane) – LARA would kick-in and command a 3–3.8g 'fly-up', automatically. For example, with a 1,000ft (300m) SCP selected, if LARA sensed that the aircraft had gone below 680ft (210m) AGL (the 68 per cent setting) the fly-up to the MEA would ensue. The fly-up manoeuvre was terminated by depressing the autopilot release lever on the stick, at which point the pilot would assume control while the crew fathomed out what was wrong, before resuming Auto TF flight.

LET-DOWN AND SET CLEARANCE PLANES Initial let-down from cruise height to the MEA was rapid but gentle, at a ten degree glide path, during which time the crews checked all was working 'as advertised'. Maj Jim Chamberlain described it this way;

> The airplane began a gradual descent at about a five degree nose down pitch angle until passing through 5,000ft [1,520m], where the radar altimeter detected the ground and the pitch angle increased.

When LARA locked-on to the ground, comparing height with the much lower SCP selected, the system initiated a relatively terrifying dive at 12 degrees at some 166ft/sec (50m/s), until they began to level off just before reaching the first SCP, at 1,000ft (300m) AGL.

> Almost the same procedure was followed on a night sortie except that the WSO spent more time monitoring the attack radar set [ARS], backing up the TFR and the route as best he could, given the nondescript territory over which we flew on most occasions. Mountain shadows were used to determine clearance over the knobs. As dark as the night sky was flying over the Great Desert, where there was nothing to see visually anyway. Vertigo was a constant enemy as there were very few lights on the ground so that it was very much like flying over water, where no horizon is visible. On a dark night it was far better to Auto-TF than to have in control a human, subject to vertigo, hand-flying at 1,000ft [300m] above the ground.

The crews could then 'step down' gradually to lower SCPs (thru 750, 500, 400, and 300ft) one stage at a time, culminating in as low as 200ft (60m) AGL. Cranking-down the SCPs necessitated some vigil. Jumping more than 'one click' on the knob might cause an unexpected 'fly-up' as the system would be unable to guarantee safety. Also, the 500ft (150m) SCP offered a special 'weather mode' which limited the processed scan area to about 2.5nm (4.6km) ahead of the aircraft, which was fine at speeds of up to Mach 0.85 when high terrain did not factor much (a feature used when crossing the coastline during the ingress of the attack on Libya in 1986).

RIDING THE RIDGES As Maj Chamberlain pointed out, it was the Navigator's job to inform the Pilot of impending high terrain (done as a matter of course, by looking at 'radar shadows' on the ARS and saying 'I see terrain we should be climbing over'), and to anticipate the really big climbs where extra thrust might be needed. The TF30 engines featured five-zone augmented thrust operation to assist with this, and engaging a modicum of augmentation (afterburner) was sometimes required. An aural tone was available to inform the crew of the ups and downs by 'beeps' and 'boops' on their headsets, which increased in intensity relative to the rate of climb or dive (at twenty pulses/sec per g), selected at the individual crew's discretion. 'High-Timer' Maj Dick Brown was unimpressed by it and remarked, 'I never turned it on in the aircraft. I found it extremely distracting, especially when listening to the RHAWS scope for threats. The primary terrain avoidance instrument was the E-Scope and if one was flying in the WX [weather] or at night then this scope should have been monitored constantly!'. Brad Insley, with slightly more hours in the left-hand 'command seat', reckoned that 'Most crews generally listened to the TFR aural commands. I know I did. You could monitor TFR performance while you moved your attention momentarily to other duties. You had to know what you expected to hear, of course, so that any change would get your immediate attention'.

DISPLAYS AND RIDE As Maj Brown emphasized, there were a number of cockpit instruments which were crucial in maintaining safety. In addition to the ARS under the Navigator's scrutiny, the TFR systems had their own dedicated scope located at the top of the instrument panel which furnished an E-Scope presentation, offering two distinct lines: a 'command line' denoting aircraft trajectory, and a lower 'video' or 'terrain line'. The idea was to keep the upper one from the lower one so as to avoid hitting the ground, without 'ballooning' excessively over ridges as that would show you up on enemy radar. With the Instrument System Coupler switched on, repeat pull-up and nose-over bars would appear on the gunsight (LCOS) and artificial horizon (ADI) display. Pilots often found the ADI 'sloppy' and so used the LCOS command bar and E-Scope, also monitoring altitude on the AVVI and listening to the right-hand seaters. In addition, the TFR scope could be switched to a SIT (Situation Display) mode (similar to the Ground-Mapping mode, a third option, used as back-up to the ARS), but which would show only terrain at or above the F-111's altitude, a handy quick reference for terrain avoidance. How close the aircraft would actually balloon over depended on the 'ride mode' selected: Soft, Medium or Hard. Medium was normal, with Hard being reserved for certain combat situations, as it was inclined to generate a zero-g cockpit environment during the nose-overs, when everything in the cockpit – maps, charts and other paraphernalia – would go flying about. It also only guaranteed clearing the terrain by 170ft (50m) at the 200ft (60m) SCP, quite disconcerting at transonic speeds of some 900ft/s (275m/s)! It is important to appreciate that Pilots, at all times, kept a vigil with their hands on the stick and throttles to apply power and pull-up (or nose over, if necessary). It was not literally a 'hands off' system as, despite an excellent track record of reliability, there were a number of well-known 'funnies' which could degrade the TFR.

PRECIPITATION Heavy rain or thunderstorm activity could seriously degrade the system, so crews used their main mapping radar, the ARS, to avoid weather cells whenever possible too. Crews were also instructed to climb to the MEA if the TFR display went blank under such conditions. 'Blanking' was routine over water or very flat ground, when the system reverted to LARA and safely assumed the terrain beneath was flat, thus bypassing the pull-up command. However, if weather (or sand- or snow-covered 'no show' terrain) caused 'blanking', the system might have made the same assumption and fly the crew into a hill or other obstacle! Crews thus had to be aware at all times of the terrain they were flying over, which is why so much time went into mission planning,

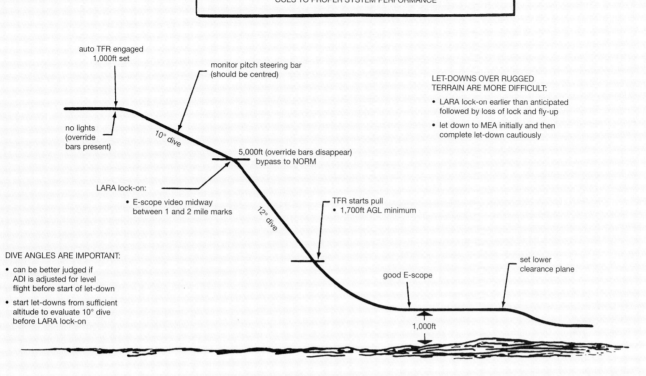

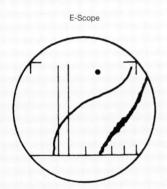
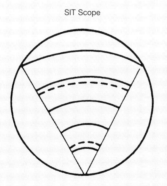

Typical auto TFR let-down profile.

and why the MEA was prescribed as a fail-safe. During the testing years, at least one crew flew right through a snowdrift lacing a gutter between two mountain peaks!

Other quirks of the TFR were encountered when overflying sparsely wooded areas. In the latter instance, tall, isolated trees would not be picked up and the aircraft might slam into one if it was taller than the lowest clearance of the 68 or 83 per cent fly-up threshold. Clumps of woods could also drive the TFR momentarily 'schizo', causing mini fly-ups. It all required considerable vigilance but a well coordinated crew seldom encountered any real problems. However, it explains many crews' particular dislike of trees and power lines, long after they have moved on from 'the program'!

OTHER LIMITATIONS The TFR scanners were programmed to 'look' into turns so that the crew would not slam into terrain they might not otherwise see during such a manoeuvre, and this effectively limited the aircraft to 30 degrees of bank (initially only 10 degrees of bank). The bank angle had a direct relationship with actual turning performance at different speeds and wing settings during 'hands off' flight, so crews had to study 'the curves' in advance and factor them in during Flight Planning. The TF would work on its own, but it would be no good asking the flight controls for such-and-such an input if the crew 'goofed' on the wing and powerplant settings, and the aircraft was unable to oblige! Much of the test-flying plotted these curves, to help crews avoid mismatched sweep/airspeed.

The next major area of technological advancement was the TF30 turbofan. Although it was based on an established powerplant it generated serious problems for GD and Pratt & Whitney, some of which were never fully resolved.

The first symptom of incipient design problems with the aircraft became apparent in its considerable and rapid weight increases. For the USAF the maximum weight ceiling rose considerably from the hoped-for 45,000lb (20,400kg) between the initial SOR proposal and mock-up construction. This was also considerably in excess of the USN's target. Partly, the weight originated from the more muscular structure to withstand Mach 1.2 at low altitude. Also it soon became clear from wind-tunnel testing that aerodynamic drag at the upper end of the performance envelope was higher than expected. The designers therefore found themselves entering the deadly syndrome of adding more power, therefore more fuel, therefore more weight, therefore more power, etc. Unlike the USN, the Air Force could live with a certain amount of extra bulk on its runways rather than sacrificing the all-important range criterion. However, the F-111 soon began to look less like a fighter, if dog-fighting and zippy manoeuvres are what fighters are all about.

Pratt & Whitney TF30 Turbofan

BACKGROUND Sir Frank Whittle's early jet engines were the first to use pure jet propulsion with no thought of using the jet turbine to turn a propeller. However, he also explored projects involving ducted fan and bypass engines where the airflow from a large first-stage fan at the front of the engine, driven by a core axial turbojet, was directed partly into a 'hot' gas turbine for combustion while the remainder passed around the core of the engine and mixed with the hot exhaust gases. Whittle's research from the mid-1930s was largely ignored for thirty years until General Electric and then Rolls-Royce began to design engines using a significant proportion of bypass air. The turbofan was seen to offer greater fuel economy and, with a very large front fan, reduced noise, despite having increased thrust. In the 1990s turbofans have largely replaced the older axial-flow turbojet. Pratt & Whitney's JTF10 two-shaft, single-spool turbofan was designed in 1958 for a four-engined airliner planned, but not built, by Douglas Aircraft. Its fuel economy and high thrust suggested military applications for TFX and the result was the TF30-P-1 (JTF-10A-20).

CONSTRUCTION The engine's three-stage titanium fan section, generating a mass flow of 247lb/sec (260lb/sec in the P-100 version) was constructed integrally with a six-stage, low-pressure compressor section. The seven-stage high-pressure compressor was connected to a 'can-annular' combustion chamber and eight Hastelloy-X flame cans. Its forty guide vanes (stators) and ninety-eight aircooled blades were of cobalt-based alloy (single crystal alloys in the P-100) allowing temperatures up to 2,000°F (1,090°C). An intermediate low-pressure turbine had three stages. The engine was used in this form as the TF30-P-6/8 in the A-7A/B Corsair II.[1] For the F-111A and later the F-14A Tomcat P&W added afterburning. For the P-1 thru P-12 variants this comprised a five-zone, double-wall unit with three spraybars, variable-area exhaust with six ram-actuated segments and an ejector nozzle with six blow-in doors. For the final variant, the TF30-P-100, a different nozzle was installed with eighteen 'petals' which slid along tracks of curved profile to increase or decrease nozzle area. At 3,900lb (1,770kg) weight, the TF30-P-100 was actually over 100lb (45kg) lighter than the much less powerful TF30-P-7.

SERVICE RECORD As the first practical military turbofan the TF30 was generally successful in offering high specific thrust for low fuel burn, plus strength and reliability. However, it suffered its share of problems.[2] Essentially, P&W designed compressors which were prone to stall (breakdown of smooth airflow through the engine leading to loss of power and probable engine damage). Like many jet engines it emitted a loud bang when stalled. The engine's military applications had only been explored in wind-tunnel tests and the problems were not revealed until it was flown in an F-111, which had intakes that exacerbated the problem. In service use the stalling problem was overcome by training in the selection of correct power settings. Improvements in power for the P-100 were attained with a new fan and LP compressor to handle increased airflow, a different (smokeless) combustion chamber and an improved afterburner. However, this 'hotter' TF30 also suffered reliability problems.[3]

TF30 VARIANTS

USAF Designation	P&W Designation	Thrust in A/B	Installation
TF30-P-1	JTF10A-20	18,500lb (8,390kg)	Early RDT&E F-111A/B
TF30-P-3/-103	JTF10A-21	18,500lb (8,390kg)	F-111A/C/E
TF30-P-7/-107	JTF10A-27D	20,350lb (9,320kg)	FB-111A (F-111G)
TF30-P-9/-109	JTF10A-36	20,840lb (9,450kg)	F-111D, EF-111A
TF30-P-12	JTF10A-27A	20,250lb (9,180kg)	Late F-111B
TF30-P-100	JTF10A-32C	25,100lb (1,1380kg)	F-111F

Notes:
1: Use of the TF30 for the A-7 was another offshoot of McNamara's commonality policy. Although it offered good range characteristics it left the A-7A/B underpowered and was replaced in the A-7E (USN) and A-7D (USAF) 'common' variants by the more powerful Rolls-Royce/Allison Spey-derived TF41-A-1.
2: In the F-14 these led to many aircraft losses through compressor stall and blade-loss problems. Navy Secretary John F. Lehman commented angrily that it was 'the worst engine/airplane mismatch in history'. The final TF30-P-414A had 200lb (90kg) of extra steel armour to prevent compressor blades from penetrating the engine case if they flew off. The USAF would have like a follow-on engine for its F-111 fleet. Veteran Aardvark pilot Brad Insley commented, 'Everyone who flew the F-111 would have liked the GE F110 engine'. USN Tomcat pilots had to wait until 1986 before its F-14B first flew with this engine and a limited re-engining programme began.
3: 'Century Series' engine designations were applied to TF30 models in 1988.

Flight Testing

YF-111A 63-9766 rolled out at Fort Worth on 16 October 1964, two weeks ahead of schedule. It flew for the first time on 21 December. GD's Chief of Flight Testing, Dick Johnson and flight test engineer Val Prahl kept the wings spread at twenty-six degrees and 'everything down' for a flight which was cut short at twenty-two minutes after a compressor stall on take-off. Wing sweep worked well for the second flight on 6 January 1965 but both engines stalled when Johnson attempted supersonic flight, forcing him to 'bug out' at 460kt (850kph). Supersonic flight was not achieved until 5 March and it seemed that engine stall problems would prevent the new 'Mach 2.5 fighter' from going any faster than Mach 1.2. Some serious re-thinking of the engine/intake combination was obviously needed. Initially, attention turned to the TF30 engine.

Although P&W had engineered the TF30 rather too close to the 'surge line' in the quest for maximum thrust, contributing to the stall problem, there were certainly difficulties with the intakes. A long, carefully contoured intake (such as the F-4 Phantom's) can 'discipline' the airflow into a smooth, steady stream before it hits the front of the engine, ironing out flow inconsistencies due to angle of attack or large throttle movements. But this is usually at the cost of reduced overall efficiency, and intake design is normally a finely balanced trade-off between maximum engine performance and reliable operation in all flight regimes. GD chose an extremely short intake with marked changes in cross section between the outer 'lips' and the engine, which permitted little time for

Richard L. Johnson

'Dick' Johnson flew the F-111 on its maiden flight on 21 December 1964, and was instrumental in easing the aircraft through its complex, painful growing phase in the 1960s, heading the General Dynamics test team during the Category I (contractor) F-111A flight test programme. He also was the first to demonstrate the swing-wing system in the aircraft, and made the first ever supersonic sortie in the aircraft.

A native of Cooperstown, North Dakota, Johnson entered the Air Force in 1942 and flew 180 missions as a fighter pilot in the Mediterranean Theater of Operations before going on to qualify as a USAF test pilot, accumulating 4,500 hours in multiple aircraft types at Edwards AFB, and retiring with the rank of Lieutenant Colonel. In 1953 he joined General Dynamics' Convair plant in San Diego, California, and became chief engineering test pilot for the F-102 and F-106 programmes, before heading-up their Fort Worth, Texas, F-111 programme.

In October 1967 he was awarded the coveted Iven C. Kincheloe Award at the annual SETP (Society of Experimental Test Pilots) meeting in Los Angeles. By that stage he had accrued 230 flying hours in the F-111, and was cited for 'Consistently flying F-111 aircraft on their most demanding missions'. These included solving the engine/airframe matching process, supersonic flutter tests, refining the flight control system, and low-level TFR radar trials. At the time of the award he had led the GD contractor team through more than 1,800 accident-free flying hours – an astonishing feat.

A confident wave from GD Test Pilot Dick Johnson following the first flight in YF-111A (63-9766), which he undertook with co-pilot Val Prahl.

the airflow to be 'smoothed' inside the duct. Stalls were occurring in straight and level flight, let alone the violent manoeuvres which had originally been planned for the 'fighter' end of the F-111's performance specification. At East Hartford the TF30-P-1 was modified with more stall-tolerant blade angles and a sixth-stage bleed-air vent to prevent 'choking' at high speeds. This became the USAF-standard P-3 engine, though the modifications did little to reduce stalling. GD set about redesigning the intake, a task which eventually cost $100m without providing a full solution. Fortunately, however, GD's modifications worked best for the low-level, high-speed flight regime which became the F-111's primary mission and for which the intake had originally been optimized. Through extended tests of a wide selection of intake configurations, the 'Triple Plow' intake evolved.

As these development problems slowed the programme and pushed up costs, McNamara's dream of 'saving a billion dollars' began to fade. In simple terms the cost

TF30: An Engineer's View

Ed Rossman worked on TF30 development at Pratt & Whitney Aircraft from 1962 and described a few of the problems to the authors:

> TF30 was one hell of a challenge. The early years of development were very frustrating partly because the firm didn't receive an F-111 flight test-bed [aircraft No 2, 63-9767] until 1966. Previously, engine testing had to be done in a B-45 bomber with the engine deployed on retractable banana links from the bomb bay. Hundreds of pressure taps and temperature pickups were employed on each test engine. We never had a catastrophic failure in the air, but exploded some test-cell engines big-time on the ground.
>
> When the YF-111A test-bed was received, testing moved from the East Hartford company runway to the Connecticut Air National Guard facility at Bradley Field Airport.
>
> The F-111 carried a test pod in its weapons bay which resembled a coffin. It was loaded in by brute manpower and we used rather primitive instrumentation. Our 'constant temperature base' of 32°F [0°C] was a Thermos jug filled with ice and water with probes installed through the lid. All temperature data was compared to this. When the YF-111A made its first test flight it could not get power up at the end of the runway. It had numerous compressor stalls before the fifth zone afterburner could be engaged. Commercial aircraft were backed up at the terminal and the airport manager was furious! Finally, the P&W test pilots put their feet against the throttles as the throttle cables were binding and blasted off.
>
> Later they said they knew they had made a mistake – it was a battle to retard the throttles! The stalling on acceleration was an intake design fault. We at the P&W factory had done inlet distortion tests and we later proved this to General Dynamics, although there were some harsh words between GD and P&W folks over this point. The intakes were changed.

The formal date for going ahead with the revised inlets, called Triple Plow I, is recorded on former GDFW documentation as having been made on 29 April 1967. Production of the even more tolerant, but slightly 'draggier' Triple Plow II inlet began in March 1969.

F-111 Intake Variants

TRIPLE PLOW I The top of the splitter-plate was curved in towards the fuselage and the intake's inner face had a notched side-plate and twenty vortex-generators. The intake lip had increased radius. The front cowl of the intake translated hydraulically fore and aft. This intake actually allowed the highest top speed.

Application: late RDT&E F-111, first FB-111A (67-0159) and all production F-111A/C (and EF-111As, which were adapted from production F-111A airframes).

SUPER PLOW An interim version of the Triple Plow II with only two blow-in doors.

Application: F-111Bs No 7 (152715) and FB-111A No 2 (67-0160).

TRIPLE PLOW II Triple blow-in doors, no splitter plate. Cross-sectional intake area 10 per cent bigger and relocated 4in (10cm) from the fuselage side (away from the troublesome boundary-layer airflow near the fuselage), causing extra frontal drag. This version required redesign of the entire intake and several fuselage frames. Intake 'spikes' were lengthened by 18in (46cm). RAM (Radar Absorbent Material) panels were also added inside the intake to reduce frontal radar signature.

Application: FB-111A No 3 (67-0161) and up, and all F-111D/E/F.

(Right) **With wings set in the 'cruise' position the F-111A's relatively small wing area and large tail are more apparent.** Lockheed-Martin

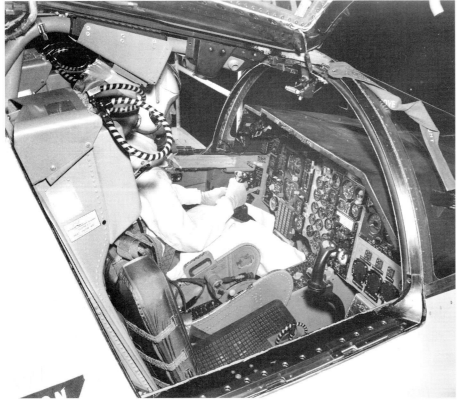

An early RDT&E cockpit shot. The right-hand portion of the cockpit was filled with monitoring dials rather than the radar and Bomb-Nav switches of later builds. The early Escapac ejection seats are also noteworthy. Lockheed-Martin

of a single F-111 rose from $4.5m at the beginning of the programme to over $10m when the last new aircraft was rolled out in November 1976.[11] Rising cost estimates had already damaged the prospect of a long production run when the original production contract was signed on 12 April, 1965, reducing the total envisaged buy to 431 aircraft; a cut of 50 per cent. One consequence was cancellation of the RF-111A reconnaissance version.[12] Testing all the F-111A's revolutionary systems required no fewer than twenty-nine Research, Development, Test and Evaluation (RDT&E) aircraft plus the prototype (six more than originally planned) of which seventeen were later upgraded for service use, albeit as ongoing trials platforms and initial training aircraft. Part of the problem was that McNamara, with the understandably eager support of the manufacturers, had given the go-ahead for production before the F-111's first flight. Squadron aircraft were flowing from the production *before* the RDT&E team had resolved all the complex problems facing this revolutionary design. Modifications therefore had to be

(Above) **F-111A 65-5708, the 26th RDT&E airframe, was the first with a fully operational ECM fit including the ALR-23 fin-tip CMRS/IRRS.**
Lee P. Dodd

A dramatic time-lapse photo showing the extent to which the F-111's wings were flexed by hydraulic rams during cold-proof testing. Freezing gaseous nitrogen was circulated over the airframe by the ranks of electric fans. Lockheed-Martin

retrospective, rather than on the production line, adding still more to the bill.

The test programme was vast in its scope nevertheless. Aircraft No. 4 was 'tufted' for aerodynamic research, testing swivelling pylons, which could stay front-facing while the wing swept, and carrying dummy Phoenix missiles for the USN programme. No. 7 trialled a twin-Sidewinder missile installation, extended from the new weapons bay trapeze, similar to that in the F-106. Other test machines demonstrated the aircraft's warload with up to thirty 250lb (115kg) bombs on eight pylons (two pylons were later deleted, owing to stores flutter problems at lower airspeeds). However, by the end of December 1966, when the last development aircraft had been delivered, major systems, including the crew escape capsule, Terrain-Following Radar (TFR) and internal M61A-1 gun were still far from

completing their trials. The F-111A was only eighteen months away from its combat debut in Vietnam. In March 1967 Dr J.S. Foster, Director of the Defense Department's Research & Engineering, stated that the F-111A had failed to meet altitude, rate of climb and manoeuvrability requirements. Weight increases had taken it more than 12,000lb (5,400kg) above the contractor's guaranteed gross take-off figure of 69,122lb (31,347kg). It was also down on ferry range, though the expectations on that issue were always unrealistic. Although the No. 2 aircraft had reached Mach 2.5 on 9 July 1966, compressor stalls above Mach 2.2 still occurred. Sensibly, Dr Foster still sanctioned $989m for initial production, although he may not have sensed that high altitude and interception at Mach 2.5 were soon to be seen as total irrelevances for an aircraft which would become the world's premier low-level striker. Although much progress had been made, many people would at that stage have concurred with the views of the *Armed Forces Journal* Editor, Ben Schemmer, that TFX could well have stood for *Terrible F***** Experience*.

F-111E production gathers pace at General Dynamics' huge assembly building in 1970.
Lockheed-Martin

(Below)
The RF-111A testbed which first flew on 17 December 1967 was intended as the first of many reconnaissance examples; however, discounting four much later and completely different RAAF RF-111Cs, it was unique. It ended its days as Gate Guardian at Mountain Home AFB in Idaho.
Lockheed-Martin

CHAPTER TWO

Missileers

Today, some thirty-one years after project pilots Ralph Donnell and Ernie Von Der Heyden took their promising, bright and shiny F-111B (Article A2-01/BuNo 151970, the first Navalized Aardvark) into the skies above Calverton, there remains just the remnants of two heavily dilapidated TFX-Navy testbeds. Neither has received the slightest bit of attention since they were unceremoniously dumped at the conclusion of their test programme in May 1971, and the two hulks have since all but corroded away at McClellan and China Lake, California. Yet ironically, it was this aborted and long since forgotten model which was primarily responsible for determining some of the more peculiar physical characteristics of the F-111.

The cancellation of the FADF left a gaping hole open to farsighted systems developers. Aware of the potential, and a Navy paper called *Fighter Study I*, Grumman had already been at work on a design concept since May 1960 and were liaising with Hughes, who were rapidly developing the kind of radar and missile technology needed to satisfy the requirement.[1] Although the Air Force would eventually be responsible on a *de jure* basis for managing the TFX project, it seemed that it was the behind-the-scenes work by Hughes and Grumman engineers which really convinced the new Kennedy Administration of the need to buy their weapons system package to meet Navy requirements, and which got the whole show on the road. The Air Force was essentially instructed to incorporate the Navy's needs into the subsequent Joint-Service RFP (Request For Proposals) and get on with it, adapting SOR-183 as needs be. Individuals such as Hughes Radars' Jim Ferrero, assistant programme manager to Meade Livesay, and Allen Lange, toured umpteen Navy and Government offices for well over a year and no doubt helped precipitate McNamara's 'shock' pronouncement of 11 November 1962, which effectively overrode the Air Force's plans to proceed with development of what they saw as the 'less undesirable' Boeing proposals.

Based on their experience with the Douglas F3D Skyknight in which the pilot and radar operator had been able to work in concert in a side-by-side cockpit, the Navy and the Marines favoured this arrangement for operations at night and in inclement weather, rather than the tandem arrangement the Air Force wanted. The fact that the radar would need a huge antenna to provide adequate search range inevitably also influenced this seating arrangement and, even before the issue of the RFP on 29 September 1961, General Dynamics, recognizing the need to bring a specialized Navy contractor onboard to help with its own tender, asked Grumman to team up. It all fell into place very quickly with GD, Grumman and Hughes proposing the most credible seagoing fighter package and adding the Air Force 'swing wing' feature, further refined with sealed fuel-containing aerofoils equipped with leading-edge slats and double-slotted Fowler flaps originally developed for the A2F-1 (A-6) Intruder. This would ideally suit shipborne launches and recoveries while providing extended loiter in the FADF mode at the BARCAP (Barrier Combat Air Patrol) coordinates, together with the option of sweeping the wings back for a fast zoom intercept.

Boeing's delightful offering was essentially 'two airplanes for the price of one' with 60.7 per cent commonality (versus the 83.7 per cent of the General Dynamics/Grumman single baseline-aircraft-with-different-avionics concept) but was dismissed by McNamara as loaded with potential risk. The new Secretary for Defense was mostly interested in bottom-line economic appraisals, and later cited Boeing's cost estimates as being unduly optimistic. There probably also existed fears that some of the materials technology – particularly Boeing's proposed extensive use of titanium alloys – would present potential problems with strategic mineral reserves and exotic alloy supply at a time when Lockheed were busy at work on the strategically vital but covert *Oxcart* effort, which would spawn the all-titanium Mach 3 Blackbird series.[2]

Although the USAF did not care much for the GD-Grumman submission, the choice of steel for extensive use deep in the structure of their proposal must also have appealed to McNamara's 'think tank'.[3] General Dynamics also had the factory floor space and an established track record at producing complete 'weapons systems', such as the F-102/F-106 and brand-new majestic B-58 Hustler. Grumman, on its own turf, was fast developing a reputation as a superb systems integrator on the emerging A2F-1 (later A-6) Intruder and W2F-1 (later E-2) Hawkeye programmes to add to its fine heritage as a Navy airframe manufacturer, a 'double whammy'. And, as Secretary for the Navy Paul H. Nitz commented during the F-111B's roll-out at Peconic River on 11 May 1965 three years later, this greatly influenced Naval planners. Grumman would be able to fully integrate the Hawkeye AEW (Airborne Early Warning) 'Eyes of the Fleet' with TFX-N to create what became known some years later, when its similarly-equipped VFX (Navy Fighter Experimental) successor was entering service, as 'The Clean Air Act' team.

Ironically, TFX-N would barely survive beyond July 1968 and only ten airframes were ever built: one dedicated F-111B static test example (Article A7), seven flying examples (Articles A2-01 onwards) and two production machines which were never completed and which were scrapped before they could fly – a far cry from the originally envisaged 231 F-111B production run, and all the more irritating to the Air Force as TFX-N would merely act as catalyst to pave the way for development of Grumman's VFX V-G winged, TF30-powered, Hughes radar/missile-equipped *tandem seat* Design 303 – the remarkable F-14 Tomcat.

Bravos

As chief subcontractor to GD under the new arrangement, Grumman was responsible for building the horizontal stabilizers, undercarriage and aft fuselage sections for

Fresh from the paintshop, the first F-111B (BuNo 151970) complete with 'barbershop pole' test boom ... Northrop-Grumman

... and on its 1hr 19min maiden flight on 18 May 1965, with bespectacled GAC Project Pilot Ralph 'Dixie' Donnell and Ernie Von Der Heyden at the controls. The finer aspect ratio of the longer wings are evident here. Northrop-Grumman

F-111B A2-05, BuNo 151974, the fifth RDT&E 'Bravo', with Chief Test Pilot 'Dixie' Donnell and GFAD co-pilot Dave Cook onboard in November 1966. The bare metal aircraft crash-landed at Point Mugu in October 1968 and was subsequently scrapped.
Northrop-Grumman

all TFX/TFX-N aircraft built, and eventually produced 557 ship sets of these items. They also were responsible for integrating the avionics and final assembly of the Navy version – which became known as the F-111B in October 1962 as part of the US Department of Defence weapons systems nomenclature changes – at Bethpage.

As already outlined, the ostensibly 'common' TFX-N design similarly traded off out-of-cockpit visibility and aircraft manoeuvrability in favour of range/loiter, cruise economy and a capacious airframe capable of taking aloft a heavy avionics package and missile load – in this instance the Hughes Aircraft Company 4ft (1.2m) diameter AN/AWG-9 long-range search radar and allied fire control systems which would help guide the company's promising new active radar-guided AIM-54 Phoenix missiles. Optimized for the FADF requirement, up to six of these mighty weapons could be carried underwing on the pivot-pylons and in the weapons bay. The length of the aircraft was reduced by 6ft 9ins (2m) by means of a shorter nose barrel and much squatter radome, to enable it to use standard Navy carrier deck elevators, and the wings were extended by 7ft (2.1m) and consequently increased in area from 525sq.ft to 550sq.ft (49sq.m to 51sq.m) to endow the machine with longer on-station endurance. In addition, a carrier-compatible arresting hook, bigger tail bumper, undercarriage tie-down rings and nose catapult tow bar were all gradually incorporated, alongside changes to the CNI (Communications, Navigation and Identification) equipment. A Hughes nasal Infra-Red Search and Track (IRST) detector was added to assist with target discrimination amidst heavy radar-jamming, and engine specifications were altered to accommodate lower-volatility JP5 and slightly different power-generating requirements. Finally, the MLG wheels were redesigned from scratch (the Air Force version used C-130 stock). These measured 42in × 13in (106cm × 33cm), some 5in (13cm) narrower and smaller in diameter than the lower pressure Air Force equivalents.

Many of these features evolved through the test programme, but most were apparent by the time mock-up approval was granted in August 1963, authorizing the fabrication of five RDT&E aircraft for Fleet trials and systems integration. Following the 1hr 19min maiden flight on 18 May 1965, A2-01/BuNo 151970 continued its solo tests to log an additional 44 flights/63.6hr (including nine supersonic runs, one of them sustained for a testing 37 minutes), before any companions joined the effort. On 24 October the second F-111B joined the programme and Navy Preliminary Evaluations began. By early Spring 1967 there were five aircraft working full-time on the programme, with test flights conducted adjacent to the Calverton Plant 6 in Long Island (the aircraft were assembled at Bethpage and transported to Calverton for maiden functional flight tests), Hughes' facility at Culver City, California (where the testbeds were kitted-out with the radar systems and displays), NATF (Naval Air Test Field) Lakehurst, New Jersey and the Naval Missile Test Center at Point Mugu, California, and also Edwards AFB, the latter supported by Plant 74 GFAD (Government Flight Acceptance Department), stationed in Building 1870 with a hangar and administrative space. Edwards offered a faster-paced flight test environment than the East Coast and F-111B A2-01 moved there in September 1967, with A2-05 joining it at the end of the year. The flying was undertaken by GFAD chief pilot John Norris, engineering test pilot Bill Miller and flight engineer Doug Reynolds, supported by ground staff and six engineering specialists, with GD and AFFTC personnel also climbing aboard to wring the aircraft out. There was only one stick, so the right-hand seater was either there for the ride, or to work the CNI and intercept avionics.

The Hughes radar/missile package worked almost flawlessly, and the big F-111B airframe certainly met the revised FADF role. Much of the trials work undertaken with AEW and shipborne platforms remains classified to this day: the datalinks used to exchange information were incredibly sophisticated and could be coupled to the 'Seavark' for hands-off target vectoring and even the dispatch of missiles by remote control, even amidst extensive RF-spectrum jamming.

F-111B Intercept Avionics

V/HUD, TID AND DDD COCKPIT DISPLAYS Grumman, in partnership with Kaiser Industries, developed the World's first TV-style contact-analogue display for use in the A-6 Intruder, known as the 'pilot's highway in the sky', which effectively replaced the traditional ADI instrument and combined attitude director information with target attack data. Combining this technology with the Hughes AN/AWG-9 fire control system plus Litton INS and the Central Air Data Computer, optimized for an air-to-air format was a natural evolutionary step for the F-111B. This advanced package resulted in a set of displays which offered synthetically processed flight and target data rather than 'needles and dials' or raw, direct view radarscope imagery (though there existed a set of back-up instruments and modes).

The pilot was furnished with a Vertical Display Indicator/Head-Up Display (V/HUD), comprising a circular HUD combining glass and TV video, and the Missile Control Officer with a Tactical Information Display (TID) and Detail Data Display (DDD) to handle the AWG-9 radar and Phoenix missiles. The two sets of displays were fused so that the MCO could provide the pilot with accurate target vectors and navigational steering cues for interception and carrier recovery. Similarly, the MCO would also 'talk' electronically, via secure aerial or Naval Tactical Data Link (A/NTDS), with E-2 Hawkeye Airborne Early Warning and Fleet ship-based fire control centres to pass or receive information on potential enemy 'bogeys' (unidentified targets) and 'bandits' (confirmed hostile aircraft), at the push of a button. AN/ASW-27 A/NTDS could even be used with the F-111B in autopilot to fly the 'Seavark' on an optimum intercept course to unleash its deadly cargo of Phoenix missiles, and to help with carrier landings, feeding the pilot with Automatic Carrier Landing System (ACLS) glidescope information.

The package evolved during the course of the F-111B trials programme, 1965–71, with alphanumerics later added to the TID display to provide detailed target data at a quick glance, while the 'tadpole tails' grew with bead and rectangle markers to denote maximum, optimum and minimum missile launch parameters for the individual targets, along with related time to launch. Weapons launch itself relied on selecting the weapons one at a time via a station select knob, and pushing a large red button on the right-hand side of the cockpit, all under MCO control. The follow-on F-14A Tomcat shared virtually common systems at the cross-over point, 1970–71, including the V/HUD and DDD/TID displays, but with expanded weapons capability encompassing an M61A-1 20mm gun, plus AIM-9 Sidewinder and AIM-7 Sparrow missiles. More significantly perhaps, it offered expanded V/HUD radar auto-acquisition for Sparrow, a Honeywell-mounted VTAS sight for Sidewinder (in the early years), and thus full pilot authority over the weapons. The right-hand 'Missile/Mission Control Officer' in the F-111B was replaced by a less grandiosely titled rear seater known as the 'Naval Flight Officer' or 'Radar Intercept Officer' in the Tomcat. Antipathy by pilots towards the Navigator 'running the show' was no help to the TFX-N effort either!

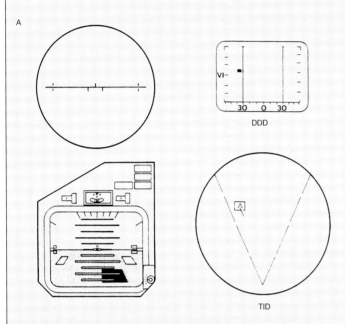

A. V/HUD Displays at left are in the 'Normal' mode, used for navigation and monitoring aircraft attitude, altitude and airspeed. (*Further flight director information is described in B and C below.*)

The DDD (upper right) could be used to display single targets in a number of modes: 'range rate' – relative target velocity and bearing, as depicted; radar or infra-red C-Scan (depicting relative target elevation and bearing from a radome's-eye-view) and radar/IFF B-Scan, similar to the bigger TID display below, as back-up.

The 10in (2.5cm) TID below it, the primary MCO radar display, was optimized for a synthesized 'god's-eye-view' showing multiple target options simultaneously, including relative bearing between the F-111B and its target plus target status (as depicted, in much simplified form). It could be rotated so that the top of the video represented North in a geostabilized fashion, and in either instance the F-111B's position was represented by the base of the vertex or large 'V' denoting the horizontal radar fan-scan or 'pie slice' limits. This pattern could be switched to selective range increments out to 25, 50, 100, 200 and even 400 nautical miles (drawing on the F-111B's massive electrical power reserves), in sweeps of between 10° and up to 65° either side of the nose (to generate 'pie slices' ranging between 20° and 130° wide), and scan in 1, 2, 4, or 8 vertical 'bars' (superimposed, stacked-up 'pie slices'), in low, medium and high Pulse Repetition Frequency rates, depending on the mode selected. 'Low' pulse was best for detection at maximum range in 'look up' long-range search, and high PRF pulse-Doppler for discriminating targets against ground clutter, in a 'look down' manner, albeit at much reduced ranges. The radar tracking handle would be used to tilt the AN/AWG-9 antenna, and to help manually slew radar and IRSTS, with IRSTS coming into play primarily to acquire targets or maintain radar lock in the event of extensive enemy jamming. Cogwheel cursor slewing on the DDD was also an option.

The AN/AWG-9's most versatile mode was 'Track-While-Scan', whereby it monitored up to two dozen targets simultaneously, prioritized them on the TID, and conveyed mid-course guidance (held in separate 'track files') for up to six AIM-54 Phoenix air-to-air missiles. The latter were guided towards the target by midcourse data-link in the first instance, before achieving independent lock-on when their intended prey came within range of their DSQ-26 processor-driven active missile radar seekers.

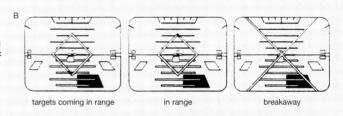

targets coming in range — in range — breakaway

B. Typical pilot's VDI sequence during a Phoenix missile attack, with the diamond cursor and marker (which ticked counterclockwise) to depict time to optimum Phoenix launch range. The 'Breakaway X' signified that the target had closed within minimum missile firing range. Note the artificial horizon, in this case showing that the aircraft was in level flight. The horizontal lines were 5° pitch attitude reference markers (10° between the longer ones), and the vertical ones atop the display depicted 10°, 20°, 30° and 60° roll (via a marker which moved left and right). Both were used in conjunction with the artificial horizon behind them, which shifted about according to aircraft attitude (dive/climb and roll) relative to the ground, just like a traditional, gyro-driven ADI instrument.

The Phoenix diamond, along with heading data etc, was repeated on the HUD combining glass for a missile attack. For attack with air-to-surface weaponry, the HUD provided an octagonal display with a gap in it, which moved to denote range to target for the optimum weapons 'pickle' (which was manual). Air-to-ground stores station and weapons ballistics were selected on a panel in front of the pilot's control stick. In the 'Landing' mode, the HUD furnished glidescope markers to assist with optimum airspeed, radar altitude and angle-of-attack to ensure a safe recovery on ship in inclement weather; a 'Breakaway X', which flashed at two cycles per second based on signals from the ACLS, would appear to signify a 'wave off', instructing the pilot to apply thrust and go around for a second attempt.

F-111B Intercept Avionics (continued)

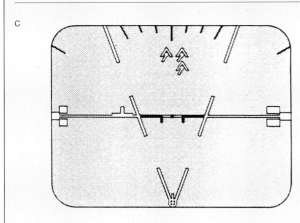

C. Pilot's 'Simultaneous' VDI mode, combining a simplified version of the MCO's TID display with a command line. In this instance the 'inverted T' heading cue was instructing the pilot to turn to port to intercept the targets. The white squares at left denoted desired airspeed and the right-hand white rectangles denoted the correct altitude for the intercept. If they had moved above or below the horizontal reference line that would have meant more or less power or height was required, respectively. In this instance the pilot was at the right height and airspeed.

On the full-sized TID, on the right-hand cockpit radar video, the MCO would have been using a more sophisticated version of the big synthetic 'V' scan and target symbols shown here, and for the purposes of analysis let us assume we are looking at this display on the TID instead. The three target returns are hostile because they carry 'inverted V' icons or 'hats' (whereas unidentified targets would have borne an 'inverted U' 'hat'), this information having been ascertained by the lack of friendly IFF (Identification Friend or Foe) 'squawk' signals by either the onboard AN/AWG-9 or via A/NTDS. The 'tadpole tails' are pointing in the direction of the targets' heading, in this case closing and heading to port.

Simulated carrier trials began with BuNo 151974 in late 1967, conducted at Calverton as part of Grumman's Glidescope Controllability Program. It engaged seven test pilots (five USN, one Grumman and one from General Dynamics) in 216 passes on a simulated carrier deck complete with 'meatball' mirror landing aid, and went very smoothly. However, aircraft take-off weight had long since become an issue as it had grown to an alarming 79,000lb (35,830kg) by this point, roughly ten tons over the ideal, and a series of structural-pruning efforts followed, which progressively denuded commonality with the Air Force version. This commonality fell to a nominal 29 per cent by the time the Super Weight Improvement Program (SWIP) and three successive Colossal Weight Improvement Programs (CWIPs I–III) had all been effected. These, in fact, had been initiated as early as February 1964 (finding their way into the airframe with A2-04/BuNo 151973 beginning in 1966), close on the heels of Chief of the Bureau of Weapons Admiral Masterson's pleas that production be suspended pending gross redesign, on the basis that meeting both Air Force and Navy requirements with a common airframe was absurd. Cynics observed that the US Navy, who may have been more politically astute than their Air Force counterparts, understood that fighting McNamara with objections would do no good, whereas by adding further 'essential' avionics systems to the F-111B to deliberately raise its weight, they could kill the effort through the back door. The best and final effort by Grumman, caught in the middle, only reduced take-off weight by 4,000lb (1,810kg). While poor cockpit visibility was theoretically offset by the advanced

Early F-111B cockpits originally featured traditional, basic flight controls (many outlined in fire-engine red!) and flutter test equipment. This is BuNo 151973, the fourth in the series, the first aircraft to be fitted with the escape module. It crashed on 21 April 1967. *Northrop-Grumman*

V/HUD (Vertical Display Indicator/Head-Up-Display) approach symbology which included cues for the ACLS (Automatic Carrier Landing System, then in advanced development), crews were concerned how they would handle a 'systems out' approach, and authorization to study a new module design with better forward vision was given the go-ahead in March 1967 (as a spin-off from the CWIPs, which also re-examined the undercarriage arrangement). Test pilots John Norris and Ted Tate experienced just such a total systems 'black out' during a ferry flight from California to NATF Lakehurst, forcing them to 'MAYDAY' and conduct a 'hairy' hydroplaning landing, with only fuel vapours feeding the engines, on a very soggy diversionary field: McGuire, New Jersey.

Carrier qualification trials on the USS *Coral Sea* conducted from May 1968 (during which time BuNo 151974 made nine catapult launches and ten arrested landings or 'traps') also highlighted earlier weight concerns: it was considered too complex and expensive an aircraft to be deployed twenty at a time on the Navy's carriers as Fleet Defense 'missileer'; and in the air superiority MiGCAP (MiG Combat Air Patrol) role, where it would be expected to escort strike packages and engage enemy fighters in close-quarters combat, it was judged too heavy and lacking in manoeuvrability to replace the McDonnell F-4 Phantom. And it too possessed no gun, nor even Sidewinder capability: it was strictly a long-reaching heavy puncher. Although the aircraft behaved well in the carrier circuit in the hands of competent test pilots, turning a squadron of them around on deck could place the whole launch and recovery cycle in a logjam, and there would be hard wear and tear on the catapult shuttles and pendants (arresting wires). Most carrier crews were used to spotting and cycling just a token handful of 'heavies' like the A-3 Skywarrior and RA-5 Vigilante, which were in the same weight class. The Navy contended that the decks of its carriers, and the aircraft elevators and launch and recovery equipment, would have to be substantially strengthened at a cost of over a billion dollars. The TF30-P-12 engines and Triple Plow II inlets envisaged for the production examples (A2-07/BuNo 152715 introduced the interim 'Superplow' version) still would be apt to cough and splutter if abused, and the whole powerplant remained short on 'oomph' even with a combined 40,500lb (18,400kg) thrust in afterburner offered by the 'dash Twelves'. Using the original 'dash Ones', with a full load of four Phoenix missiles suspended on the pivot-pylons, it was hard work going much past Mach 1; Grumman pilot Don Evans, accompanied by GD flight engineer Grover 'Ted' Tate, were at Edwards and scheduled to break the double-sonic barrier with the weapons aboard. Building up energy in a wild zoom, the engines conked out at 45,000ft (13,720m), and were not lit again until the bird had plummeted to a mere 7,000ft (2,130m) above the hard terrain.

Response times between throttle inputs and the engines piling on the thrust was also much slower with the 'One-Eleven's' new turbofan engine compared to a traditional quick-reacting but heavy fuel-burning turbojet, creating potentially terrifying situations during wave-offs and bolters in a single engine scenario. It was a problem that was also to plague the much lighter Tomcat (58,000lb/26,300kg) at normal take-off weights, the original design goal for F-111B) for many years.

The CP-741/A secondary armament computer, interfaced with the V/HUD to provide radar range to target for a 'canned'

(Above) With full-span slats and double-slotted Fowler flaps out, BuNo 151974 conducts a simulated carrier bolter during Navy Preliminary Evaluation trials. Carrier trials demonstrated superb handling characteristics despite very little wind-over-deck. (One USAF officer noted that for the subsequent Intruder launch, the carrier had to generate considerably more steam!) However, the aircraft's weight remained contentious. Northrop-Grumman

John Norris and Doug Reynolds of the Edwards-based GFAD pose by one of the black-nosed F-111Bs, the latter a trademark of a Hughes AN/AWG-9-retrofitted aircraft. Curiously, at around this time Grumman switched Intruder radome coatings to creamy-white neoprene. Northrop-Grumman

Hughes at Culver City, California, refitted the 'baseline' GAC F-111Bs with the all-up Phoenix missile and radar, and IRSTS gear. Up to six AIM-54A missiles could be carried: four on pivot-pylons and two in the weapons bay. *Northrop-Grumman*

manual bomb or rocket attack, was another piece of kit which added to the overall weight and cost and was built-in as a secondary mission mostly to satisfy an alleged CAS (Close Air Support) requirement, with the US Marines in mind. However, as early as July 1966 it was clear that they were not going get their hands on the $8 million aircraft (the price of four Phantoms in then-year money) and the Commandant of the Marines pulled them out of the programme. As with the F-111A, the 'Seavark's' quarter-circle intakes were heavy FOD-eaters and the machine would be totally incompatible with operations from rough, forward fields such as the new SATS (Short Airfield Tactical Support). These comprised interlocked aluminium matting and a mobile arresting device, and all sorts of hazards would have occurred if the F-111B attempted to use such a facility.

Conversely, using prepared fields would decrease reaction times too much for the machine to be of use to the Marines on the ground, despite its potentially impressive warload. The Navy never took the air-to-ground function seriously either, and it was gradually whittled away.

Stop Work

At this point in its development, 1967–68, a series of problems beset the F-111B effort, and the F-111 in general. A2-05/BuNo 151974 had crashed at Calverton on 21 April 1967 when both engines flamed-out with a compressor stall on what was otherwise a routine take-off, resulting in a six-month programme setback and much consternation at Grumman at the loss of the two test pilots, who did not appear to have attempted ejection in the new module. More worrying to GD, during the previous January a WCTB (Wing Carry Through Box) test example suffered severe buckling. This occurred at a wing sweep of 16 degrees and at a loading of 130 per cent of the operational design limit (equivalent to 7.33g). The box was required to cope with 150 per cent of the operational limit. Structural remedies ensued including the addition of 3×8in (7.6×20cm) reinforcing gussets which added a nominal 34lb (15kg) but also much more greatly to time and cost. There were further delays and costs after a WCTB failed completely the following summer, necessitating revised design of the wing box. There were other equally serious problems that needed remedying, related elsewhere in the book, while an ongoing Congressional inquiry hung like a spectre over the whole F-111B programme.

Grumman quietly began work on its more nimble Design 303, taking the best features from the F-111B and leaving out the worst and superfluous, aware that the axe was about to fall. Amongst these developments was an electron beam-welded titanium WCTB developed for the new fighter (Grumman also later produced the boxes for European Tornado fighters under contract to Panavia). However, as the woes and wails in Washington reached their crescendo, some of it fuelled by the realization that buying the F-111B would necessitate costly and time-consuming modifications to the aircraft carriers, Congress refused further production funding (the US Senate declining authorization in April, and the US House in July) and on 9 July 1968 the contractors were formally notified to stop work. Orders for the remaining machines in the initial thirty-seven aircraft buy were cancelled. However, bought and paid for pending formal contract termination of the remaining aircraft on the order books on 14 December, Articles A2-06 and -07 were completed and handed over to the US Navy for follow-on Hughes radar/missile trials which continued until May 1971. Although the Navy did not want the F-111B, it desperately wanted the Hughes AN/AWG-9 and Phoenix radar/missile system.

There was a price to pay for the continued research and development: F-111B A2-02, out on a test sortie from Point Mugu, plunged into the Pacific on 11 September 1968 with its occupants, and A2-05 suffered a heavy landing the following month on 11 October, injuring radar operator Bill Bush. Deemed uneconomic to repair, the machine was reduced to spares before it was scrapped to keep the four others flying. The Navy was effectively done testing aerodynamics and carrier suitability and all four machines were allocated exclusively to

A close-up view of BuNo 152715, the seventh and last F-111B to fly, which was equipped with the interim double blow-in door 'Superplow' inlets and TF30-P-12 engines. It was active on Phoenix trials until May 1971, and an inert captive XAIM-54A round (sans tail fins) is shown mounted on the F-111B's unique missile-launching pivot-pylons. Hughes Radars & Missiles

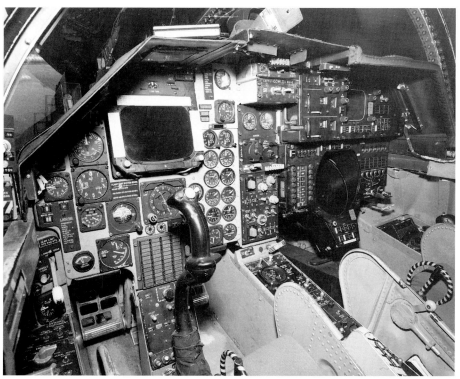

(Right)
BuNo 151972 was representative of the 'all-up' F-111B cockpit from an avionics perspective, complete with V/HUD, DDD and TID displays and controls; however, in common with the first two F-111Bs it retained its Douglas Escapac 'bucket' ejection seats. Hughes Radars & Missiles

support the radar/missile effort, which went from strength to strength.

In March 1969, one of the Hughes F-111Bs engaged two Firebee drones successfully, opening up a series of live trials which climaxed with six-on-six. Pilots and their Missile Control Officers (as they were known in those days) had merely to wait for the 'in range' lamp to light up before unleashing their deadly rocket cargo, which pulled manoeuvres of up to 17g to catch the inbound targets. The overall pK (probability of a kill) was 82 per cent, against subsonic and supersonic targets hugging the earth or zooming at 120,000ft (35,600m). During the great 'drone shoots' of the ensuing years the heading in the instruction manual simply stated 'How to become an Ace on your first pass'!

Phoenix emerged from the ashes as the legend prophesied, alongside a newer, more extensively transistorised model of the AN/AWG-9 for installation in the VFX Tomcat, none of which would have been possible without the trouble-plagued F-111B airframes lending a hand. That, undoubtedly, was their greatest contribution; problem-solving and fine-tuning the advanced radar/weapons package formed a hefty chunk of the eventual 1,748hr/1,173 test sortie tally, when the Tomcats could take over completely. There may have been many Air Force pilots who cussed the aircraft for the legacy of the limited view out of the cockpit, but many more who are grateful for the limb- and life-saving escape module which would not have otherwise been fully realised without the quirky Navy seating arrangement.

CHAPTER THREE

Aces

It's 2am; the sky is overcast at 500ft [150m]; the valleys are full of fog and the hills and ridges are shrouded in clouds. It's pouring rain. Virtual blackness surrounds the cockpit which is glowing reds and ambers, the canopy reflecting this light in an eerie, shimmering dance. Greenish amber images sweep the radar scopes presenting impressions of the terrain ahead. Positive Gs tug at you, followed by a negative release and weightless slide down the backside of a ridge. Airspeed reads 520kt [963kph], with altimeter and vertical speed tapes in constant movement. The radar altimeter is fluctuating like a windshield wiper, generally reading 200ft [60m]. Your crewmate's breathing is heavy and quick over the unicom. It's thirty seconds to target. You feel the heavy bombs swaying on the pylons, causing the aircraft to wobble and shudder. Your radar homing and warning gear is squawking, flashing signals of enemy radars trying to track and kill. The autopilot controls your destiny; your left hand is on the throttle and your right hand near the stick as you hurtle to the target at 1,000ft [300m] per second. It's time. You press and hold and the bomb release button on the stick. 5, 4, 3, 2, 1. You feel a pulsing shaking of the aircraft as bombs ripple from the pylons. The canopy flashes blue and yellow with each detonation somewhere behind. You sweep the wings to 72 degrees, push up the throttles and accelerate to supersonic speed in a desperate search for safety. Streaks of orange, green, blue and white criss-cross your path and suddenly it's black again. You pull your sweat-soaked mask from your face and pick up a heading for home. Piece of cake!

Col Roger J. Mathiasen, former Commander of the 429th TFS, describing a combat mission from Takhli RTAB in 1972.

As the RDT&E force of F-111As pushed ahead with their Category II test programme in 1966–67 they began to explore the operational potential of the F-111 concept more fully. On 25 March 1966, a convincing demonstration of its long-range, low-level penetration capability was given in a 1,203-mile (1,936km) flight, half of it on TFR at under 1,000ft (300m) AGL. At Edwards AFB, shortly after the flight of the first pilot-production aircraft (65-5701) on 12 February 1967, an evaluation programme named *Combat Bull's-eye 1* tested the F-111A's ability to strike targets in poor weather. Ferry range was demonstrated by the two aircraft which flew to the Paris Air Show on 22 May 1967. Col Tom Wheeler, Capt John D. Phillips and their crewmates flew from Loring AFB, Maine, to Paris without tankers or external tanks.

Among the first generation of trainees the F-111A's revolutionary features still caught aircrew off guard at times. Col Roger Mathiasen was one of the USAF's initial cadre of six F-111 pilots. After a 100-mission war tour on the F-105 at Takhli RTAB he reported to Edwards AFB and 'checked out in one of the three test aircraft' before moving to Nellis AFB to help establish their first F-111A training unit, the 4527th CCTS (Combat Crew Training Squadron).

During that period our Detachment Commander, Col Don McCance was involved in a crash-landing at Edwards [in F-111A A1-09, 63-9774]. The Instructor Pilot was killed and McCance badly burned. The wing-sweep handle was the cause, since at that time movement of the handle forward moved the wings aft. That design deficiency was corrected so that forward handle motion moved the wings forward.

The aircraft had landed with 50 degree sweep at a low airspeed suitable for a 16 degree angle and its pilot forgot which way to move the 'trombone action' handle in order to spread the wings.

Even experienced test pilots were fooled by the F-111's usually docile landing characteristics. At Holloman AFB's Open Day on 18 May 1968 Kent Roberts, an Alamogordo Radio Station reporter was announcing to his public the arrival of the 'extremely news-worthy, very controversial plane... and here it comes down right in front of you...'. Sadly, GD's test pilot Fred Voorhies let his speed drop too low on a 'dirty' approach and the aircraft 'came down', but short of the runway, very hard and 'doggone close' to Ken Roberts' radio van. Although the damage was not severe it earned one more Sunday headline: 'Another F-111 Crashes'.

In the early stages of USAF acceptance of the F-111 one of the original criteria which was quietly forgotten was the 'rough field' capability. This had shaped the aircraft's Herculean undercarriage and, to some extent, its swing-wing. Short-field landings could still be done though. Capt Brad Insley judged that 'you could land with the brakes depressed before touchdown and get landing rolls of less than 2,000ft (610m)'.

The USAF's Category III tests, the operational phase, was brought forward (partly as a result of the encouraging *Combat Bull's-eye* results) in response to a JCS (Joint Chiefs of Staff) proposal of 24 April 1967 to send up to ten F-111As to S.E. Asia before the end of that year 'to silence its critics by proving the aircraft's combat capability'. At the time, Senator John L. McClellan was making strenuous efforts to end funding for the F-111B.

At Nellis AFB, Nevada, the 4480th TFW was established on 15 July 1967, receiving its first F-111A two days later. It was collected by Col Ivan Dethman, Commander of Detachment 1 of the Wing's only squadron, the 4481st TFS. Its Commanding Officer, Col Bobby J. Mead was charged with organizing *Combat Trident*, a rushed programme to prepare the F-111A for combat. GD's side of the programme, clearly a vital one for the aircraft's future, was headed by George Davis, a former test pilot and a senior figure at the company. Six F-111As were delivered to the unit equipped to carry AN/ALQ-87 noise-jamming pods to cope with Soviet SA-2 missile guidance radars. As part of the preparation, under the nomenclature *Harvest Reaper*, their undersides were given a coat of FS 24079 Dark Green in place of the usual FS 36622 Grey.[1] Col Mathiasen's team, under Col Gabriel Bartholemew, had 'as their first training task to check out and prepare *Harvest Reaper* aircrews, whose aircraft were ready by January, 1968'. There was some initial resistance among the trainee fighter pilots, including Capt Rick Matteis.

> I was not pleased to be selected for the F-111 for two reasons. The first was that nine of us who were fully checked out and combat ready in the F-4 Phantom front seat were selected to occupy the right seat of the F-111. We flew as Integrated Crews, composed of an Aircraft Commander (AC) and Pilot-Navigator. However, we perceived ourselves as having been downgraded from ACs in the F-4 to 'pilots' in the F-111. We had been trained to take full responsibility for the safety of an aircraft and its mission and now we were being asked to take orders from someone else during flight operations. The second reason for being disappointed was the fact that we were trained as fighter pilots and enjoyed the prestige that goes along with flying a fighter.

When Col Mead advised his new crews that 'one of the biggest problems is to get used to that guy in the seat next to you' he was surely aware that all nine 'Navigator/Pilots' had asked to resign, but had their requests refused. Fellow trainee Lee J. Dodd described them as a 'very unhappy bunch of guys'.

All the aircrew chosen for the first Vietnam deployment, *Combat Lancer*, were very experienced, partly as a way of reducing the training time before they could take the new aircraft into combat. There was plenty for them to learn, nevertheless. Col Mathiasen:

> As you might expect, the most dangerous aspect of flying the F-111 was ground proximity. The Nellis range complex is loaded with mountain ranges, many over 10,000ft [3,050m], and this proved to be invaluable in our training missions. We found we had much to learn about all the systems, specifically the TFR. Snow-topped mountains became a TFR danger, so did dry lake beds, while heavy rain and snow showers caused hazards. In five years of instructing over these ranges, day and night, I became intimately involved with the F-111 and privileged to see it evolve.

Flyers were, in IP (Instructor Pilot) Charlie Coker's opinion: 'surprised at how close the systems would take the aircraft to a mountain before it would command a pull-up to fly over the terrain. We would have pulled up sooner if we had been hand-flying it'. Roger E. Peterson, training at Nellis a few years later, 'used to take new pilots and navigators into the canyons of the South-West USA on TFR and make them put their hands on their helmets as we rode TFR "hard ride" – just to build their confidence in an excellent system. Manual flying was too demanding for combat and we always flew auto-TFR or we cancelled the mission if it malfunctioned'.

They also discovered the Aardvark's extraordinary rapidity at low level. Roger Peterson remembered reaching above Mach 1.5 below 100ft (30m) AGL over Mud Lake, Nevada. 'I flew 1.2 Mach, 200ft [60m] bomb-drops at night on auto-TFR in Fighter Weapons School. No other aircraft in the

---

Lead-computing Optical Sight

BACKGROUND While the Pilot (more correctly termed the AC) enjoyed access to a whole bank of instruments, the GE(USA) AN/ASG-23 LCOS was a very useful device in the mould of what later became known as the 'head-up display'. It received a host of inputs from the other subsystems and its own lead-computing gyro and computing amplifier, depending on what mode it was working in, to provide astonishingly accurate indicators. This 'first generation HUD' package was evolved by General Electric over many years for several aircraft, including the Phantom, and reached its zenith during the F-111 programme.

The ASG-23 LCOS was fitted as part of the F-111A/C/E Mark I bomb-nav system as standard, and the ostensibly similar ODS (Optical Display Sight) equipped the Mk IIB avionics-equipped FB-111A and F-111F in the guise of ASG-25 and -27, respectively.

OPERATION The LCOS (and very similar ODS) provided two, superimposed collimated images focused at infinity on the 'gunsight glass' in front of the AC: an aiming reticule and allied deviation indicators (in red), and a set of command steering bars (in green). To set it up at the correct line of sight, bearing in mind that the aviators included people of all sizes, the AC would simply adjust the height of his seat pan so that he saw the tip of the pitot probe 'just touching' the horizontal bevel marked on the combining glass.

Essentially, the aiming reticule (or 'pipper') provided lead-computed angles by moving about in the AC's line of sight to correct for weapons ballistics in air-to-air gunnery and visual CCIP (Continuously Computed Impact Point) bombing, plus a depressed sight for manual strafing and bombing. It also provided attitude reference roll tabs, deviation indicators and steering bars to help guide the pilot, and an analogue radar range bar which wound-down clockwise between the 3 o'clock and 9 o'clock positions to assist with dropping or firing weapons in-range to target. Most of these functions are aired in other boxes specifically describing the gun, TFR flight, and bombing procedures.

Many of these steering indicators were repeated on the AC's main instrument panel's ADI (Attitude Director Indicator) and HSI (Horizontal Situation Indicator) instruments, but 'heads up' in a combat environment always provided an edge. Experienced pilots came to use the LCOS a great deal during attack patterns while giving the steering cues on the ADI and HSI a mere cursory glance. As high-time combat Instructor Pilot Maj Dick Brown remarked, 'A little known fact is that the steering presented on the

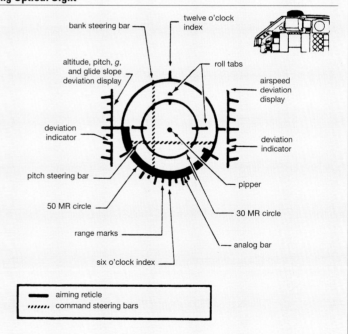

Aiming reticle and steering bar presentations.

LCOS gave the most precise steering indications and pilots were supposed to follow its indications to achieve greater azimuth accuracy. I do not think many people knew this and that little bit of knowledge helped me and WSOs get better bombs on the range than other flight members!'

world could do that then and few can do it today'. Nellis had its lighter diversions too. 'I remember making supersonic passes at low altitude in the Nellis range area – often surprising wild horses, cattle, and trespassers or cattle rustlers. We would make low altitude passes on the houses of ill repute out in the Nevada desert; Sally's and Sherries'. Night-flying training soon became the primary aim in 1968, concentrating, as Charlie Coker pointed out, 'on flight instruments, the TFR and radar and only occasionally looking out to avoid other aircraft. Looking out was really a waste of time because no-one else would possibly be fool enough to fly that close to the ground at night!'.

Familiarization with instruments was a byword to safe aircraft operation, and the F-111 boasted a comprehensive cockpit, including a new LCOS gunsight which was more than just a weapons aiming device. Part of the *Harvest Reaper* preparations involved an intensive trial of another new feature, the F-111A's comprehensive

---

Penetration Aids

BACKGROUND The F-111 was the first TAC fighter-bomber to incorporate a fully integrated Electronic Warfare suite (sometimes known as the DEWS, or Defensive Electronic Warfare System). This comprised five different items, and became fully operational during the inaugural F-111A *Combat Lancer* deployment in early 1968. Subsequent updates added digital processing, refined displays and newer external pods.

RADAR HOMING AND WARNING SYSTEM Built into the nose barrel, wing glove and horizontal stabilators, the Dalmo-Victor AN/APS-109 (and follow-on ALR-62 Countermeasures Receiving Set, an update incorporated from the very late 1970s under TO 1F-111-1168) alerted the crew to low-, mid- and high-band frequency friendly and enemy (and unknown) radar activity. This would encompass the full gamut of fighter, AAA and gun-laying radars known and programmed into the receivers. Threats were presented as warning lamps and alphanumerics on a compass rose indicator, together with audio warnings on the crew's headset, and could be handed-off to the jammers and chaff/flare dispensers, based on what had been selected in the Pen-Aid control panels. Alternatively the crew would intervene manually and select countermeasures at their discretion. It also provided a Homer Set/Homer Track radar-triangulating function in the early days to help knock out hostile emitters, though this was never properly exploited. At the present time, the RAAF has a requirement for an Anti-Radar Missile (ARM), to achieve IOC by 2001, and a new interface is on the cards.

COUNTERMEASURES RECEIVER SET Allied with the RHAWS was the Cincinnati Electronics AN/AAR-34 CMRS (also known as the Infrared Receiver or IRRS, and as the AN/ALR-23 prior to September 1968). Manifested as a rear-facing 'glass' dome mounted in the pod atop the vertical stabilizer, this was a refrigerated unit, gas-cooled to 77K (−196°C) to pick up fighters and missiles in the aircraft's rear hemisphere. It also would present the 'infrared threats' on the RHAWS/CRS scope, and similarly could be tied to the other self-defence equipment for automatic dispensing of chaff and flares. However, the system was constantly plagued by 'false alarm' problems and tended to be used purely for warning. Not long after the RHAWS had been updated to the AN/ALR-62 CRS configuration it was decided to remove the IRRS as a maintenance-saving move, and all USAF aircraft relinquished it in the early 1980s. Plans by Cincinnati Electronics to 'revisit' the stored devices with newer ultra-violet spectrum MAWS (Missile Approach Warning System) technology was shelved as a cost-cutting measure, and the USAF Aardvarks ended their days with a plastic plug cap in the fin instead. RAAF F-111C/Gs, however, are likely to receive just such an update in the near future, which will include the ability to detect laser beam-riding and passive heat-seeking missiles with a great degree of reliability.

COUNTERMEASURES DISPENSING SET The General Dynamics AN/ALE-28 CMDS was an explosive train pyrotechnic dispenser built into the F-111's 'speed bumps', immediately aft of the horizontal stabilator roots. It was stuffed with TBC (Track Breaking Chaff) and flares. TBC was designed to foil 'terminal threat' radars – those actually guiding flak or missiles by remote control – and to similarly provide a false 'painted target' for semi-active/active-guided missiles to lock on to. It could be activated automatically by the CMRS/RHAWS, or manually by the crew. As one 'high-timer' noted, 'Two bundles of TBC equated to the size of an F-111 – so therefore we always dispensed two bundles each time'. A Special Purpose Chaff (SPC) option was also available, to cater for specific Soviet threats. It would have been installed in combat aircraft in USAFE in the event that hostilities broke out, and was standard on the FB-111A alert variant. SPC was essentially 'top secret' stuff and security surrounds it to this day. Flares, a fierce-burning disposable decoy, were always selected manually, as a night-time release might actually alert ground gunners to the F-111's whereabouts; however, they were the only effective defence against heat-seeking missiles if they had locked onto the F-111.

Additionally, two batches of 'Mod O' F-111As (66-0016 thru 66-0024, and 67-0037 thru 67-0057) were modified so that the pilot could select chaff/flares instead of the gun and either crewmember squeeze the trigger to activate the CMDS. Brad Insley recalled that this was introduced as 'An easy way to fire the chaff and flares without having to go "heads down". They tried to include more aircraft but could never come up with the money, to the crews' dismay. Only those few A models ever got the Mod.'

All the same, the CMDS was apt to jam and, as a sideline to the much later AMP (Avionics Modernization Program) and Pacer Strike avionics updates of the late 1980s and early 1990s, the fleet switched to new Tracor AN/ALE-40 'ice cube tray' fittings in the same location, housing eight 'square shooters' offering a combined capacity of 120 chaff and 60 flare cartridges. If one cartridge failed, it would not impede the release of subsequently-triggered pyrotechnics.

ELECTRONIC COUNTERMEASURES TRACK-BREAKER Completing the internal suite was the Sanders AN/ALQ-94 ECM deception jammer. This radio-frequency spectrum device was designed to use modulated jamming tailored to match the enemy radars' PRF and PRI (Pulse Repetition Frequency/Interval), creating copy-cat fake 'echoes' out of phase with the emitter so as to generate spurious azimuth and range returns. Fighter radars, missiles and flak relying on mid- and high-frequency guidance could thus be 'walked away' from the F-111, and lower frequency early warning and height-finder systems similarly fed false information. It was a 'switch on when necessary' system which was largely pre-programmed by EW specialists from what later became known in the USAF as the CNPA (Communications, Navigation, Penetration Aids) branch. Beginning in the very late 1970s, FB-111As, and later EF-111As (neither of which were equipped to carry external ECM pods), received the updated AN/ALQ-137 version. This offered faster response times and increased ERP (effective radiated power), by means of 'power management' techniques (better ECM directional output tailored to the most serious threats, based on those picked-up by the ALR-62/Compass Sail updated RHAWS/CRS).

ECM PODS Beginning with the *Combat Lancer* deployment, the F-111 was modified under a QRC (Quick Reaction Capability) programme to carry external jamming devices. These, initially, comprised a pair of General Electric AN/ALQ-87 'Beacon' noise-jamming pods, mounted between the strakes and under the left-hand weapons bay doors. This jamming was tailored to defeat SA-2 Guideline SAM command guidance, and to swamp acquisition radars with noise, effectively masking the F-111's position. The pods were gradually superseded by the more capable Westinghouse AN/ALQ-101(V)2/3, -119(V)14/17 and -131(V)13 two-band (mid and upper) devices for operations over the electronically-intense Eastern European combat theatre. F-111Ds, once they had achieved 'mobility capability', received QRC-80-01 pods (externally identical to the ALQ-119(V)15 'long' pod, programmed to counter threats in the areas they might have been deployed to for contingency operations). One of these pods, which would be constantly checked and updated by CNPA, was carried between the strakes to provide noise or deception jamming to defeat 'terminal threat' radars. The later Westinghouse models offered 'power management' and could cope with up to forty different wave forms simultaneously. To a large measure, they actually proved far more useful than the internal track-breaking jammer during the final years of operations, and aircraft with 'down' pods would always abort, whereas those with defunct internal jammers would sometimes 'press on regardless'.

internal self-protection equipment, at Eglin AFB, Florida. In practice, aircrew were suspicious of the CMRS and ALE-28 CMDS even at the training stage. The ALR-23 warning device tended to give too many false alarms, triggering off the ALE-28's chaff and flares automatically and thereby revealing the F-111A's position to potential attackers. Pilots rightly predicted that releasing flares at low altitude would make them 'flak magnets' in combat. Use of afterburner at low level was avoided for the same reason.

While the 250 men involved in the *Harvest Reaper* programme 'flew the legs off the F-111' (as one pilot put it) a difficulty arose concerning weapons delivery. Severe vibration was experienced with bomb racks carrying partial loads at transonic speeds. It was reported that in some cases they were 'shaking the shackle pins off the bombs'. Col Charles W. Reed, F-111A Project Officer at Nellis, explained that this only occurred when high-drag bombs were carried. For *Combat Lancer* the aircraft were to use their new purpose-built Bomb Release Unit the BRU-3/A, which was aerodynamically tailored for lower drag. It also offered a snugger fit using square metal bomb lugs which 'snapped' into place (rather than 'D-rings' and the anti-sway braces used on the older Multiple Ejection Rack).

Combat Lancer

On 20 January 1968 the 4480th TFW became the 474th TFW *Roadrunners* under Col Chester van Etten, and its 428th TFS was formed from the 4481st TFS, the *Harvest Reaper* cohort. On 14 March Col Ivan Dethman, an F-86 pilot in the Korean War, briefed the Squadron's Detachment 1 for the 7,000 mile (11,260km) trip to Takhli RTAB, Thailand, where it would attach itself to the Thunderchief-flying 355th TFW. The unit had trained for about eight months; not long enough according to Col Tom Germscheid who was aboard one of the six Aardvarks heading out to war.

The early F-111As that we took to South-East Asia were undoubtedly pressed into combat too quickly. *Combat Lancer* was a flight test, and problems were to be expected as indeed they were encountered. Tactics were being developed while under hostile as well as political fire. The weapon system was in its infancy, automatic terrain following was new to the world and crew members had less than 100 hrs in the bird.

Generally, the airmen realised that they were under pressure to prove the F-111 concept. Commanding officer Ike Dethman was diplomatic on that issue when he climbed out of his specially-marked aircraft, 66-0018 into the 95°F (35°C) heat at Takhli. 'The F-111As are here for a mission, not for a test', he told the microphones. The *Takhli Times* reported the event as a 'great day for the Irish' (it was St Patrick's Day) 'and for the 355th TFW', whose boss Col John C. Giraudo greeted Dethman in front of a crowd of 1,000 and some huge 'Welcome *Combat Lancer*' banners. The event was officially seen as the first stage in replacing the wing's F-105s, which had carried the bombing offensive to North Vietnam since the beginning of the war. The Press got a clearer impression of the F-111A shortly afterwards when Lt Col Dean E. Salmeier and USN exchange pilot Lt Cdr Spade Cooley made a supersonic pass at 150ft (45m) above Takhli's runway. The *Bangkok World* observed that this 'left the visiting press-men massaging their ears in agony'.

The first real mission for the 'big ugly bird with loose wings' [2] was flown on Monday 25 March by Col Dethman with Rick Matteis as his Navigator/Pilot.

The target was a bomb dump on a small island known as Tiger Island off the coast of South Vietnam. We planned the mission to approach from the west so that we would be heading out to sea as our bombs went off. We flew at high altitude from Takhli to the Laos border, then descended to 1,000ft (300m) over Laos.

Although heavy cloud prevented effective BDA (Bomb Damage Assessment) for this

Col Ivan Dethman relaxes with a cigar and scotch in Takhli's crew room. via Col Tom Germscheid

(Below)
Close formation by Combat Lancer **F-111As with two AN/ALQ-87 pods apiece and the distinctive yellow and blue fin emblem worn by the Lancer Detachment.** Col Tom Germscheid

The original Combat Lancer line-up at Takhli on 26 March 1968. Two days later Spade Cooley and Ed Palmgren were the first combat losses. From left to right, *standing:* Mac Armstrong, Charlie Arnet, Rick Matteis, Joe Keene, Les Holland, Sandy Marquardt, Bill Coltman, Hank McCann, Bill Soule, Denny Graham, Spade Cooley, Ken Powell, Norm Rice, Chuck Tosten. *Kneeling:* Tom Germsheid, Joe Hodges, Col Ike Dethman, Dean Salmier, Ed Palmgren, Bruce Ashley, Roger Nunemaker. via Col Tom Germscheid

and the other sorties that night, the opening strikes were generally considered successful. All were single-ship missions to reduce the risk of detection. Col Edrin D. Palmgren, the 'Ops' Officer flew slightly later that night to targets near Dong Hoi and reported that 'The only time they knew we were there was when the bombs went off'. The pattern for the next three decades of F-111 interdiction operations was effectively established that night.

Sadly, Ed Palmgren's luck ran out three days later. Flying 66-0022 with Spade Cooley against a truck convoy they vanished without trace. Theories about their loss still abound. Initially, the North Vietnamese claimed to have 'shattered down' the F-111, but Rick Matteis felt that the USAF's official 'pilot error' verdict might have been more likely:

> We never knew for certain what happened to this crew, but we all knew that they felt they could fly the aircraft at a lower altitude than the auto-TFR would permit. We surmised that they probably flew their aircraft into the ground.

Tom Germscheid reinforced the point that Ed Palmgren 'was indeed an advocate of hand-flying terrain following. It may have gotten him into tall jungle trees'. It was the 813th US aircraft lost in the war but it made the headlines throughout the USA as if it was the first. When Hank McCann and Dennis Graham went down with 66-0017 on 30 March a new note of hysteria crept into the press reporting. 'Race with the Reds for F-111 Secrets' was a typical headline. Once again the NVA claimed a shoot-down, this time over Ha Tinh Province, 150 miles (240km) north of the DMZ (Demilitarized Zone), and there were concerns that the wreck might be probed by Soviet specialists. Analysis of radar plots by two technicians who had watched the

(Above) **Six M117 bombs hang from the BRU-3/A racks of this Lancer F-111A in its Takhli revetment in March 1968.** Col Tom Germscheid

Rick Matteis (*left*) and Tom Germscheid, ready for action at Takhli on 2 October 1968.
Col Tom Germscheid

'visible' section of '0017's last flight told a different tale. After flying north from the check-out point at Nakon Phanom to the Vietnam border the aircraft entered a figure-of-eight pattern, apparently trying to make the necessary contact with a ground command post to cross the border. It then turned back towards Takhli and flew about 140 miles (225km) before going off the screen. Despite daily flights by 'Psy War' Cessnas broadcasting offers of $50 rewards to the local people for any information, nothing was found. The 'official' theory was that a capsule of fuel-tank sealant had been left in the aircraft and had 'become lodged in the controls', causing the crash. Col Germscheid was doubtful that the unfortunate pair were orbiting at the border because of a communications problem: 'The mission was pretty much radio-silent. Rick [Matteis] and I were fifteen minutes ahead of Hank and Dennis. We were on the same assigned frequency and heard nothing. We talked to no-one, successfully hit our assigned target and encountered no ground fire'. Possibly they were grappling with some other systems failure which eventually caused them to turn back.

Generally unremarked by the media were the Detachment's next twenty-two days of successful combat sorties in which no F-111A suffered more than a scuffed tyre. From March, 1968 President Johnson's 'bombing pause' had limited the air war to the southern panhandle coastal strip of North Vietnam, divided into Route Packs 1 and 2 in 1965, rather than the tougher Route Packs V and VI around Hanoi. Most of the targets were hidden in the jungle and identified by coordinates as possible arms and supply caches or truck parks. Damage assessment was difficult as often there was no-one in a position to judge whether secondary explosions occurred. Two fresh F-111As (66-0024 and 66-0025) were delivered on 5 April with replacement crewman Capt Fred H. De Jong, 'The Flying Dutchman'. With him was Lt Col Ben Murph, CO of the 428th TFS who took over the Detachment. Both men were 100-mission F-105 veterans. With the restored force of six aircraft, one or two sorties per night were flown on average, though some were inevitably little more than tree-clearance exercises due to inadequate reconnaissance data on elusive targets. A slightly more relaxed atmosphere prevailed for a while as Tom Germscheid recollected:

We had a couple of Aussies join our unit at Takhli as observers. Shortly after the arrival of Flt Lt Spitzkowski, an engineering officer, small kangaroo stencils began appearing on our F-111As. It was quite evident who the culprit was. At the going away party for Spitzkowski we managed to stencil a bald eagle on his bald ass with indelible blue magenta ink. I'm sure this decal accompanied him through quite a few showers. We were very grateful to the Aussies for rescuing about fifty cases of black label scotch from the RAAF club at Ubon when that unit returned 'down under'.

Four F-111 sorties went out on the night of 22 April, but one crew, Maj Alexander A. Marquardt and Capt Joseph W. Hodges returned by a different method. Maj Wade Oldermann's HH-3E *Jolly Green Giant* rescue helicopter pulled them out of the jungle in a 'very smooth rescue' after their aircraft (66-0024) fell from the sky at 09.29, Saigon time. Thinking they were in Laos and alarmed by 'gunfire', which was actually 20mm shells from their own gun 'cooking off', Sandy Marquardt and Joe Hodges fought their way into the jungle. When Maj Oldermann located them they had covered less than a mile and were relieved to find that they had landed in Thailand after all.

M61A-1 Vulcan Gun

BACKGROUND The GE(USA) electrically driven M61A-1 gun was a six-barrelled weapon offering a nominal rate of fire of 6,000spm (shells per minute) at a muzzle velocity of 3,400ft/s (1,040m/s). It originated in 1949 at the company's Burlington, Vermont plant as the T-171, and was named Vulcan after the Roman god of fire. Introduced to service as a defensive weapon for bombers in 1958, it rapidly became the standard USAF gun, replacing traditional cannon in all new fighter designs, fitted internally or in gunpods for air-to-air combat and ground strafing.

LCOS AIMING As part of the 'F-111 Weapons System Package', GDFW incorporated the Vulcan into a module which could be fitted to the right-hand side of the weapons bay, complete with 2,087-round (2,000-usable) ammunition drum, muzzle shroud plus venting and flush-fitting skin which substituted the detachable starboard weapons bay doors. Although gun firing could be effected using either stick trigger (a feature realized on the F-111D, with its twin, 'second generation' HUDs), aiming and firing was traditionally the exclusive province of the AC, accomplished using the LCOS gunsight (or later models' ODS or HUD) 'pipper':

GUN LIMITS There were many limiting factors to using the Vulcan. Firstly, during Vietnam era combat, the left-hand weapons bay door was rigged to carry an AN/ALQ-87 ECM pod. The gun could not be used when this was installed though the vibration would shake-up the pod and render it inoperative. A maximum bursts length of 2.5 seconds, with intervening cooling periods of 1 minute, were also prescribed. A more serious problem was that the gun was apt to cause engine compressor stalls when fired during manoeuvring flight in the stall-thru-400kt speed regime, especially with afterburner engaged (which the pilot would have been obliged to select under those circumstances). The gun was also down-rated to 5,000 spm to help with this problem. It was fine when used in the 400-thru-680kt (up to Mach 1) Indicated Airspeed regime at heights above 9,000ft (2,740m) in 'mil' power, but that would have required a 'sitting duck' target. Not surprisingly, it was never actually used in combat!

The gun was removed from the aircraft as a self-defence item as soon as the more useful AIM-9 Sidewinder missile became widely available to the F-111 fleet, beginning in the early 1980s (a factor precipitated by many of the guns reaching their twenty-year life cycle, which would have necessitated expensive maintenance refurbishment). F-111A/Es had the weapons put in indefinite storage, F-111Ds retained only the gutted 'pack' to use as a luggage rack, and F-111C/Fs and RF-111Cs ditched it altogether in favour of the new *Pave Tack* targeting pod and weapons bay cradle, or reconnaissance pallet, respectively. However, as several crewmen told the authors, 'It was nice to know it was there, just in case, but I'd rather have had an AIM-9'.

SIDEWINDER F-111As were originally given the capability to use this weapon, but only AIM-9B versions were generally available (fighters absorbing the better models). The Mach 1 limits imposed by this missile, which was also only effective from the enemy's six o'clock position, made it less useful and reliable than the gun. Even the famous 'trapeze' was deleted from the inventory shortly after its service introduction,

• With the LCOS set to GUN A/A and the ARS set to AIR/AIR, this aiming reticule provided a lead-computed angle to assist with air-to-air shooting, to compensate for bullet ballistics. Also, the semi-circular LCOS analogue ranging bar would 'unwind' from the 3 o'clock to 9 o'clock position to indicate range to target in 1,000ft/300m (250ft/76m between 5 and 7 o'clock) increments. The pilot thus manoeuvred the aircraft within firing range of the target and 'flew' the pipper onto it, attempted to hold it in place for a couple of seconds to help it stabilize for maximum accuracy, and then pressed the trigger.

The 9 o'clock position of the analogue bar represented the firing range set into the LCOS Preset Range counter beforehand, less 3,000ft (910m), so that the weapon was at the desired firing range when it had receded clockwise to the 6 o'clock position. If radar lock-on was lost, the analogue bar disappeared from view and the 'pipper' lead angle automatically was adjusted for this preselected range (and not actual range to target). Thus, it was customary to set the range counter for the pilot's preferred, optimum gun firing range. For example, for a setting of 1,500ft (455m), the 5 thru 7 o'clock positions of the analogue bar would represent range to target cranking down from 2,500ft (760m) thru 500ft (150m). If the radar then lost lock, the pilot usually had a good idea of 'how big' the target should be in his sights to hit it. Outside of visual range, with the radar locked-on and instruments coupled, the LCOS steering bars would help guide the pilot to the target. (This air-to-air mode could thus be used to find friendly aircraft, particularly tankers, at night or 'in the weather'.)

• With the LCOS set to GUN A/G for strafing, the 'pipper' acted as a fixed, manually depressed aiming reference, using commensurate altitude, airspeed and depression angles preset or 'cranked' into it prior to the gun pass. The pilot would then follow the prescribed attack parameters as precisely as possible for the chosen dive angle, a process assisted by following the altitude and airspeed deviation indicators on the sides of the LCOSS reticule, while radar-ranging was furnished on the analogue bar. The pilot lined the 'pipper' up on the target, and when the analogue bar had receded to the 6 o'clock position the aircraft was in gun firing range.

Later tac-air versions of the F-111 used a very similar set-up for 'guns', except that the F-111F ODS and F-111D (with its different switchology and HUD displays) provided full CCIP capability in all modes, with manual sightline depression merely there as back-up.

owing to problems at Nellis with them getting 'stuck down occasionally, so they decided to eliminate the problem by removing them'. When later AIM-9P models became available to the F-111 fleet in the early 1980s, the missile was reintroduced, these models providing 'forward hemisphere defence', and a much better defence than the gun. Indications on the LCOS for optimum ranging etc. was pretty much the same as for guns, except that the weapons 'growled' when they had achieved lock-on, making it a 'point in roughly the right direction' weapon, after which time it would do its own thing. AIM-9s were carried on Aero-3/A rails attached to the outer faces of the outer pivot-pylons (Stations 3A and 6A). Crews liked the missile at that stage as it gave credence to the F-111 being an 'attack aircraft rather than a bomber'.

Det 1's Ops Briefing Room set up for briefing the five missions which were launched on 20 May 1968. Take-off times were thirty minutes apart. *Col Tom Germscheid*

(Below)
Two of Det 1's Aardvarks provide a tanker crew with some practice. Col Dethman's aircraft is 'on the boom'. *Col Tom Germscheid*

(Below)
Rolling out at Takhli, this Harvest Reaper F-111A shows its AN/ALQ-87 mounting and M61A-1 gun fairing. The noise-jamming pods were added under a Quick Reaction Capability initiative as part of the Harvest Reaper configuration. Groundcrew names appear in black on the olive drab nosewheel doors, initiating a long F-111 tradition. *Col Tom Germscheid*

Structural Woes

In describing the *Combat Lancer* deployment it is inevitable that the three losses will colour any account of an otherwise successful deployment. The third crash was the most crucial and it effectively ended the operation because it became obvious that it resulted from a structural problem. In otherwise normal flight 66-0024 had suddenly gone out of control when an elevon swung to its maximum deflection. Examination of the wreck was possible this time and it revealed a broken weld in a hydraulic control-valve rod. Speculation mounted that McCann and Graham might have gone down the same way. Back home the newspapers hit new levels of hysteria, blazoning headlines such as 'Do Everything Plane Fails in its Mission' and 'Senators Urge Recall of Suicide F-111'. When a 4527th CCTS F-111A crashed in Lincoln County near Nellis on 8 May, Maj Charles van Driel and Maj Kenneth A. Schuppe ejected and reported a similar tail failure. Inspection of the F-111A fleet revealed forty-two aircraft with potentially defective valve welds. Although the *Combat Lancer* aircraft remained in Thailand until 22 November they were unable to add to their fifty-five combat sorties and were restricted to sporadic local training flights. The 428th TFS nameplate was altered by a deviant humorist to read '428 TKS' (Tactical Kamikaze Squadron), but spirits remained fairly high among those who knew the F-111's true worth. As Tom Germscheid observed, 'We didn't bring the war to a quick end but we achieved many other accomplishments. We proved the low-level, night, adverse weather, long-range (the F-111 didn't need tankers) interdiction capability of the F-111'. When Lt Col Ben Murph led the five surviving aircraft back to Nellis he took the Press microphone in a firm grasp and said of the F-111, 'This is a hell of a fine airplane. I hope to see something good in print about it'.

Sadly, the good news was still overshadowed by a continued series of high-profile accidents at Nellis. On 23 September Lt Neal Pollock RAAF and Lt John M. Nash, a USN exchange pilot, were picked up by a Huskie rescue helicopter when their F-111A crashed inverted just short of Nellis's runway. Loss of control on approach had been caused by an inoperative fuel gauge leading to fuel transfer imbalance and a shift of centre of gravity. It was the ninth crash in

Laotian karst terrain, photographed from an F-111A and a challenge to the aircraft's TFR system.
via Lockheed-Martin

(Below)
The *Combat Lancer* Commander's aircraft with its blue and golden-yellow diagonal pinstripes replaced by a vertical black one.
Col Tom Germscheid

(Bottom)
Tom Germscheid at the helm of the F-111A which he and Rick Matteis usually crewed. The simple restraint strap arrangement and basic aircrew seats are in contrast with the capsule's close-fitting array of complex controls and equipment.
Col Tom Germscheid

A historic view of an M117-laden F-111A taxiing out past an EB-66 jammer for one of the first Combat Lancer **missions on the evening of 25 March 1968.** USAF

(Below) **A 'party clowns' parade outside the squadron building as the** Lancers **prepare for a session in the Takhli 'O' Club. (*From the left*: Mac Armstrong, Les Holland, Joe Hodges, Rick Matteis, Bill Soule, Bill Coltman, Ken Powell, Charlie Arnet, Chuck Foster.)** via Col Tom Germscheid

Going home. The Lancers **head back to Nellis AFB with supporting KC-135As.** Col Tom Germscheid

Towards the end of the Takhli deployment the revised Lancer line-up:
back row: **Paul Fierman, Joe Keene, Fred de Jong*, Ken Powell, Charlie Arnet, Bill Coltman, Bill Soule;**
middle: **Sandy Marquardt, Norm Rice, Tom Germscheid, Rick Matteis, Joe Hodges, Mac Armstrong;**
front: **Chuck Tosten, Les Holland, Ben Murph (CO)*, Dean Salmeir, Roger Nunemaker.**
* Replacement aircrew. via Col Tom Germscheid

two years. Although the USAF demonstrated that F-111 accident statistics were far lower than those for other 'Century Series' fighters, the fight for approval was far from over.[3] On 22 December 1969 came the worst blow of all. Brig Gen 'Boots' Blesse, Commander of the 474th TFW at Nellis, was leading a four-ship of F-111As which were conducting tests to explore the F-111's CAS potential. The flights involved strafing, low-angle bombing and rocket-projectile firing. Aircraft 66-0049 pulled up from a rocket-firing pass on Range 65 at Indian Springs but, as Col Mathiasen explained, 'The right wing snapped clean off. Right-seater Maj Jim Anthony and his pilot instantly ejected but the aircraft had already gone into a violent roll. It hit the ground at 12 o'clock to the target and the module, ejected while inverted, impacted short killing both crew members'. Their F-111 was one of a batch which had already been modified with a pair of steel gusset reinforcements on its WCTB. Buckling and cracks around bolt-holes during fatigue tests on GD test article wing boxes earlier in the year resulted in F-111s being progressively reinforced as a precaution, with 3.5g limits in place on unmodified examples, but it was not regarded as a potentially fatal flaw.

The crash of 66-0049 changed all that. Grounded for seven months, the F-111 fleet was subjected to a massive structural test and inspection programme. GD built cold-proof chambers at Sacramento ALC, Waco and Fort Worth in which the aircraft's wings were flexed at –40°C. Although only three further failures of WCTBs or tails occurred in these tests and all were satisfactorily repaired, the confidence of the USAF, and new customer the RAAF, had to be won back by this drastic and costly method.

Constant Guard V

From 1968 to 1972 the 'pause' in bombing North Vietnam meant that the F-111's special capabilities were not required there, regardless of its other problems. However, in the summer of 1972 President Richard Nixon decided to respond to the North Vietnamese invasion of parts of the South by resuming the air war. *Linebacker I* began on 10 May and on 14 August the 474th TFW received orders to return to Takhli RTAB in force. The 1970 grounding had interfered with training for a time while each F-111 was put through the lengthy cold-test routine. During that period, as 429th TFS veteran Don Laing remembered, trainees 'were put on a Permanent Change of Station to avoid having to pay them Temporary Duty allowance'. Meanwhile, 'Boots' Blesse persuaded TAC to lend him seventy-five AT-33 trainers so that his men could keep up some sort of flying currency. That lasted for about a year. Lt Col Lee P. Dodd Jr was one of the students during that awkward period. Having been assigned as a PWSO (Pilot-Weapons Systems Officer, or right-seater) in May 1968, Lee and his friend Jack Gawelko had persuaded their way onto the Aircraft Commanders' course and were half-way through their proficiency checks when the Range 65 crash occurred:

Don Laing with his F-111A on a visit to Cannon AFB from Nellis. Don Laing

Constant Guard **F-111As in their revetments at Takhli, with KC-135A tankers beyond.**
Lee P. Dodd

> Our squadron, the 430th TFS was the last to receive its F-111As but in the meantime Jack and I had accumulated another 300 hours in AT-33s which were considered by TAC as fighter time. Bill Coltman was one of my IPs in AT-33s. As soon as we started getting our F-111s back I transferred to the 428th to help get them combat ready. As 'Alpha' squadron we got the highest priority in aircraft deliveries from maintenance and I found myself flying almost every day or night for about a year. By early 1972 I had over 1,000 hours of jet fighter time and was asked to check out an IP with the 442nd TTS. The flying in the 442nd was even more intensive since we were the only training squadron [for three F-111 Wings at that juncture]. By the fall of 1972 it looked certain that the 474th would deploy to S.E. Asia (after about two years of being jerked around by our political leadership) and I asked my 442nd Commander if he would allow me back to my old squadron so that I could get combat experience. I was allowed to transfer to the 429th which, with the 430th TFS was selected to participate in the Constant Guard V deployment.

On 27 September 1972 the deployment got under way. Col Roger 'Mat' Mathiasen, who commanded the 429th TFS *Black Falcons* felt confident that his men were genuinely well prepared:

> When we deployed in 1972 we were extremely well-trained and knowledgeable, ready for combat. We knew that the environment we were heading to would hold more challenges, and it did. I departed Nellis in late September on a C-141 along with twenty-four of my *Black Falcon* crew members. We offloaded at Guam. Also aboard the C-141 were twelve other aircrews

429th TFS F-111A 67-0065 with sixteen CBU-58s in 'slant four' configuration, with the inboard stations empty. Notice the offset M61A-1 gun location and black undersides. USAF

(Right) **WSO Capt Richard B. Tourtellott lends his support to a full BRU of Mk 82 'slicks'.**
Lee P. Dodd

who flew on to Takhli to prepare to fly the first combat missions. I waited with my mates for the arrival of twelve F-111As which were flown non-stop to Guam from Nellis. Our groundcrew quickly turned the aircraft around and we launched for Takhli a short time later. The flight was about six hours and I had the privilege of landing the first F-111A (67-0086) at Takhli, ready for combat. Six aircraft were rapidly turned around, armed and launched that evening on the first missions. At this time Col Nelson [474th CO] and the rest were somewhere en route from Nellis.

Lee Dodd remembered that the transit flight was not without its moments of excitement:

Our first leg was from Nellis to Hickam AFB, Hawaii. The USAF officer who greeted us stated that Henry Kissinger had reached agreement with the North Vietnamese and we would probably head back to Nellis tomorrow. I was very disappointed. Nevertheless we left next morning on the longest leg of the deployment, to Clark AFB in the Philippines. The join-up with KC-135 tankers was truly exciting; they kept aborting right and left. Finally, my cell got its turn. I think I was a two-ship lead since it was my responsibility to join up on the tanker. In all the excitement, I forgot all about the KC-135's climb speed being so slow and passed my tanker with over 100kts [180kph] of overtake. Needless to say, I had my hands full trying to get us back behind him without stalling. I somehow managed just before we went into the clouds and we stayed in cloud all the way through the climbout, maintaining our separation by using a *Thunderbirds* Bomb-Burst manoeuver with F-111s going in every direction trying not to overtake their tankers.

Some staff officer decided that we should carry our bomb racks [BRU-3/As] on this deployment and we carried four. We were told that our refuelling had been adjusted to take account of this. Wrong! I think we had to refuel four, maybe five times crossing the Pacific. It became obvious at the first refuelling event that things were not working out. First, it was impossible to stay on the tanker without using afterburner on one engine. We had never tried this before. Our four-ship lead demonstrated that it could be done and each of us had a chance to learn this procedure under very stressful conditions. The last guy to take gas was Capt H, and for good reason: we had our doubts about H. After he fell off the tanker about four times, Flight Lead told him to either plug in next time or plan to swim back. H suddenly got the courage to light off one afterburner and top-off.

I was flying with [a junior Lieutenant] rather than my usual PWSO. He had asked Flight Lead if he and another WSO could entertain themselves by playing chess, using the HF radio. 'Hell, no!' was his response, I think. Nevertheless they decided to do it anyway. They tried to keep it a secret from me, but I was on to them. I pulled up my HF button on the ICS and listened now and then, but pretended I did not notice. They were using tiny little chessboards with magnetic chess pieces. [My right-seater hid his by keeping it out of sight on his right rear sub-panel, which happened to be near the cockpit ECS [environmental control system] air duct. After a few hours of this the ECS got clogged with ice and dislodged itself into the right ear of [the Lieutenant]. Tiny little chess pieces went all over the right side of the cockpit. [The WSO] spent the rest of the flight unstrapped with his knees in his seat, standing on his head, looking for chess pieces that had lodged under his seat. I never even let on that I noticed.

This was a very long flight. All told, I logged nearly eleven hours for this flight, not including the four hours of pre-flight preparation. We were issued 'stop' and 'go' pills for the flight. Most of us decided we would save our pills until after landing so that we could have the energy to do a little partying at the Clark AFB 'O' Club.

Nellis deployed two squadrons to Takhli, totalling forty-eight F-111As. The 430th TFS *Tigers*, under Lt Col Eugene Martin headed out at the end of the month via Clark AFB. Among their number was PWSO Roger E. Peterson. Just before departure he had spent a pleasant day sailing on Lake Mead, Nevada, with his Flight Commander, 'Lefty' Brett, Bill Coltman and their wives. Suddenly, the urgency of war impinged:

The deployment brought us into Clark AFB just prior to a typhoon. We spent several days there (mostly in the bar) waiting for the storm to leave. I ran into a good friend, Skip Bennett, who was returning from a tour on the Cessna A-37 in South Vietnam. My feeling when he went to war was that he would return. I had the same feeling about myself. I believe most young men going to war feel they will survive. Too bad so many were wrong.

429th TFS Aardvarks with 'NB' codes, changed to 'NA' in time for the 1972 S.E. Asia deployment. This was the aircraft in which Wilson and Sponeybarger went down over Hanoi on 22 December 1972. Don Laing

our radar. During the climbout I heard some frantic pleas for more airspeed from one of my following flights. It happened that one of the wingmen picked up pitot-tube icing during the climb and saw less than 100 KIAS every time he looked back into the cockpit while flying formation on his lead. Every time he saw his airspeed indicator he transmitted 'Airspeed too low. PUSH IT UP, Lead!' and of course every flight pushed it up. When we popped out of the clouds at about 25,000ft [7,620m] it looked like

Takhli had been sadly neglected since the departure of the *Combat Lancer* personnel four years previously. Wiring and water-pipes had been 'borrowed' by the local population and crews were more likely to find a poisonous snake than hot water in the showers. Roger Peterson: 'We arrived at Takhli, an F-4 base with limited support facilities, no "O" Club, a pool full of scummy water used for fire-fighting and no night support operations'. However, there were more urgent considerations. The first

Roger Peterson in G-suit ready for a mission. Part of his kit was a .38 pistol with five rounds, though he remembered variations on this; 'Some carried hundreds of rounds to fight the enemy, others only one round in case they were soon captured'.
Roger Peterson

(Right) **Mk 84s on a 430th TFS Tiger F-111A at Takhli RTAB.**
Roger Peterson

Constant Guard missions were launched on the night of 28 September within twenty-four hours of the first aircraft leaving Nellis. Col Jon Jordan felt that there may have been a wish to establish a new TAC record for bombs-on-target at the start of a deployment. The targets were mostly in the heavily defended Route Pack VI within 50 miles (80km) of Hanoi and the crews who had prepositioned for the missions had a couple of days to study the target data. When their aircraft arrived from Guam, just before sunset, six were bombed-up and replenished immediately, but the urgency led to problems. The first aircraft was delayed nearly an hour while suitable fittings to hang its ALQ-87 jammers were lashed-up. Thirty six minutes after launch it lost contact with the ground, causing the last two launches to be aborted. Only two of the six aircraft reached their targets and one of those only made its secondary objective.

It soon became horribly apparent that F-111A 67-0078 with Maj William C. 'Horse' Coltman, a *Combat Lancer* veteran, and Lt 'Lefty' Brett (an excellent pilot in Roger Peterson's view) had gone down. Theories still circulate regarding the tragic start to the deployment. Lee Dodd:

> It is my opinion that they flew TFR all the way into North Vietnam. They dropped their bombs on target and forgot to pull up to clear the 'frag' pattern [debris from the explosion]. They were carrying Mk 84s which required 1,300ft (400m)

AGL to clear the 'frag'. I nearly did the same myself a few days later.

It is possible that they suffered disorientation by going 'hard ride' TFR all the way. After the first night's missions, 'Capt Bob Sponeybarger (who was in the number two F-111A) briefed us on his experiences. He was just about to enter North Vietnam when he was called back. He said that he and his WSO were basket cases by the time they got to North Vietnam. They had gone hard TFR all the way through Laos'.

Although the Nellis training had been very thorough there were still areas where it could not offer adequate background for the S.E. Asia experience. Col Robert F. Wendrock, who later became Deputy Commander for Operations at the 20th TFW in England, had 'never been lower than 1,000ft (300m) at night and I had never been on instrument conditions on TFR because neither was allowed in training. That was why a guy could end up hitting the ground at 200–300ft [60–90m]'. Col Mathiasen was well aware of the difficulties with terrain:

> Although we had trained in 'night, low-level' over the mountains of Nevada we found the topography of the S.E. Asian jungles very different and challenging. We encountered TFR difficulties early on, negotiating the steep karst; undulating vertical masses of stone cliffs. Each precipice put heavy climb/dive commands on the TFR in rapid order and with heavy bomb loads it was difficult indeed. Tree canopies, often 200ft [90m] above the ground, confused radar signals due to reflection and 'skipping' of the energy. The result was often unknown tree clearance, which was disconcerting. Exiting the land mass on the deck [many missions went out over the coast – 'Feet Wet' – after their attacks] was a high hazard as well. We found that the TFR could command a nose-down response as forward loss of signal returns resulted from the radar energy skipping off the smooth water. Our basic skills carried us through and we were able to adjust quickly to these anomalies.

Another possibility for that first loss was the weather. Capt Brad Insley, who flew seventy-five combat missions with the 430th TFS, pointed out that the deployment began at the height of the monsoon season. Heavy rain caused the TFR and ARS screens to go blank as the rain attenuation soaked up the radar energy without giving the receiving antennae a hardenough return to signal a fail-safe pull-up. Sometimes, in extremely heavy rain, the TFR/autopilot reverted to LARA, flying the aircraft straight and level as if over the sea, while the precipitation was actually disguising sheer karst inclines that required very rapid manual pull-ups. F-111 crews claim to have invented the expression 'granite overcast'.[4] There was a standard fall-back procedure for rain-TFR failures, as Brad Insley explained:

> We immediately climbed to a predetermined MEA (Minimum En-route Altitude) for that portion of the route. The night this actually happened to me we flew all the way to Thud Ridge before returning to bomb an alternate target in Laos. The weather apparently knocked out the enemy radars as well as ours because we were never 'illuminated' by their radar'.

When things worked well, as they usually did, the result was still an exciting ride. Roger Peterson:

> We would come into North Vietnam over Laos at medium altitude, then let down to TFR in the Western mountains. Often there was a low-altitude cloud layer of fog and you would slide down the mountains into the clouds only to pop up above the clouds intermittently as you climbed over some ridge. It would send your heart racing as you first entered those clouds because they often signalled the threat area where the Vietnamese would start shooting. Triple-A would light up the clouds like lightning.
>
> The skies were so black on a moonless night due to lack of light pollution that the stars were incredible. The St Elmo's fire was almost beyond description in terms of beauty. Often, in a two-ship formation, you would back away from your wingman's F-111 to avoid the static discharge from one aircraft to another. If you got caught in a rainstorm, they were intense, with rain so loud you could hear it in the cockpit despite wearing a helmet.

Tactics and Weapons Reassessed

After that first night of combat flying a five-day pause was ordered to reassess tactics. All incoming aircrew were made to wait three days before beginning combat, and their first mission had to be over the 'softer' Route Pack (RP) I before going north to the tougher areas. Even the 'lower' RPs could pose unexpected threats, as Roger Peterson discovered before he went on to win two DFCs over the North:

> My first combat mission with pilot Doug Kodak was at medium altitude. We were struck by lightning sixty seconds from the target and lost control of the aircraft. We recovered 2,000ft [610m] above the ground and managed to return to Takhli with only a radio and magnetic compass; all other electronics were lost. We could not jettison our bombs, twenty-four Mk 82s, and had to land with them.

Another consequence of the re-think was the abandonment of TFR'ing over Laos. 'Instead we would fly what we called a "No sh** MEA". Each crew worked out their own MEA based on their route. Our MEA was 500ft [150m] above the highest terrain along the leg of the route'. The more senior, experienced officers explored Route Pack VI targets first and then opened up the way to the rest of the troops. This also helped to establish a basic library of reliable RSP (Radarscope Photography) snapshots to assist newcomers. Lee Dodd:

> Many of our more experienced F-111A pilots had recently completed combat tours in S.E. Asia. Some will admit that the experience of flying a combat mission to Route Pack VI in the F-111A was totally unique and terrifying. My first target in RP VI was a North Vietnamese Army training camp in the hills just north of the city of Thai Nuegent, about 20nm [36km] from downtown Hanoi. The mission was a piece of cake until we started our final bomb run. We were carrying four Mk 84s on the pivot pylons. The Mk 84 is a 'slick' bomb. When released it will fly along at nearly the same speed as the airplane. At the point of impact the bomb is only a few hundred feet behind the airplane. To avoid getting 'fragged' by our own bombs our tactic was to start a 15-degree climb at 20 seconds TTG (Time-To-Go), using the Auto Bomb delivery mode. This gave the BCU a chance to recompute bomb range during the manoeuvre so that the bombs had the correct range data at release.
>
> Our bomb-run was on auto TFR at 500ft [150m] AGL. As we cleared the last rise at 30 seconds TTG the complete target complex came into sight. I told Bruce [Tourtellott, WSO] to look up and see it and he did. The camp was completely surrounded by a lighted perimeter fence and we were heading for the centre of the camp. About that time we both looked back in the cockpit and saw about 15 seconds TTG. Bruce put his head back in the scope, trying to refine his offset aimpoint and I pulled the nose up to start the climb to release. The TTG meter went to zero immediately and the bombs came off. I looked at the LARA and it read 600ft

Mk I Bombing Navigation System

The heart of the F-111A's navigation and offensive avionics was the Litton AN/AJQ-20A, which included an Inertial Navigation System (INS, known as the 'stabilized platform') linked to a Navigation Computer Unit (NCU) panel, bomb-nav distance time indicator and Ballistics Computer Unit (BCU). These worked in cooperation with a host of other subsystems, including the AC's ADI and HSI flight instruments, LCOS, and the autopilot to provide automatic or manual steering. It also was linked to the WSO's Attack Radar Set, enabling him to keep track of aircraft position, update it, guide the pilot and aircraft in the dark and through virtually all weathers, and perform precision-bombing and radar-assisted landings to boot. Known as the Mk I Bomb-Nav System, it similarly formed the basis of the F-111C/E core avionics, and first became operational onboard the Harvest Reaper F-111A fleet in early 1968.

MISSION WAYPOINTS Dominating the right-hand side main instrument panel in front of the WSO was the Bomb-Nav NCU panel, comprising a series of push-buttons, knobs, and 'windows', the latter consisting of a series of car odometer-type spinning digital counters. The WSO could, to all intents and purposes, fly the aircraft in the horizontal plane and bomb the target using this box of tricks.

During mission planning, the crew would plot a series of waypoints to the target and back, in a join-the-dots fashion. This plotted a course-line, bypassing known 'hot spots' of enemy SAMs and AAA batteries based on an EOB (Electronic Order of Battle), as provided by 'Intel'. They included all the relevant geographical coordinates on the map, including diversionary fields in the event of an emergency landing, for their 'route folder' which they would later take with them on the mission. This planning, which took up to four hours' work on the maps and charts, also embraced Offset Aimpoints (OAPs), landmarks which would be readily recognizable on radar to a skilled 'Wizzo', especially when flying over otherwise unfamiliar territory. Night or weather usually precluded reliance on visual sighting, and enemy defences meant that more circuitous routes often had to be chosen, making OAPs all the more important. These 'radar significant' features would comprise things like a riverbend or church, conspicuous ridge, or some other item which tended not to change much, rather than something relatively fragile or exotic. Along with coordinates, range and bearing of OAPs to the target or a key waypoint (such as the Initial Point, which would provide a reliable heading for the final leg to the target), OAP terrain elevation differences with the key waypoint and target was also jotted down. In determining the routes, crews made extensive use of RSP snapshots (radarscope photography gleaned from prior missions), while 'radar prediction' specialists were on hand in the early days to provide sketches of how the radar return should look on the cockpit radarscope. Final run-in headings to the target were usually prescribed by those overseeing the whole planning operation, to allow deconfliction – avoiding aircraft bumping into one another – in the target area, but the rest of the planning was left to the crews' discretion.

Prior to take-off, as part of the 'power on' checks which consumed up to an hour, the right-seater would align the inertial system with north and present position (the latter often being fine-tuned at the EOR or End-of-Runway), and this would provide a basis for the INS to subsequently update position on the instruments, based on aircraft movement. The AN/AJQ-20A 'sensed' speed and left/right movement via gyros and accelerometers and computed these with other inputs via the Central Air Data Computer to keep abreast of the aircraft's whereabouts at any given time.

Once in flight, the WSO would reach over to the NCU panel and enter the coordinates of the next destination – the next turn-point along the course-line – into the appropriate 'window'. With the navigation system coupled to the autopilot, this would take the aircraft to that destination automatically, whereupon the WSO would enter the next destination, and so on, all the way to target and back. However, it was customary for the ACs to be in charge of the actual turns and simply take a heading from the WSO, uncouple the roll autopilot and manually bank the aircraft onto the next heading, before letting it fly on its own to the next point. Steering cues were available on both the HSI and LCOS, if selected, for complete 'hands on' piloting, and pilots could uncouple the system to bypass unexpected enemy defences. And at any time it could be interrupted for such essential tasks as aerial refuelling. By entering the next intended destination or waypoint after 'gassing up', the NCU/INS system was simply instructed to 'go there', by comparing current and intended geographical coordinates. Timing mattered a great deal, so the WSO would keep an eye 'on the clock' and take short-cuts, or ask the pilot to throttle-up or down to make good time, which was always accomplished by dead-reckoning. A 'destination storage' capability was available too, providing three stored coordinates, but this was rarely used and it always proved just as easy for the WSO to enter the next destination one at a time, into the 'windows'. With the TFR taking care of pitch inputs to the autopilot, and the NCU furnishing steering, the system was akin to 'flying by buttons'.

If the navigation systems went awry, the crew would fly manually using map and radar dead-reckoning methods (an auxiliary flight reference system was available to help with this), though a fully functioning NCU/INS, just like a fully serviceable set of radar scanners to help navigate by and avoid the hard terrain ahead, was usually a prerequisite to continuing a combat mission. Manual and semi-automatic updating was possible using overflight of a prominent waypoint, and radar would also be used a good deal, as described below, to assist this process as well as for keeping a watch. Drift in the inertial system, albeit originally very low at about 0.5nm (0.9km)/hour, necessitated constant updating, and the system could 'crash', requiring in-flight realignment and updating from scratch. A novice WSO could wind up getting lost and missing his Time-Over-Target, and receive censure from both a grumpy AC and his fellows if he was not careful. For longer-legged sorties such as ferry trips at altitude, 'Great Circle' curved-earth navigation was available, but en route to a target the NCU/INS was operated in the 'Short Range' mode, which used a flat-earth model effective for legs of up to 200nm (370km). When approaching the target, the NCU would be switched over to 'Visual CCIP' (providing inputs to the gunsight for visual bombing), or 'Auto Bomb' (for automatic 'blind' bombing with the nasally housed BCU computer), or a 'Manual Ballistics' option if some of the automated systems were 'on the blink'.

The other data, including target coordinates, offset range and bearing, and heights, were all similarly fed into various 'windows' on the NCU panel, and the system would in turn generate useful feedback in the form of commensurate 'windows' expressing nautical miles to the next destination, present position, and so on. There were seventeen 'windows' in all, related purely to navigation and targeting. And, from 1972, a new 'Offset Box' dedicated to holding six offset coordinates was added, providing a pool of useful OAPs for critical waypoints and the primary and secondary targets.

ATTACK RADAR SET The GE(USA) AN/APQ-113 ARS was the primary navigation and attack look-out sensor installed in the F-111A/C/E (with very similar APQ-114 & -144 models later equipping the FB-111A and F-111F variants, respectively). Its importance was reflected in its nickname, *The Big Eye*. Without it, the crew were effectively fumbling in the dark when flying at night or 'in the weather'. The scanner was mounted above the two TFR radar sensors behind the radome on the same roll/pitch stabilizing unit which automatically compensated for aircraft rolling moments and different nose attitudes (within limits) to provide a steady radar image in the cockpit. It scanned 45 degrees either side of the nose at ranges of between 5nm (9km) and up to 160nm (300km) to provide four modes: air-to-air, plus two stabilized, wind-corrected high-definition PPI (Plan Position Indicator) radar ground maps, known as Ground Automatic Stabilized ('Ground Auto'), and Ground Velocity Stabilized ('Ground Vel'). The fourth option was a manual mapping mode known as 'Ground Manual', similar in most respects to 'Ground Auto' but without automatic correction for wind, and used purely as back-up. The radar map imagery was displayed in eerie electric-amber on the WSO's ARS scope panel, located just above the NCU panel, and he spent a good deal of time scrutinizing its 'paintbrush smear-like' radar returns, checking on navigation points, updating the systems, and watching for terrain obstacles.

CROSSHAIRS The bomb-nav system was highly automated and interlinked, but there was always a 'Wizzo in the loop' to maintain supreme control at all times. A vital tool was his right sill pedestal-mounted radar tracking handle, which could be used to tilt the ARS, and move the NCU/INS-driven crosshairs – comprising a straight azimuth one and a curved range cursor – about the radar display, to fine-adjust their position over the next destination waypoint, OAP, or the actual target when prominent during the final stages of an attack run. The coordinates for these points were set into the NCU 'windows' as described elsewhere and, by pressing the relevant grey buttons –

'target', 'offset', etc – on the instrument panel the crosshairs would automatically slide into place , confirming the aircraft was on track and that all was well. However, inertial system drift usually crept in during the course of the mission, so the crosshairs would shift 'out of whack'. The WSO would thus periodically update the navigation systems by taking the radar tracking handle, squeezing its enable bar, and move the handle about to synchronize the crosshairs precisely over the next destination, or sometimes a more prominent OAP (whichever was currently selected). Updating by overflight of a prominent landmark was also possible. When the handle was released, everything was automatically updated, including the counters or 'windows'.

Indeed, later in its career (from around 1987) the F-111's largely redundant 'Homer Set/Track' NCU button options (originally designed to plot enemy radar positions in conjunction with the RHAWS/CRS) were used for the 'Cursor Direct' and 'Ground Enter Visual Fix' (G-EVF) modes, respectively. The former allowed the aircraft to fly to its destination based on cursor position instead of NCU/INS coordinates in the navigation modes (as it normally did during weapons delivery), while the latter permitted a high quality fix to be taken at the end of the runway before takeoff. 'Both of these mods were designed to help out the cantankerous INS' according to Maj Jim Rotramel, in the days before the digital updates arrived. Scrutinizing the radarscope display and manipulating crosshair position was both a highly skilled science and something of an art which normally took at least six months' worth of operational flying to perfect.

It is worth noting here that in the ARS' 'Ground Auto' mode (and reversionary 'Ground Manual' mode), use of the tracking handle and its enable bar trigger moved the crosshairs about or 'over' the radarscope imagery. This mode could be used for attack but was generally employed for navigation, taking fixes and updates and getting lined-up on the target. In the 'Ground Vel' mode, which offered a specially expanded display for precision radar bombing, moving the tracking handle to make fine, last-minute adjustments actually shifted the radarscope imagery 'underneath' the crosshairs, which remained centred in the display. The area under scrutiny was selectively limited too, according to the range setting. For example, the 15nm (28km) radar range ('5/15') offered a scan showing a 5nm (9km) diameter about the crosshairs, effectively expanding the radar image threefold. The sweep would also be narrowed from the 90 degree big PPI pie slice shape to a narrower 20 degree one for a more rapid, freshly updated scan by switching the 'select' button forward on top of the radar control handle. As for target scrutiny, Col Richard Matteis recalled that 'More often than not the target was not radar-significant and we were required to carry an offset. We would try to select a point that would be clearly predictable on the radar and which was beyond the target. Once this was done you could move the radar crosshairs from the offset point to the target with only one button depression for each change [by pressing the 'target' and 'offset' buttons on the NCU panel, as described above]. It was normal to select the offset and once that was found the crosshairs would be moved to place them directly on that point on the radar. Then the operator would switch from the offset to the target and back. When the target broke out on the radar the operator would stay on the target until bomb release'.

With the crosshairs synchronized on the target and the aircraft zooming towards it, the system could be coupled to the autopilot (using 'heading nav') to fly it automatically to the target, but many ACs customarily preferred to be in control and maintain course via the steering deviation cues presented on the HSI and LCOS, just as they did with general navigation, as the target sometimes became visible through the windshield, making fine course corrections possible.

ARMAMENT SELECT PANEL As the time/distance-to-target counters wound-down, if he had not accomplished this in advance, the WSO would have been very busy at this juncture setting up the weapons ready for the bomb pass. The ASP (later known as the Weapons Control Panel) was located on the WSO's right instrument console, and comprised an array of large grey knobs and stops to configure the aircraft for weapons release. These embraced ordnance type, weapons station (pivot-pylons for the most part) and weapons fuzing (nose, tail or both). The release mode ('Step', 'Train' or 'Salvo') had to be selected. In combat, 'Step' would be used when there was more than one target, as bombs could be dropped in singles and pairs from selected stations during different bomb runs with each press of the 'pickle' (stick bomb release) button. 'Train' was similar in most respects, but release continued as long as the 'pickle' button continued to be held down. The release sequence was staggered between the bomb racks, with bombs being dropped at preset intervals set into the ASP intervalometer, so that the WSO could guarantee to straddle the target with ordnance. The intervalometer setting was based on the crew's preplanned attack speed and the target's characteristics. For example, during a low-level Snakeye bomb run at 480kt (890kph) with a setting of 125 (milliseconds), the bombs hit the ground some 100ft (30m) apart, resulting in twelve bombs producing a strike pattern measuring some 400yd (370m) by the width of the bomb blasts. 'Salvo' dumped all stores from the selected stations in one fell swoop and was a bit adventurous, apt to produce 'overkill' or a miss, or even problems with aircraft symmetry in the event of 'hung bombs' (resulting from a defective BRU-3/A rack or MAU-12C/A). Crucially, the ASP panel also contained the 'Master Arm' switch, without which a bomb run would have remained 'dry'; and, equally important, the 'Delivery Mode' knob. With the aircraft working as advertised for an 'all-up systems' bomb pass, the WSO would customarily have selected 'Nav' on the ASP (and 'Auto Bomb' on the NCU), to provide automatic 'blind' weapons release over the target.

BOMBS OFF! Maintaining target heading, the pilot then selected 'Level Bomb' on his LCOS gunsight to receive steering cues there and simply pressed and held down his stick-mounted 'pickle' button all the way through weapons release, to give consent to the AN/AJQ-20A to deposit weapons when its BCU had 'sensed' all the correct parameters – radar slant-range, aircraft speed etc – had been met to hit the target. Bombs would then come off the racks as programmed by the WSO in the ASP. Last-minute changes to airspeed and altitude/delivery angle were possible, provided the BCU was given enough time to chew over the new parameters being fed to it. It was not a 'canned' system, providing respect for its limits was observed by the Pilot; ultimately, however, crew and aircraft survival was paramount and it would be better to mess up an attack run and come back later for another attempt, rather than risk a dicey bomb drop for the sake of accuracy.

Releasing the 'pickle' button at any time during 'Auto Bomb' deliveries would effectively abort the bomb run, and a good cockpit rapport entailed systematic, succinct communication between the crewmen. At sixty seconds-to-target, the 'Master Arm' was usually thrown and switch modes confirmed. From now on, the AC would call off time-to-target at ten second intervals. 'Pickle point' varied with crews, depending on how clearly the WSO saw the target in the display during the last critical half-minute. Maj Dick Brown reckoned he usually pressed the consent button during the last 10–20 seconds, and continued with the countdown at ten second intervals until ten seconds-to-target, when the countdown ran by the second. 'If live ordnance was expended then we would execute the appropriate maneuver, turn to our egress heading and the WSO would select the next navigation point in the nav computer. In the case of most bombs one could feel the weapon(s) come off the aircraft'. WSOs would also switch the radar sweep back to 'norm' at this point, to avoid the dish banging against the stops and trashing the drive mechanism.

As an alternative, if it was clearly identifiable target, the AC (usually a high-ranker in these circumstances) might have instructed the WSO to switch over to 'Visual CCIP' on the NCU (in lieu of 'Auto Bomb'). In this instance, the pilot simply flew the wind- and drift-corrected LCOS 'pipper' to the target and pressed the 'pickle' button when they intersected in his line of sight, with the bombs coming off the racks instantly and theoretically hitting the ground exactly where the CCIP 'pipper' had been pointing at the time. A manual reversionary method was also used when the BCU was suspect, or sometimes when hitting the target was akin to shooting a barn door at three paces. Here the AC would ask the WSO to select 'Manual' (in lieu of 'Nav') on the ASP, which meant simply dropping bombs by eye. Weapons would then come off in 'train' as long as the 'pickle' button remained depressed, or a one-shot load would be deposited in the 'step' mode. It was a good, flexible system with plenty of leeway for the crews to intervene and take all sorts of compensating measures for 'down systems'. However, the Mk I Bomb-Nav System always remained highly 'task-saturated', and one incorrect switch setting could result in a goofed target pass. The theoretical 'switchology' described above barely touches upon the degree of training that went into preparing a mission-ready crew, and the coordination par excellence required in live combat situations which tested the mettle of men beyond the norm.

[180m]. I knew we were probably not going to survive the bomb 'frag'.

I pulled the nose up as hard as I dared. When I saw the first bomb flash I looked at the LARA and it read 1,300ft [400m]. I rolled us inverted at this point to 'split-S' back down to TF altitude. At this point I was mostly afraid I would depart the airplane, get spatial disorientation or get fired at by a SAM, none of which appealed to me. During this time Bruce got the show of a lifetime. The bombs hit several seconds apart and each impact lit up the whole target complex. Bruce swears he saw one make a direct hit on a large building. I was too busy to enjoy the fireworks. We got back on auto-TFR, smoked across the Delta as fast as that airplane would go (in fact, faster than it should have) and flew into Northern Laos. When I started the climbout I noticed that we were in one stage of afterburner on the left engine and making better than 0.9 Mach. This was not our original plan, but I didn't really care at this point. I would worry about fuel later.

In planning their missions Col Mathiasen let his men make many of their own detailed decisions on routes, deconfliction, timing and choice of radar offsets:

Target coordinates and suggested run-in headings were provided in the frag orders but I allowed aircrews full autonomy in route selection. I established a procedure whereby each crew briefed the entire squadron in detail the night following their mission, with emphasis on any surprising or unplanned circumstances they encountered. I believe these debriefings contributed greatly to our success.

Meticulous planning could ensure that each crew had an excellent chance of completing its task, but obviously there could be no real cure for the inevitable tension which each exceptionally demanding mission caused for some individuals. 'We had twenty-four hours to plan a mission', Lee Dodd explained. 'This obviously helped in the planning, but it was also psychologically stressing. Some of our crews were unable to sleep before a mission, others got nauseous and had to vomit before they could fly. Others had to get drunk'. Roger Peterson agreed:

Alcohol was a way of life for many of us, although most never flew under the influence. The missions would end any time at night or early morning and we would hit the bar for drinks and or food. Then sleep; prepare for the next mission, and fly. We generally flew every other night.

Time became meaningless during night operations. The Chaplain had to post a notice in the street to notify everyone whenever Sunday came about, otherwise there was little to tell one day from another. We closed off all our windows to give total darkness so we could sleep during the day. Our quarters (two persons to a room) had a huge air conditioner. We kept the temperature in the 60s.

By the end of October the F-111As and their crews were attaining the planned mission rates, which soon topped thirty per 24-hour period. Takhli's FOD-generating, crumbly runways were repaired, new revetments were built and logistics improved. Spares supplies were good, though often at the expense of home-based units. There was even a visiting delegation from the UK-based 20th TFW to study combat tactics. Aircraft reliability was problematic in the humid conditions. 'It was not uncommon to abort three airplanes before we got airborne. This,' Lee reckoned 'was exhausting'. A failed ALQ-94 track-breaker or APS-109 RHAWS was enough to cause an abort if it did not pass the 'squirt' check prior to take-off. All radar systems had to be fully operational and the humidity and lack of shelter for maintenance worked against this. Generally, the F-111A's basic structure held up well, though the few exceptions sometimes had spectacular consequences.

We lost one aircraft [67-0072] on takeoff due to a broken [undercarriage] strut. The F-111 came sliding to a stop on its bomb-load (twenty-four Mk 82s) off the side of the runway at just below take-off speed. The subsequent fire and explosions continued all night, with no fire-fighters able to approach the inferno. The crew survived, with one spending the night in a Thai Army bunker and the other being rescued in a brave move by the Air Police in an armored truck. He was running so fast down the runway that the armoured vehicle, with a top speed of 15mph [24kph], had to call to him to slow down so they could catch him. The armored truck had moved between him and the explosions to protect him. We resumed normal operations the next day.

Bombloads were initially four 2,000lb (900kg) Mk 84s, soon changed to twenty-four 500lb (225kg) Mk 82 LDGP (Low Drag General Purpose) 'slicks' or a dozen Mk 82 retarded Snakeyes which had to be dropped at speeds below Mach 0.8 to stop their fins being ripped off.[5] The Mk 84s became unpopular after several release system malfunctions which caused them to come off, armed, at low altitude with no warning. The carrier aircraft could be hit by 'frag', and this may have explained a couple of the early losses, including the first of only two from the 429th TFS. Capt James Hockridge and Lt Al Graham, in 67-0060, were carrying four Mk 84s against Phuc Yen airfield on 16 October. Although the prodigious ground defences may have hit them, bomb blast was an equally plausible reason for their loss. The North Vietnamese claimed to have discovered the crew, still in their module.

The heavier bombs were often saved for medium-altitude drops over Laos. Ground-based radar beacons were frequently used for these missions. The equipment used was similar to the USMC's TPQ-10 unit and there were five main sites in Laos. Col Mathiasen: 'We dropped the weapons using azimuth and distance instructions provided by the beacon operator'. Lee Dodd thought the system worked well:

Beacon bombing worked out great. Actually, we never had a chance to practice or train in it prior to our deployment. Our procedure was to fly to our target area and contact our 'friendly' on the radio. The friendly was typically a Laotian (or sometimes an American) sitting on top of a karst outcrop surrounded by bad Laotians or North Vietnamese. Friendlies were always glad to talk to us. We would drop a single bomb on the first pass of the first guess at the desired offset bearing and range. 'Friendly' would spot the splash and give us corrected range and bearing for the next pass. Next time around we would let everything go and return to base. We would usually have several more F-111s coming after us on the same target if it was under attack. Planning the Laotian missions became 'no brainers' after a while. We called these missions 'combat dumps'. We bombed offset using the radar beacon mode whenever we had a friendly to give us the desired offset bearing and distance. Accuracy approached LGB (Laser Guided Bomb) deliveries.

Col Tony Sobol of the 430th TFS told the authors that on these missions the F-111s 'dropped a lot of ordnance. I think we changed the magnetic anomaly of the earth there! There was a pretty good war going on down there and we would drop off CBU-58s (the primary ordnance) or 500lb [225kg] and 2,000lb [900kg] bombs'.

It was during operations over the Plain of Jars that the nickname *Whispering Death* was applied to the F-111 by the Royal Laotian Army, as Tony Sobol remembered. 'The reason was that we came in at medium altitude and the first time they heard us was when the bombs went off'.

One variation in procedure, though not a popular one, was Pathfinder or 'buddy' bombing. Single F-111As were used to lead small formations of other tactical aircraft to their targets. Roger Peterson explained:

We used to fly Pathfinder missions for F-4s but only during bad weather. In these missions we would lead a flight of F-4s to a target and drop in unison off the F-111's radar since the F-4 air-to-ground radar was so bad. These were all medium altitude missions. For fun, we would often turn on our automatic deception jammers (ALQ-94) during the join up to play with the F-4s' air-to-air radar. When they couldn't lock us up we would dump fuel and torch it, then ask the F-4s 'Can you find us now?' Usually, an F-4 pilot would spot the 150ft [46m] of flame coming out of the back of the F-111 and succeed in joining on us. The USAF 'threatened' to have us fly Pathfinder missions over North Vietnam with A-7s and F-4s. We were strongly opposed to this because of the extremely slow speeds they flew at medium altitudes. It gave us little manoeuvrability in case we had to evade a SAM. However, these missions never came about. There may have been a revolt if they had.

Lee Dodd was dismissive of this attempt to coordinate TAC's fighters: 'We hated these missions. No challenge or no targets killed; just monkeys and snakes'.

'Torching' fuel had its uses on other occasions too. Brad Insley remembers:

It was used for several reasons including visual ID for formation join-up, checking bomb-racks for hung bombs (bombs hung on rear outboard stations of the BRU were hard to see), impressing tanker crews who would ask to see our Zippo trick and, I am told, creating UFO sightings.[6] It usually took at least three stages of afterburner to torch off the fuel.

Wings were usually swept forward for the 'hung bomb' inspection as returning aircraft neared home base. Occasional encounters with KC-135A tankers were a frequent excuse for a little gratuitous fuel-flaming, sometimes seen from the tankers' viewpoint. Roger Peterson considered:

In between missions we were sometimes scheduled for tanker rides to be exposed to their mission requirements as passengers. These were a pain in the butt and dangerous because of the large fuel load and the extreme take-off distance required. If an engine failed on takeoff you were sure to be a 'crispy critter'. We needed no air refuelling but were more often scheduled to meet a tanker to give them practice. Afterwards we would torch the fuel. You could see someone else doing that 100 miles [160km] away. Often the light from the 'torch' exposed the crew of the KC-135 at the windows taking pictures.

F-111A 67-0085 returns from a Linebacker II **mission in December 1972.** USAF

Linebacker II

Despite the destruction wrought on North Vietnam by the renewed air campaign President Nixon could detect little change in that country's reluctance to negotiate a peace. He approved a JCS directive on 17 December 1972 which was designed to force the North Vietnamese to the negotiating table with a 'maximum effort of B-52 and TACAIR strikes against targets in the Hanoi/Haiphong area'. All the targets which many pilots had regarded as priorities since 1965 were released for attack. Between 18–29 December, 700 sorties by B-52 bombers poured explosive onto those targets, supported by 613 tactical missions. Suddenly, the Pentagon saw the F-111's role as being crucial to the campaign. Having proven itself in the *Linebacker I* phase the *Constant Guard* V force was unleashed on railway yards, the nineteen MiG-capable airfields, army barracks and SAM sites among many other vital targets. They were probably the most heavily defended targets ever tackled by US aircraft.

Triple-A (AAA) presented the main threat, some of it radar-directed ZSU-23 but mostly sheer volumes of flak, hosed into the path of each solo F-111 or aimed at its noise.

On one mission we were attacking a target near Hanoi from the north and my Squadron Commander Lt Col Martin was hitting a target nearby from the south at the same time. We could follow his flight-path by the amount of AAA following his aircraft and after the mission we remarked on this to him. He stated, 'Hell, you should have seen the AAA being shot at you!'. They generally fired behind us due to our speed and the difficulty in picking us up visually or on radar. The intensity of the AAA was similar to, and visually demonstrated by, the CNN videos of the AAA over Baghdad in the Gulf War. It was beautiful in a strange and scary way. It seemed to be in slow motion like a firework show. At times it was so close that it shook the airplane and you could hear the explosions.

Direct retaliation was not an option; other aircraft were usually tasked with flak suppression and in any case the F-111As could not shoot back. Like their *Combat Lancer* predecessors they carried the M61A-1 gun, but at that stage it was seldom loaded. 'They didn't want us strafing the enemy with a $15m airplane', Roger Peterson reflected. Mainly, the gun was retained to preserve cg balance. Similarly, 'Dropping on enemy AAA was strongly discouraged since we were to hit our primary targets or alternates only'.

Lee Dodd's memory of ZSU-23 AAA was of a 'terrifying experience. They produced a solid wall of tracers when they got a lock-on. We had no defences against this weapon. If the Soviets were to load it with non-tracer ammunition no-one would know they were getting hosed until the airplane disintegrated'. Brad Insley had particular recollections of it at Phuc Yen airfield, on a mission where he had to return to Takhli and switch to another aircraft, having lost everything but his standby instruments over North Vietnam. He still managed to make a very tight time on target (TOT). Phuc Yen communications centre controlled the air defence assets north of Hanoi.

We had very strict timing on this sortie as we had to arrive ahead of the B-52s and be off target five minutes before their TOT. We let down after entering North Vietnam and flew a route through the mountains north of the Delta, and were headed almost due west at 400ft [120m] as we approached the target. After about a minute we saw an 85mm gun start firing, which seemed ridiculous at our altitude. As we approached bomb release, weapons of all calibers began firing at us from the right side. We released our twelve Snakeyes and concentrated on getting out of there. The tracers looked like fire hoses streaming water at us. A bullet with your name on it will look initially like it is being fired in front of you, which of course it is. We had been briefed that the Vietnamese had one of their two ZSU-23-4s at Phuc Yen and we spent a lot of time trying to decide which way to turn off target to try and avoid it. We eventually said, 'What the hell, let's fly right over it'. We got some pretty accurate and intense fire from one gun position which I believe was the ZSU-23-4. We crossed back into the mountains east of Hanoi and climbed up to return home when a warning went out about 'two blue bandits [MiGs] on the 270 degree radial at 75 miles [120km]'. Since that was our approximate position I started looking around and saw two planes go by in the opposite direction. One turned north and other turned on us. We started a descent back to low level with the TFR but he locked us up in the descent. The ALQ-94 started working and it dropped his radar off in space somewhere. I was a great believer in that band of the ECM after that. In most cases I believed in silent running as we felt they often fired at us to get us to jam in order to locate us.

Suppression of the thousand-plus SA-2 missiles which were fired during *Linebacker II*, mostly at B-52s, was one of the *Roadrunners'* other missions. 'Single pass, haul ass' attacks using CBU-58s were made against launch sites and SAM assembly or storage locations. Lee Dodd flew against a SAM complex 7 miles (11km) northwest of Hanoi on 20/21 December and two nights later. On the second mission another 429th TFS F-111A (67-0068, callsign *Jackal* 33), crewed by Capt Robert D. Sponeybarger and Lt William F. Wilson followed thirty minutes behind Lee in the same area, but against a Hanoi river docks target. They succeeded in putting twelve Snakeyes on target but lost their right engine on egress. Possibly it took a 'barrage' flak hit though the crew were not aware of this. A rapidly developing fire and loss of hydraulic pressure made a quick exit their only choice. Bob Sponeybarger was caught after two days in hiding while Bill Wilson managed a whole week on the loose in which he used virtually every trick in the survival handbook. After two attempted helicopter rescues he was caught out by one of the enemy's own ruses, a trip-wire attached to an explosive charge to alert the search-party. Both men saw out the war in the 'Hanoi Hilton'.

Several of the other 1972 losses were as mysterious as those of *Combat Lancer*. Because F-111A operations were virtually all single-ship and radio-silent, apart from occasional check-in calls to *Moonbeam*, the ABCCC (Airborne Command and Control Center) aircraft, which were not always made. They also flew without the F-105G *Wild Weasel*, EB/RB-66C Destroyer jammers or KC-135A tankers which could normally keep track of strike aircraft. Establishing the cause of a crash usually began with zero evidence and many theories are still debated by ex-*Roadrunners*. A recurrent interpretation, based on experience, involved the TFR and its tendency to induce insidious height loss. Col Rob Balph, then a Lt WSO with the 429th TFS, recalled one pilot, Jerry A. Fetter, who had set his TFR to the 200ft (60m) minimum, expecting it to signal an automatic fail-safe fly-up at about 135ft (40m). His F-111A was down to 70ft (21m) when he caught the fault. Lee Dodd had a similar experience:

The auto TFR normally worked well over terrain. Over surfaces such as water or snow-covered lakes the system would go into LARA override which usually worked OK but had a very dangerous failure mode. In LARA override the TFR climb/dive commands were generated by the position of the LARA pointer. If this 'froze', which it did when it malfunctioned, at an altitude above the one which had been selected, the auto TF system would descend the airplane into the water or ground. I experienced this one night going 'feet wet' out of North Vietnam. Fortunately, I was looking for this to happen when it did. A 400ft [120m] AGL ride was selected when we went 'feet wet'. The LARA was reading about 30ft [9m] high. I cross-checked the barometric altitude, which was not a normal part of the TFR cross-check, just as we were descending through 200ft [60m] AGL.

At least three of the six *Constant Guard V* combat losses could conceivably have been connected with this phenomenon. Stafford and Caffarelli (in 67-0092) went 'feet wet' after a 21 November mission in RP I. Normally they set 200ft (60m) on the TFR, and wreckage washed ashore in South Vietnam suggested that the aircraft had impacted the sea at a shallow angle with no attempt at ejection. Roger Peterson had a simple, poignant memory of their passing:

They lived across the hall from me and Doug Kodak. The first time I heard of their loss was when the maid told me in the morning, 'They no come back last night'.

I remember being on R&R at Pattaya Beach with three other crews during one of the bombing halts over the North. Feinberg stated that he had a dream in which Ward and McIlvane were lost on a mission. We told him he was nuts since there were no combat operations. We called the base and were told to return since operations were resuming – and that we had lost a crew: Ward and McIlvane.

It is thought that Ops Officer Dick Ward's aircraft (67-0099) had also entered a shallow descent while egressing its target on the first night of *Linebacker II*. Maj Brown and WSO Morrissey of the 430th TFS were also going 'feet wet' on TFR after a November RP I mission (in 67-063) when they disappeared.

One threat which never really affected most F-111 crews was North Vietnam's MiG force. Interceptions were attempted against a few crews, including Brad Insley, but were easily out-run by going auto-TFR and into full military thrust.[7] In any case, the MiGs were preoccupied with the B-52 formations during December. However, as Lt Col Jon Jordan told the authors, MiGs could be a distraction and he attributed one of the early losses to a crew who were 'inordinately concerned about MiGs', and may have overlooked a crucial TFR warning at low level as a result. Roger Peterson was adamant that, 'there was no chance a North Vietnamese pilot would attempt to attack a low-altitude F-111 at night, and no chance for him to catch a high-altitude supersonic F-111'.

Overall, the two Takhli squadrons sustained a remarkably low loss rate. At 0.15 per cent it was better than the peacetime training attrition for many units. Their 4,000 combat sorties between October 1972 and March 1973 were some of the most demanding in the Air Force's history and concerns about the defences were often marginalized by the basic tasks of flying the aircraft to the target. Roger Peterson:

Generally, low-altitude combat missions overloaded the crews due to the intensity of the missions and the multiple tasks to be accomplished. As a result, often we would mentally 'tune out' the lesser demanding tasks, such as radio calls at turn points and ECM warnings of SAM and radar activity. Our typical counter to SAMs and radar was to go lower until the signal disappeared off the RHAWS scope.

During *Linebacker II* the F-111 finally and conspicuously proved itself as a new and vital asset, able to hit heavily defended, pinpoint targets with great accuracy and with minimal risk of being intercepted or hit. Pentagon officials who had so recently regarded it is a 'lemon' began to appreciate its qualities, and even on occasion over-estimate them! Jon Jordan was given an ammunition storage area 20 feet (6m) square as one of his targets: 'A bit extreme for an aircraft dropping bombs 100ft [30m] apart'.

It was an evolutionary process, as Brad explained: 'The longer we were flying sorties the more they discovered our capabilities. We started getting targets that only we could effectively hit, such as airfields and SAM sites. The crews knew what the airplane could do and how to do it, but the planners had to be convinced'. Brad also echoed a view which the authors have frequently heard from two generations of F-111 aircrew: 'I can think of no other aircraft I would rather have taken into combat'.

Post-War Conflict

Linebacker II forced a peace agreement but the F-111s remained in Thailand. The 430th TFS was replaced by the 428th TFS *Buccaneers* on 22 March 1973 and combat missions continued against insurgent forces in Laos, most of them medium-altitude drops. By this stage the beacons were usually operated by 'indigenous personnel' with call-signs such as *Red Dog*. One of these sorties ended in a mid-air collision, a very rare occurrence for the normally-solo F-111. On this occasion an F-111A with radar failure asked a second aircraft to 'pathfind' their target for them. Col Ken M. Alley and pilot Glen Perry lost 6ft (2m) off the wing from 67-0066 and made a 240kt (444kph) landing at Udorn, ripping out the mid-field BAK-9 arresting cable but catching the departure-end BAK-12 successfully. Major Robert P. McConnell and Dick Skeels ejected from the other aircraft, 67-0111.

On 30 July 1973 the Takhli squadrons were taken over by the 347th TFW at the base, causing a code change from NA to HG. As the wider war wound down twelve aircraft were returned to Nellis in September and in June 1974 the remaining F-111As were moved to the other ex-Thunderchief base, Korat RTAB. Until the cessation of operations on 15 August 1974 they continued to attack targets in Cambodia. Roger Peterson flew many of these sorties from Korat, remaining there until October.

These beacon-guided targets were seldom seen directly by aircrews before we released bombs. If there was trouble communicating with the 'indigenous personnel', a Yank (possibly CIA – we were never told) would get on the radio to straighten out the communications. Releases were always above 15,000ft [4,600m] to avoid enemy shoulder-fired SAMs and AAA.

F-111A 67-0013 of the Takhli-based 428th TFS, which was under 347th TFW control by 15 August 1973 when this aircraft was photographed flying its last combat mission in S.E. Asia. USAF

However, after release we would often go low and fast (600kt plus) to check out damage and the target – not always the same. I remember one F-111 (not mine) accidentally striking friendly forces when a crew put an inverse radial [bearing] into their BCU.

These missions were quite mundane with little threat. Often we would take high-speed tours of Ankor Watt. We were told if we ejected over the Tonle Sap to remain near the middle of the lake and wait for rescue: the crocodiles had control of all the shores and they were huge.

Before the Aardvarks finally returned to Nellis in June 1975 there was a final flurry of activity: the *Mayaguez* Incident.

Hunting the *Mayaguez*

In May 1975 the Cambodian Navy boarded the US merchantman *Mayaguez* and took the crew as prisoners, causing a major international incident which dominated the US media. Lt Col Kenneth S. Law, who flew F-111As with the 347th TFW at Korat, describes his part in locating the vessel:

The hot, steamy air of the tropical environment hung heavy over the tennis courts of Camp Friendship, our little fenced-off living compound located several miles from Korat AFB. The rythmical ca-thung, ca-thung of the ball bouncing and meeting my racket echoed through the still, sultry, early morning jungle heat as I started the ritual of another day in my one-year tour of duty on the F-111A.

It seemed that I had no more than started my conquest on the tennis court when someone had the audacity to yell at me to jump into my 'green bag' (flight suit and boots) and pedal my posterior down to the squadron for an unscheduled flight to look for a cargo ship with a name that no two people pronounced in the same manner – the *Mayaguez*. It was somewhat exciting to receive an intelligence update which placed three of my fellow officers and myself in the unique position of possibly being the first to locate the shanghai'd vessel. Intelligence briefed us with the latest known information on where the ship was not located. Air Force C-130 and Navy aircraft had been out searching but to no avail. The F-111 was selected because of its duration, speed and radar/radio equipment.

After a quick briefing and an hour of mission planning we grabbed our helmets, tested our oxygen masks, donned our G-suits and boarded the step van heading for the flight line. Exterior pre-flight finished, my pilot and I strapped in, started through our checklists, completed engine checks, brought the INS up to speed and waited for radio check-in with Ellis 1, the lead aircraft of our two-ship flight. Check-in accomplished, we rolled out to the main taxi-way for join-up and a final quick-check from maintenance personnel when a staff car pulled up and a fellow jumped out waving a 35mm camera. It seems that no-one had the forethought to come up with the idea that it would be nice to have some pictures to verify what might be found. After the No. 2 engine 'rolled back' I opened the canopy and was handed the camera and roll of film. This was the nearest thing to a shooting mechanism that the Flight had. A few minutes later we lined up on the runway and sat in pulsating thunder of Lead's afterburners which thrust him down the runway fifteen seconds ahead of our brake release.

It wasn't until we were in radar range of the position where the *Mayaguez* was thought to be (Paulo-Wai Island) that I could feel the adrenalin start to flow. It was also then, after a few hard jinks, that I discovered my radar azimuth stabilization was gone and my radar kept sectoring off the scope. This negated the use of my radar, but with good radios, an updated INS and a VFR day we were still in good shape. Ellis 1 had a good radar but his HF radio was inoperative. This meant that I would be the one to maintain contact with Blue Chip, the Tactical Air Force S.E. Asia Communication Center.

We stayed in loose visual formation at around 5,000ft (1,524m) and turned towards another island on my navigation chart named Ko Tang. It was only a minute later that Lead advised us that he had a bright blip on his scope which could be nothing but a large ocean-going vessel. My scope sectored around and the ship's return banged in; there was no doubt! We stayed up and idled back to conserve fuel. Lead went on down for a low pass to get a look at the name… it was definitely the *Mayaguez*. Raising Blue Chip on radio I confirmed our find and also related that several small PT-type boats were near her hull. As Ellis 1 screamed by her deck top level the gnat-like parasites peeled away and headed for the Cambodian mainland. Blue Chip advised us to try and divert them by making low passes over their bow. Shooting at them with a 35mm Nikon had no effect! After the gnats had departed we went down to take a closer look at the anchored behemoth… no sign of life could be seen.

The ship was later boarded by US Marines from the USS *Holt*. Three of the gunboats were sunk, one by a direct hit with a Mk 84 dropped from Lt Col Peacock's F-111A. 'All that was left', Roger Peterson recalled, 'was smoke on the water'.

This 428th TFS F-111A earned its 'F-for-fighter' designation. Armed with four AIM-9B Sidewinder training rounds it duelled with Northrop F-5s at the Fighter Weapons School. Roger Peterson

CHAPTER FOUR

Bullet Bombers

The eighteenth RDT&E F-111A later served as initial FB-111A testbed and also conducted SRAM-A captive-carry trials. The markings are calibration dots, not SAC 'Milky Way' markings. USAF

In keeping with his devotion to 'commonality', on 10 December 1965 McNamara pressed TFX on Strategic Air Command, the full-time nuclear alert arm of the USAF. 210 older models of the B-52 'Buff', and the 'hot' but complex silver B-58A Hustler were all to go by 1971, replaced one-for-one by a production run of 263 of the FB-111A model, allowing 53 for training and attrition reserve – the 'B for Bomber' in the prefix being largely a subtle change of designation to assuage SAC chiefs. In meeting the operational demands of SAC, General Dynamics was once again obliged to stretch 'commonality' further, producing an aircraft with a gross takeoff weight approaching fifty-five tons, although weight gains in the 'baseline' F-111A, which featured progressively increased internal fuel capacity, soon placed this within easy reach. However, in the absence of the intended Rockwell Mk II Bomb-Nav system, which was behind schedule, SAC opted for the hybrid analogue-digital Mk IIB, requiring a wholly new, subsidiary avionics development initiative to tie the new package together and provide it with hardening against nuclear electromagnetic pulse (a feature B-52s lacked). That was the right decision, but the delays inevitably resulted in a scaling-down of orders to 112 aircraft, pending availability of the revised avionics. And following McNamara's resignation as Secretary for Defense in 1968 (to become President of the World Bank, a post he held until his retirement in 1981), the incoming Nixon Administration's new Sec-Def Melvin Laird chopped these down further to the definitive figure of seventy-six machines on 11 April 1969, 'to salvage work in progress'. As a consequence, thirty-six further assemblies in production at that stage were diverted to TAC F-111D production instead, a version with which it shared some common internal structural characteristics.

It was during the lead-up to all this, a time wrought with political angst over TFX/TFX-N in Canberra, Washington and London, that Britain's Royal Air Force pulled out of the TFX programme. The Wilson Cabinet, having cancelled the impressive BAC TSR-2 six months after forming their Government in October 1964, later promised fifty F-111Ks in their stead. The order for the aircraft, to be equipped with the promised Mk II systems, was announced on 1 February 1967 – and then was subsequently cancelled on 17 January the following year, when the first two machines, YF-111K testbeds equipped with mostly trials avionics, were virtually ready for roll-out. These were deemed uneconomic to adapt for American service use and were unceremoniously reduced to spares.[1] However, some forty-eight capsules and nineteen part-built F-111K airframes were turned over to FB-111A production, without the slightest raise of the UK Defence Minister Dennis Healey's famous eyebrows.

GD was obliged to juggle airframes based on these numerous changes to Contract 13403 (that which eventually encompassed Lots 5 thru 20, comprising 491 of the eventual 562 production tally), which in turn further escalated costs because of the loss in flow-through rates and economies of scale which had been the jewel in McNamara's original vision of 1,500 'common' aircraft. The seventy-six run of FB-111As funded in Fiscal Years 1967 thru 1969 thus wound up costing $1.2 billion, 700 per cent of the planned cost of the originally envisaged 263 SAC-model aircraft run! A patient cadre of frustrated engineers and job-nervous shop fitters, part of the 30,000 GD work force engaged on the TFX programme during its heyday, began to wonder what the airframes they were working on at the time would eventually emerge as. It was fortunate for GD, in their own words at the time, 'that 82 per cent of the airframe parts are common to two or more versions'. However, rework required some considerable 'gutting' of electronics, and expensive refitting as airframes rolled down the mile-long GDFW final assembly line, and the FB-111A remained utterly unique while TAC redrafted plans to distribute 'Wing-plus attrition' sized batches of follow-on models, the F-111D, E and F, described in the ensuing Chapters, for one-model-per-Wing operations.

Features

Structurally, the FB-111A differed from its tactical cousins in featuring a redesigned rear hourglass fairing and fuel vent (part of a rear fuselage redesign which housed revised long-range communications electronics, shunted through the HF/UHF in the fin), the extended wings of the Navy version for greater turning performance, lift and cruise economy, and stronger landing gear and brakes – and adjacent fuselage frames – to permit takeoffs at up to 119,240lb, (54,075kg) and landings at gross weights of up 109,000lb (49,431kg) at an 8ft/s (2.5m/s) sink rate. Two non-flying articles were specifically fabricated at Fort Worth to wring-out the beefier airframe and gear, including B6 as a landing gear fatigue example, and B5 which was subjected to destructive drop tests. In service, this structure has only failed when abused. Range was enhanced by increased provisions for jettisoning fuel tanks and pylons on the fixed, outboard stations (which the tactical models never used in practice, just as the FB-111A only ever used six of its eight stations), and pylons were redesigned specifically for a snugger fit with drop tanks and nuclear weapons, the only envisaged stores.

The first airworthy SAC model was actually a modified RDT&E F-111A, A1-18 (63-9763), which first flew on 31 July 1967 with GDFW test pilot Val Prahl at the helm. This machine, adapted for preliminary test work with the added external fuel 'baggage' necessary to increase range, was joined by two further, fully fledged prototypes: FB-111A B1-01 (67-0159), still equipped with Triple Plow I inlets, and B1-02 (67-0160), which featured the interim 'Superplow' version with double blow-in doors. B1-01 first flew on 13 July 1968, the second in the fall, and all three slightly different aircraft spent the remainder of their service lives engaged purely on test duties, including trials of the Boeing AGM-69A Short Range Attack Missile (SRAM-A) which would form the heart of the FB-111A's weapons arsenal in operational service, alongside the gravity devices.[2] Fully fledged production examples kicked-off with B1-03 (67-0161), delivered in June 1969. By mid-December there were seven all-up FB-111As pounding the paving. Four

FB-111A 68-0247 in the original 'SAC SIOP' scheme of greens and anti-flash white, with tiny 509th BW(M) badge on its flank. The aircraft later became one of two AMP testbeds. Lockheed-Martin

GDFW F-111 Production Delivery History

Month	Monthly Del.	RDT&EF-111A	TACF-111A	TACF-111E	TACF-111D	TACF-111F	SACFB-111A	RAAFF-111C	Cum. Total
Dec '64	1	1							1
Jan '65									
Feb	1	1							2
Mar									
Apr	1	1							3
May									
Jun	1	1							4
Jul	1	1							4
Aug									
Sep									
Oct	1	1							4
Nov									
Dec	2	2							8
Jan '66	1	1							9
Feb	1	1							10
Mar	1	1							11
Apr									
May	1	1							12
Jun									
Jul	1	1							13
Aug	2	2							15
Sep									
Oct									
Nov									
Dec	3	3							18
Jan '67									
Feb									
Mar									
Apr	2		2						20
May	2		2						22
Jun	1		1						23
Jul	3		3						26
Aug	3		3						29
Sep									
Oct	1		1						30
Nov	6		6						36
Dec	2		2						38
Jan '68	4		4						42
Feb	3		3						45
Mar	5		5						50
Apr	7		7						57
May	1		1						58
Jun	1		1						59
Jul	7		7						66
Aug	14		13					1		80
Sep	3		2					1		83
Oct	8		7					1		91
Nov	12		12						103
Dec	3		3						106
Jan '69	4		4						110
Feb	4		4						114
Mar	8		8						122
Apr	8		8						130
May	8		8						138

BULLET BOMBERS

Month	Monthly Del.	RDT&EF-111A	TACF-111A	TACF-111E	TACF-111D	TACF-111F	SACFB-111A	RAAFF-111C	Cum. Total
Jun	11		10				1		149
Jul	9		8				1		158
Aug	12		6	2				4	170
Sep	16			2			1	13	186
Oct	4			2				2	190
Nov	21			14			3	4	211
Dec	12			11			1		223
Jan '70									
Feb									
Mar									
Apr									
May									
Jun	1				1				224
Jul	1			1					225
Aug	19			12			7		244
Sep	20			8			12		264
Oct	19			10			9		283
Nov	18			10			8		301
Dec	18			12			6		319
Jan '71	11			7			4		330
Feb	10			1			9		340
Mar	8						8		348
Apr	2						2		350
May	3			2			1		353
Jun	1						1		354
Jul	1				1				355
Aug	1				1				356
Sep	3					3			359
Oct	9				1	8			368
Nov	10				1	9			378
Dec	10				2	8			388
Jan '72	9				2	7			397
Feb	10				2	8			407
Mar	10				2	8			417
Apr	13				5	8			430
May	14				6	8			444
Jun	8				5	3			452
Jul	5				5				457
Aug	7				7				464
Sep	9				9				473
Oct	11				11				484
Nov	9				9				493
Dec	10				10				503
Jan '73	8				8				511
Feb	9				8	1			520
Mar	2					2			522
Apr	1					1			523
May	1					1			524
Jun	1					1			525
Jul	1					1			526
Aug	1					1			527
Sep	1					1			528
Oct	1					1			529
Nov	1					1			530
Dec	1					1			531

Month	Monthly Del.	RDT&EF-111A	TACF-111A	TACF-111E	TACF-111D	TACF-111F	SACFB-111A	RAAFF-111C	Cum. Total
Jan '74									
Feb	1					1			532
Mar									
Apr	1					1			533
May									
Jun	1					1			534
Jul	1					1			535
Aug									
Sep	1					1			536
Oct	1					1			537
Nov									
Dec	1					1			538
Jan '75	1					1			539
Feb									
Mar	1					1			540
Apr									
May	1					1			541
Jun	1					1			542
Jul	1					1			543
Aug									
Sep	1					1			544
Oct									
Nov	1					1			545
Dec	1					1			546
Jan '76									
Feb	1					1			547
Mar	1					1			548
Apr						1			
May	1					1			549
Jun	1					1			550
Jul	1					1			551
Aug	1					1			552
Sep	1					1			553
Oct	1					1			554
Nov	1					1			555
Totals		18	141	94	96	106	76	24	555

of these were engaged in full-time Category II USAF preliminary service trials at Edwards – and Carswell, adjacent to GDFW, where an additional three had been assigned to the newly formed 4007th CCTS (Combat Crew Training Squadron). The parent Wing, the 340th Bomb Group, was headed-up by Col Winston E. Moore, who personally accepted 'tail' 67-7193 on 29 September 1969. The new Mk IIB navigation and bombing system showed promise. However, things barely got off to a start before the frightful 'Aircraft 94 Incident' at Nellis grounded the entire fleet for seven months.

Tanks and Tankers

When fleetwide operations resumed at the end of July 1970, the production bottleneck was unstopped and SAC maintenance took delivery of no fewer than sixty-seven further aircraft through June 1971. Training had continued unabated with ground academics and Singer Link Division simulator procedural training and, as minimum crew entry qualifications consisted of 2,000hrs logged flying time for Pilots and 1,500hrs for Navigators, the aviators – mostly ex-B-52 'Buff' or B-58A Hustler – rapidly made up for lost time. As was the case throughout the F-111 community right to the end, Navigators (they were never called 'Wizzos' in SAC service) were drawn from the top 10 per cent of their peers. Pilots were mostly hand-picked and SAC had a great 'pool' from which to siphon the required talent. Most of them were incredibly enthusiastic, particularly the 'Navs' who were accustomed to working in confined, dark corners of SAC 'heavies' in a psychologically alarming, downward-firing ejection seat, or cocooned in a Hustler's claustrophobic escape bucket wearing a *Dr Who* 'Cyberman' outfit with windows which merely cast distracting light on the

A 509th BW(M) 'Bullet Bomber' hooked-up, in this instance with inert AGM-69 SRAM-A training rounds underwing, which could also be carried in the weapons bay ... via Lockheed-Martin

... And delivered at supersonic speeds *(below)*. The FB-111A introduced the AGM-69A to service under Project Bullet Blitz, which included live firings over the White Sands Missile Range in New Mexico, beginning in 1971. via Lockheed-Martin

instrument panel rather than offering any diversion. GD's 'shirtsleeve environment' in the '111 was a major revelation. In 1971 Maj Harold M. Donahue judged that a SAC 'Nav could never before see out while he was working, and now, instead of being a navigator who does dead reckoning and figures Estimated Times of Arrival with a pencil, he's a computer operator. Also, he's a flight engineer, a co-pilot and a defensive systems expert. His world really changed in this airplane – and he can see outside!' It was like entering a new century. The high degree of automation available via the Mk IIB Bomb-Nav system was a great novelty, turning navigators into 'Whiz Kids', and placing them in a position where they would actually be in *de facto* control of much of the mission. Sitting next to the driver, they could develop a genuine rapport with the pilot in charge, rather than merely respond to curt orders over the intercom from somebody 'up front'.

For the SAC pilots, the *g* they pulled, the sprightly handling characteristics of the Aardvark (a name SAC adopted only very late in the aircraft's career) and the kudos attendant in flying a brand-new machine were all attractions which had volunteers banging at the door of the more correctly termed 'FB-111A Program'. By this stage all of the aircraft featured the definitive powerplant: Triple Plow II inlets and TF30-P-7 engines, rated at a useful 20,350lb (9,230kg) each in afterburner for take-off, and 10,800lb (4,900kg) each in continuous cruise once up to speed. The newfound enthusiasm in the right seats acted as a catalyst to the pilots, with the instructors responding very quickly by honing basic proficiency on the 'nav switches' and radar too, so that they could fly from either seat. In common with all but the cancelled Navy machines, Aardvarks could be flown from the right seat, though the left command position offered primary access to several critical controls.[3] The professional interrelationship generated in the cockpit set new standards: the ability to look across and see what was going on, especially in the days before interactive multifunction cockpit displays became available, was a definite bonus, and sharpened wits with massive payoffs to mission prowess and safety. There was no time for daydreaming and either crewmember could give the other a gentle nudge, or helpful pointers which might have gone amiss in a tandem cockpit arrangement. It was a unique set-up within the SAC community.

The 70ft (21m) span wings of the FB-111A are clearly evident here, as its engines fight the drag created by the MLG door-cum-airbrake which opens up the bay to swallow the folded trunnion and landing gear 'as if by magic'. Frank B. Mormillo

(Below)
Tanking was essential to the FB-111A community and the introduction of the KC-10A Great White to Aardvark operations from 1986 proved a boon.
USAF photo by Walt Weible

SAC Mk IIB Avionics

BACKGROUND Designed as a stop-gap system, the SAC Mk IIB avionics package installed in the FB-111A proved so successful that a similar TAC Mk IIB was evolved for the definitive model, the tactical F-111F. It possessed many features of the Mk I package, including a virtually identical Texas Instruments AN/APQ-134 TFR and Honeywell AN/APN-167 LARA, plus GE APQ-114 ARS with its familiar 'Ground Auto', 'Ground Vel' and 'Ground Manual' ground-mapping modes, although processed mapping range extended out further to 200nm (370km). Married to this were those components from the Mk II system that worked early on in that development effort: the Rockwell AN/AJN-16 INS, and IBM Digital Computer Complex (DCC). Together, they created a hybrid cockpit which at a glance looked very similar to the F-111A's, but on closer inspection contained an extensively revised right-hand 'office'.

The sensor suite was also expanded with the addition of two new devices in the nose barrel, embracing the Singer-Kearfott AN/APN-185 downwards-radiating Doppler radar, which helped provide additional data on aircraft velocity and drift (by measuring the change in Doppler frequency reflected back into its horn antenna); and the upwards-looking Litton AN/ASQ-119 Astrotracker, which could take a positional fix based on sightings of up to 57 stars through its Cassegrain optics, day or night, which were compared with stored celestial patterns held in its memory. These provided supplementary positional update data to the INS, but could also help build a redundant 'navigational model' in the event the INS went 'on the blink' – a not irregular occurrence.

DCC The heart of the Mk IIB, which replaced much of 'the old cogs, gears and pulleys' of the Mk I, was the DCC, comprising two IBM 48K AN/AYK-6 computers. They were mutually redundant devices, with one serving as General Navigation Computer (GNC) and the other as Weapons Delivery Computer (WDC) at any one time. The computers were capable of using both digital and analogue inputs (converting the latter, as required), and offered redundancy in navigation and targeting as the DCC would use inputs from the subsidiary systems, including the Central Air Data Computer, Doppler and Astrotracker, and the Auxiliary flight reference system, in the event of INS failure, to generate the all-essential 'navigation model'. However, the AJN-16 INS remained crucial for absolute accuracy, this being aligned to within one hundredth of a minute (60ft/18m) for takeoff coordinates, with only marginal drift thereafter. Providing it worked, creeping errors were easily erased by means of ARS radar crosshair fixes, or inputs from the Astrotracker.

Another crucial difference between the Mk I and Mk IIB was that the GNC could be fed with a complete mission flightplan in advance of take-off. The Navigator did not have to enter destinations one at a time in flight, after each turn-point. Instead, these could be keyed-in in sequence on the right instrument panel during the power-on start-up phase on the ground. Alternatively a 'bigger than deep freezer'-sized computer in the operations section could be given the flight-plan coordinates, including multiple offsets etc, in turn churning out a punched paper-tape containing all the required information. Ground specialists would then take the tape, housed in a suitcase-sized device, and plug it into the DCC complex in the nose, to transfer the information directly. Once fed in, the aircraft then knew where to go from takeoff all the way to the target back home, based on up to 150 navigational data points encompassing the complete flight-plan – and up to four OAPs per turnpoint or target. All aircraft on nuclear alert were preened this way, containing data for the SIOP flightplan and offsets well in advance. A later AMP computer update massively expanded this capacity during the last few years of the FB-111A's career.

NAVIGATION DISPLAY UNIT The NDU replaced the old 'Navigation and Attack' NCU panel with a slightly more compact configuration, and represented the most obvious physical change introduced by the Mk IIB in the cockpit. Instead of the 'windows' featuring spinning cogs with numbers on them, there was a new bank of LED (Light Emitting Diode) digital displays, much like those found on domestic radio-alarm clocks or VCRs. These included most of the familiar 'window' based data, including present position and the next (or other selected) sequence point coordinates, speed, heading, wind, and time and nm to the next destination. It also flashed up a brand new LED readout showing the next destination number: each turnpoint, including those for the IP and target, was given a 'sequence number', and the computers would follow these in the correct order unless the Navigator elected to bypass some ('Sequence Interrupt') to take a more direct route, or command a completely different change of heading.

The key factor here was that the aircraft would not only fly from one destination to the next in sequence, automatically, but it would also execute the appropriate bank-to-turn movements all by itself with the autopilot switches engaged. Of course, pilots were still at liberty to uncouple the roll autopilot and bank the aircraft onto its new heading manually, while letting TFR provide automatic pitch inputs. Here, the navigators would call out changes of heading a few degrees right or left, while watching for terrain in the main radarscope, so that the crew might take advantage of a valley or ridgeline rather than blaze over the top of it and expose themselves to enemy defences. Re-engaged, the computers would then swing the aircraft back on course to the next destination point all by themselves. This, combined with the TFR automatically taking care of terrain following, created 'an other worldly experience...', with the rock-steady, glassy-smooth flight control system and high wing-loading giving crews '...the impression that the earth was moving beneath them, rather than the other way around'. But it was no arcade game. Systems had to be monitored with just the same degree of vigilance as before, including wing-sweep and throttle settings to ensure the aircraft would clear the peaks and pull up in the valleys and gullies, as hitting the ground at transonic speeds meant almost certain death.

GREEN THE NUKES For attack, the Navigator would select stores stations using a new push-button array on his right console, including a special SRAM master control panel to select the delivery mode for that weapon. Also, 'consent' was required from both crewmembers to arm nuclear weapons via a switch, with the navigator also having to enter a series of Permissive Action Link codes, based on those contained in the EWO folder and cross-referenced with the mission codes conveyed over radio. These would have been dispatched by the US Defense Department's WWMCCS (Worldwide Military Command & Control System), including airborne Looking Glass EC-135s and NEACP (pronounced 'kneecap', National Emergency Airborne Command Post) E-4s, in which the JCS and Presidential Staff and aides would have orbited at altitude following a SIOP launch. From their lofty perches they would have conveyed the final 'go' or recall codes to the FB-111As, prior to them reaching enemy airspace and the LLEP. At that juncture the crew would have probably dropped below line-of-sight for radio communication and would have become literally incommunicado. From March 1979, AFSATCOM (Air Force Satellite Communications) was introduced, including a new digital teletype panel in the cockpit. This bypassed the possibility of radio communications jamming, and also permitted crews to be recalled, or retargetted, even after having begun Auto TF'ing operations, as they would always remain within line-of-sight to at least one satellite to receive Emergency Action Messages (EAMs).

Weapons fuzing was also crucial, and not just a simple 'nose or tail, or both' as with conventional ironmongery, but a more complex affair selected on the Discrete Control Unit 137/A in the right-hand corner, which offered multiple FUFO (Full Fuzing Options) using a large safety-latched knob: 'Freefall' or 'Retarded' bomb deliveries in 'Air Burst' or 'Ground Burst'. Calling up target and OAP positions on the NDU, and synchronizing the ARS crosshairs on OAPs and target during the bomb run by means of the radar control handle was procedurally similar to a conventional attack using the Mk I avionics package; the main difference was that there existed four little grey Offset buttons on the NDU to tinker with, to help define target position that much more precisely, and it was customary to use at least two of them. While nuclear warheads might appear to render such accuracy something of an irrelevancy, targets embraced underground missile silos and command and control bunkers where pinpoint targeting was crucial. An error of only a couple of hundred yards might leave a hardened facility 'dug up' but otherwise intact and operational. For this reason accuracy was judged paramount, and rigorously evaluated by means of RBS scoring during ORIs. Some 'overkill' was also prescribed, calling for up to two bombs or three SRAMs per hardened target.

With the target tracked by the radar crosshairs and the FB-111A's Mk IIB Nav mode systems switched to 'Bomb' or 'SRAM', weapons selected and fuzed, and master arm 'on' the computers would have flown the aircraft to target, and then taken care of weapons release automatically at the correct time. This would have taken into account the chosen weapons ballistics: retarded or freefall bomb delivery, or SRAM-A mode, factoring-in the missile's 'strike footprint' at ranges of up to 100nm (185km) from the release point. The pilot would have to keep the 'pickle' button pressed on the stick to provide 'consent' for weapons release, and would have been in complete control of executing the relevant aircraft delivery manoeuvre – e.g. a low-angle pull-up, or high-angle 'toss' – to help the weapons on their way. Timing was also closely monitored, with the customary digital Bomb Nav Distance Timer Indicator furnishing seconds-to-go to weapons release in the normal manner. Either crewmember could effectively abort the run by removing consent, although the crew were clearly within easy punching distance of one another!

It was during this lead-in phase with simultaneous Category II–III testing that much unique FB-111A doctrine was evolved. First, to extend range but also permit a useful payload, the FB-111A had to perform one of aviation's more curious sights on takeoff in the combat configuration: a compromise 16 degree wing lock-out with the outboard, fixed pylons (stations 2 and 7) housing external fuel 'bags' pre-set at 26 degrees, obliging FB-111As to roar down the runway and take to the air with the outboard tanks pigeon-toed. (Australia adopted this technique for its RF/F-111C operations too.) Minimum Interval Takeoffs (MITOs) of 7.5 seconds between aircraft were possible, at double the rate of the B-52 and KC-135. With wings reset at the 26 degree lock-out as soon as the gear was up and speed had risen to a healthy margin, the aircraft would become less sensitive to roll inputs.

required a far better rehearsed join-up, with a much tighter 'time gate' at the RZIP (Rendezvous Initial Point). Hanging the aircraft in the sky when it desired to go much faster required constant trimming with the slightly more fore c/g (centre of gravity) but it behaved well and its 'solid' flight characteristics actually made it a much easier refuelling receiver than its big, flexible-winged Boeing counterpart. The FB-111A and its tanker would attempt to arrive at the same spot in space simultaneously. The KC-135s, which would have already MITO'd in advance of the bombers and climbed to 25,000ft (7,620m) ahead of them, would dive to build up speed, while the bomber performed a similar manoeuvre from 20,000 down to 19,000ft (6,100 to 5,790m). They would steer to meet the tanker, before popping-up behind to go 'on the apple' and absorb pumped fuel through the telescopic metal straw, to bring them

would employ the standard point-parallel refuelling method, whereby the tanker held a racetrack orbit at the pre-established ARCP (Aerial Refuelling Control Point) and the FB-111A slid in up behind, standing by on its wing if others were there first. That technique would have been accomplished on the return legs from a nuclear strike.

For alert purposes, tanker-bomber ratios had to be high, usually one-for-one plus spares for the RZIP, with a similar set-up at two locations during the return journey. Unplugged, the FB-111A crew would make maximum use of Great Circle transpolar navigation direct to the carefully pre-planned LLEP (Low Level Entry Point), to squeeze top range out of the aircraft. It involved meticulous preparation and timing, and little scope for error. Crews on alert, to all intents and purposes locked away from their families and friends for

The FB-111A usually carried four nuclear weapons – two in its belly and two on the inner wing pivot-pylons, freeing the outer pivoting- and two fixed-pylons for drop tanks. The outboard tanks were thus carried 'pigeon-toed' (just discernible here) in line with the 26 degree wing lock-out, creating a most peculiar sight at take-off. USAF photo by Walt Weible

The first event after takeoff was to 'gas-up'. Customarily, a B-52 'Buff' embarked on its initial cruise-climb at a fairly leisurely pace using its giant wing to gain altitude gracefully and join up with the kerosene-donor, using easily-matched speeds, whereas racier FB-111As, loaded with external nuclear weapons and drop tanks,

to an AUW (all-up weight) of some sixty tons (notionally 122,900lb/55,730kg). The selective use of afterburner on one engine (a technique perfected by TAC crews carrying stores on a mere four stations) could be used to stop the heavy FB-111A dropping through the air. For routine missions, and return top-ups, crews

days at a time, were able to study radar predictions (and later, satellite photos) and focus on their potential mission, which was one little cog in the giant SAC SIOP (Strategic Air Command Single Integrated Operations Plan). Klaxon-commanded MITO takeoffs rang through the bases up to four times a month, and gruelling ORIs

(Operational Readiness Inspections) were sprung on the crews at roughly 12–15 month intervals.[4] In a live target-venturing Aardvark, outboard tanks and the intermediate tanks would be jettisoned as fuel was consumed and the 'bags' ran dry, with fixed outboard pylons being dumped also to permit greater wing-sweep settings, leaving the aircraft with only internal fuel, four nuclear weapons (up to two in the weapons bay and two on the inboard pivot-pylons), and two empty pivot-pylons, in a relatively 'slick' configuration for a live target-venturing Aardvark. However, with only a 4,150nm (6,680km) range after top-up at the RZIP, basing plans were soon established to provide a little further reach, and New England was chosen. Basing here placed the aircraft closer to the Soviet Union via polar navigation routes, while the cold winter air would provide sprightly takeoff performance for part of the year as an added bonus. It also placed them closer to Europe.

FB-111A 67-7194 was severely damaged in a hard landing and ensuing fire in February 1976. It was later restored to new at Fort Worth *(below)* using the rear end of the second FB-111A prototype, 67-0160, and was subsequently nicknamed Franken'Vark! It was the beginnings of the Fort Worth 'Plane Hospital'.
both Lockheed-Martin

Pease and the 'Burgh

The 4007th CCTS' seven month-long courses began with daytime flying and progressed on to night-time/instrument low-level work, to provide the nucleus of the new training cadre. They were aided a little by the TAC community at Nellis who provided much in the way of ground academics.

First to equip on the type was the 509th Bomb Wing (Medium) *Enola Gay* at Pease AFB, New Hampshire (the wing taking its name from Paul Tibbetts' Hiroshima-striking B-29). The 509th received its first aircraft in December 1970 and tentatively achieved its ORI the following year, just after Upper Heyford's F-111Es became nuclear-qualified, owing to the FB-111A pioneers having to do 'exam resits'. That experience sharpened skills and by 1973 the 509th boasted two operational squadrons, the 393rd BMS *Tigers* and 715th BMS *Eagles* and was nominally furnishing eight of its thirty aircraft on full-time nuclear alert. Under Col Paul W. Maul's direction, it added SRAM-A to its repertoire later that year under an operational test programme codenamed *Bullet Blitz*, which included seventeen launches of inert weapons at the White Sands missile range in New Mexico, the first of which was performed by the *Eagles* in early 1974. Annual SRAM launches were conducted subsequently, though with a limited stock of missiles this meant two per year for the whole FB-111A community.

Meanwhile Plattsburgh AFB, with an Authorized Unit Establishment of thirty-eight aircraft and the appropriate callsign *Heat*, pressed ahead with the formation of

Nuclear Weaponry

SIOP PHILOSOPHY SAC's Emergency War Orders for the mission of Armageddon were heavily integrated under what was known as the Single Integrated Operations Plan (SIOP). This embraced tankers, command, control & communications posts, and even strategic reconnaissance assets. Orchestrating the SIOP relied upon very precise timing, to coordinate tankers and strikers and to overwhelm enemy defences with a maximum blow. Although communications (e.g. AFSATCOM) improved during the FB-111A's alert career, allowing ever greater flexibility, the nuclear doctrine remained much the same throughout the FB-111A's tenure with SAC, embracing a sequence of command- and clock-related 'milestones' crucial to the perceived success of the mission:

- 'Go Code', otherwise known as the Positive Control Turnaround Point, when the crew would verify orders as to whether to return, remain in a holding pattern pending further orders, or proceed to target.

- Hour Control Line. Every attack aircraft would have had to pass through a line, drawn around enemy territory, within a 3-minute assigned 'time gate' for precise timing.

- Low-Level Entry Point. The coordinates where the FB-111As would have let-down to radar-evasive low altitude in Auto-TFR.

- Start Countermeasures. The point in time where the force would 'switch on the music' – electronic countermeasures – to have overwhelmed enemy radar, missile and fighter defences.

Crews would fly to their assigned targets autonomously rather than in flights, with the FB-111As relying on speed, low-level flight and their comparatively low radar cross-section to evade enemy defences.

Typically, a combination of SRAM missiles and gravity bombs would have been carried. As larger industrial and military targets were assigned to the B-52s' cruise missiles, the FB-111A increasingly was tasked to use gravity bombs and SRAMs against first- and second-tier defences in a Strategic 'Swing Wing Wild Weasel' role, destroying heavily defended targets like enemy radar complexes, MiG airfields and command and control centres, as part of the SIOP philosophy of 'rolling back the defences' to open up corridors for the few heavies assigned to penetration, and fellow FB-111As.

SILVER BULLETS There were three, overlapping generations of nuclear gravity weapons employed by the FB-111A, the first two having been compatible with the Tactical F-111 fleet, and utilised on *Victor Alert* F-111E/Fs in USAFE between 1971 and 1985, when the alert tasking was usurped by the Ground Launched Cruise Missile.

The first of these was the late 1950s-generation Mk/B-43 (the prefix 'Mk' and 'B' being interchangeable). The B-43 was a high-yield (Megatonnage) device, measured 12.5ft (3.8m) long and was fitted with a steel spike in its nose to penetrate hardened targets. It could also be employed for air burst. Keeping the weapon upgraded became a constant headache and it was soon supplemented in FB-111A service by the more modern and compact 11.5ft (3.5m), much lighter B-61, which became the mainstay Aardvark nuclear bomb. Its design and evolution, like SRAM-A, more or less paralleled that of the F-111 'family'.

Known as the 'Silver Bullet' because, 'like its Coors beer namesake, it doesn't slow you down!', the B-61 came in a sinister natural metal finish with a red-brown fibreglass radome concealing the radar fuze, behind which was a hardened penetrator nose. It did not limit aircraft performance one iota, and FB-111A crews were cleared to fly the aircraft as if it was 'clean' (no stores, with optional pivot-pylons, assuming the tanks had been 'punched off'). Its origins can be traced back to August 1960 when initial feasibility studies began, and the weapon was designated TX-61 on 18 January 1963 when the design had been completed. The first freefall ballistic tests were conducted at the Atomic Energy Commission's Tonopah Test Range site in Nevada on 20 August, production engineering of the 'Mod 0' version began in May 1965 and full-scale production in October 1966. By 1987, when production ended, some 3,150 had been built in 'Mod 0' thru 'Mod 5' format (with 'Mod 6/8' versions following, based on updated earlier models, including a 'Mod 7' high-yield type). The Conventional Forces in Europe (CFE) Treaty and Bush-Yeltsin Strategic Weapons accords later effectively put a stop to the programme, though over 900 remain in the USAF inventory today, the remainder having been dismantled and destroyed. Later versions contained some 4,000 parts in 1,800 subassemblies manufactured by 570 suppliers and nine primary contractors, and it is astonishing the details of the weaponry was such a well-kept secret for so long.

During the Aardvark's heyday, the weapon came in two fundamentally different internal formats, employed using 'angular', 'laydown' or 'toss' deliveries based on radar/INS and the Dual Bombing Timer. The 'Mod 0/1/2' employed a 17ft (5m) diameter nylon parachute for 'retarded' (airbraked) deliveries in low-angle drogue and laydown modes, enabling the FB-111A to escape the shockwave. Such deliveries could be conducted supersonically, and as low as 200ft (60m) AGL or as high as 5,000ft (1,520m) AGL and offered 'air burst' and delayed surface burst options. The parachute remained stored for 'freefall' 'slick' deliveries, invariably conducted in a 'toss' manoeuvre, permitting a rapid change of course after release while the bomb arced up in the air and then down towards the target. This mode offered either airburst or ground contact burst. In a nutshell, an air burst would be used to destroy a large, sprawling target (such as a factory, docks, marshalling yards, air defence complex or airfield), with detonation set from ground level at ground zero up to nearly 10,000ft (3,050m). A ground contact burst was designed to take out pinpoint targets such as missile silos and command and control bunkers, by partially penetrating the target before detonation. Delayed surface burst meant the bomb would settle down and go off at ground level over half a minute later. These earlier models were in widespread use with the FB-111A force as soon as they became available for operations, while USAFE F-111E/Fs assigned to *Victor Alert* soldiered on with the B-43 and tactical-only B-57.

The 'Mod 3/4/5' B-61, in production from May 1979, effectively supplanted remaining B-43 models in the '111 community, and introduced a new nylon-Kevlar 24ft (7.3m) diameter parachute for supersonic deliveries as low as 50ft (15m) AGL. With its new microprocessor-based FUFO (Full Fuzing Options) this permitted FB/F-111s, flying supersonically, to conduct a laydown retarded ground contact burst attack, making full use of their speedy on-the-deck delivery capability to hit hardened targets with precision. Equally important, FUFO offered crews the flexibility to select fuzing mode and yield in flight (which was hitherto accomplished on the ground, before takeoff). Yield could be switched between 100 and 500 kilotons with a special low 10kT option for tactical nuclear warfare applications.

Routine training in USAFE made full use of BDU-33 and Mk 106 practice weapons to emulate 'freefall' and 'retarded' deliveries, respectively, but FB-111As tended to employ electronic Radar Bombing Scoring, whereby the aircraft transmitted a 1,020 Hertz signal over its UHF radio to signal time-of-release to a ground scoring receiver, which was plotting aircraft position. All the crew saw was the green 'bombs away' lamp. RBS was better suited to judging accuracy and polishing techniques with the Strategic Aardvark as the aircraft practised both simulated gravity weapons ballistic drops and SRAM releases. WTD Range sorties and exercises employed the Douglas BDU-38/B, in all respects identical to a B-61 in terms of shape, weight (and even featuring its telescoping parachute deployment rod and nylon-Kevlar retarding 'chute), but with the entire device painted in an innocuous gloss white colour 'so as not to alarm the natives', as Maj Fred Zeitz put it.

The B-77 high-yield thermonuclear bomb, designed for deliveries at speeds of up to Mach 2.2, was trialled by FB-111As in the mid-1970s but cancelled in December 1977. In its place came the Livermore Laboratory's B-83 after Congress became fed up funding expensive B-43 and B-61 updates to keep the high-yield versions viable, and the weapon was on the verge of entering the FB-111A arsenal in the late 1980s, just before aircraft retirement. Only a few of its BDU-46/B training shape equivalents were deployed before the FB-111A bowed out of strategic operations.

SRAM-A The AGM-69A Short Range Attack Missile (SRAM) evolved almost in parallel with the FB-111A programme. In the aftermath of the cancelled B-52 Skybolt programme, Boeing undertook studies beginning in December 1963 towards a Short-Range Attack Missile. Not entirely coincidentally, the following year the USAF developed SOR-212 resulting in the drafting of Weapons System 104A, stipulating just such a weapon offering a rocket-assisted range of 100nm (185m). With its head start, Boeing won the contract on 31 October 1966, and live firings (with inert warheads) were well underway by the summer of 1969. Initially SRAM equipped only B-52s, which desperately needed the standoff capability, but studies suggested that the FB-111A would actually prove to be an excellent launch platform, because of its more accurate INS and more stable, high-speed flight performance. Missile capability was thus built in to the Mk IIB specifications by adding CAE (SRAM Carrier Aircraft Equipment). The first

> **Nuclear Weaponry** *(continued)*
>
> supersonic launch was made as early as 22 September 1970, bearing out predictions: SRAM could be launched at up to Mach 1.1 at low-level to impart extra range, and offered double the accuracy compared to the B-52. Close on the heels of equipping 'Buff' units, SRAM-A entered service with the FB-111As of the 509th BW(M) during 1973 and remained a mainstay weapon for seventeen years.
>
> Internal missile guidance employed a Singer-Kearfott KT-76 Inertial Measurement Unit (IMU) married to a Delco onboard computer to command varied, pre-programmed flight profiles, all of them being possible following weapons release at low-level:
>
> - Semi-Ballistic. Launched straight at the target, whereafter the missile flew an arc-like trajectory up, and then down towards the target. This was the least accurate but offered maximum range, at around 100nm (184km).
> - Terrain-Sensor. Low-level flight after launch using a radar altimeter for terrain-avoidance, keeping it under the enemy's radar umbrella to reduce the chances of detection.
> - Inertial. Launched at a set altitude and bearing for optimum accuracy.
> - Combined inertial and terrain-sensor. The most sneaky and accurate, but it limited range to about 35nm (65km).
>
> Original plans called for selected numbers of SRAMs to be equipped with the Sylvania AN/ALR-37 Radiating Site Target Acquisition System (RASTAS), to turn the missiles into dedicated anti-radar missiles with a nuclear punch. However, the programme was dropped, as SRAM inertial accuracy was deemed sufficiently potent to enable crews to fire them against radar targets acquired on the AN/APS-109 RHAWS (and later AN/ALR-62 CRS), which could be linked with the ARS crosshairs to plot target position on the radarscope, for target-locating accuracies of about half a mile – sufficient to knock out most radar and SAM complexes. However, most launches would have been against pre-planned coordinates set out in the EWO using radar-inertial targeting, just as was done with gravity bombs, and the traditional methods offered much greater accuracy.
>
> Alert FB-111As could carry up to six of the 14ft (4.3m) long, 2,230lb (1011kg) million-dollar SRAMs, but a maximum of four was more typical: two in the weapons bay and two more on the inboard wing pivot pylons (stations 4 and 5). When mixed with gravity weapons, the SRAMs were carried in the weapons bay.
>
> Launch procedures were lengthy, with missile warm-up taking place well in advance of release. This required the Navigator to select each missile in turn, and then feed its KT-76 with a 'navigational model' supplied directly by the FB-111A's Mk IIB. This gave the weapon present position and velocity, and target coordinates, based on the INS-driven ARS crosshairs. (In the mid-1970s, following the FB-13 SRAM computer software update, the system was not entirely INS dependant and similarly could be fed with a navigation model derived from the auxiliary sensors). The missile then began 'thinking', aligning its IMU while the pilot would make small manual changes of heading every quarter of an hour or so to 'torque' the weapon, keeping it alert and accurate, right up until the planned release coordinates; the missile itself knew where to go after release by comparing present position at launch with the target coordinates it was given. Ideally, release was fully automatic, with multiple launches in 'Train' employing overlapping countdown sequences, at intervals of 2.5 seconds. A back-up 'SRAM manual' mode also permitted launches at 5 second intervals (such manual reversionary methods becoming increasingly available with later 'FB' software packages, as part of its annual systems updates). Immediately following release a Lockheed, later Thiokol, hydroxyl-terminated polybutadiene rocket motor ignited to accelerate the weapon up to Mach 3, the missile using body lift to maximize range after rocket burn-out. Fine changes to course heading were accomplished using its three chunky tail fins, to deliver its W69 warhead which packed a persuasive yield of 170kT.
>
> With their anti-flash curtains lowered over the clamshell hoods, the FB-111A crew would not have waited to witness the results and would run for home.

two operational squadrons of its own, also to maintain a minimum eight-aircraft alert commitment: the 528th and 529th BMS, which began their transition to the new 'swinger' on 17 July 1971. They achieved IOC on 1 January 1972 and were declared ready to support SAC's EWO (Emergency War Order) by the branch's Inspector General on 6 June that year. In September 1973 they absorbed the 4007th CCTS, which by that time had logged 3,179 sorties and 13,312 flying hours.

Another change introduced by the FB-111A had to do with operating philosophy: whereas TAC crews would fly training sorties with maximum systems and abort if things went awry, SAC crews flew training missions with deliberately degraded systems and trusted that the alert aircraft preened for maximum readiness, and exchanged for other aircraft following a routine Klaxon alert launch, would function fully most of the way to the target (with dead-reckoning probably entering the equation by the time they were ready for a recovery in Iceland or Turkey, failing post-strike aerial refuelling). The need for this open approach to systems arose after it became clear that avionics MTBF (Mean-Time Between Failure) was 4.5 hours. To the SAC community it spelled trouble, and the 509th actually failed its first ORI when eight of its twenty-three aircraft achieved poor bombing scores owing to failed INS equipment. It was soon realised that combat mission duration would almost certainly involve flight times of up to twelve hours, during which time two key items would likely break down. 'Degraded' training, introduced shortly after and adopted FB-111A fleetwide, thus involved 'no INS', the main culprit, whereby a Navigation model had to be created using only the auxiliary sensors, and 'INS autonomous', which assumed that the DCC had failed, resulting in manual bombing (a much less likely event as the computers exhibited 98 per cent reliability). However, learning to derive a position 'hack' for manual weapons release, by manipulating radar crosshairs purely manually over key offset aimpoints was also practised regularly, in case the bombing circuitry went awry, and that explains why FB-111A 'Navs' enjoyed access to four offset aimpoints per turn point and target, all selectable on the NDU instrument panel as individual little grey buttons. With all working to order, only two were usually required. Later software updates to the systems allowed crews to switch selected systems to standby rather than 'off', making safe night-time and Auto TFR operations possible with degraded avionics, something TAC crews were never expected to accomplish even in peacetime training in night and the weather.

The Singer 'Swinger' simulators – one at Pease and two at Plattsburgh – played a big part in routine training, especially in helping crews through the process of learning not to become too reliant on a fully-functioning aircraft. Crews would have 3–3.5 hour sessions in them eighteen times a year. Beginning in August 1977 'out of the window' vision was added to the simulators for extra realism, and the three devices and their operators were some of the busiest at the base, working in two daily shifts over fifteen hours, with any necessary maintenance taking place in the night hours.

Proud Shield

Crews usually 'pulled' one alert session each month, put in a restful week wrapped around that, and then crammed in all their real flying time in the twelve or so flying days left each month. Training missions, in common with the Stateside TAC

An artist's rendition of the proposed FB-111H version, which never happened. The FB-111B/C variants were externally identical, and even a Sea Lane Interdiction version, using the Navy's Phoenix missile system, was proposed. Lockheed-Martin

community, involved sporty flying over the wilderness, using specific corridors available on Military Training Routes, embracing Instrument Routes (IRs) where the crews could fly by night and in the weather, and Visual-only Routes (VRs). As Jim Rotramel noted some years ago, 'Unlike Britain, where we're told where we can't fly, in the US the FAA (Federal Aviation Administration) and environmentalists have teamed up to tell us where we are allowed to fly'. Many of the routes transited the Strategic Training Route Complex, which included *Olive Branch* (formerly bearing the more war-like name *Oil Burner*) Radar Bomb Scoring (RBS) facilities. Rather than 'pickling' off a practice bomb, the aircraft transmitted a signal from which the RBS personnel could deduce weapons delivery accuracy, based on the strength and timing of the signal relative to their radar plot. For SAC crews, an error of a mere two seconds was 'off the mark'. The training routes had the environmental advantage that they served as sanctuary for much of America's wildlife, so were very sparsely populated too, but the disadvantage that the fauna included buzzards and eagles which could present a serious birdstrike hazard. Nevertheless, FB-111A crews flew all-out a good deal of their time, as their 'ordnance' did not present the same encumbrance as six-packs of conventional bombs, and would be 'dropped' during transonic-supersonic dashes to practice shockwave evasion. As Capt Tom 'TJ' Johnson recalled, 'From the exhilaration of "bending" the 'Vark through the valleys in tac formation to the intense concentration of a night IFR/TFR radar laydown, the FB-111A was a total joy to fly. A 'Vark at 1.2 Mach at 50ft (15m) is a sight that will water your eyes'.

Despite all the excitement and intensity of getting things right, it was mostly a low-profile profession, with crews working their way up from initial novice status to attain 'Mission Ready', then 'Senior' or 'Select' status (which ironically usually resulted in gradually fewer flying hours): 13, 12 and 11 sorties a month each, respectively. This was punctuated with occasional publicity for a few of them at the annual SAC Bombing and Navigation Competition. Managed by the 1st Combat Evaluation Group, personnel selected from nominees were given only five days' notice prior to the event, to rule out advance preparation. The FB-111A's digital technology enabled it to excel, with the '111 crews customarily collecting many of the nine trophies up for grabs. They were initiated to the *Giant Voice* competition (later retitled *Proud Shield*) in 1970, when 340th BG crews put in an appearance, complete with large 'flying deuces' painted on their tails, signifying their attachment to 2nd Air Force. The two operational Wings passed to 8th Air Force control on 1 January 1975, and that was when participation started to become a major annual event. When 'Varks from the 'Burgh were not picking up trophies – they came out top in 1974, 1976–78 and 1984 – crews from Pease were. The 509th BW(M) received top honours between 1979 and 1983 (with the exception of 1980, when the well-represented 'Buff' entrants finally got a look-in, although the wing still took the John C. Meyer Trophy for low-level excellence in bombing that year, picked up by the crew of 69-6509, *Spirit of the Seacoast*). 380th BW(M) pilot Capt Tom Johnson who finished second (behind a Pease FB-111A) during the Aardvark's final SAC Bomb-Nav Comp in 1989, flying 68-0244 *Lucky Strike*, recalled that 'This is a tribute to not only the operators, but the hundreds of maintainers whose hard work and sweat made that jet fly like it was brand new'. In fact, during that *Proud Shield*, '111s from the 'Burgh, Pease and Cannon swept up all three top placings for the LeMay trophy (most bombing points earned by an individual crew). It was an outstanding aircraft crewed and maintained by outstanding people, and its later success has been unparalleled.

As well as regular participation in *Red Flag* and *Green Flag* wargames at Nellis, Nevada, the 393rd BMS *Tigers* made a couple of European appearances to take part in the NATO 'Tiger Meets'. FB-111A 68-0247 took part in the 1978 'do' at Kleine Brogel, Belgium with a complete tiger tail, and in the 1987 meet at Montijo, Portugal, *Dave's Dream* (69-6508) and *The Wild Hare* (68-0272) featured feline striped yellow rudders. Their round trip took them to Belgium and Lakenheath before returning to Pease.

The Big Stretch

Despite its unquestionable prowess, many further up the chain of command viewed the FB-111A as mere institutional preparation for the up-and-coming 200-ton AMSA (Advanced Manned Strategic Aircraft), the Rockwell B-1A bomber. This swing-wing design was to utilise the same low-level, terrain-masking doctrine as the FB-111 and would take over the penetration mission in the early 1980s, but with a commensurately bigger payload (including the new SRAM-B) and longer range. However, the B-1A project was terminated by President Carter's Administration in July 1977, leaving the USAF to scratch around for a replacement. The FB-111A seemed like a good place to start as it was the only SAC aircraft offering true high performance. SAC had already anticipated this scenario and dusted off some older studies, while GD began to explore the possibilities of an enlarged FB-111 variant in earnest. By 1977 this included the proposition of withdrawing the sixty-seven strong operational fleet and modifying them into further-reaching FB-111Hs. This was dismissed at first, mostly on the grounds that it comprised an unfeasibly small number of airframes unless production was reinstated (manufacture of an extra ninety-eight aircraft was considered, and rejected by Congress). However, GD

Ground crews at the 'Burgh load a BDU-46/B 'training shape'. This innocuous white object, filled with concrete ballast rather than a nuclear warhead, enabled crews to practice deliveries of the ostensibly similar, all-up **Mk/B83 nuclear gravity bomb**. USAF

stuck to their guns and proceeded with design work and some 805 hours of wind-tunnel tests, resulting in a revised proposal at the end of the following year to modify (by then) sixty-six ostensibly similar FB-111B conversions, along with eighty-nine of the troubled F-111D force, the retirement of which was being studied seriously at that juncture, into FB-111C marks. This number of aircraft, 155 in all, would be sufficient to fill the gap left by the cancelled Rockwell bomber and GD argued that the programme cost, estimated at $5.5 billion in FY 1980 values, would offer the same capability as 100 B-1As for less than half the money. GD's proposals were backed by Jim Wright, Democratic Representative for Texas and House majority leader, who pleaded the case with President Carter.

The concept involved adding a 15ft (4.6m) extension to the fuselage fore and aft of the WCTB structure, and widening by 1.5ft (.46m) in the rear empennage by a longitudinal fuselage plug to accommodate a pair of GE F101 afterburning turbofans. Thus enlarged, the aircraft would possess the capacity for 68,000lb (30,840kg) of fuel and the ability to tote a dozen nuclear gravity weapons or SRAMs on a rotary launcher and external fuselage hardpoints. According to GDFW it would also offer a Mach 0.85 cruise capability at 200ft (60m) AGL. The existing avionics suite would also be outfitted with the emerging B-52-standard Honeywell SPN/GEANS (Standard Precision Navigation/Gimballed Electrostatic Aircraft Navigation System) for greater commonality.[5] And, unlike the FB-111A at that stage, the aircraft would be capable of carrying the full gamut of conventional ordnance, including magnetic and acoustic weapons for the mining of harbours and anti-submarine warfare, or a conventional bomb load of up to three dozen Mk 82s or Mk II Rockeyes for battle area interdiction.

The fuselage stretch also promised to provide some 40 cu.ft (1.12m^3) of spare room for future growth. GDFW even postulated the need for an AN/AWG-9 Fire Control System-equipped derivative, complete with 12–18 Phoenix missiles,

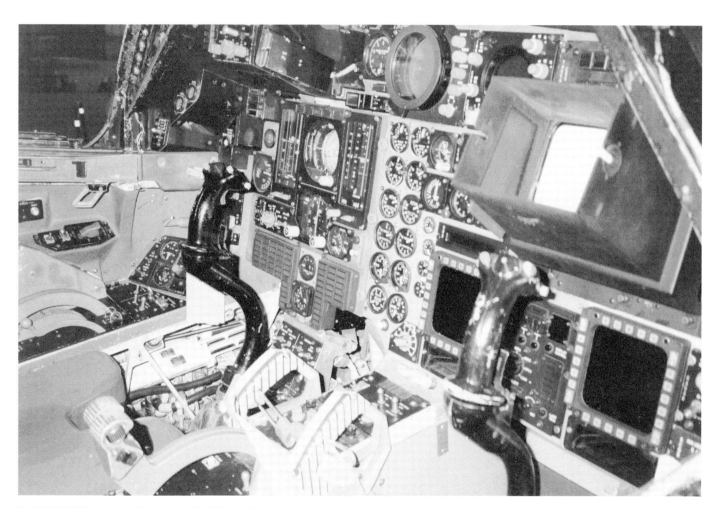

The FB-111A AMP cockpit, with new right-hand Central Display Unit and Multifunction displays; the pilot's instrumentation remaining unchanged. Note the padlocked ejection handles! Tom Johnson

designed to cruise the world's oceans and be capable of hunting and downing Soviet SUAWACS aerial command posts and Tu-22M *Backfire* bombers![6] If the FB-111B/C effort had been funded, work would have started in October 1980 and the conversion programme completed in the summer of 1986. However, to many on Capitol Hill it seemed like the F-111 saga resurrected, or 'fixing the shortcomings of TFX by stretching it' as some put it.

When the FB-111A force shifted its emphasis to conventional bombing, NATO became its chief focus of operation. Here, 'Dark 'Varks' jostle for take-off position during a deployment to RAF Lakenheath in August 1986, while a Mk IIB systems-equipped cousin, the F-111F, comes in to land. Tim P. Laming

the earliest opportunity, as an economy measure. Avionics maintenance was proving extremely costly on both models, resulting in many 'hangar queens' which had accumulated as little as 700 hours apiece at that stage. The greater emphasis that the FB-111A community placed on short supersonic dashes as part of fighter evasive training and nuclear laydown deliveries – crews were required to perform at least one supersonic sortie annually, and usually far exceeded that – also meant their powerplants were being subjected to greater demands. For most of its first decade of service the FB-111A was averaging 280 hours mean fleet engine hours between removals (a fifth of that of the B-52H's TF33-P-3 turbofans, for example) and the fleet was being subjected to around 150 unscheduled engine removals annually – more than two per aircraft. It was a labour-intensive machine from the ground troops' perspective, requiring at best some 44 MMH/FH in the mid-1970s, this when the equipment was still new and mission specialists were well up the 'learning curve'. It also was heavily reliant on tanker support, which did not come cheap.

The force remained under critical review, and was probably saved from premature extinction by eventual FB-111A high-timer Lt Col John Plantikow. He spent the last fourteen years of his career doing nothing but flying the Strategic Aardvark, mostly in Stan/Eval where he could accrue a great deal of flying time, and eventually logged a staggering 3,170 hours in the aircraft (the highest anyone achieved in one variant).[7] Dr Hans Mark, Secretary for the Air Force, flew a familiarization ride with Plantikow on a 'decently crummy, snowy and rainy [day], with clouds all the way up to refuelling altitude and all the way down to 300–400ft [90–120m]'. Gen Pringle had instructed Plantikow to fly the aircraft like it was meant to be flown – all out. Joining with the tanker RZIP as planned, and missing the LLEP by a mere four seconds (bearing in mind that Plantikow was effectively flying and navigating, single-handed), they rode TFR over the Adirondack Mountains at virtually the minimum SCP, and conducted a simulated bomb drop at 650kt (1,050kph)over Fort Drum, with everything working absolutely flawlessly. Massively impressed by it all, Hans Mark became instrumental in ensuring that the seeds were sewn for the FB-111A force to stay in place for the ensuing twelve years. His sound advice was taken onboard the FB-111A community too: 'Get a bigger profile'. Moving into the realm of conventional weapons expertise was a starter. But, arguably more important, project studies began in earnest which would give every line-pilot the chance of flying the FB-111A the way Plantikow had: off the tarmac and everything functioning as would be expected in an ideal world.

Pre-update Interlude

Unlike the tactical versions of the '111, which were manufactured in wing-plus sized batches and thus offered some attrition leeway, by 1978 some half-dozen of the FB-111A operationally capable production run had been stricken from the inventory, and the force could not sustain many more losses without seriously stretching resources. Every tail counted, and on 17 July 1978 GDFW was contracted by SMALC to begin reworking

After a second, intense but short debate at committee level, the project faltered in favour of continued development of the Boeing AGM-86B ALCM (Air Launched Cruise Missile), to extend the aged B-52 fleet's credibility into the 1980s, and the inauguration of top secret 'Stealth' aircraft development, to which only a few senior people were privy at the time, which would spawn the B-2A (and F-117A). The F-111 possessed the RCS (Radar Cross-section) of only a small car or bicycle but, just around the corner, 'Stealth' technology was beginning to promise aircraft with an RCS smaller than that of a hummingbird.

The idea of removing the aircraft for conversion having already been entertained in 1979–80, serious consideration was now being given to simply pensioning off the FB-111A and TAC F-111D fleets at

damaged airframes and restoring them to as-new. FB-111A B1-08 (67-7194) was the first. This aircraft had been involved in a heavy landing in February 1976, resulting in its main undercarriage collapsing and a severe fire which gutted its port flank and wing, after which time it was left languishing at Sacramento for two and half years. In an extraordinary rebuild which took a year to complete, beginning on 1 September 1978, GDFW had the aircraft shipped to Fort Worth and set about removing its entire forward fuselage and other recyclable components. FB-111A B1-02, one of the two trials aircraft, was similarly dismembered, its fuselage spliced in place, a redundant Australian WCTB added, and the ensemble reworked to a finished standard incorporating all the intervening TCTOs/TOs (Time Compliance/Technical Orders), including a new lick of paint. It returned to duty at Plattsburgh on 18 September 1980, and later sported the artwork *Virgin Abroad* on its sides – though to the crews at the base the aircraft became known as *Franken'Vark*!

By 1988 GDFW had rebuilt a further dozen of what they described as 'basket cases' back to their former glory, including an additional FB-111A that had suffered serious internal ruptures from a rogue BDU-38/B drogue chute rod. Two F-111As, three 'Es and no fewer than six 'Ds were also salvaged from near-scrap, for an average unit cost of $4m, one tenth of the price of a new-build F-111 from a reopened line. However, further casualties accrued, and the two SAC Wings were able only to sustain training and operations at the required tempo by means of reliability updates, which kept a bigger proportion of the fleet airworthy. These formed the biggest item on the agenda during the aircraft's second decade of service when, to many, the aircraft 'really came into its own'. American success – and failures – during Operation *El Dorado Canyon*, the F-111F strike on Libya in 1986, which employed the kind of sortie FB-111A crews could expect to fly, also added further impetus to a long-overdue systems upgrade.

Going Tactical

Beginning in December 1986 the FB-111A fleet began to receive a General Dynamics-designed, digital update known as AMP (Avionics Modernization Program). Col Rick Matteis recalled that the 'main thrust was to improve reliability'. Amongst the new kit were revisions to the TFR, LARA (replaced by a Combined Radar Altimeter, or CARA multiplex) and ARS to reduce 'maintenance downtime'. Central to the update was the new 64K Weapons/Navigation Computer for the DCC, along with a new digital databus to tie the systems all together, with the ultimate goal of reducing dependency on INS – the bane of mission reliability. The Navigator was also provided with a pair of multifunction displays and a revised ARS display (complete with pilot 'peephole'), while related mods to the ECM kit, including AN/ALE-40 chaff/flare dispensers, cured some of the remaining ills with the DEWS. SAC-AMP served as nothing less than a model for the follow-on tactical models' Rockwell and Grumman AMP, AUP and *Pacer Strike* updates.

68-0247 had the honour of serving as trailblazer, followed by 68-0272 as the 'kit proof' aircraft. So valuable was the testbed that on early test flights the aircraft flew with padlocked ejection handles! The key feature, as mentioned above, was the new navigation computer, which could hold up to 350 navigation data points and three sets of 100 sequence points (triple the previous capacity). It made for easier loading of 'mission tapes' too, which actually became completely digitized, by means of cockpit-loadable solid-state Data Transfer Modules so there was no actual 'tape' as such. DTMs would be prepared by ground specialists involved in converting Emergency War Orders into the necessary package, so that alert aircraft could be armed and preened with all the SIOP data they required for tanker RZIPs, navigation points and offsets, targets and diversionary fields, with plenty of spare capacity. Plug-in power kept them on alert, ready for launch. Crews could similarly prepare routine, day-to-day flightplans which were held on DTMs for the 'stock birds' – those not currently assigned to alert commitments – avoiding the need laboriously to enter long strings of coordinates into the cockpit console. The old cumbersome punched paper formatting and loading process was given the heave-ho.

It turned what was fundamentally a good system into a superb one, offering 100+ hours' flying time before a malfunction occurred, according to the crews who flew them (despite an already respectable forty-hour MTBF guarantee). To make life even easier, Astrocompass was deleted and twin, virtually unbreakable and extremely accurate Honeywell Ring-Laser Gyro inertial systems were added in lieu of the old INS. As a result the previous 3g manoeuvring limit imposed by the Astro-tracker was removed, and the system gave virtually 'SNAFU-less' navigation and bombing. Concurrent with AMP, a 'lizard' camouflage began to appear, known to its crews as the 'Dark Vark' scheme, which was offset by a renewed flurry of artwork skilfully airbrushed on the machines' flanks by proud Crew Chiefs. A new influx of Mission Specialists (MX) in the support shops, specifically trained on the new systems and ignorant of its past woes in terms of slogging in the 'barns', further added to 'Dark Vark' kudos.[8]

AMP also heralded a newfound use of conventional weapons, and in July 1988 the, by then, operational fleet of fifty-nine aircraft were committed in support of European tactical air power as part of NATO's new 'flexible response strategy'. At this juncture, 100 of the resurrected Rockwell B-1B, a slightly simplified version of the 1970s B-1A, had been fielded at Carswell, and Ellsworth, South Dakota, in a rush programme that had received the personal backing of President Reagan, and was poised to assume the nuclear penetration mission as soon as its troubled AN/ALQ-161 defensive countermeasures could be made to work satisfactorily (something still to be fully accomplished at the time of writing). Conventional weapons employment, which the FB-111A force had 'merely dabbled with since around 1980', according to Plantikow, on the heels of Dr Hans Mark's visit, also was expanded, giving the FB-111A a vast armoury. Alas, this new lease of life endured for just two years.

Phase-out from SAC, after twenty years of auspicious service, finally began during 1990 during the climax of the AMP updates. The effective break-up of the Soviet Union and defrosting of the 'Cold War', further pushed along by dollar-saving base contractions, would turn Pease into a lower-key Air National Guard facility, with a substantial chunk of the freshly updated FB-111A fleet being flown out to Davis Monthan AMARC, for retirement. The loss of SRAM was a further factor. The weapon was withdrawn from FB-111A alert use on 7 June 1990, under the express orders of Defense Secretary Richard B. Cheney, and there seemed little left for them to do in the 'New World

FB-111As became F-111Gs after their transfer to TAC's 428th TFTS Buccaneers **at Cannon AFB. The bump on the nose barrel previously housed the Astrocompass. The squat pods are SUU-20/A practice bomb dispensers.** Craig Brown

Order'. To some, it all seemed to come down to SRAM weapons leaks: the weapon's rocket compound was guaranteed for ten years and 'Buff' units got most of the updated Thiokol-equipped versions with more stable hydroxyl-terminated polybutadiene propellant, making selected numbers good for a few more years, allowing further time to fiddle about with the B-1B's wretched countermeasures.

During the SAC draw-down, twenty-eight FB-111As, redesignated F-111Gs for TAC use, were transferred to the 428th TFTS Buccaneers, 27th TFW, at Cannon AFB, for much less exacting duties as RTU trainers in a purely conventional capacity. The unit formed in April 1990 to provide a new training nucleus for the emerging digital, tactical Aardvark fleet, receiving its aircraft from 1 June.[9] With the new assignment came yet another paint job: overall 'Gunship Quality Gray', which was pioneered on these ex-SAC 'swingers'. It was hastily applied in the base's own 'paint barn', and the ensuing peeling under the engine area merely underscored the aircraft's short lease of life: they were replaced by two dozen former USAFE AMP'ed F-111Es during 1993. The remainder of the valiant old 'Bullet Bombers' were shipped off to Museums (no fewer than eight, including the gaudy SMALC example), or were decommissioned and stripped of useful spares at Davis-Monthan, the last such 'boneyard-bound' example (68-0249, nicknamed Little Joe) departing Plattsburgh on 10 July 1991 with its former wing boss Col J. Paul Malandrino, and Navigator Capt Mark McCausland, at the controls. Little Joe would never fly again, branded BF-18 as scrap, alongside thirty-five others. There would have been fifty languishing in the desert but for an unexpected turn of events: beginning in late 1992, fifteen of the aircraft were sold overseas, many of which still fly to this day under wholly new ownership in the Southern Hemisphere.[10]

CHAPTER FIVE

Echoes at Upper Heyford

For twelve years before moving to Upper Heyford in December 1969 the 20th TFW had flown the F-100 Super Sabre, first of the 'Century Series' fighters. In 1970 it began to transition to the last of the Series, the F-111. Despite their initial reservations about an aircraft which was 50 per cent longer than their F-100s and nearly three times as heavy, the aircrew found that they had a fighter which, relatively 'clean', was 100kt (185kph) faster at low level and left the 'Hun' standing at altitude.[1] It also had a much bigger bonus of more than double the F-100D's combat range. The arrival of the first two F-111Es (68-0035 and 68-0045), led in by 20th TFW Commander Col Grant A. Smith, took place on a wet 12 September 1970. Like most of the F-111's period of service in the UK this event was generally overlooked by the Press but it introduced NATO's most decisive strike element for the following twenty-three years.

First flown on 20 August 1969, the 'E' or 'Echo' model was a stop-gap to keep the production line flowing while GDFW wrestled with the Mk II avionics of the F-111D. Basically a slightly enhanced F-111A, the 'E' had Triple Plow II intakes, a better Stores Management System using a new WCP, and a KB-18A strike camera to supplement radarscope photography. It also introduced many Pen-Aids which had to be retrofitted to F-111As, such as the alphanumeric AN/APS-109 RHAWS (which replaced primitive strobe lines with threat icons on the cockpit threat indicator) and Westinghouse's deception jamming-capable AN/ALQ-101 pod. By

F-111E 68-0012, one of the few to serve with 27th TFW tail codes before transfer to the 20th TFW in 1970. C Moggeridge

The 'UT' codes worn briefly by the 77th TFS in 1970. F-111E 68-0019 was lost to a bird-strike in 1984. MAP

the end of 1969 thirty of the ninety-four production F-111Es had been checked off the Fort Worth line and some had winged north-west to Cannon AFB, New Mexico, and the 27th TFW. Equipped initially with ten loaned 474th TFW F-111As, the 522nd TFS *Fireballs* expected to be the first of Cannon's three squadrons to receive the new F-111E. Their first aircraft did arrive on 30 September 1969, but a combination of circumstances soon altered the big plan. Re-equipment was delayed primarily by the grounding of the whole F-111 fleet, following the fateful Nellis loss on 22 December. Fewer than twenty F-111Es had arrived before the grounding order, a few of them receiving 'CA' or 'CC' base codes.

following WCTB failures. With production batches averaging 100 for each major variant it made sense to make a single USAF wing sole user of each type. After a short soak in the New Mexico sun, the F-111Es were therefore redirected to a cloudier, wetter place: England.

The Cannon wing resumed operations with a handful of F-111As and had to wait a further two years before it reached IOC on its designated Aardvark model, the F-111D.[2] In many ways Upper Heyford was the right place for the innovative F-111. Thirty-five years previously an RAF bomber, the Handley-Page Heyford (named after its base) was flown in a direct line towards the BBC's short-wave transmitter at Daventry to establish whether it would

Mainly Training

First to be selected for the new type (in October 1969) was the 79th TFS *Tigers*, which received its full complement by January 1971 and became the first *fully* operational F-111 squadron anywhere. F-111Es 68-0019 and 68-0021 arrived in the same month to start the conversion process for the 77th TFS *Gamblers*, commanded by Lt Col Jude McNamara (no relation to the politician), with the 55th TFS *Fightin' Fifty Fifth* last to make the change. Appropriately, both Wing Commander, Col Smith, and DO Col Richard Baughn had flown P-51s in Europe during WWII (though not with the 20th FG). When the last example of the P-51's grandson, the F-100, left Upper

'UT' codes changed to 'JT' in 1971 and 'UH' a year later. Robin A. Walker

Wings of Swingers

The second factor in limiting the 27th TFW's operation of the 'Echo' to a few months was a change in USAF policy. It had become clear that delays in service entry, cost overruns and a number of major changes in specification were going to reduce F-111 production to a series of short runs, each one yielding a different variant. To achieve McNamara's original aims would have meant stopping production altogether until all the 'faults' were cured, as suggested by Senator McClellan, who led the investigation into the F-111

reflect radio waves off its metal surfaces. That experiment led to the building of an early warning radar chain just in time for the Battle of Britain. Upper Heyford had been a bomber base throughout its RAF years and home to many a USAF B-47 and B-52 thereafter. The pilots of the 20th TFW, with a long tradition of single-seat fighter operations, were under no illusions about the nature of the their new heavyweight charger. Designed to fly under the radar chain of Eastern Bloc countries and deliver nuclear or conventional weapons against deep strategic targets, the F-111E was destined to spend little time on fighter-like activities.

Heyford there were still ten months of hard training ahead before the wing became fully operational. Each squadron had a nominal strength of twenty-four F-111Es, requiring a $20m building and equipment upgrade at the base, which also absorbed a new communications centre at RAF Croughton and a dispersal site at RAF Greenham Common.[3] Later in the 1970s, fifty-six TAB-V (Theater Air Base, Vulnerability) shelters were installed by Italian contractors. Each 'shell' offered a 124ft × 82ft (38m × 25m) floor area and heavy protective doors.[4] 'TAB-Vees', as they were known, despite their external uniformity, often became

F-111E Armament Control Differences

WEAPONS CONTROL PANEL The F-111E's Mk I Bomb-Nav-System was fundamentally the same as that fitted to the F-111A, except for some subtle differences. First, it featured a revised Armament Select Panel on the WSO's right console, known as the WCP, to offer automatically-set ballistics. This replaced the old grey knobs and 'organ stops' with a new push-button array, including four new weapons select cassettes. According to Lt Col Terry Simpson, who briefed the authors on the 'E's cockpit late in the aircraft's career, these held the weapons ballistics for fourteen different types of munitions each, each encompassing a specific set of stores stations (though there was slight overlap, for back-up purposes). The tape loops for the cassettes were prepared by ground crew specialists and periodically updated. To select a particular weapon, the WSO simply pressed and held down the 'SEL' select button until the desired weapon appeared in the corresponding loop-tape display window. Individual, specific stores station, weapons fuzing, release pattern and attack mode buttons were then pressed to configure the system for weapons release (or 'READY' in the weapons cassette windows). The F-111E WCP similarly featured other separate push-buttons for the delivery mode ('Manual', 'Nav', 'Angle' or 'Timer'), and buttons for jettisoning ordnance, BRUs or pylons. The only 'old-fashioned' selection that had to be made concerned the milliseconds weapons release interval, which was 'thumbed-in' using little cog wheels and counters as before. The WCP looked one step nearer digital technology, but still was '1960s technology'.

DUAL BOMBING TIMER Also available to the F-111E (in common with the 'A' version, and built-into the F-111D/F's slightly different digital-based avionics) was the ability to use the back-up Dual Bombing Timer (DBT) for both a pull-up 'loft' bombing manoeuvre and for a flyover Laydown Drogued Delivery (LADD). Using the Timer was strictly 'canned' in terms of the pilot having to maintain altitude, airspeed and g precisely, but it was practised a fair bit in USAFE as it offered exactly the high-speed deliveries required of nuclear weaponry for freefall (slick) or retarded (Nylon/Kevlar parabraked) drops, with the bomb fuzed for either an air or surface burst.

The DBT worked using time-to-target in seconds cranked into the 'Timer Box' situated in front of the AC, measured from a preplanned, prominent IP (Initial Point). The AC pressed his 'pickle' button at the IP, to set the timer going and, still holding down the bomb release button to maintain consent, then followed the 'canned' bomb run on the correct heading and airspeed until the weapons were released automatically when the system had sensed the correct elapsed time. The method actually used two separate, consecutively running timer settings, one set for time from the IP to the 'pull-up' point (which was indicated by a pull-up light on the instrument panel for the 4g exertion), and a second timer window set for the calculated time between pull-up and weapons release. As an aid to accuracy, the AC would follow the g accelerometer tape on his AMI (Airspeed Mach Indicator) instrument initially, and then look up to the gunsight LCOS indicators, attempting to maintain the pitch steering bar and left-hand deviation indicator at centre (which in this mode indicated deviation from the optimum $4g$, necessary to toss the weapon to target). The Timer release point equated to when the gunsight range bar had receded to the six o'clock position, with actual weapons release indicated by a 'Bomb Release' light on the instrument panel, cueing the pilot to effect evasive manoeuvres (although all pilots commented that it was easy to 'feel' the bomb(s) leaving the racks).

Brad Insley explained that the 'DBT was used on the LADD delivery as a primary delivery mode. This allowed an airburst of a nuclear weapon when overflying the target at low-level. The delivery involved a $4g$ pull to a 45 degree climb until timer expiration, then an inverted pull to a nose-low position and re-engaging the TFR [after rolling the wings upright] for a low-level escape'. He also explained that the 'timer could be used to raise the LCOS pipper in the CCIP mode or to manually raise the pipper in other modes' too. This latter facility enabled the pilot to 'pickle' the bombs as normal but with the timer compensating for the difference, in situations where the LCOS 'pipper's' CCIP referencing would otherwise have been somewhere in the glareshield area, too low in the pilot's line-of-sight to be of any practical use. Timer values thus simply represented a difference between pilot 'pickle' and actual CCIP 'bombs away', with the aiming mark being raised according to the time set-in.

'Angular' deliveries were also available, whereby time from IP to pull-up was set as before on the DBT, but the weapon was released automatically when the system had 'sensed' that the correct preset pitch angle and g had been achieved, rather than elapsed pull-up time. Different angles were practised.

The preset timer values were actually all carefully tabulated and worked out in minute detail down to a tenth of a second, based on aircraft speed and altitude; but to give a general idea of how the timer worked, if the distance between IP and target was 5nm (9km) and the aircraft was flying low-level at 600kt (1,110kph), then the Timer would be set for a total value of 30 seconds. Countdown to initiating the Timer itself was based on time-to-the-IP, based on normal radar-INS navigation methods (or back-up dead reckoning), and as usual required the kind of rapport between crewmen which only the F-111 community tended to foster as routine.

Weapons stores, types and so on were set up as normal on the WCP (and nuclear panel if required) beforehand, with the delivery mode set to 'Timer' (instead of the commonly used 'Nav', or reversionary 'Manual' mode).

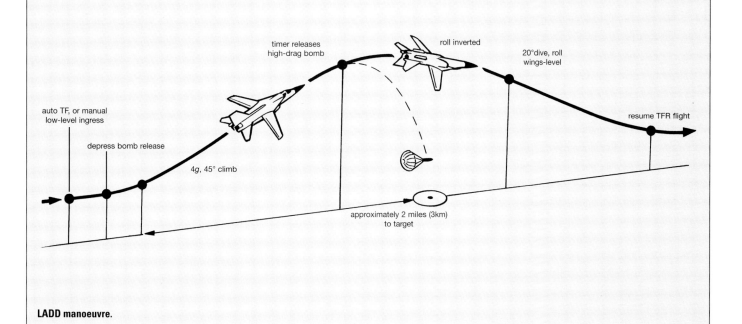

LADD manoeuvre.

> ### F-111E Armament Control Differences *(continued)*
>
> **'BLUE BOMBS AND BEER CANS'** Another main difference concerning weapons 'switchology' between the F-111A and the F-111E had to do with USAFE safety procedures (and was applied to the far more sophisticated F-111F too). As one former WSO noted, when describing the preparations that were made for transferring the units to England, 'We began using the [Suspension Underwing Unit] SUU-21 bomb dispenser instead of the previously used SUU-20. The SUU-20 was an open pylon mounted dispenser that carried six practice bombs, usually a mix of BDU-33 and Mk 106, and had four single rocket tubes on the corners. It made use of the regular conventional bomb circuitry so that dropping a practice bomb from it was exactly like dropping a conventional bomb [using the appropriate loop-tape window command]. The SUU-21, also pylon mounted, was a closed dispenser which provided an added safety feature over populated areas in that it was impossible for a bomb to drop from it unless the doors were opened by use of the nuclear bomb circuitry'. Located in the right-hand corner of the cockpit, a safe lock lever had to be unlatched and the knob set one of the arming positions. To this extent, daily range practice also helped crews prepare for possible nuclear procedures, in a limited fashion – what the F-111E was all about in the first fifteen years of USAFE operations.
>
> The orange 10lb (5kg) Mk 106 (alias the '*Beer Can*') emulated the aerodynamic ballistic characteristics of a nylon/Kevlar parachute-retarded nuclear weapon as well as that of a Mk 80 series Snakeye or later AIR; and the 25lb (11kg) BDU-33 (also known as the Mk 76, or '*Blue Bomb*') behaved just like a full-sized 'slick' bomb, and also could be lobbed to emulate the trajectory of a Paveway laser-guided munition, or nuclear bomb being 'lofted' in 'freefall' mode. On the F-111E in USAFE, each SUU-21/A was loaded with six of one type only. These miniature weapons were the 'meat and potatoes' of the 'E's sorties over the UK ranges. That they made only little puffs when they hit the ground instead of bigger ear-splitting tritonol bangs or huge nuclear fireballs did not matter much; they would behave the same way as the real thing, ballistically. Drops of full-sized, inert conventional ordnance was reserved for WTDs and Flag deployments, when ACs could get accustomed to the slightly different weights and handling characteristics of the all-up combat configuration, and WSOs with the more complex intervalometer release settings associated with dropping BRU-fuls of bombs in train.

canvases for quite elaborate ground crew 'shelter art' inside, based on the name or artwork on the resident aircraft.

Similarities between the F-111A and F-111E were such that training could be conducted on Nellis-based 442nd TFTS F-111As, and eight F-111Es which that unit also owned for a couple of years until they were reassigned to Upper Heyford or the 442nd FWS. In a three-month conversion course aircrew with 1,000hr flying time, including 750hr on jets, flew a total of 45 hours on the F-111 followed by another 45 hours or thirteen sorties (Phase 2) at Upper Heyford. A Singer Link Division simulator based on a GPB4 computer was in place at Upper Heyford soon after training began. It was later described as a 'trainer' rather than a 'simulator' by 55th TFS CO Col Terry Simpson, who saw it as 'useful for practising emergency procedures and getting new guys up to speed'.[5]

One of the first jobs for Col Smith, and Col Baughn when he took over the wing in June, 1971, was to establish realistic European training routes. They needed routes which could combine the aircraft's impressive range characteristics with terrain which allowed low-level TFR flying; all to simulate radar-evasive penetration into the sort of landscape which F-111E crews might have to face 'for real'. A series of eleven Combat Profile Mission (CPM) routes was devised for the squadrons, taking them out to ranges at Aviano and Sardinia, Italy, or more locally to Wainfleet (The Wash), Jurby (Isle of Man) and Scotland. CPMs were mainly tests of precise navigation and timing. Crews' performances were evaluated by the squadrons' Radar Systems Section which examined radarscope photography of targets and offsets (actual or simulated bomb release generating a photo marker).

Endurance could be further extended by hanging two side-by-side 'Tokyo' fuel tanks from the pallet-like roof of the weapons bay. Their use tended to be restricted to special missions, such as SAC Bomb & Nav Comps where six or seven hour flights were made without inflight refuelling. A disadvantage

The 'Wizzo's' side of the 'office' differed little from that of the F-111A/C models, except for the WCP on his right console. The hole in the dashboard is where the RSP film camera magazine is inserted prior to missions. Note the large grey knobs and digital counter 'windows'. Authors

was that they prevented the bay from being used for anything else. They also took several hours to fit and check, as opposed to about fifteen minutes for drop tanks.

Splitting the syllabus equally between Nellis and Upper Heyford was necessary in view of the big differences between the two training scenarios. Pilots who could do well on daylight auto-TFR over the empty expanses of sunny Nevada had much to learn when they encountered the UK's cloudy, crowded conditions. Some of the problems began the moment they left Upper Heyford's runway. Capt Brad Insley, who ended his USAF career as the all-time, high-time F-111 flyer with 5,056.9 hours and 2,009 sorties on the type, later recalled some of the local restraints encountered during his two tours at the Cotswold base:

> Flying from Upper Heyford presented several problems that most bases don't have. The towns of Steeple Aston and Middle Aston caused us to fly a very precise course on departure from Runway 27 [heading West], starting with a turn shortly after takeoff which was considered unsafe by visiting crews from the [Nellis] 430th TFS during a Coronet Daytona deployment to the base. We maintained a heading until past Duns Tews from which time we would continue a normal departure. In 1988 the Wing Commander ordered us to discontinue the noise abatement departure and the resulting uproar was on the news nightly for a while. Even Parliament was involved and we eventually started a modified but safer procedure.
>
> We were told that historically Upper Heyford had the second worst weather of the bases in Europe, so that was always a challenge to operations. The fog was much worse during my first tour (1975–78) but it snowed more during the second (1984–89)! In fact the roads into Upper Heyford were closed a couple of times.
>
> Upper Heyford also was a very busy traffic area with twenty active airfields within a 20 mile [32km] radius and being located beneath the [civil ATC] Amber airways caused departure and arrival problems. Gliders at RAF Bicester and Enstone created numerous collision hazards on the 360 initial and straight-in final approach. Light aircraft were always sneaking up the Cherwell valley below the clouds causing us to manoeuvre to avoid them. There were two ultra-light fields near Brackley right under the visual downwind approach. All these groups cooperated to some extent but someone was forever off course creating a hazard.

On his second tour Brad was a member of

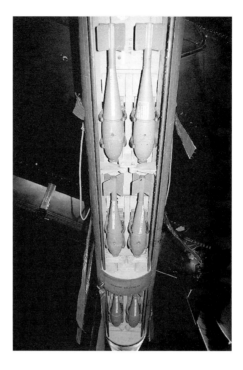

The SUU-21/A dispenser, with closing doors, was used by all USAFE Aardvarks for day-to-day practice bombing. BDU-33 'blue bombs' are shown here.
Authors

the wing-based Instructors Unit (known as the CTU or Consolidated Training Unit) which trained crews for all three squadrons and provided other specialist skills. In later years, training, like maintenance, became a squadron responsibility again.

The CPMs remained in use throughout most of the 20th TFW's stay, though initial F-111 training moved from Nellis to Mountain Home when the 474th TFW traded-in its F-111As for Phantoms in August 1977, and the 'Aces' shifted to Mountain Home under the auspices of the 388th and 389th Tactical Fighter Training Squadrons.[6] There, Pilots and WSOs entered a six-month training process which covered handling, safety procedures, basic attack profiles and TFR flying by day and night. The local Saylor Creek Range provided bombing practice. For WSOs the flying training qualified them to handle the aircraft above 1,000ft (300m). Officially, this was to give them the ability to get home in case of incapacitation of the AC, but many WSOs were 'allowed' to fly the aircraft the 300 miles (480km) or so back from a range practice. However, like Nellis, Mountain Home was only part-preparation for Europe. Col Tom Barnes, training there in 1972, described it as 'a base in high desert and very isolated. Coyotes roamed through the base at night and were seen on the golf course, along with a few snakes. The flying weather was clear almost all of the time'.

Aircrew who were assigned to Upper Heyford were 'in-processed' in much the same way in 1972 as they were in 1988 when Lt Col David Skakal described their initiation. They had 'three or four rides to show them the UK. They then entered a Mission Qualification Training program, making another five rides before their check ride with the Standardization & Evaluation (Stan/Eval, or "Stanley Evils") to certify that they were ready to fly the mission. It took them about forty-five days to be normal soldiers: mission-ready'.

The F-111A and F-111E were so similar that crews needed only a checkout rather than actual flying training before beginning Mission Qualification. One difference was that the 'Echo's' more widely spaced intakes caused greater parasitic drag, making it a little slower than the F-111A and giving a bigger head-on radar signature (partly reduced by installing RAM in the intake areas). Most aircrew rate the F-111A as the fastest Aardvark, even over the rapid-acceleration F-111F.

One point about handling was constantly reinforced: the need to keep wing sweep at the correct angle for the flight situation. Capt George Kelman, who later flew the F-117A *Nighthawk* in Desert Storm, felt that 'the only thing that will really bite you is wing sweep. It will induce a lot of problems if a pilot forgets his wing sweep or tries to manoeuvre with his wing aft or forward'. Wing sweep tricks were also among the

68-0080 Strange Brew.

67-0121 Night Stalker.

68-0059 The Mad Bomber.

68-0079 Tiger Lil'.

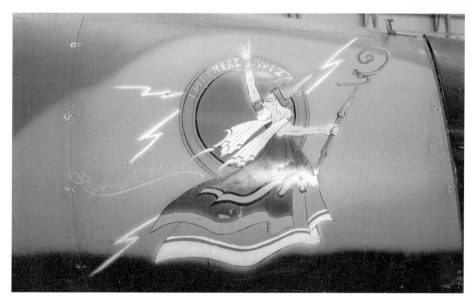

68-0002 Imperial Wizard.

68-0047 Till We Meet Again.

All photographs by Authors or via Mike Gibson

defensive techniques which new aircrew learned as they prepared to 'do battle' with nimble NATO fighters in exercises which provided the bulk of their training for war. George Kelman, describing these tactics to the authors in 1988, said 'You can set the wings to fake somebody out. If someone's attacking and he sees the big airplane down there with its wings back, even though you're going at a relatively slow speed (480–500kts/890–925kph), he may think you're going 600kt [1,110kph] and leave you alone'. Normally wings were set at 35–40 degree sweep for range operations.

A Day's Duty

Brad Insley, who often flew his assigned F-111E, 68-0033 *Hat Trick*, describes a typical sortie from Upper Heyford:

We generally showed up four hours prior to the scheduled take-off time to start planning the mission. Normally we only had a range time scheduled so everything that happened was planned according to the weather and the crew training requirements. Weather was always the most important factor in deciding a course of action. Once we had decided where to go and what to do the Flight Lead would assign everyone a duty. Normally someone would draw up the route, someone would coordinate the range times and someone else the low-level attack. We generally tried to do a coordinated attack on a realistic 'target' on the low-level route since they weren't practical or possible on the overwater ranges. [These were known simply as RTTs, or Realistic Target Training features]. Then we would proceed to the coastal range, dropping the practice bombs according to the needs of the crews in the flight. Often we had to work around available range times so the range might come first in many cases.

We generally briefed the flight two or two-and-a-half hours prior to take-off. Then we would meet for our desk brief about an hour and a quarter later. The aircraft was pre-flighted and engines started thirty minutes before take-off and we taxied out 15–20 minutes before take-off. Once airborne we would check each other over for damage; missing panels or fuel leaks. After level-off we would do the TFR checks and get a weather update if it was marginal. If the weather is bad over large sections of the UK a large proportion of the tactical aircraft are likely to be low-level in the same training area. Generally we would be in tactical formation and you got lots of visual training looking out for these hazards and light aircraft.

The low level attack was the crux of the training. We wanted minimum time over the (land) target but the spacing had to be right or you could kill the crew following you or be killed arriving too early after the aircraft ahead of you. With most weapons you had to arrive 23–35 seconds after the aircraft ahead of you to avoid being killed, or killing those following you. To evaluate our success we would call 'off target' and the lead WSO would time the calls. Most crews could hit their planned time within three seconds. In competitions the winning crews were generally within two seconds. After a successful egress we would join up and head for an overwater range.

There we would generally split the deliveries between radar and visual methods including level, toss, LADD and diving deliveries, each requiring ballistic computations during pre-flight planning and adjustment for wind and density altitude once on the range. All through the sortie, fuel and weather would be checked to determine when to return to base. Several ranges would be briefed in case the planned one was 'weathered out' and another became available. We would generally fly formation and instrumented approaches upon returning home, even in good weather to keep in practice. After landing, the aircraft was post-flighted and a maintenance debrief carried out. Then there would be a debrief of the sortie, including the planning to see what went right and what needed improvement. The whole process could take nine to ten hours in all for a typical mission.

Mission planning was usually done in the squadron's 'hard ops' area, a central complex sealed off from the base by sinister decontamination chambers and blast doors. Individual crews pored over maps, ring-back books of 'target' photos taken with the F-111E's KB-18 camera, and filing cabinets full of RSP shots. Targets might have been bridges, dams or isolated historic monuments. Many a Scottish castle became the unwitting recipient of a simulated nuclear attack! One priority, as Maj Fred Zeitz pointed out, was checking whether the 'Royals' were airborne and avoiding their route. Aircrew, who were normally 'paired' for a whole tour, tended to have their own sets of pre-planned routes. Once a launch of two or four Aardvarks was decided call-signs and mission numbers were 'chalked-up' on the Squadron Ops board for the day. Although most crews only averaged 15–20 hours flying time per month it was important to maintain 'currency'. Fred Zeitz: 'A certain number of sorties was required per month and per quarter. If you fell below that you were no longer prepared to go to war'. The success of a mission depended very much on accurate planning by the whole team. As George Kelman observed, just before setting off on a range trip, 'If one person's eating his lunch when he should be drawing little threads on a map it may be the reason why we lose an airplane and a crew. Everyone takes their job very seriously'. Waypoints for each sortie were usually entered into the aircraft's NCU/INS one at a time in flight, using a computer read-out of coordinates supplied pre-mission.

Pre-flight checks of the 'green airplane' (as crews often called the F-111E, distinguishing them that way from the EF-111A 'gray airplanes' which arrived in 1984–85) required all systems to be 100 per cent functioning for a night TFR sortie. Any doubts on that score meant stepping over to the spare jet.[7] Start-up was supervised by the aircraft's Dedicated Crew Chief (DCC). After the crew walk-around (the preferred pathway for this was prescribed in the manuals!), review of documents and strap-in they would ask for electrical power and compressed air to start up the systems and run through their checks. The call, 'Ready for a start, Chief', would then come over the DCC's headset. He checked that the cavernous shelter behind the F-111 was clear and then called 'Air on two', as the snaking, silver air hose powered up the No.2 TF30. The other engine would either be started by cross-feed from No. 2 or with starter trolley air. At bases without the equipment to provide air over the blades an internal cartridge-based 'cart start' could be used.

All being well, the Aardvark could then nose out of its lair and swing onto the taxiway for pre-takeoff visual checks and pin-pulling to de-safe any weapons aboard. Rolling to the 'piano keys' on the active runway, the Aardvarks then took off singly or in pairs, with full afterburner *de rigeur* in all conditions. Rotation occurred at around 142kt (263kph) and lift-off at 157kt (291kph), depending on weights.

Riding the Ranges

Whenever possible, training routes were calculated to include landscape which resembled the kind that the 20th TFW might have to 'ski' across in time of war. Without conspicuous manoeuvrability,

77th TFS 'squadron' aircraft 68-0077 and partner on approach to RAF Upper Heyford in 1983. Aircraft names (e.g. 077 Red Alpha) **sometimes appeared in the white flashes on the nosewheel doors.** T. Shia

and with a large radar signature viewed side-on, the Aardvark had to rely on terrain masking to protect it from defending radars whenever possible. 'Unfortunately, there isn't much "terrain" in Europe', as 77th TFS WSO Greg Lowrimore once observed. 'We try to stay away from the flat areas so that we have something vertical to hide behind'. This also meant flying round the highest peaks rather than making a highly-visible 'pop-up' over them.

In situations where diversion to a handy piece of cover was required, it was possible to use manual headings supplied by the WSO.[8] Reversion to fully automatic mode could then be made with a couple of reswitching operations. Although the F-111's auto-TFR modes were all 'hands off', and did not require manual control inputs, pilots always kept a hand on the stick, partly for psychological reassurance. As George Kelman said of the TFR:

You never trust it to go entirely on its own because at any one time it monitors itself between all its different functions and it can tell when it's making a mistake. But at other times it visually presents something for you to diagnose and say, "Yes, that's wrong and I'm going to have to take action". So you then have to override it and if your hands are doing something else you may not be quick enough.

A 600kt (1,110kph) flight over the ground meant vaulting over the highland crags and into gulleys at 1,013ft/s (309m/s).

Riding on Faith

Flying night TFR in the Scottish valleys ('probably the most dangerous thing we do', according to George during his 'Kelmaniac' days at Upper Heyford) required a high degree of situational awareness (SA) and cockpit coordination. Chris Ross, son of a Georgia Tech Sports Coach, and on his first tour as Wizzo in 1988 before going to fly F-111Ds at Cannon AFB, remarked that the experience was disorientating at first. 'Down low I've always found that if you get "low SA" you feel that you're really zooming. Stuff's just flying by and you can't keep up with the airplane'. To George Kelman it could also be 'Better than a Double-E ticket at Disneyland'.

You go up in the Scottish Highlands; there's no moon and you descend through a cloud deck, and now you are underneath the weather. The right-seater's very intent upon his job, so is the pilot. And then, out of the corner of your eye, you'll see a red flash. That's the aircraft's rotating beacon reflecting off a mountain peak only about 70ft [20m] off your left side. This is about 15ft [4.5m] more than the machine is guaranteed for, so you're doing OK. When you fly the same thing in daytime you say "Holy S***!" Look how close I was to this thing. It's huge! It's granite! But the hundredth time you do it you're still as exhilarated and scared as the first.

David Skakal added, 'I noticed that in transitioning from day to night TFR I had a tendency to look outside the airplane. I learned very quickly that this does two things. Number one, it scares you even more than you already are, and number two, it disorients you. You don't look outside. You place complete faith in the airplane and the systems and watch it closely'. Crew coordination relied on a series of routines which each pair devised for itself. Maj Dick Brown, who became the USAF's High-time Instructor Pilot with 3,454 hours, reviewed that issue.

Techniques were wide and varied among many crews. We were a community of 'many ways to skin a cat'. Some procedures were better than others and the best techniques were incorporated among many crews as… kind of the way of doing business. In my opinion the F-111 community was probably the most disciplined of all the aircraft I flew with or against. One reason was the high threat of night and all-weather low-level flying and its inherent risks! Additionally, we often 'policed our own' by demanding high standards from those present – and new to the F-111. The temperament and personal skills of crews varied immensely, and by chance when two talented aircrew members were crewed together they formed an awesome combat weapon. The best WSO I flew with was Dudley 'Squid' Lowery, who was in Upper Heyford's Stan/Eval crew in 1979–81. What made 'Squid' so exemplary was not only his ability to 'run the right seat', drop good bombs and be an expert in aircraft bombing systems, but the fact that he could always intimate my next move. I never had to ask him to 'sequence to the next point', it was already there.

Despite the visibility problems caused by the side-by-side seating in terms of watching for fighters, Chris Ross liked the 'subtle things, like when the pilot's talking on the radio and he's coming up to a set altitude. I can just point to the altimeter and he'll known what I'm talking about'. 'Plus', added Dave Skakal, 'You can always reach over and shake him – beat him a little!'. In critical phases of TFR or weapons delivery crews usually relied on standard 'hot mike' contact.

Weapons practice tended to take place on the northern ranges such as Tain. Wainfleet, a well-equipped sea range near the Wash, tended to be dominated by RAF Tornado units, but few southern-based aircraft apart from the F-111 had the endurance to use the Scottish ranges as part of a day's training. Sometimes a crew would 'bootleg' another range by briefing a mission that included it, and then calling

---

WTDs to Spain and Turkey

Maj Dick 'Downtown' Brown reckoned that:

The main reason we went to WTD was to drop numerous training bombs and fly in VFR weather. Most of the deployments were during the bad weather months in Europe. The planning involved was fairly simple for the deployment, and for the local missions there. However, the logistics involving spare parts and equipment to repair and test aircraft were always to the detriment of the F-111. Spare parts, even at the home station, were a constant source of headaches to commanders and aircrew.

Day to day sorties at the WTDs were similar to UK sorties except that the weather was usually much better and we got to fly what we planned. Turkey was generally less restrictive than Spain over low-level flying and presented a variety of terrain. Most 'low-levels' concluded at the local range, with anywhere from 30 to 45 minutes of scheduled range time and two or four SUU-20/21s of training ordnance. For the crews, a major benefit came from flying in a strange environment and to strange ranges. Repetition is a tremendous propagator of complacency and the unrealistic 250ft [80m] low flying restriction in the UK and on over-water ranges did not help. Face it, it was not too hard to bomb a raft located by itself in the middle of the ocean. The main challenge presented by UK flying was the ability to avoid all the restricted airspace, avoid the bad weather found on the low-level routes, and still accomplish the mission. Strangely, this in itself aided one in perfecting SA, which helped in combat. What should have been learned from the WTDs was that, given an unrestricted environment the F-111 could take off, fly to its target, kill the target and return to do it again. Furthermore, one got to buy all kinds of rugs and copper!

Maj James E. 'Rotro' Rotramel, describing the WTD specialities specifically with the other UK-based F-111 Wing, the 48th TFW Statue of Liberty, with LGB capability in mind, surmised that:

Prior to the Libya Raid in April 1986, there was never enough money or incentive to send European-based F-111s to Red Flag exercises at Nellis. (After Libya, Red Flag deployments became much more frequent until *Desert Shield* kicked off.) Instead, each squadron would take turns heading south to (hopefully) better weather in either Turkey or Spain for about three weeks. The real highlight was the ability to fly with and deliver full-size (albeit inert) practice bombs, often fitted with laser guidance kits. Also, these deployments led to some spirited evenings in the bar and a lot of much-needed camaraderie. Generally, the first couple of weeks were great fun, but everyone was more than ready to go home after the third.

In Spain, we deployed to Zaragoza AB, in the north-eastern part of the country. We often flew our deployment sorties through France at low-level. (The key words for getting along with the French air traffic controllers were 'I see the ground', which meant they could stop talking… while you tried to find your way across their unfamiliar countryside without causing an international incident!). Once in Spain, low level was usually restricted to some nose-bleed altitude like 2,000ft [610m] above the ground. One deployment, we investigated medium-level tactics with the Pave Tack system, finding various targets around the base and in downtown Zaragoza from 20,000ft [6,100m] or so. It was abundantly clear that, if F-111Fs ever were given the opportunity to attack targets in that manner, it would be almost impossible to miss. The Iraqis found this out a few years later. Normally, though, the most useful training came from going to Bardenas Range and dropping bombs, which was fun enough. Also, quite often we stayed in real hotels downtown instead of on base, giving us ample opportunity to sample the shopping, cuisine, and night life of a Southern European city.

In Turkey, we deployed to Incirlik CDI [Air Base], near the city of Adana in the south-central part of the country, near the Mediterranean. We could fly unrestricted low levels within 50 miles [80km] of the base (except for the Syrian buffer zone) and selected low level routes that led to Konya bombing range, about 150 miles [240km] away. The frustrating part was that the charts were woefully out of date and inaccurate TPCs (as were some 1:50,000s dating back to WWII). Also, being the allies, we always got the (literally) sunrise takeoffs (which meant waking up at about 0300 to get ready for the mission) and the sunset landings, which made for some very long duty days for those not flying. But, if the weather held, the flying was great, the scenery spectacular, and the shopping during the Fall deployments made everyone a hero at Christmas time! We always stayed on base, and the living conditions tended to be a little on the primitive side. Nightly cookouts were generally preferred over the local fast food or O-Club fare. We also took weekend tours to visit some of the historical sites in that part of the world, of which there are many. After our leaders snatched defeat from the jaws of victory during the Gulf War Incirlik became a strategically vital base for Operation *Provide Comfort*. Unending rotations for months at a time have undoubtedly made its name dreaded now for all concerned with this vital mission. Saddam has put an end to the good times in Turkey for a very long time.

it up during the flight to see if it had a vacancy. Most UK ranges, unlike those on the Continent, were over-water and consisted of a raft with a single reflector on it. Much more realistic over-land training was to be gained on the squadron's annual 'big event', the Weapons/Tactics Deployments (WTDs).

Generally, the F-111Es behaved extremely well. A fleetwide grounding order came into effect in 1977 owing to the ejection capsule nozzle problem, following the loss of two crewmen at nearby Lakenheath, and all but the F-111Es were grounded several times in 1975–76 for engine failures. Brad Insley noted:

> Nellis lost about six aircraft due to catastrophic engine failure in less than a year. At Upper Heyford we were having no engine failures using the same engines. We were impacted some while they grounded engines with over 350 hours and then all engines with less than 350 when someone pointed out that all the failed engines had less than 350 hours. Eventually TAC sent an engine team to Upper Heyford and asked our engine people why our engines weren't failing. Their response was to ask 'what percentage of the engines from Depot are you rejecting?' The TAC team wanted to know why they should reject an engine from Depot and the Upper Heyford engine shop said that they rejected 55 per cent of Depot engines for excessive vibration. The TAC team immediately went to the Depot and found that they didn't balance the engine blades when they rebuilt the engines.

Red Flag

When USAFE F-111 units were allowed to attend *Red Flag* exercises at Nellis they gained their most valuable experience of 'near-combat' conditions. In Dick Brown's estimation, 'It's as close to combat as you can get. The difference between 450kt [830kph] at 250ft [60m] over Europe and 600–700kt [1,110–1,295kph] at 100ft [30m] in the desert is like day and night. It's like driving slowly through town and then going out on the motorway for the first time'. Brad Insley offered more information on the tactics employed there.

> Generally *Red Flag* sorties involved coordinated attacks with different types of aircraft against a series of targets in one area in an attempt to saturate the defences.
>
> The details of the attack were the responsibility of the Mission Commander, a position which rotated with each sortie. We tried to vary our attacks so as not to be predictable, with occasional feints to try and get the defenders to commit in the wrong direction, or to commit to an attack on our air-to-air aircraft. We worked up gradually to dropping live ordnance. This allowed everyone to settle in and get used to the adrenalin rush before they dropped bombs that could kill you as well as your target. Drop at too low an altitude or at the wrong airspeed, or with the wrong spacing and the enemy gets a kill without firing a shot.

Closer to home, routine NATO exercises kept crews in shape. These ranged from mass launch exercises to Tiger Meets ('largely social events where allies got to know one another and the capabilities, requirements and limitations of each aircraft, weapon and aircrew', according to Brad). During its twenty-three years in the UK, the 20th TFW took part in *Midlink* Exercises to Iran and Pakistan in support of CENTO. A *Reforger* exercise allowed the F-111 units to show that they could fly 166 out of 194 allocated sorties in weather which kept virtually all other tactical aircraft on the ground. Eighty-six per cent of the successful missions on that occasion were by F-111Es (which had been allocated only 30 per cent), and 145 hit their 'targets'. *Excalibur* exercises in the 1980s pitted F-111Es against a range of other USAFE units with some much younger and more sophisticated hardware. In the April 1988 *Excalibur III* the four-ship 20th TFW team came first and second on timing, beating all the F-16 wings. Hahn AFB's *Excalibur II* the previous year gave the F-111Es a resounding victory over the F-16s in low-angle, low-drag bombing scores. *Hammer* exercises in the 1980s included thunderous mass launches of up to fifty-eight F-111Es and Ravens from Upper Heyford's runway in simulated war conditions. Otterburn range was the location for a series of *Mallet Blow* exercises when F-111Es experienced the UK's version of *Red Flag*, with land targets and simulated SAM and fighter threats.

F-111E 68-0062 earned the name Land Shark **on a** Red Flag **deployment where its ground-hugging target approaches often left only its tail-fin visible to observers on the ground.** Authors

Raven

ORIGINS In the early 1970s the USAF found itself without a dedicated radar-jamming support aircraft. The venerable EB-66C Destroyer had already been deemed obsolescent by the time of *Linebacker* operations where it was mostly relegated to standoff work, and was retired from service during 1974. The USAF believed that podded jammers, carried by the fighters themselves, would provide adequate protection. This was proved horribly wrong during the Arab-Israeli War of Attrition and to a much greater extent during Yom Kippur conflict of 1973, when US-designed pods used by the *Hey'l Ha'Avir* failed to make much impression on a new generation of Soviet-supplied radar-guided SAMs and AAA, many manned by Soviet technicians. Continuous wave radar illumination for semi-active SAMs like the SA-6 *Gainful*, and batteries of the ZSU-23/4 AAA proved lethal if given a 'free hand'. On the basis that 'if it could happen to them, it could happen to us', the Pentagon funded USAF Project *Pave Strike*, an all-embracing effort which included amongst its key components (there were eleven in all), the impetus to develop a new dedicated jamming platform.

The possibility of acquiring US Navy/Grumman EA-6B Prowlers was explored first. This carrier-compatible derivative of the A-6 Intruder packed an Eaton AIL AN/ALQ-99 which offered a 'Closed-Loop' system capable or working in 'Lookthrough': the ability passively both to acquire and analyse simultaneously enemy radar signals and respond with effective 'noise' jamming, without the latter disrupting critical reception (causing Electromagnetic Interference, or EMI). The company's invention also offered impressive, massive waveband coverage, from about 0.1 to 10.5 gigaCycles or gigaHertz (military bands A thru J), covering the full gamut of enemy systems from early warning and height-finder emitters through to high-frequency airborne intercept radars. It had been combat proven during *Linebacker II*, providing electronic smokescreens for waves of USAF B-52 'Buffs', and updates were in progress based on Sigint (Signals intelligence) of the latest Soviet hardware, and studies of captured equipment in the Sinai. However, the Prowler used giant underwing airstream turbine-generating propellor-equipped pods to do the jamming, which were high on drag. The USAF thus re-explored the idea of using a completely internalized package. The conclusion was to give the fighters and attackers self-protection using their own pods against 'terminal threats', those trying actually to kill them at any given moment, but also develop the idea of an all-encompassing jammer which could provide an electronic 'cloak' or 'smokescreen' to mask crucial headings, altitude and numbers, and mitigate the hazards of the enemy defences.

The ALQ-99's noise jamming itself worked by 'whiting-out' enemy radar screens on the ground and in the air, by overriding their receivers and automatic gain control systems with so much static that they had no hope of obtaining aircraft position, let alone a 'lock on'. However, it required rapid analysis of the signals and effective, timely jamming.

Not enamoured with the four-man Prowler, because of its subsonic performance and limited endurance, but rather taken by its electronic 'bag of tricks', the USAF set about examining incorporation of a more automated version of the noise jamming system into a twin-seat aircraft, whereby one EW Officer would handle all bands using automation (rather than apportioning different frequencies to two or three crewmen, as was the Prowler philosophy). Eaton AIL of Deer Park, New York, obliged with the creation of the AN/ALQ-99E Jamming Sub System (JSS), tailor made for the obvious candidate: converted F-111A airframes.

SPARK'VARK In this mission the Aardvark would offer penetration capability, and had the room to contain the JSS and its cooling plumbing within a gutted weapons bay and exterior ventral 'canoe' (comprising the jamming component), and yet still provide supersonic dash: Mach 2 at 44,000ft (13,400m) and transonic at sea-level, together with 32,000lb (14,500kg) of fuel, allowing it to stay airborne for more than four hours without aerial refuelling. The receiver portion of the JSS was to be housed within a new 'football' fairing spliced to the top of the fin, similar to the Prowler's. In all, the equipment would weigh-in at two and a half tons, eventually requiring 700lb (317kg) of lead ballast to be carried in the nose as counterbalancing deadweight. Primary contractor responsibility was given to the Grumman Corporation (now Northrop-Grumman) which it ably performed at its Long Island facilities, and evolved both the aircraft modifications there and performed all the hardware and software integration work.

This began with a Phase 1A study contract which established a common baseline design using F-111A 66-0041, drawn from operations at Nellis. Work shifted to Phase 1B from December 1974 when Grumman was awarded a follow-on contract to produce two prototypes, which absorbed F-111A 66-0049 into the effort. At this stage the 'canoe' was trialled and the cockpit redesigned, but most of the work with the airframe was embroiled in studying electromagnetic patterns, to ensure the design would minimize EMI. It is also worth noting here that, while the 'Ace's' days were not numbered as an attack machine, this new programme would ultimately siphon forty-two airframes away from the force. Following the conclusion of operations in S.E. Asia, the F-111As would live out the rest of their days as either jamming platforms or as RTU trainers, with just one operational squadron to represent the 'Vietnam Vet airframes' on exercises. On the tactical conventional and nuclear bombing Aardvark front, attention shifted decidedly towards the F-111D, 'E and 'F models, with the latter's production trickling on at this time with the vague prospect of new, follow-on marks.

TRONS GO... AT THE SPEED OF LIGHT The jamming mission is known nowadays under the broader banner of SEAD (Suppression of Enemy Air Defences), but formerly was known simply as 'soft kill' defence suppression, as the combat itself was performed using electrons. First, enemy emissions across a broad range of frequencies were detected and analysed. Their pulse frequency and interval indicated threat type, and by means of interferometry and triangulation, their angle of arrival could be used to deduce the threat's azimuth and approximate range. The system was very similar to that used by the F-111's onboard APS-109 RHAWS and later ALR-62 CRS, but far more sensitive, and able to cover not only 'terminal threat' systems likely to guide flak or missiles, but the fuller gamut of devices like early warning, height-finder, GCI systems and SUAWACS.

Threats would be displayed on a new Data Display Indicator (DDI) mounted in the WSO's side of the cockpit, complete with a jammer control console and 'master radiate' switch, plus new pedestal control computer entry panel — which replaced the right-hand stick — with a series of buttons and a DDI cursor-controlling 'coolie hat' switch, similar to a stick trim button. This way, the right-hand seater, known as an Electronic Warfare Officer or 'Ewoe' (to distinguish him from ordinary WSOs who had not undergone a course in the bizarre art of Electronic Warfare) could monitor the threats as they emerged and assign specific jammers to counter them. Selection was highly automated based on the IBM AN/AYA-6 computer which managed receivers and jammers; but manual override was built-in, so that the EWO could respond for specific calls for help, or use his 'sixth sense' to counter threats the computer was not seemingly able to prioritize. It involved looking at a giant PPI 'threat map', a sort of 360° dartboard arrangement laced with threats to get the 'big picture', and constantly switching between this display on the DDI display to another showing a roster of threats with up-and-down 'carrots' marking what the antennae were taking on in which frequency band (and intervening accordingly), all the while pushing jammer activation buttons on the right-hand console which replaced the traditional ASP/WCP, tapping entries into the pedestal keyboard to command different computer display functions, and using the 'coolie hat' switch to shift the priority cursor. It was a completely new profession. EWOs originally needed 1,500hr flight-time to qualify for the programme, but it was later discovered that young, fresh minds, weaned on computers and still able to adapt to somebody else's complex theory, tended to make the best candidates.

Raven (continued)

ACES GO SPARKY Two testbeds were adapted from F-111As, M-1 (66-0049) initially serving as aerodynamics trials aircraft in overall white with red and blue cheat lines and trim, first flying on 10 March 1977, and M-2 (66-0041) which first flew in the all-up systems configuration the following 17 May, painted in ghostly greys with red insignia panels. Grumman and USAF DT&E trials consumed nine and a half months and 162 sorties/473 flight hours in two overlapping stages before IOT&E commenced under the auspices of Det 3 of the Eglin-based TAWC – in this instance, the term 'Detachment' was apt as the aircraft effectively toured the States – beginning in September 1977. FOT&E, using 'blue shirt' Air Force personnel rather than GAC workers to support the aircraft on simulated operational trials, were conducted between April and October 1979, adding a further 86 sorties/261 flight hours. These established the aircraft's credibility to a worried DAB (Defense Acquisition Board) who felt concerned that the aircraft might be too sophisticated for field operations: FOT&E established that the aircraft needed less than the 20 MMH/FH stipulated; MTBF was double that predicted at 5.7 hours; and DCCs and MX ground personnel required an average of only 2.4 hours to isolate and repair any faults that cropped up, also half that originally anticipated,. This was all in spite of M-2 having the bear the brunt of these trials pending M-1 being reworked to a systems-capable configuration (eventually accomplished by November 1981), during which time the aircraft had to miss a scheduled PDM and began to suffer from minor fuel leaks! Grumman claimed with some pride that four Ravens flying 'racetrack' orbits in Western Europe could generate 'an unbroken electronic screen across Europe, from the Baltic to the Adriatic'.

As Col Rick Matteis, a Systems Progress Officer Program Director at the ASD at the time noted:

> The test program was described by the US Congress and DoD as the most extensive test of an electronic warfare system ever attempted. There was an element in our Govt that was trying to make a point of the fact that we did not have the test ranges that would fully test a system such as this prior to committing to production. The rest of us felt that you would have to actually go to war, or at least ask the Russians to let us fly over the ground-based systems, to satisfy those people that were looking for complete realism!

Actually, the EF-111A performed flawlessly. With its systems working at near full power (the ALQ-99E was powered by two 90kVa generators that replaced the 60kVA devices fitted to stock F-111As), M-2 simultaneously and momentarily jammed not only every radar within reach of its jammers, but accidentally blanketed out all commercial radio, traffic control and TV systems on the West Coast! With several aircraft working in concert in 'lookthrough' mode, supplementing each other using refined, spot-noise jamming properly tailored to the threats, it was agreed that the aircraft could handle the mission with considerable finesse. In all, three roles were laid down: escort-penetration deep behind enemy lines, CAS support jamming, and standoff, 'racetrack' orbit jamming. In practice, crews performed whatever was required of them and thought along two lines: the 'frag' (what they were expected to do) and 'ad hoc' (meeting new threats as they emerged on the airwaves), in any of those scenarios. Ground specialists, given access to a threat library based on anticipated hostile radars, could update the EF-111A for the given mission.

An initial six conversions were authorized in March 1979, followed by orders for the remaining thirty-four machines (including the two, reworked testbeds) thru FY 1983. Airframes selected for conversion were withdrawn from operations at Mountain Home AFB and flown direct to GAC's Calverton facility for a complete tear-down and rework, which included all the key facets of PDM. Conversion gestation took an average of nine and a half months, 'involving a 25 per cent change to the aircraft', including 25,000 new cables and 100 antennae as part of the JSS kit plus additional Dalmo-Victor AN/ALR-62(V)4 TTWS and updated Sanders AN/ALQ-137(V)4 SPS. These latter upgrades were based on FB-111A systems, and designed to help provide individual aircraft protection while the Raven plied its art of protecting others. 'Mod O' integrity on those airframes given the stick-controlled pyrotechnic-dumping feature was maintained. Stripped down to bare metal and repainted in epoxy-primer undercoats and a two-tone matt grey acrylic top coat, the newly renamed Raven – a name with strong USAF electronic combat associations – required up to six FCFs (Functional Check-Flights) to wring out its systems prior to acceptance. These embraced electronic trials against Grumman's 'Campsite', a DoD-funded Range, and the full spectrum of Raven performance, which climaxed with a TFR run against the sheer cliffs and crags on 'No Man's Land', an Island off the tip of Martha's Vineyard, Massachusetts, followed by a zoom climb to 35,000ft (10,700m), a dive and supersonic dash, and then wing/flap/slat checks in the circuit around Suffolk County Airport, prior to recovery at Calverton. All aircraft were signed for by FCF crews between 4 November 1981 and 23 December 1984.

Access to the TF30 powerplant was facilitated by massive doors incorporating the rear fuselage strakes. The over-wing fairing, raised for access in this view, was held down by a cable and pulley. The 'lips' around the wing-fold (known as 'boots') inflated to form a seal as the wing moved in and out of the 'fold' area. In high-*g* conditions the wing-fold fairings could rise up slightly from the fuselage top-surface. Authors

Electronic Warriors

GRIFFINS Raven deliveries went initially to the 388th ECS *Griffins* at Mountain Home, beginning with the first arrival (66-0051) on 5 November 1981. Commanded initially by Aardvark and Destroyer Vietnam combat veteran Lt Col Tom Pickering, the unit was redesignated the 390th ECS *Deny, Deceive, Defeat* the following December. Initial inductees for the first eleven crews possessed an average of 2,000 hours flying time in the Aardvark, and formed the nucleus of the new establishment. By Christmas 1984, when all forty-two aircraft had been completed, the 390th ECS had thirty qualified aircrews and twenty-seven Ravens, offering both an operational commitment and Raven conversion training.

The remaining forty-three 366th TFW F-111As, half of which were assigned to the 389th TFTS *Thunderbolts* for RTU training, provided not only basic and conversion training for crews bound for 20th TFW F-111E operations in England, but also conversion and refresher requalification training for the 'Raven track'. EWOs, who unlike their pilots later came in increasing numbers straight from 'Fightergator College' and Electronic Warfare Courses at Mather AFB, would then spend an additional 127 hours of academics and 30 hours of simulator time. A minimum of twenty hours' flying time was then accrued with the 390th ECS before being passed for operational duties, with most of it being taken up 'learning the switches' at a tremendous rate of knots over Mountain Home's 109,468-acre Saylor Creek bombing and EW range in Southern Idaho. This included a host of simulated radar threats, and scrutiny of performance in this ethereal form of warfare was performed by personnel from the 392nd ECRS using data processed from the MUTES (Multiple Threat Emitter Simulators) and MSR-T4 analysers.

The 390th ECS perfected their art for eight years, each aircraft flying some 112 sorties/255 hours annually, a tempo that began to increase markedly with time. Excursions included overseas deployments and *Run Fast* rapid deployment and surge sortie tests as well as regular appearances for *Red/Green Flag* manoeuvres at Nellis. Ravens first ventured to Europe in the late summer of 1986, operating from RAF Boscombe Down for four weeks as part of *Coronet Papago*, and flew to Iwakuni, Japan for a four-weeker under *Coronet West* between 14 March and 10 April 1988. This was the first time that any Aardvarks had operated from that country, as the Japanese would not countenance the presence of nuclear weapons on their soil and were deeply suspicious of all but the conspicuously unarmed Ravens. This pattern of training and building systems expertise, regularly incorporating software updates to the TJS to take account of new threats, continued unabated until the call came to test their knowledge in combat.

This began with small-scale but essential jamming support over Panama beginning on the night of 20 December 1989, codenamed Operation *Just Cause*. Because the attackers – F-117A Stealth fighters and AC-130 *Pave Specter* gunships – primarily employed electro-optic targeting aids, the Ravens could jam virtually at will. Things were rather different when the big test came and the 390th ECS(Provisional) joined forces with the 48th TFW(P) at Taif, Saudi Arabia, for *Desert Storm* operations (described more fully in Chapter 8) alongside radar-toting Coalition fighters. The Ravens' jamming had to be precisely executed. Although each jet's ten, computer-steered 1,000 Watt transmitters contained behind the JSS 'canoe' meant that jamming could be directed specifically at the threats, thereby reducing undesirable EMI interference and maximizing Effective Radiated Power to boot, it nonetheless required meticulous SA; there were other SEAD aircraft duelling with SAM complexes in deadly HARM shoot-outs and these had to be able to use their 'senses' unimpeded. Judicious spot-bursts of noise had to be generated in accordance with the rigid 'frags' to mask ingress/egress routes, while EWOs maintained a vigil and 'rubbed-up some static' when specific pleas for assistance were called for, to confound 'terminal threat' emitters and keep the occasional enemy fighter guessing. Of the thirty-eight coalition fixed-wing losses, only three were downed by radar-directed SAMs and none of them was under Raven protection at the time. The end score within the Raven community was parity: one Iraqi Mirage was goaded into flying into the ground by a skilled Raven crew, Capts James Denton and (EWO) Brent Brandon (flying 66-0016); but an EF-111A met a similar fate while executing a 'threat reaction manoeuvre' on 14 February 1991. 390th ECS(P) crewmen Capts D.L. Bradt and P.R. Eichenlaub perished after an unsuccessful, fraction-of-a-second-too-late tug at the tiger-striped ejection handles.

The Raven establishment at Mountain Home wound down after the Gulf War, on the heels of the disestablishment of the two 366th FW F-111A squadrons. These aircraft had led a relatively tame existence flying from Idaho, though Upper Heyford could not have filled its ranks without them, including ground crews who received 'hands on' training on the F-111As under its Field Training Detachment. It was a well-deserved peacetime flying roster for the Vietnam veteran airframes, before they were despatched to AMARC during 1991. Their reworked Raven stablemates enjoyed no such luxury. In their wake, the 390th ECS Ravens were redesignated the 429th ECS on 11 September 1992 and the aircraft and its crews were transferred to Cannon AFB, New Mexico. To this day, in terms of their TDY commitments, EF-111A crewmen remain some of the most hard-worked in the USAF.

NATO RAVENS USAFE also received its quota of Ravens to meet the Warsaw Pact threat, following the reactivation of the 42nd ECS, renamed *NATO Ravens*, at RAF Upper Heyford on 1 July 1983. Preparations began in March with the arrival of a SATAF (Site Activation Task Force), which oversaw the necessary reconstruction of facilities and emplacement of Raven-dedicated materiel, including Grumman AN/ALM-204 test benches, necessary to check the health of the EF-111A's forty-nine separate LRUs. The squadron was initially commanded by Lt Col David Vesely, and he and Maj Roger Brooks brought the first aircraft (66-0037, named *NATO Raven One*) to the base on the afternoon of 3 February 1984. Sixty aircrew and 225 MX people made up the squadron cadre by 1 July 1985, when control of the force passed to 17th Air Force and the 66th ECW at Sembach, West Germany, home of the 43rd ECS and its EC-130 *Compass Call* Hercules. The Ravens were optimized to concentrate on the full spectrum of emitters, paying special attention to the mid- and high-frequency band devices used by AAA, SAMs and fighter GCI networks on an ad hoc basis after disrupting early warning and GCI systems during ingress, while the '*Herky Birds*' would take care of communications-jamming. The units were worlds apart otherwise, and only shared common grey paint schemes. NATO-wide operations from outside of the British coastline began with Exercise *Distant Hammer* 85, flown from Italy, in time to prepare the *NATO Ravens* for its pivotal support role in Operation *El Diablo*, their contribution to the April 1986 retaliatory strike on Libya, *El Dorado Canyon*. Star of the raid was '052 *Cherry Bomb*, which consistently offered one of the best availability rates of all the Ravens, one of two that provided beautifully-executed spot-noise jamming. However, they could do nothing to deter electro-optically guided missiles (the 'blindspot' of the Ravens), which were mostly aimed using rack-of-the-eye lock-on methods, especially after Washington insanely ordered a trail of F-111Fs against the one small target, precipitating the sole Libya loss. It was doubly frustrating for the Raven force sent there to protect them.

Five years later the 42nd ECS provided jamming assets for the 7440th Composite Wing at Incirlik, for *Proven Force* Persian Gulf combat. A quartet had flown there on 1 September 1990 for an already planned Exercise *Display Determination*, and numbers were increased on 17 January, just in time for hostilities. The two Raven detachments located at Incirlik and Taif flew 400 combat sorties, totalling 2,150 hours. After the cease-fire, the Gulf Ravens continued to maintain a presence in S.W. Asia in support of *Provide Comfort* and *Southern Watch*, operating from both Incirlik, and from Dhahran, Saudi Arabia, under the 4404th CW.

Ongoing USAFE operations continued unabated in parallel, placing a great burden on the crews and maintainers. Tail '056 *Jam Master* crashed near the base on 2 April 1992 after suffering an engine fire shortly after takeoff, but to everyone's delight the crew ejected successfully: Capts Jeff Coombe and (EWO) David Genevish made a bumpy but safe landing by capsule as their wingman circled overhead. In the 42nd ECS' bar, named the *Ravensden* (announced by a poached English town sign of the same name), remnants of the aircraft were retained as a reminder of a lucky escape.

Gulf commitments became the sole responsibility of the 390th ECS after the last three Upper Heyford-based Ravens (callsign *Volt 1/2/3*) returned to Oxfordshire on 26 June 1992. Raven boss Col James N. Worth was there to greet the returnees, which included Capt Dave Vish Genevish, who had recovered from his earlier trauma and subsequently had deployed to Incirlik, undaunted. A final ceremony to mark the squadron's official deactivation took place on 10 July 1992 when seven more Ravens exited the base, many already bearing Mountain Home insignia, to be absorbed into the 390th ECS (later 429th ECS) in the 'Gem State'. The very last to leave was the squadron bird, 67-0042 *The Old Crow*, which departed for Wright-Patterson AFB on 7 August, due for eventual reassignment to Cannon AFB, where the entire Raven force was destined to recongregate under 27th FW headquartership for its final few years of operations.

Better Bombs, Stronger Screens

While the F-111E remained relatively unchanged throughout its service life, its operational capability was significantly enhanced by the introduction, late in its life, of some new weapons and improved delivery techniques. These were of greater importance when the wing gave up its nuclear strike role in the mid-1980s. This roughly coincided with the arrival of an additional dozen 'swingers' swelling its ranks: EF-111A Ravens, which formed under the 42nd ECS *NATO Ravens*, initially under the command of Lt Col David Vesely.

In place of *Victor Alert* F-111Es standing ready around the clock with a pair of F-111As in Vietnam. Even the retarded Snakeye Mk 82, which fell behind the aircraft's flightpath satisfactorily, imposed a 500kt (930kph) drop limit to prevent the bombs' retarding fins failing. F-111 crews, particularly those honed on nuclear deliveries, preferred much higher speeds over the target. Air Inflatable Retards (AIRs) solved the problem. In place of Snakeye's mechanically-extending cruciform airbrakes a Goodyear (later Loral) BSU-49 tube was fitted to the bomb's tail. This contained a canvas 'balloon/parachute' (Ballute) to slow down the Mk 82 bombs. The larger Mk 84 had a BSU-50 equivalent. Each BSU incorporated a spring-loaded cover at its rear with lanyards, hooked to solenoids on the BRU or pylon, which withdrew pins from the cover on release. The Ballute then blossomed, extending and drop nose down, where they fired a rocket motor, blowing away the 'chute, and charging into the target to rip up paving and tarmac. A good-sized drop would include eight or twelve of them, train-released from a pair of BRUs.

At the same time, new weapons delivery modes were added to the training syllabus, including Low Angle Drogued Delivery (LADD) and 'Toss' bombing, all in anticipation of the AMP update. LADD was based on the DBT and could be done visually, or using radar at night or in bad weather.

Among the structural improvements incorporated into the aircraft was one crucial change. The F-111s' original windshield proved very susceptible to birdstrike damage. Initially it was felt that its very steep rake would deflect birds over the air-

For almost twenty-two years Aardvarks were a familiar sight over Britain, practising their skills on 'targets' such as the bridge in this photo. In wartime, the aircraft would have operated at much lower altitudes than this. via John Roberts

Mk/B.61 nuclear weapons under the inner wing-pivot pylons, USAFE introduced Tomahawk GLCM (Ground-Launched Cruise Missile) at the wing's satellite airfield, and the USAFE Aardvarks finally began to take conventional bombing a bit more seriously. Low-level bombing with conventional weapons always meant a serious risk of damage to the dropper from a faulty delivery, as was established by the about 4ft (1.3m) behind the bomb. Its big advantage, in Dick Brown's opinion was that you could 'drop it lower and faster. It's about the best improvement we had. You could use it at 100ft [30m] at the speed of heat – as fast as the old jet would go'.

Matra Durandal BLU-107/B boosted runway cratering weapons also entered service during the mid-1980s. After release, they would be braked by parachute craft but, in practice, even small birds were damaging or penetrating canopies and causing aircraft losses, particularly in low-level flight over water. Developing stronger polycarbonate replacements of the required degree of transparency took a while. In 1978 Upper Heyford's fleet had three trial windshields fitted, recognizable by red edges to the panels. The rest of the fleet was gradually retrofitted during Programmed

Repainted as Heartbreaker, the name it first wore in 1987-88, F-111E 68-0055 is obligingly positioned for photography outside its TAB-V in September 1993. The aircraft nose art (devised by a woman, in case feminists are offended!), was echoed in paintings on the rear shelter doors and floor. Authors

A GBU-12D/B LGB training weapon is suspended from this 77th TFS F-111E in September 1991. After the Gulf War, F-111Es sometimes carried LGBs although they were unable to laser-mark their targets and relied on a 'buddy' laser or ground forces to do the job. Authors

Depot Maintenance at BAe Filton, north Bristol, or at SMALC in California. More obvious visible external additions, fitted to all marks, included the *Compass Sail* AN/ALR-62 RHAWS/CRS 'knob' antenna, installed just ahead of the KB-18 camera housing (with further new antennae built into the wing 'glove', all put in as part of TO 1F-111-1168). The new system proved more reliable than the APS-109, and also helped the AN/ALQ-131 ECM pod – the third-generation external jammer bolted between the strakes – optimize its jamming output. Another external change included the gradual adoption of electroluminescent formation strip lights (under TO 1F111-1209), to help wingmen see others during night formation join-ups. The 'glow' factor was variable, by means of a rheostat switch.

Late-life Update

The F-111E force had to wait until the last few years of its USAFE service before it was thought appropriate to spend major dollars

F-111E 68-0084 proudly bears its '6,000 HOURS' logo in July 1993. Although the aircraft was less than two years away from retirement it had used up little over half its actual fatigue life. Its WSO, Capt Mike Nuss later delivered F-111E 67-0120 The Chief to Duxford Museum with Frank Rossi as pilot.
Authors

on more serious upgrading. The TF30-P-3/9 engines had proved reliable and replacement could not have been funded, though aircrew would have welcomed a superior engine such as the GE F110, which replaced the TF30 in later F-14D Tomcats. However, the F-111A/E's 'cog-and-crankshaft' Mk I analogue Bombing & Navigation systems had become dated and unreliable by the mid-1980s and better systems were needed to keep the aircraft current. The result was AMP, using digital avionics for the cockpit and computer hardware derived from the FB-111A's SAC-AMP update kit. Software was written in Jovial language instead of the newer USAF-wide Ada language (a common ailment of the avionics upgrading programmes), though anything new to analogue Aardvarks in this department was welcomed. Even so, WSOs and MX specialists had not had to suffer the complexities of Assembly language which Mk II/IIB specialists had endured for so long. F-111Es received the new 'digital trio' of two cockpit MFDs and a revised radar Central Display Unit, tied in through databuses with a single RLG INS which could accept GPS updates. A five-channel AN/ARN-151(V) Navstar receiver was wired in, adding an external trademark: a round bump on the glareshield. Grumman was awarded contracts for new hardware installation and for designing the computer software, though this took much longer than expected owing to the need to develop the system for both the F-111E and Raven. SMALC's F-111E (68-0040) was used for lengthy flight tests and the intention was to upgrade all the F-111As of the 366th TFW as well as the surviving F-111Es. However, the programme was effectively put on the chopping block when East-West tensions began to relax in 1990, and the final outcome was only twenty-five F-111E conversions and a similar number of Ravens. Most of the 'Echoes' were modified at BAe Filton during routine PDM work, on a 'first come, first served basis' according to Lt Col Terry Simpson, using the first SMALC production AMP F-111E, 68-0050 as an exemplar. This machine featured a temporary 'Gunship Gray' scheme which was also to have been a fleet-wide change, but events in the Persian Gulf put an end to that. 'Zero-Five-Zero' was later returned to standard finish and operated by the 77th TFS (as were all other AMP'ed examples), and flew the last mission in *Desert Storm*. AMP gave the F-111E marked improvements in navigation and weapons delivery as well as reliability, akin to the GD SAC-AMP'ed FB-111A although, picking up a minor point, Terry Simpson noted that 'AMP left out the obvious: a simple estimated time of arrival indicator'. Even with AMP, Wizzos were obliged to mentally compute this based on indicated speed and distance. In the same update programme the aircraft received the Tracor AN/ALE-40 CMDS in place of the AN/ALE-28 in the 'speed bumps', another fleetwide upgrade effort designed to give the Aardvark better protection, and that received a universal thumbs-up.

Grooming Mud-pigs

Upper Heyford's maintenance was initially organized on a squadron basis, then went to a wing-based pattern in 1972 with the 20th Organizational Maintenance Squadron (OMS) looking after all the Aardvarks. Codes became standardized as 'UH' and aircraft were effectively pooled. After several changes of title, the maintenance structure evolved into three main elements.

The 20th Aircraft Generation Squadron (AGS) was tasked with the day-to-day business of keeping the aircraft flying. It handled launches, recoveries and replenishment (rearming and refuelling) and conducted minor repairs – the latter being possible not only in ICT (Integrated Combat Turn-around) fashion, but also 'hot' (with the engines in idle). This meant that a subsequent crew could climb into a 'warmed up' cockpit and launch in under an hour from the previous recovery, with the aircraft kept running for up to four consecutive sorties.

The second element was the 20th Component Repair Squadron (CRS), which looked after the complex avionics and the flight simulator, and 'tweaked' and reprogrammed the penetration aids.

Thirdly, the 20th Equipment Maintenance Squadron (EMS) tended to handle wheels, tyres, capsules, munitions and all the ground-handling equipment collectively called AGE (Aerospace Ground Equipment).

In a further USAF-wide change following the introduction of TAMS (Tactical Aircraft Maintenance System) in USAFE at the turn of the 1980s, AGS maintenance devolved to a squadron basis once more, with each assigned its own similarly colour-coded troop for TAB-Vee organic tasks, these later becoming known as Air Maintenance Units (AMUs). The practice of applying individual squadron codes and badges was not resumed, but the squadrons' 'flagships' (68-0055 for the 55th TFS and 68-0077 for the 77th TFS) proudly bore 55th or 77th AMU logos adjacent to their doctored serials, while the 79th AMU made do with one or both *Chiefs* (67-0120 & 68-0020), as squadron and wing representatives. The 'gray airplane' community on the north side of the base, with their exotic Ravens, similarly acquired a '42nd ECS/AMU' designator on an assigned tail following legal adoption of the jamming assets by their *de facto* operators the 20th TFW, immediately after *Desert Storm*. For six years the Ravens had technically been under 66th ECW control at Sembach, Germany, which managed EC-130H *Compass Call* Hercules specializing in low frequency radar- and communications-jamming, and were decorated in a similar two-tone grey camouflage to that on the Ravens.

Throughout all these paper upheavals the force stayed put and the basic responsibility for each EF/F-111 rested with its DCC. He or she worked with 'their' tail number almost all of the time and got to know its individual eccentricities. As recognition of this relationship, *Project Warrior* in 1987–88 encouraged DCCs to participate in naming and applying nose art to their aircraft, often based on WWII origins. Some of these reflected interests close to the Chiefs' lives. For example, F-111E 68-0040 (later transferred to SMALC as an AMP and, sadly, written off during later 428th FS duties at Cannon AFB) became *The Other Woman* because SSgt Larry Casteel's wife felt that he spent too much time with his 'swinger'. F-111E 68-0072 was *Strange Music* because of the range of minor ailments it generated when put on *Victor Alert* duty.

The TF30-P-3 was generally regarded as a trouble-free engine thanks to the exemplary tuning conducted at Upper Heyford, and its detachable components made it easier to service than the J79, which many maintainers had previously worked on in USAFE Phantom squadrons. Ground-running tests were done in a test-rig building where the strapped-down engine could be run in fifth-stage afterburner, its efflux venting onto a water-cooled metal grid and generating a plume of steam which was visible for miles, as if a mystical dragon lived on the base. More serious maintenance or repair to engines was done at OAAALC, Tinker AFB, Oklahoma. Mission avionics 'black boxes' and scanners were in the overall charge of WRALC, Warner-Robins AFB, Georgia.

Major Maintenance

Every forty-eight months each F-111 was required to undergo the 'III SIP' *Speedline* inspection of its crucial wing-pivot areas, or a full PDM at either SMALC or BAe Filton. The timing was dictated mainly by the need to replace pyrotechnics in the escape capsule. When both centres were operating, from the late 1970s to 1992, around twenty-five F-111s of various marks would be 'under the wrench' at each facility. USAFE F-111E/Fs went through

EF-111A 67-0052 in landing configuration. This aircraft flew in support of the El Dorado Canyon/El Diablo **mission and carried the name** Cherry Bomb **in 1987–88.** USAFE photo by Sgt David Nolan

Filton originally, but F-111Fs were flown back to Sacramento for specialist modifications (*Pave Tack* or other avionics upgrades) during the early 1980s and during the last five years of their USAFE service. The Ravens were the exclusive bailiwick of Sacramento. Filton, which would have served as a major repair facility in the event of war in Europe, returned its last F-111E (68-0076), callsign *Sapphire 22*, to Upper Heyford on 16 September 1992.

Both facilities were equipped to deal with maintenance and repair problems, including major component replacement. Filton replaced a WCTB in F-111E

Arguably the most valuable of all Aardvark variants, the EF-111A Raven rapidly became a vital part of USAFE's combat strength and an indispensable asset in the Libyan, Persian Gulf and Bosnian war scenarios. Authors

69-0043, and a major tail frame in 68-0001 when structural failures were detected, establishing a good reputation with AFLC (Air Force Logistics Command) which scrutinized the mainframe reels of tapes generated by the cold-proof chamber computer. Aircraft were given a full strip-and-paint every other PDM, including separated subassemblies such as MLG and NLG. Within the 13,000 to 16,000 manhours needed for a PDM (21,000 for the Raven), two major specialized jobs were done; deseal/reseal and cold proof-testing.

Because sealing compound in the aircraft's wing and fuselage tanks perished after a few years, causing leaks, it had to be patched or completely replaced. A full replacement involved softening the existing compound with a highly toxic chemical cocktail and then cutting away the residue with 6,000psi water lances. Desealing the internal fuselage tanks involved the lance operator working inside the tank area, a job which the supervisor called a 'bloody revolting activity' and one which

Gulf War veteran EF-111A 66-0037 was the first to be assigned to USAFE. Its early Triple Plow intakes, high-lift devices, EW antennae and heavy-duty undercarriage are all in evidence here. Authors

most workers could only stand for 15 to 20 minutes at a stretch despite full protective clothing. Wing tanks were treated after first removing the wing skins and then fastening them back in a hurry before the fresh sealing compound set.

Cold proof-testing was introduced after the wing-box problems of the F-111A,

Duxford Delivery

On 19 October 1993 *The Chief* (F-111E 67-0120) was handed over to the Imperial War Museum's collection of American aircraft at Duxford. Its last pilot, Capt Frank Rossi, who went on to fly the F-16C, gives his account of the final flight.

> First off, it was a big team effort. My WSO was Capt Michael 'Pickle' Nuss, who is now a Major and F-15E Instructor/WSO. According to regulations the minimum runway length for an F-111E is 7,500ft [2,290m]. Obviously, the 4,500ft [1,370m] strip at Duxford presented some problems. We got into our Technical Orders and computed that with 4,500lb [2,040kg] of fuel we could land in 3,000ft [910m] without getting hot brakes. As a precaution we would have a departure-end cable in place. Well, Third Air Force HQ didn't think that was safe enough and they directed us to land using an approach-end cable engagement with the departure-end as back-up. Their main concern was hot brakes. [Hot brakes meant that the big, fat F-111's tyres were apt to explode and potential wheel well hydraulic fires were another problem nobody wanted to contend with.]
>
> We practised approaches the day before to familiarize ourselves with the visual cues at Duxford. There was also the challenge of communicating with air traffic control facilities in the area since they operated on VHF in that sector and all we had was UHF. A telephone relay was devised with a UHF-equipped facility and a mobile radio had to be set up at Duxford for the same reason. 'Pickle' Nuss also did some outstanding radar work and was able to use the airborne instrument landing approach system on the F-111 to give us a normal glidepath reference. The day of the delivery we took off with 10,000lb [4,540kg] of fuel and flew some more practice approaches (everybody wanted to make sure we didn't miss that cable). We even had another aircraft as 'chase' in case we needed some assistance (though of what kind I don't know!). I'm sure the spectators thought we were providing an airshow for the delivery. Fortunately, practice makes perfect and it was probably one of my best landings ever (which isn't saying much!). It was also the first approach-end cable arrestment for either 'Pickle' or myself. Everybody was just fantastic in their support of the delivery and you could feel the warmth and admiration the crowd had for the F-111. My wife was on hand and afterwards the Museum staff gave us and some of the 20th FW staff a personal tour of the Museum. It was a very 'feel good', memorable day which I'll never forget.

when GDFW and the USAF constructed facilities at SMALC and Fort Worth to fatigue-test WCTBs and tail mechanisms. In September 1986 a similar facility was constructed, at BAe's expense, at Filton. Each aircraft was clamped to underfloor fixtures by its undercarriage, taileron spigots and wing pylons. Seventy-ton arms clamped to the wings moved them to various sweep angles. The building was then chilled to −40°C, using 7,000gal (32,000l) of liquid nitrogen. Massive jacks bent the wings through a total vertical travel of 5ft (1.5m) at their tips to simulate the greatest aerodynamic load they might encounter. Any tiny cracks would become visible under this 'accelerated fatigue' regime and component failure could occur safely there, rather than in flight. Replacement WCTBs, on the rarer occasions that they were needed after these tests, were hard to find and usually had to be salvaged from derelict F-111s.[9] Towards the end of the Aardvark's service life SMALC introduced a less labour-intensive, more environmentally acceptable inspection process using radiographic and ultrasonic equipment.

During their twenty-three years of tenure in England, the F-111Es of the 20th TFW kept the 'Bear at Bay' and championed myriad systems and doctrinal improvements, many vitally important to both safety and mission success. Despite the type's essentially first-generation Mk I Bombing & Navigation package, it was the F-111E model which gave rise to one of the Aardvark's lesser known but more flattering sobriquets, 'The Cadillac of the Air Force'. To many past, and likely also future key commanders who cut their teeth at the base, it is remembered with special affection.

Heyford's 'Swing Wing' Finale

Around 09.00 on the morning of 7 December 1993 the skies above Oxfordshire began to clear. When the sun broke, it described a full rainbow which appeared to hang above RAF Upper Heyford for a quarter of an hour, serving as a beacon for all those venturing there to witness the departure of the 20th Fighter Wing's last trio of F-111E Aardvarks. Amongst those saying farewell were MSgt William 'Bill' Daley, a Crew Chief who had been on the rain-dampened Upper Heyford apron when the first arrivals had come just over twenty-three years previously. His father had flown as a B-17 ball-turret gunner with the 8th Air Force during WWII, and he was in perhaps a unique position to appreciate the sentiment of the busloads of troops, 620th Air Base families and enthusiasts who turned up to bid their farewells to another classic aircraft, one which had also 'beaten up' the skies over Europe, but in much happier times for all concerned; with the Aardvarks' big, fat tyres, green hues and metal airframes glinting in the breaking sunshine, the authors could not help thinking of the many farewells that had taken place during the mid-1940s.

In July 1992 the last of the 42 ECS *NATO Ravens* had left their Oxfordshire enclave, with the seventy veteran 'Echoes' following suit in phases throughout 1993. First to disband were the 79 FS *Tigers*, on 23 April. The 77 FS *Gamblers* bowed out on 9 July and the 55 FS *Fighting Fifty-Fifth* followed suit on 15 October. The last deployment had drawn to a close precisely a week beforehand when the last jets on *Dynamic Guard* 93 returned from Incirlik, leaving just a token establishment.

The long-established Anglo-American 'Vark Institution' finally succumbed on that windy, but welcomely sunny December morning. The wing's last three F-111Es, squatted plugged into their start-up carts with wings spread-eagle, all resplendent with nose art and carefully painted crew names specially applied for the last trip. Electrical 'power on' checks proceeded with haste and by 10.20 piped air hosed into the aircraft was beginning to push the three aircraft's massive turbofans into motion too. There was no official ceremony. It was as if few could bear to acknowledge the final farewell, which the crews concerned described euphemistically as the 'beginning of our mission transition from flying support to drawdown and closure objectives'. All three formal squadron farewells had already taken place, and it was better just to crank up and go.

Just before 11.00 the first of the last to leave town took to the air, thundering west. 68-061 *Last Roll of the Dice* was first to flex its wings, piloted by Wing Vice-Commander Col Patrick Nolte and Capt David Bikker. Twenty seconds later 68-055 *Heartbreaker* (alias *Slack Alice*) flown by Lt Col Ken Holder, 55 FS boss, and Maj Brian Ramsey made a non-nonsense takeoff in reheat. The duo joined up, and performed a wide circuit, as if on finals. Then, at 11.01Z, just as the pair shot over the assembled crowd in formation with their wings swept, 68-020 *The Chief* vaulted off Heyford's runway. It was crewed appropriately enough by the wing boss Col Randall 'Mark' Schmidt, and 20th Operations Group commander Lt Col Daniel Clark. The Chief caught up rapidly to assume the lead position in reheat and the three F-111Es soon left only smoky flecks to mark their position, which dissipated all too quickly in the distant wind, '061 being the last to leave the onlookers' gaze. '020 was bound for display at Hill AFB, Utah, and '055 for a similar fate at Robins AFB, Georgia. '061's future was less prosperous: its final destination was to join over two hundred 'Varks already forever dormant at the dusty Davis-Monthan 'Bone Yard' in Arizona.

Back at Upper Heyford, with the tenants having quit notice from their cavernous TAB-Vee shelters (effectively welded shut), a mass of crew access steps and drop tanks lay stacked or laid in patterns like old bones, a sad reminder of the wing's almost exclusive ownership of the F-111Es for over two decades. The wing, at one time or another, had operated no fewer than eighty-eight of the ninety-four 'Echo' models built. Ironically, all three squadrons celebrated their diamond anniversaries shortly before or during the draw-down, as did RAF Upper Heyford, whose heritage stretches back to WWI. The facility was handed back to the UK MoD the following September and is now in the process of being dismantled to create space for commercial land development. An era is being wiped off the map, but not off the history books.

CHAPTER SIX

High Plains Deltas

In the pre-microchip age, a computer offering 2K binary number-crunching was pretty impressive. IBM's AN/AYK-6 8K system was thus considered 'state of the art' in the late 1960s, and formed the heart of the world's first fully transistorized, all solid-state avionics package: the Mark II bombing and navigation system developed for the F-111D. However, it presented its systems-integrators, Rockwell Autonetics and General Dynamics, with an immense challenge, as the Mk II involved a host of sensors and subsystems, including Norden cockpit TV displays and twin-HUDs, and Rockwell's own INS and attack and terrain-following package. Many of these represented major advances in their own right and all of them had to be able to communicate with each other via a twin AYK-6 network called the Digital Computer Complex (DCC). Stuffing all the computer routines into the limited space meant extremely skilful software programming matched to hardware development, and this took a great deal longer than anyone envisaged. Ultimately, the F-111D's Mk II package evolved almost in parallel with the rest of the Aardvark programme rather than as an evolutionary progression (although the Mk IIB-derived aircraft the FB-111A and F-111F shared its DCC 'black boxes'), not only later rendering it incompatible with many later USAF weapons and sensor upgrades, but also making the F-111D very much a 'one off' exclusive variant with its own peculiar strengths and weaknesses.

An artist's perspective of the aborted RAF F-111K. The aircraft was to have the longer-span wings of the FB-111A and the Mk II avionics systems of the F-111D. Only two heavily instrumented YF-111K prototypes were produced, and scrapped before final completion following Britain's pull-out from the TFX effort.
Lockheed-Martin

'D' for Delayed

The system was originally intended as the next-in-line package following completion of the F-111A run and its Mk I BNS systems, which at that stage were considered mere operational trials aircraft and 'international show case' machines to spur potential NATO exports pending a thousand-plus production run of Mk II avionics-equipped Aardvarks. But the near unfathomable complexities involved in completing development of this system were already surfacing at the same time that major structural problems became contentious in 1968–69. This was probably the key factor in McNamara not fulfilling his dreams. Britain's RAF pulled out of the programme when Mk II delays and cost increases beset the effort, and the USAF, impatient to replenish its Vietnam-depleted 'Thud' interdictor force with a faster and more survivable nuclear bomber than the multi-role Phantom, instead opted to 'leap frog' over the Mk II-equipped F-111D and continue Mk I systems production in the form of the F-111E. A planned force of sixty RF-111D reconnaissance models was shelved, while the F-111D order book was reduced from 315 to a mere ninety-six examples, all financed under funds obligated in FY 1968. But even the reduced number being built ended up sitting at Fort Worth in a part-built state pending Mk II systems availability, and were eventually finished only when the line had double-leaped onto initial manufacture of the definitive variant: the F-111F. F-111D final assembly then was stretched to provide a bridge for follow-on F-111F orders. What it all boiled down to is that most F-111Ds were four years newer than their 'AF' tail numbers suggested![1]

In all fairness, as Col Tom Runge noted of the Mk II systems, 'We were a tad too ambitious'. With hindsight, many also rightly point out that, had F-111 production seen its originally envisaged numbers, would there have existed the talent to make it work the way it eventually did? In all probability, no. Those who pioneered the F-111 thought as hard as they flew, helping to place the Aardvark at the peak of its profession. Many stayed with the 'F-111 Program' after their first assignment, and built up its institutional knowledge, helping to establish an elite with its own stringent standards which would not otherwise have been realized with massively swollen ranks. A thousand-plus production run all in one fell swoop might have proved to be a complete disaster.

'D' for Digital

Col C.E. Francis, 27th TFW commander, piloted the first F-111D to arrive at its new home, Cannon AFB in New Mexico, on 12 November 1971. 68-0090 was one of four arrivals that day, all bound for the squadron nominated to introduce the new bird to TAC: the 4427th TFRS. The base had previously resounded to the thunder of nearly thirty analogue models in a preliminary 'false start' work-up effort before the bulk of this force – twenty-nine F-111Es – sped east for England. In their wake the 27th TFW had continued to fly the venerable F-100D/F 'Hun', the last of which departed in July 1972 for service with the Air National Guard, and made do with another ten F-111As on loan from Nellis. By the time F-111D production was finally completed and the last example delivered to Cannon on 28 February 1973, the wing had four squadrons getting to grips with the machines. First to achieve IOC was the *Fireballs* which had begun conversion in May 1972 and was declared operational that November. On its heels, in overlap fashion that August, was the 524th TFS *Hounds*, followed by the ephemeral 481st TFS *Green Knights* which assumed training duties for only a few months to supplement the 4427th before it metamorphosed into the definitive operational squadron on 31 August 1973, the 523rd TFS *Crusaders*.[2] Achieving IOC was accomplished remarkably quickly given the long periods of idleness to which the aircraft had been subjected pending final assembly. No fewer than twenty-one F-111Ds were further held in storage at Cannon until their cracked fuel tank sealant could be patched or stripped out and replaced. Engines, on the other hand, comprising the uprated TF30-P-9, offered 20,840lb (9,450kg) thrust in afterburner, and quickly became popular. Rated as a 'vast improvement' over the TF30-P-3 powering the F-111 A/E, it quickly established itself as being more reliable than its predecessor and fifteen years later formed the basis of an 'upgrade kit' which was used to enhance the P-3s installed in the Ravens.

In the cockpit, the crews confronted a radically different display set-up, both physically and procedurally. Collectively, the system was known as the AN/AVA-9 Integrated Display Set (IDS). The Pilot's LCOS/ODS was replaced by two HUDs (Head-Up Displays), one for each crew-member, and in place of most of the needles and dials the pilot was given a 7in (18cm) Vertical Situation Display (VSD) and the Wizzo a hoodless 11in (28cm) Multi-Sensor Display (MSD), both easy-on-the-eyes green TV presentations. Although offering multiple display options, depending on the mode selected, the pilot would use his as a flight situation display (in lieu of the old ADI) laced with additional symbology, while the WSO's served primarily as a fancy radar display. The guts of the Norden IDS package was a nose barrel-mounted Signal Transfer Unit (STU), which converted sensor data derived from the attack and terrain-following radars, and other subsystems, into the magical synthetic displays through a display mode system coupler. As Dick Brown noted when interviewed by the authors several years ago, the interactive nature of the VSD and MSD was especially welcomed: 'If you wanted to bomb from the left seat the pilot can do that; you could put the attack radar display in front

Motto of the 27th TFW was Intelligent Strength **and this F-111D wore a bigger than usual New Mexican Zia with the wing badge superimposed.**
Jim Rotramel

(Above) Complete with Harpoon anti-ship missile and GBU-12/B Paveway LGB, which exemplify its overland interdiction and maritime strike capabilities, and adorned with *Supersonic Kookaburra* fin flash, the RAAF's No 1 Sqn 'flagship' generates a 'ton of con' in a low-level high-speed dash. RAAF

Last Roll of the Dice, F-111E 68-061, on the day the 20th bade farewell to its Aardvarks. The big swing-wing jets were resident at RAF Upper Heyford for over 23 years! Authors

(Below)
A production F-111A, 67-0091, seen at Hickam AFB in May 1971. 'NC' codes were worn by the 430th TFS until April 1972. Five months later this aircraft joined the *Constant Guard* deployment to SE Asia. Col Tom Barnes

A four-ship 79th TFS launch prepares to leave. The three aircraft on the left are doing 'last chance' checks, while the F-111E on the right has had to pull out for slightly more extensive therapy. Authors

Hard-pressed 63-9772 also tested the GD Sidewinder trapeze, fitted to the right-hand weapons bay in lieu of the Vulcan gun. The system went into production but was removed from operational use after several 'froze' in the deployed position. Lockheed-Martin

(Above) **Transferring first to the 390th ECS (later 429th ECS), under the 366th TFW at Mountain Home in July 1992 and then to Cannon's newly formed 430th ECS in mid-1993, Upper Heyford's Ravens became part of a small, centralized pool of EF-111As which will outlive all other USAF F-111 variants.**
Craig Brown

(Left) **Col Dethman's aircraft, 68-0018, was distinguished by thin blue and yellow stripes running diagonally back from the cockpit. In 1983 it was reborn as an EF-111A Raven.** Col Tom Germscheid

(Below) **From the late 1970s, F-111As stationed at Mountain Home, Idaho, provided 'analogue Aardvark' training for its resident units and RAF Upper Heyford's mighty F-111E establishment.**
Frank B Mormillo

82 Strike Wing's instrumented F-111C (which wears the ARDU trials badge on its fin) is one of the hardest-working 'Pigs' in the inventory. One of its many projects was a GBU-15 evaluation. White undersides and wing-sweep position indicators help with weapons-separation data recording. The aircraft has since gone on to serve as the AUP testbed. RAAF

(Right) **F-111Gs** serve with the RAAF as 'iron' haulers, but at the speed of sound. RAAF

(Left)
The F-111F Pave Tack upgrade involved some complex reworking of the weapon bay area, including new outer doors and a central rotating cradle. Jim Rotramel

(Above) The age-old tradition of bomb graffiti was revived during Desert Storm, in this case with neatly applied squadron patches too. Fitted with a BLU-109/B warhead, this GBU-24A/B Paveway III weapon has large pop-out fins (which extend from slots visible on the stub fins at left) giving better range and allowing lower launch altitudes. This was aided by the solid-state laser-homing nose seeker which drove the forward steering fins using proportional guidance. Craig Brown

A 509th BW(M) 'Bullet Bomber' preparing to go 'on the apple'. Training sorties in this 'clean' configuration were not uncommon. via C M Reed

(Below) The 'real' Miss Liberty (**72-1448**) streaks low and fast, displaying the patches of all four Lakenheath squadrons on its flank. Adrian Walker

F-111Ds soaking up the sun between Red Flag sorties in December 1980, complete with inert Mk 84 2,000lb (900kg) bombs ready for the next mission. Frank B Mormillo

(Below) **Inert Mk 82s tumble from F-111E 68-0074 of the 55th TFS, on the range.** USAFE via Lockheed-Martin

(Bottom) **Heading out with a consignment of GBU-15s, this nocturnal Aardvark would have switched off all external illumination on crossing the border into hostile territory. The electroluminescent formation strips were added to all Aardvarks under TO 1F111-1209 during the early 1980s.** Jim Rotramel

Lucky Strike (68-0244) was a trophy-winner when serving with the 380th BW(M) at Plattsburgh, New York. The knobs and dark panels forward of the nose landing gear doors include the AN/ALR-62 CRS and Doppler radar. Note also the short rear MLG door, which was cut back beginning in late 1975 on all Aardvarks so that it could sit dropped instead of in a horizontal posture in the gear-down position. Tom Johnson

At around the time of the AMP modification, the FB-111A force began to switch to this green and grey lizard scheme, giving rise to the nickname 'Dark Varks'. This peeled AMP example (68-0262 Lady Luck) executes a roll manoeuvre under the skilful camera eye of Capt Tom 'TJ' Johnson. Tom Johnson

For the last F-111 deployment to Britain, Cannon AFB deployed eight 523rd FS Crusaders F-111Fs to RAF Fairford in June 1995 for a Salty Hammer/Central Enterprise **exercise**. Authors

(Left) A Plattsburgh FB-111A negotiates the terrain during a daylight training sortie. Missions were conducted along 'canned' Visual or Instrument Routes (VRs and IRs). Walt Weible via USAF

(Below) **Capt Tom 'TJ' Johnson titled this stunning self-portrait** Cool Reflections. **Tom was flying FB-111As at Plattsburgh AFB at the time.** Tom Johnson

of you and WSO could put the attitude indicator in front of him and fly from the right-hand seat'. This feature, combined with the dual HUDs, made the F-111D an excellent Aardvark trainer.

What was more revolutionary in many respects was the way the avionics package was interlinked through the DCC, giving a whole new meaning to the term 'integrated'. The F-111D's WCP was smaller and more compact and located on the main instrument panel. This stores management system used the 'protected memory' loop tapes pioneered on the F-111E and FB-111A, but effectively commanded the other systems to get ready for action, depending on the attack mode selected. Just by selecting stores, stations and mode, everything – radar, displays and so on – were automatically reconfigured for that mode. Dick Brown again: 'All you have to do is say "this" weapon is located on "these" stations. You just push the buttons and it gives you automatic ballistics for everything – CCIP, toss bombs, etc – pretty fancy.' The DCC handled the automatic ballistics solutions and would generate bomb release in the normal manner, with manual back-up modes also being possible. Radar and Visual level deliveries, 'Toss' and Angular modes, including LAB (Low Angle

F-111D 68-0122 of Cannon's 522nd TFS approaches RAF Boscombe Down, Wiltshire in May 1980 for Coronet Hammer, **the first of five deployments to the UK. Other TDYs took the 27th TFW to Egypt, Australia and South Korea.** Robin A. Walker

(Below) **Col Tom Germscheid** *(middle row, fifth from left)* **commanded the first operational F-111D squadron, the 524th TFS** Hounds **from February 1975.**
Col Tom Germscheid

Bombing at 10 degree dive or less), and LALD (Low Angle Low Drag, for angular deliveries above 10 degrees dive angle) were all available at a push of a button. HUD-aimed visual Continuously Computed Impact Point deliveries were also possible employing a far greater degree of sophistication than that available to the other F-111 versions. Using instructions from the Weapons Data Computer (one of the AYK-6 devices fulfilling this role), the HUD would project a steering and a bomb fall line alongside aircraft attitude, guiding the pilot through the entire attack sequence. Also, the DBT could be used to raise the HUD 'pipper' automatically if CCIP computations would have otherwise placed the aiming reference mark on the glareshield (for example, during deliveries of high-drag ordnance). 'The F-111D computers would automatically add time, if needed, during CCIP deliveries and would display the time added in the HUD' according to Brad Insley. Pressing the 'pickle' button when the target and aiming mark intersected, '…all you had to do was hold the button until release', recalled Dick Brown. In the analogue F-111A/E variants, this value had to be worked out by the pilot in advance and entered manually – another event taken out of the equation in the automated F-111D.

The WSO's Navigation Data Display Panel (NDDP), located under his MSD, was similarly more compact on the F-111D and generated green LED numbers pertaining to coordinates and timing, in lieu of the old 'spinning counters'. Tied to this, the other DCC device served as General Navigation Computer (GNC) and held up to 150 navigation data points (later greatly expanded), fed in using a punched paper tape system, or manually inserted or altered by the WSO using a navigation keyboard. As with the derivative Mk IIB system which actually preceded the Mk II to service, this computer-based flightplan provided 'hands off' flight from point to point along the programmed route, with up to two offsets each. Updates to the AN/AJN-16 INS would be effected via radar in the customary manner (a LORAN system originally slated for the Mk II package having been deleted during development), by placing radar cursors precisely over the present position or destination (depending upon which was selected) to automatically 'tweak' the system back on track. But the GNC was also capable of producing a navigation model based on inputs from the other systems, as back-up

In use at SMALC in October 1974, F-111D 68-0175, flown by Lt Col R.W. Petitjean and Capt P. Renaud, tested a modification to the F-111's undercarriage which later became standard – the rear MLG trunnion door, which was cut back for a better fit and which greatly eased the use of larger ECM pods between the strakes.
via Col Tom Germscheid

if the INS failed, so long as some fix could be established, either by use of the attack radar or by overflying a known point and depressing the Enter Visual Fix button. While it usually required a series of updates to the GNC, it could compute all the variables of the INS (ground speed and drift) using inputs from other systems such as the Doppler radar so that, given a long enough route and good definable ARS fix points for updates, the GNC could stand in for the INS, if required.

Moreover, the radars tucked behind the duckbill radome were all-new. The Rockwell AN/APQ-130 offered traditional PPI ground maps to keep a look-out for terrain and navigate and conduct weapons deliveries, by means of calling up and scrutinizing the position of the crosshairs over prominent offsets and the target; but it also offered a HRGM (High Resolution Ground Map mode), which generated expanded patch and strip maps, giving much higher definition for fixes and targeting. The antenna would work well at long range – selectable from 2.5nm (4.6km) out to 200nm (370km) – at very low grazing angles. Radar maps could also be frozen, and the radar could employ Doppler processing to offer a Moving Target Indicator (MTI) mode. This made the F-111D capable of tracking trains or convoys. If the attack radar played up, the display could be switched to TFBU (Terrain-Following Back-Up) mode and the AN/APQ-128 TFR used to generate a ground map at 5, 10 or 15nm (9, 18 or 27km) range for attack purposes, something the TFRs in the other models were incapable of doing (where they provided just terrain-monitoring ground maps and situational displays). In E-Scan mode it furnished a terrain avoidance monitor display for auto TF operations. Overall, it was a superb piece of kit, but Mission Capable Rates (MCR) were a constant headache throughout the 1970s. The Mark II required highly specialized maintenance that was not always lavished on the package.

Ironing out the availability kinks in the system began when the STUs were replaced with new ones beginning in 1979. The distinctive Zia-marked F-111D then quickly began to excel. Dick Brown:

The early 'Ds' had what was called an 'analog' STU. Its function was to convert digital signals to analog and the F-111D had tremendous problems with its avionics because of this poorly designed piece of equipment. The fix was to introduce the 'digital' STU. It helped the 'D' become more reliable. In 1983 we received new MSDs and the reliability improved immediately. The 'D's main problem during its whole career came from poorly trained technicians (MX avionics specialists). Whenever one of them became proficient the Air Force would promote them and make them supervisors and take their talent out of the maintainer's loop. The 'D' had a complicated avionics package and when it worked it was the best of all the F-111s. I flew it in *Proud Shield* 1988 and 1989. This was SAC's worldwide bombing competition in which the 'D' did outstanding.

The 27th TFW participants picked up the LeMay, best crew, and Mitchell best conventional bombing trophies in 1988, and the following year an F-111D crew came in amongst the top three LeMay placings (the other two being FB-111As from Plattsburgh and Pease).

One reason we did so well is that we got all the best MX people – from avionics to Crew Chiefs. However, it took us about two to three weeks to bring our aircraft up to competition standards: actually to the place that the 'D' was intended to always function. Once we got them there the 'D' was an amazing aircraft. Many crews who flew the 'D' never got to see it perform at this level. The 'D' usually ran with the radar at 70–80 per cent capability. We got to use it at near 100 per cent! If I would pick an 'all-star' F-111, I would choose the 'D' avionics, the 'F's engines and reliability. As far as the statement 'least reliable variant' I would say that it would be better for history to say the F-111D had the greatest potential but was the 'poorest maintained variant'.

To ease the maintenance workload further, parts of the system were decommissioned when spares went out of circulation. The Astonautics Corp AN/AYN-3 Horizontal

Maj James E. Rotramel next to F-111D 68-0153 in December 1981. Jim Rotramel introduced many changes to flight-planning which revolutionized F-111D/F prowess according to many of his contemporaries. He finished two tours at Lakenheath as well as his two stints at Cannon AFB. Jim Rotramel

(Below) **Aardvark 68-0086, one of three F-111Ds operated by the 431st TES Red Devils, 57th FWW, over Lake Mead near Nellis AFB. Before March 1980 it was known as Detachment 2. The unit was responsible for conducting trials of new equipment.** USAF photo by Ken Hackman

Situation Display, a film-based display located at the top centre of the main instrument panel and designed to show aircraft position and heading by means of a black pointer and electric green track cursor and aircraft cross symbols, overlaid on a projected moving map, was removed in 1986. It was popular and useful, but 'Kodak stopped making the 140mm film needed for it and nobody wanted to be troubled to maintain either the HSD or its maps', according to former IWSO Jim Rotramel. Jim Rotramel himself did much to enhance the aircraft's capabilities later in its career by revising training procedures, maps and charts for a more symbiotic relationship with the temperamental, but otherwise extremely accurate AN/AJN-16 INS. Nobody had realised before that if the maps used to plan missions offered commensurate accuracy, the system itself was much more likely to behave!

'D' for Deployability

Getting the F-111Ds up to peak efficiency in the first instance involved a slow learning curve which took six years; though when that moment arrived, many reckoned they had the best Aardvark of all and, like the other digital models, the F-111Ds tended to just keep getting better and better with time.

Despite an appearance at *Giant Voice* in 1975 and other sundry exercises, which included a three-week stint in May 1977 by the 522nd TFS *Fireballs* operating from Warner-Robins AFB, Georgia (flying a squadron-sized force away from home), the F-111D community did not venture abroad until September 1978, its first true deployability trial, when eight *Fireballs* flew to Gardermoen, Norway, under *Coronet Kingfisher* in support of NATO exercise *Northern Wedding*. Extra confidence in aircraft availability resulted from the 524th TFS' *Bold Eagle – Surge Delta 78* that October, which tested mass launch and turnaround procedures away from home at Homestead AFB, Florida, generating two sorties per aircraft per day, to open up a massively expanded series of deployments. This kicked off in October 1979 when the *Hounds* made an 18,000 mile (2,9000km) trip to RAAF Amberley in Queensland, Australia, where they stayed four weeks. The *Coronet Beacon* excursion culminated with a further three weeks at Sachon AB, South Korea, paving the way for follow-on deployments there by the 523rd TFS *Crusaders*. The *Crusaders* first deployed their F-111Ds to Sachon AB for PACAF *Team Spirit* manoeuvres beginning in March 1981, and returned subsequently on a biennial basis. The unit was unusual in deploying at that time inasmuch as it also had a Replacement Training Unit (RTU)

Updating the Bumpies

Maj Jim Rotramel (USAF retired), well known to many military aviation enthusiasts and historians alike, was a 'key player' in the F-111 programme, and probably understood the aircraft's avionics and computer idiosyncrasies, and how they could be solved, better than anyone else. High-time F-111 flyer Dick Brown remarked:

> Jim Rotramel was the key person in helping the Mark II avionics evolve during 1988–90. He had a keen knowledge of the intricate workings of computers and in my opinion Jim contributed more to the combat capability of the F-111 than any other WSO in its history. His revolutionary and precision update of training route folders, combat lines and avionics modifications changed the combat capability of the F-111 dramatically.

Jim Rotramel originally trained as a WSO on F-4Cs at Luke AFB before being grounded with kidney stone problems. He later qualified as an Aardvark WSO and flew four tours at Cannon and Lakenheath on the F-111D/F variants:

> With the almost-strategic range and then-unparalleled navigational accuracy of the F-111, mission planning became a science. While the charts we flew with were the same as used by other aircraft – usually 1:500,000 (TPC) charts for low-level, with IP to Target legs done on 1:250,000 (JOG) charts – the wise F-111 WSO would use the best charts available to generate his navigational and target coordinates. In Europe, that usually meant 1:50,000 scale, and in the US, 1:24,000. In other words, charts 100 to 1,000 times as detailed as the TPCs. If possible, satellite photography was used to generate coordinates, but that was usually only available for 'contingency planning'.
>
> There were two reasons for using charts showing such great detail. First was pampering on the inertial navigator (INS), which was easy to put in a bad mood. If it was going to have a bad day anyway, there wasn't much that could be done aside from being well prepared to navigate using time-distance-heading and good map reading. However, even if the INS was in good shape mechanically, putting fixes into it using sloppy coordinates (like from a TPC) could cause it to eventually get fed up and quit.
>
> The second reason to use accurate charts was to minimize the potential for confusion during a low level. If the coordinates for various offset aim-points (OAPs), destinations and targets were all derived from accurate sources, the radar crosshairs were much more likely to land neatly on top of them, building confidence in both the system, and your ability to hit the target.
>
> Maintaining all those charts was a logistical nightmare; the F-111's great range also meant that chart coverage of the 'local area' meant ALL of Europe or much of the US. It was the responsibility of the Intelligence people to stock all those charts, and it had to have been a shock for someone coming from another fighter into the F-111 community to see how much more responsibility had just been heaped on their shoulders.
>
> A squadron competition I participated in once illustrated the importance of picking good offsets. We were to attack a remote railroad station in Scotland that was located next to a bridge. The goal was to approach from behind a ridge line and do a Pave Tack toss delivery, giving the 'defences' minimal look-time at us, but also giving us minimal look-time at the 'target'. To do this required careful OAP selection. However, without telling anyone, the squadron's radar strike officer gave everyone the bridge coordinates, not those of the targeted railroad station. Like fools, we trusted him! My frustration was palpable when I switched to Pave Tack during the final few seconds of the 'bomb's' time of flight only to see the bridge, not the railroad station, squarely in the crosshairs. I learned that day that I could hit anything with the F-111F – as long as I didn't trust anyone else to give me the target coordinates!
>
> Not long after the railroad station fiasco, we attacked Rosehearty range from overland. The target was a raft in the water, but it wasn't visible on radar until the last few seconds of the bomb run because we were approaching from behind a large cliff and the target was in its shadow. However, located on the cliff was a small radio antenna which we could get a good look at. When I went 'target direct', it was a tiny adjustment to the target, which we 'shacked'.
>
> Often forgotten in the navigation equation was the importance of elevation. If the aircraft's 'Altitude Calibration' was off, even perfect alignment of the radar crosshairs on the target would result in a miss, with the bomb hitting either short or long, depending on the error. Therefore, it was important to get a good 'Alt Cal' very soon after entering the low level (keeping the latitude/longitude inputs to the INS accurate so it wouldn't sulk) and again when as close as practical to the target. The importance of 'Alt Cal' could be vividly seen in either the Pave Tack pod or the F-111D's HUD. With radar crosshairs squarely on the target, either the HUD cursor or infrared image would appear high or low – a sure sign that a calibration was required.

Almost lost against a desert background resembling a giant's cake-mixing bowl, this 4427th TFRS F-111D skims low and fast over the 'bumps'.
Col Tom Germscheid

function, which it continued to fulfil until 1 October 1983. For the most part, RTUs possessed no 'deployability' commitments, but the Aardvark community was unique in having three such units at one time or another during the 1980s (the others being the F-111F-equipped, RAF Lakenheath-based 495th TFTS, and Raven-equipped 390th ECS at Mountain Home), which functioned much like RAF Operational Conversion Units, with the instructors forming the combat-ready nucleus.

In August 1980 the 524th TFS had assumed the task of chief 'new guy' RTU from the disbanding *Green Knights*, and it relinquished its NATO commitment to the 522nd TFS *Fireballs*. Their European F-111D deployments began in earnest in May 1980, when *Coronet Hammer* brought eighteen *Fireballs* to RAF Boscombe Down, Wiltshire, where they flew 282 sorties over the first two weeks. The *Fireballs* came back for September 1983's *Coronet Archer*, and again three years later under *Coronet Comanche*, in company with half a dozen Ravens from the Mountain Home-based 390th ECS, assisted by KC-10A tanker support in lieu of the customary Stratotankers. June 1989 saw them operate from Boscombe Down for the last time, when a dozen aircraft deployed under *Coronet Diamond*. They made one more appearance in June 1992, their fifth and ultimate deployment to England, when Col Tony Sobol brought a squadron detachment to RAF Lakenheath in Suffolk. England was not the only venue. The squadron also made a habit of venturing to extreme climates: in January 1983 they operated from icy Elmendorf, Alaska for *Brim Frost*, and followed that up with a roasting summer deployment to Cairo West, Egypt for *Bright Star* exercises, as part of the wing's commitment to US Central Command (previously known as the Rapid Deployment Joint Task Force).

The Cold Lake Air Weapons Range in Alberta, Canada, also became venue for *Maple Flag* manoeuvres, the 523rd TFS's last (*Maple Flag XXV*) taking place in May 1992 when six aircraft were deployed, just in time to savour the new 'medium intensity' conflict tactics being introduced to the post-Cold War training scenario. These successful operations which endured for fourteen years enabled the wing to shrug off its previously besmirched availability record. Mission Capable Rates had risen from a meagre 34.4 per cent 'low' in the 1970s to well over double that ten years later, following the STU and MSD updates, and the crews no longer muttered 'F-111D for Dog' under their breath. A long time in the making, the force really came into its own in the 1980s.

In between excursions to more exotic locations and intense wargames fought over the skies of Nevada and Alberta, crews made do with the IR and VR training routes in the Four Corner States. Some overwater missions were also thrown in, these having begun with a joint USAF/USN COMPTUEX 3-79 exercise held in August 1979, which pitched the *Fireballs* into pathfinding and sea-lane interdiction tasks, a back-up mission the Aardvarks were qualified to perform from then on, despite it being more of an Australian Aardvark speciality. Day-to-day flying embraced pounding the nearby dedicated Melrose bombing range, 24 miles (39km) west of the base. Newcomers passing through Cannon's 'digital schoolhouse', its chief RTU from 1980 and exclusive one from 1983, the 524th TFTS *Hounds*, began with sixteen simulator sessions on one of the two Singer devices. Simulator number one was modified in 1982 with digital image generation systems which offered 'outside' vision. A radar landmass system was also used, based on 3ft (1m) square transparencies which employed light beams to convert the colour combinations into simulated radar presentations in the cockpit. It was all very 'cosmic' when it was first introduced early in the programme, but one experienced IWSO reckoned that 'it sucked!' by 1980s standards, and a digital land-mass system was later introduced to permit realistic low-level flying, visual bombing and AAR (aerial refuelling) practice. However, as was true of all simulator training, most regarded it as mere procedural preparation for the real thing: the forty-ton F-111Ds parked out in the open on the runway apron, which would introduce crews to the physiological stresses and strains of flying, and the joy and psychological burden of responsibility inherent in flying a two-man supersonic-capable striker.

Flying training was divided into four phases spread out over eighty-one flying training days, starting with basic handling. Students then progressed on to 'Strike Day' and then 'Strike Night' phases when low-level TFR and basic weapons delivery profiles were practised. Ground attack, the final stage, opened up the full vista of attack options and combined these with elementary weapons and tactics training, including terrain-masking. Altogether, novices flew an average of thirty sorties (about eighty hours) before being passed over to either 'Red' (522nd TFS *Fireballs*) or 'Blue' (523rd TFS *Crusaders*) squadrons at Cannon – or the Aardvark University (495th *Mala Ipsa Nova*) at RAF Lakenheath for transition to the F-111F – where they would receive a further two-month 'check out' to become mission-ready. A shorter, three-month-long, twenty-sortie Transition Course was also available for more experienced crews converting to the F-111D, or 'getting back in the saddle' after a long period of desk duty. Instructors were drawn from the operational squadrons and needed a minimum of 500hr flying time to qualify, flying ten sorties and undergoing 65hr academic tuition and four 'sim' rides to become fully-fledged IP/IWSO graduates. In theory, while Cannon's 'schoolhouse' was also capable of qualifying people ready for analogue Aardvark operations, that increasingly became the speciality of the 389th TFTS *Thunderbolts* at Mountain Home AFB, Idaho, home of the Vietnam veteran 'Ace' models between 1977–91, which operated under the 366th TFW *Gunfighters* banner alongside the Stateside Ravens. The *Thunderbolts*' course was fundamentally similar to that run at Cannon, except that emphasis was placed on the older analogue systems and crews generally would be posted to the collocated 391st TFS *Bold Tigers*, or to RAF Upper Heyford to fly F-111Es.[3]

Range Terminology

BOX PATTERN The flight path over the ground was rectangular. The four sides were named:
Final, the leg during which the bomb was actually dropped.
Crosswind, the leg going away from the target after a 90 degree turn.
Downwind, parallel to Final, going back to run-in again.
Base, setting up to turn to Final again for the next delivery.

BUTTERFLY PATTERN The flight path of an aircraft which dropped a bomb from one heading, such as from the north, and then turned around to immediately make another pass from the opposite direction.

'CLEARED HOT' Clearance from the Range Officer for an aircraft to make an actual bomb delivery, which resulted in a Hot Pass.

'CLEARED DRY' An order from the Range Officer for the aircrew NOT to drop a bomb on that pass, which resulted in a Dry Pass.

FLIGHT LINE-UP The names of the aircrews and the numbers of the airplanes they were flying, along with the call-signs they used.

FOUL The term used when a crew got too close to the ground during a delivery.

HUNG BOMB Where the pilot tried to release a bomb, but it did not come off due to a malfunction in the release mechanism.

IFR Instrument Flight Rules, the rules which governed operations of aircraft during IMC (Instrument Meteorological Conditions), otherwise known simply as bad weather.

IP Depending on the context in which it was used, this meant either Instructor Pilot or Initial Point, the latter being a point from which the run-in to the target was initiated.

NORTH ENTRY Entry into range airspace from the north, crossing the north IP. Ranges could also have other entry points, and Cannon's Melrose range, for example, also featured a South Entry.

OFF WET The radio call from the aircraft which indicated that a bomb was actually dropped on a pass.

OFF DRY Whether or not the aircraft was Cleared Hot or Cleared Dry, this term was used by the crew to tell the Range Officer that nothing was dropped on that particular pass.

PICKLE BUTTON The bomb release button on the stick. Pressing the button was called 'pickling'.

POP PATTERN A delivery pattern in which the aircraft entered the range at low altitude then 'popped' up in a steep climb to acquire the target, then transitioned to a diving delivery.

RCO Range Control Officer, or Range Officer. He was the one with complete authority over the aircraft in the Range airspace.

VFR/VMC Visual Flight Rules (cf IFR/IMC).

Maj Dick Brown, combat veteran and Instructor Pilot extraordinaire, with a staggering 3,454 of his 4,550 Aardvark flying hours logged as Instructor Pilot. This photo was taken during a Bright Star **deployment to Cairo West, Egypt. Keffiyeh and sunglasses were carried just in case he was obliged to eject in the middle of the desert.**
Courtesy Dick Brown

'D' for Doggoned Good

An aspect of the F-111D which operational crews would get to grips with at Cannon, and in which it stood head and shoulders above all other variants, was its air-to-air radar capability. The other models possessed only a primitive capability based on modified versions of the PPI ground-mapping presentations.

With the switches set to Air-Air on the Mk I/Mk IIB systems-toting models, the ARS assumed a search and detection pencil-shaped beam which scanned a box 2 degrees in elevation and 90 degrees wide. The WSO's radar control handle (RCH) was then gently moved forward and backwards, as required, to tilt this scan up and down for a total travel of 60 degrees (which would have been terrain-blanketed when looking down, so it was mostly used in look-up only) until a return was produced. Selecting an individual target for tracking was accomplished by moving the RCH left or right to place the straight azimuth cursor over the target return, followed by flipping the 'sector switch' on top of the RCH forwards. This reduced the fan-scan from 90 degrees down to 20 degrees, just as was done during ground attack, to focus attention on the target. The WSO would then press the 'Range Selector' button (a second button on the top of the handle, used exclusively for air-to-air) and push the handle forwards (usually) to move the curved range cursor just short of the target return. This procedure initiated auto-acquisition, whereby the radar would scan at that 'range gate' and 'step out' in increments automatically with each sweep. When it acquired the target it locked-on and stayed on it, centring the azimuth and range cursors precisely on target and feeding back range-rate (relative closure speed) and range-to-target on the ARS panel, plus LCOS steering cues to the pilot.

However, the search routine was cumbersome and the radar would easily break lock against dynamic opponents. Dick Brown reckoned it was 'not good or effective'. Thus it had no real air-to-air fighting function, although it was originally envisaged that crews could use the steering and closure rate information to set up a Sidewinder missile shot or gun volley against an unsuspecting 'sitting duck'. In the end, F-111 crews made it their business to avoid, rather than look for trade in this arena, and in the Mk I/Mk IIB systems-equipped models the package was nothing more than a handy means of finding friendly aircraft at night and in the weather. As Brad Insley put it, 'The air-to-air radar was used mostly for rejoins with wingmen, finding the tanker and trail departures where weather prevented formation join-up. We also used it to keep proper spacing between elements and formations while cruising.' It was also prescribed for avoiding weather cells, though Brad said that he preferred the ground PPI mapping mode to look for these lofty chunks of unpredictably turbulent spark-infested water.

The F-111D's APQ-130, by contrast, provided much more automated acquisition. First, it could scan automatically in 1, 2 or 4 Bars (vertically stacked-up air-to-air boxes, in effect) at up to 200nm (370km) range, in eight range increments beginning at 2.5nm (9km). As with the air-to-ground functions, by selecting air-to-air everything in the cockpit was automatically reconfigured, including the HUD and MSD displays which furnished processed alphanumerics and graphics instead of fuzzy raw radar imagery, including multiple digital LED data on the NDDP. Also, the air-to-air radar display (ARAD) presented on the TV tubes was a 'B Scan' rather than a PPI-style presentation used in the other marks. Here, the vertex or base of the 'pie slice' was spread out across the bottom of the scope, so different angles were represented by vertical and not angled lines. With the radar scan itself collapsed, relative target bearing was depicted as a solitary vertical line which moved left or right corresponding to the target's relative position. Manual target acquisition and tracking was also possible and, curiously enough, the WSO's radar tracking handle served as a model for the

F-111D 68-0127, the Cannon 'wing ship', carries the colours of all three based units and a GBU-10/B LGB underwing. The sparsely populated Texas/New Mexico plains around Cannon AFB offered almost constant good weather and visibility for low-level TFR flying; the only 'bugs' were those in the complex F-111D's Mark II avionics. 27th FW, USAF

F-111D Cockpit Displays

IN ACTION Typical AN/AVA-9 IDS displays are depicted here, to illustrate just how radically different they were from the other operational models' gear, based on the two digitally-driven TV displays, and two HUDs in the F-111D's cockpit.

HUD The twin Head-Up-Displays represented the kind of trailblazing technology that is commonplace on today's advanced fighters and attack aircraft, but which at the F-111D's introduction was extremely advanced and utterly unique. As is the case with all the cockpit diagrams depicted, we are viewing a composite of all the available green symbols. At any one time, only relevant symbols pertaining to that mode or situation (eg the 'Breakaway' symbol, signifying the aircraft had closed within minimum missile parameters) would have appeared.

PRIMARY ADI DISPLAY The cockpit TV displays were interactive; ie the WSO could access the Attitude Director Information shown on the AC's VSD, as depicted here. This particular display effectively replaced the traditional gyro-driven ADI 'black and white ball' and AVVI/AMI tape instruments to provide a fused, all-in-one TV version, also predominantly green in colour. Transistor technology-based digital number-crunching drove this system; the ostensibly similar Kaiser display employed in the US Navy's A-6 Intruder used contact-analogue technology and preprogrammed 'canned' weapons release cues, which simply instructed the pilot to go 'left a bit' or 'up a bit' or 'faster a bit' to get it right. The F-111D's cues, by contrast, were constantly adjusted to compensate for different airspeeds, dive angles and altitudes, offering flexible or 'uncanned' cues.

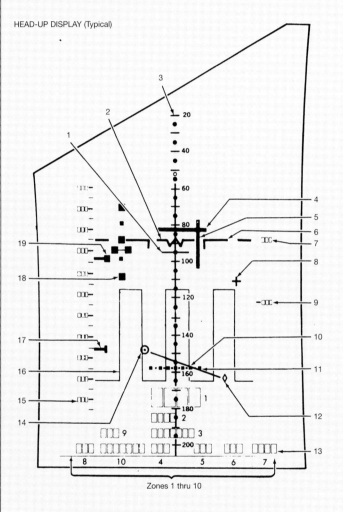

HEAD-UP DISPLAY (Typical)

Zones 1 thru 10

1 PITCH MARKER
2 MINIATURE AIRCRAFT
3 BACK-UP RETICLE
4 PITCH STEERING BAR
5 BANK STEERING BAR
6 ATTITUDE SYMBOL
7 ALTITUDE NUMBER
8 DESIGNATION CURSOR
9 PITCH NUMBER
10 BOMB FALL LINE
11 ROLL INDICES
12 FLIGHT VECTOR SYMBOL
13 SYMBOLOGY ZONES 1 THRU 10
14 CCIP OR STEERING PIPPER
15 RANGE SCALE
16 BREAKAWAY SYMBOL
17 MINIMUM RANGE MARKER
18 GLIDE SLOPE DEVIATION SCALE
19 MAXIMUM RANGE MARKER

Note
SYMBOLOGY ZONES (13)

1 Warn
2 Fuel
3 Caution
4 SOL
5 PLP/REL
6 RDY
7 BARO/RAD
8 RNG/CAS
9 True Airspeed
10 AMO (time to go)
(Display will be lost if either computer is inoperative)

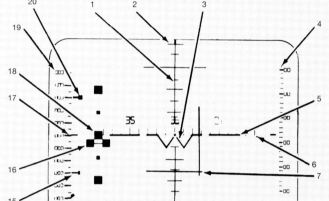

PRIMARY ADI DISPLAY

1 ROLL LUBBER LINE
2 PITCH INDEX
3 AIRCRAFT REFERENCE
4 ALTITUDE TAPE
5 ATTITUDE REFERENCE
6 HEADING SCALE
7 PITCH AND AZIMUTH STEERING BARS
8 RAD/BARO
9 RDY
10 LCH, PLP, HLD, REL
11 ROLL LUBBER LINE POINTER
12 SOL
13 ROLL INDICES
14 RNG/CAS
15 RANGE MINI
16 MOVABLE GLIDE SLOPE MARKER
17 TARGET RANGE
18 GLIDE SLOPE DEVIATION SCALE
19 RANGE AIRSPEED TAPE
20 RANGE MAX

ARAD MSD Air-to-air radar (ARAD) B-Scan displays originated in WWII with the American-designed Air Interception Mark X technology, incorporated as standard into later night-fighter versions of the British Mosquito and American P-61 Black Widow. In the early days, these displays offered a 'pie shaped' radar display showing relative target bearing and range. In its much more modern guise in the F-111D, using far more rapid and powerful signal processing and synthesized displays, annotated with steering and attitude cues to set up an optimum intercept or join-up, the bottom of the vertex or 'V' at the base of the radar presentation was effectively stretched out to the full width of the screen. Relative target bearing was denoted by means of a collapsed B-Scan vertical azimuth cursor (1), which would move left and right to denote relative target position, which also showed target range and its relative heading (4). Although much of the peripheral symbology relating to missile launch parameters was effectively redundant in the absence of Sparrow AIM-7Gs, range rate and the other circles providing steering cues remained helpful for aerial rendezvouses. Numeric digital target information is left blank in this example, and would have been repeated on the NDDP panel.

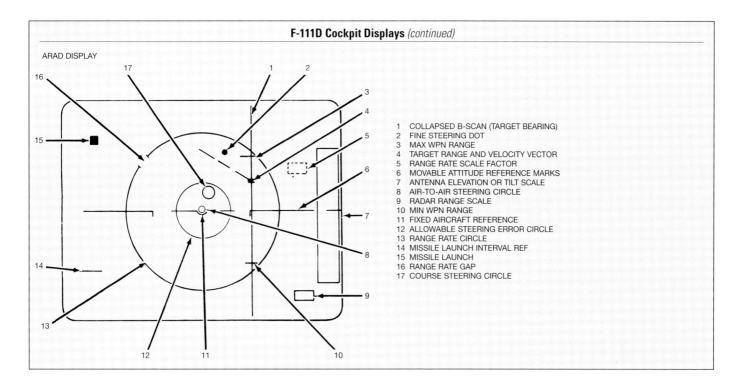

F-16's sidestick control; it was nicknamed the 'goat turd' by Aardvark fighter'gators! Range rate and steering cues were also depicted, represented as part of the multiple graphics and numerics (which would change as an intercept progressed). Originally, it was intended that the APQ-130 provide continuous wave target 'illumination' to guide Semi-Active Radar-Homing Ku-Band Raytheon AIM-7G-1 Sparrow III missiles onto such 'painted' targets at launch ranges of up to 60 miles (97km). To set up the aircraft for an optimum missile attack the crew would have flown so that the steering circle was kept inside the allowable steering error circle, thereby keeping the aircraft within missile launch parameters (just as in a Phantom). Although the XAIM-7G never progressed beyond the prototype stage and was cancelled in 1971 just prior to the aircraft entering service, the F-111D's air-to-air capability nevertheless remained far more useful than a mere glorified aerial rendezvous system, proving to be especially useful as an aid to SA. Wizzos could keep a look out for 'bogeys', interrogate their IFF (Identification Friend or Foe transponders) and gain a better overall impression of the threat situation. Brad Insley recalled that 'There was a box to dial-in a transponder code and that tied into the radar highlighting any aircraft "squawking" that code. It was very helpful finding the right tanker. It allowed more precise tracking of a target.' Hightimer and FWIC graduate Dick Brown recalled:

> It used to work great. At first the A/A [facility] was not used much. As tactics improved through the life of the F-111 its use became more and more frequent (and I feel I brought about this change in tactics using the A/A at low-level and at cruise altitudes). When I retired in 1990 we were using it constantly – even during day low-level ingress and egress. In fact, A/A in the 'D' model was used almost continually during day low-level if there were intercept threats like in Red Flag or local exercises.

The possibility of rerigging the F-111Ds with Hughes/Raytheon AIM-120 AMRAAM missiles was explored to make use of this capability, but rejected on the grounds that nobody wanted the Aardvark community loitering in racetrack patterns setting up BVR (Beyond Visual Range) 'kill boxes' when they were in high demand for dropping iron and CBUs at speed. BVR MiG-killing was the business of the F-15s, with the F-16s closing-in to mop-up enemy stragglers. Even the F-111D's gun was removed from service during 1983, although the muzzle fairing remained in place afterwards (confusing many observers), as once the Vulcan itself had been removed it was discovered the gutted 'Gat pack' unit served as a handy luggage rack! Other F-111 units had to make do with less secure underwing MXU-648 baggage pods: old napalm canisters fitted with a hinged door and latch in which to squirrel away their belongings during deployments.

Although part of the FWIC (Fighter Weapons Instructor Course) syllabus for six years, Sidewinder heat-seeking missiles were only finally introduced to operational Aardvarks beginning in May 1983 (making their debut on the F-111F models serving at RAF Lakenheath), finally ousting the Vulcan. These comprised Ford Aerospace AIM-9P-3 models, featuring active optical fuzing for point-and-shoot defence in virtually all aspects. Again, they were there purely as a self-defence item, and only two were usually carried (one each on stations 3A and 6A, the shoulder pylons fitted to the outer pivot-pylons), so an Aardvark would find itself 'Winchester' (out of ammo) fairly quickly if it attempted to hunt rather than merely bite back. As George Kelman put it to the authors back in April 1988, 'If a Soviet pilot knows that... we have that capability, he's going to stand off from you a bit more, regard you as more of a threat; and definitely if you point your nose at him and he knows you have that capability, whether you have that missile on or not, he's going to honour you'.

'D' for Determined

The F-111 FWIC, which was reformed at Cannon at the end of May 1988 as Detachment 1, 57th FWW (eleven years after its inception on the F-111A version at Mountain Home), further honed the skills of F-111 aviators as well as introducing new offensive weapons and tactics. The course contained 290 hours of academics and twenty-three flying sorties on the checquer-striped tailed beasts assigned to the unit, the flying gradually getting more intense throughout the course, climaxing with the Mission Employment Phase

Conventional 'Dumb' Weapons

STORES STATIONS The F-111A/D/E/F employed a wide variety of conventional unguided or 'dumb' munitions during the course of their operational service, of two key types: 'iron' and cluster bombs. Both categories would be carried on the wing pivot-pylons (stations 3 and 4 under the left wing, and the corresponding stations 5 and 6 under the right wing), fitted either directly to the pylons' built-in MAU-12C/A racks by means of 'D-rings' and anti-sway braces, or snapped onto McDonnell-Douglas BRU-3A/A racks using close-fitting 'square lugs'. Either type of lug could be screwed into the munition casing. The 'BRUs' had a capacity of up to six 1,000lb (450kg) category weapons each, though inboard racks were typically configured with a maximum of four outward-facing munitions each (known as 'slant four'), for a total of up to twenty munitions in the 500lb–750lb (225–340kg) class. This provided an all-up maximum load of 15,000lb (6,800kg). For sustained operations, it was more typical to limit maximum stores to between 8,000lb–10,000lb (3,630–4,500kg). This reduced drag and vulnerability, wear and tear on the undercarriage and pylons, increased range, and avoided problems with stores oscillation, to which the F-111 was prone with heavier, less aerodynamic ordnance (such as the earlier CBUs) unless flown in a relatively genteel fashion. Pilots were instructed to throttle back to 400kt (740kph) to restabilize the stores if they encountered this, and generally to avoid abrupt lateral stick movements. Symmetrical stores configurations, and release, was also necessary to preserve both aircraft integrity and weapons delivery accuracy.

IRON BOMBS chiefly comprised the Douglas/US Navy-originated Mk 82 500lb (225kg) and Mk 84 2,000lb (900kg) series of tritonal explosive-packed steel weapons which detonated much like an air-delivered grenade on impact. The similar, but less aerodynamic USAF M117 750lb (340kg) was also used in the early days. All of these could be fitted with Low Drag General Purpose (aka 'slick') fins, which required release from altitude; or, during lower-altitude drops, a 'toss' manoeuvre or dramatic pull-up after release to avoid the aircraft being struck by fragments from the exploding ordnance. For example, pull-up to above 1,600ft (490m) AGL was required after releasing the 2,000lb (900kg) Mk 84, and 1,000ft (300m) for the 500lb (450kg) Mk 82 LDGP weapon. An alternative available to the Mk 82 and M117 was to fit these with high-drag Snakeye (aka 'retard') tails to create the Mk 82 SE and M117R, respectively. These comprised steel cruciform airbrakes which opened immediately after release to enable the F-111s to avoid being 'fragged' by their own munitions during low-level drops. However, they imposed a 500kt (926kph)/Mach 0.8 limit lest the steel airbrakes fail, effectively limiting F-111 delivery speeds to well within its true capabilities, which ran contrary to the flyers' maxim that decreed 'speed is life!'. Beginning in the early 1980s, a new Goodyear (Loral) balloon-parachute 'Ballute' (officially known as the Air Inflatable Retard) tail fitting became available for both the Mk 82 and bigger Mk 84. This increased permissible low-altitude drop speeds up to 700kt (1,300kph)/Mach 1.4, revolutionizing F-111 'dumb' bombing.

CLUSTER BOMB UNITS CBUs came in a number of guises, comprising a canister packed with one or more of a variety of Bomb, Light Unit (BLU) submunitions. Based on timed-delayed or radar-based fuzing, these canisters split open at a preplanned delivery airspeed and height over the target to 'sprinkle' it with the BLUs. The CBUs evolved during and after the Vietnam war to provide a host of dedicated configurations tailored for anti-radar, -tank or -personnel uses, and were generally employed against sprawling targets, by means of a variety of submunitions. These ranged from dart-like to spherical bomblets and, depending on the type and fuzing, exploded on impact, after a time interval, or after being set-off by magnetic influences. The differences are outlined in the accompanying table. Most CBUs were USAF-evolved, but they included the Navy-originated Mk 20 Rockeye series, and F-111s could also employ British BL755s as part of NATO commonality.

A third category of weapon which was unique to USAFE F-111E/Fs and became a specialized tasking during the 1980s was the French Matra BLU-107/B Durandal rocket-boosted runway-ripper (see Chapter 5, Echoes from Upper Heyford).

Conventional 'Dumb Bomb' Stores

Type	Max. Load	Notes
Practice ordnance		
Mk 76	24	Low-drag 25lb (11kg) practice bomb, carried in up to six per SUU-20/A or -21/A. Also known as BDU-33.
Mk 106	24	High-drag 10lb (4.5kg) practice bomb, SUU details as for Mk 76.
500lb (225kg) ordnance		
Mk 82 LDGP	24	Standard low drag tail.
Mk 82 SE	24	Mk 82 with Mk 15 Snakeye high-drag tail.
Mk 36 DST	24	Mk 82 SE with delayed magnetic fuzing. Destructor mine.
Mk 82 AIR	20	Mk 82 with BSU-49 high-drag tail.
750lb (340kg) ordnance		
M117	16	Standard MAU-103 low drag tail.
M117R	16	High-drag MAU-91 high-drag tail.
2,000lb (900kg) ordnance		
Mk 84 LDGP	4	Standard low drag tail.
Mk 84 AIR	4	With BSU-50 Air Inflatable Retard tail.
Cluster Bomb Units		
Mk 20 Rockeye	20	Mk 7 canister. US Navy Mod 2/3/4 CBU containing dart-like bomblets. 490lb (220kg) all-up weight.
CBU-52	20	SUU-30H canister. 217 BLU-61 fragmentation bomblets. 790lb (360kg) all-up weight.
CBU-58	20	SUU-30H canister. 650 BLU-63 fragmentation bomblets. 810lb (370kg) all-up weight.
CBU-58A	20	SUU-30H canister. 650 BLU-63A fragmentation and incendiary bomblets. 820lb (375kg) all-up weight.
CBU-71	20	SUU-30H canister. 650 BLU-86 fragmentation and incendiary bomblets. 810lb(370kg) all-up weight.
CBU-71A	20	SUU-30H canister. 650 BLU-68 fragmentation and incendiary bomblets. 820lb (375kg) all-up weight.
CBU-87	8	SUU-65 'spinning' Tactical Munitions Dispenser (TMD). 202 BLU-97 Combined Effects munitions. 960lb (435kg) all-up weight.
CBU-89	8	SUU-64 TMD. 72 BLU-91 anti-personnel & 22 BLU-92 anti-tank bomblets. 700lb (320kg) all-up weight.
CBU-97	8	SUU-64 TMD. 10 BLU-108 anti-armour 'Skeet' smart bomblets. 920lb (435kg) all-up weight.
BL755	4	British 1,000lb (450kg) class CBU.
BLU-107/B	20	French 480lb (220kg) anti-runway boosted weapon.

For details of 'smart bomb' equivalents, refer to Chapter 7, The Sound of Freedom, *and* Chapter 8, Desert Pigs.

where the students would demonstrate that they 'were up to speed' and even experiment with new concepts. Again, the F-111D's twin-HUDs and interactive VSD/MSD displays and better air-to-air radar capabilities made it a near-perfect advanced trainer, better suited to the job than the analogue Aardvarks used previously or the 'Fs' that followed. More revolutionary defensive tactics were also introduced. One such delight was BIF (Bomb In Face). This was extremely aggressive and meant 'pickling' off a bomb in the aircraft's wake to blow away the enemy fighter trailing them at low-level. A single Mk 84 AIR was best at this, creating a mini mushroom and a quarter-mile hemisphere of hot metal and debris that would FOD (Foreign Object Damage) a MiG even if it did not blow it to pieces.

Other tactics gave renewed impetus to low-angle bombing, made available via devices like the AIR and a new range of CBUs containing Combined Effects Munitions (CEM), Gator mines, and the Sensor Fuzed Weapon (SFW). The new SUU-65 canisters housing the CEMs were capable of 'spinning' after release to optimize submunition scattering over the target, and all three types (the others using the ostensibly similar SUU-64 Tactical Munitions Dispenser canister) could be lobbed using 'mini toss' tactics. No longer were F-111s required to cruise blithely along at a given altitude and airspeed like pepper shakers, hanging in the sky over the target, to deposit CBU canisters on top. The smarter SFW 'Skeet' submunitions even sought out targets on their own using infrared target templates: 2.5 'tank kills' per CBU-97 were demonstrated in munitions trials against armoured formations. Gators were dropped to sow an anti-tank and anti-personnel minefield, while CEMs were designed to cause instant mayhem by combining incendiary fragmentation and anti-armour shaped charges. All very unpleasant and astonishingly lethal, especially given that each Aardvark could drop eight of them at a time!

FWIC was a vital catalyst in the days when the junior flyers were rising through the ranks, passing on their newfound skills to fellow crewmen at the operational bases, and later when the new weapons came on line, finally permitting the Aardvark to be used to its full potential. Graduates were nicknamed the 'patchmen', because of the FWIC cloth patch and other unit regalia velcroed to their flight-

Laden with live Mk 82 'slicks' a 27th TFW F-111D eases into the air. It has a red fin cap indicating ownership by the 522nd TFS Fireballs, **the only Cannon squadron which was exclusively operational (as opposed to having RTU duties) throughout its tenure on the Aardvark.** Jim Rotramel

suits. By the time these same men had risen to become fully-fledged instructors at the four tactical bases – Cannon, Mountain Home, Lakenheath and Upper Heyford – there existed such a high concentration of expertise at an operational level that FWIC increasingly took on additional F-111D-specific test and evaluation duties previously assigned to the McClellan AFB 57th FWW Detachment (which began to focus on just the F-111F's needs).

For several years Cannon's Project Officers had toyed with the idea of updating the F-111D with electro-optic targeting aids and new 'smart' weapons systems, several of which progressed beyond the moot stage. However, making these systems work with the F-111D's Mark II package proved problematic. The cockpit displays, for example, were supposed to feature AVE-TV (Aided Visual Element TV) and Weapons TV modes to flash-up imagery derived from infra-red and television sensors and weapons seekers. However, 'The MSD generated a different number of lines than any other television built by man', according to Jim Rotramel. 'Although we got new MSDs, the decision-makers kept the unique number of lines, which prevented us from employing GBU-15, or any other TV-guided weapon, or trading in our ancient, troublesome, ineffective and expensive film camera for a video tape system.' This latter, rather incongruous device, snapped away at selected intervals of between one second and two minutes, taking RSP pictures of the digital displays using conventional film; by contrast, the F-111F had long since switched to digital video tape. Other upgrades were tested.

Tom Yanni, who had just come from Lakenheath suggested to the TAC commander in 1986 that it would be possible for Cannon to integrate *Pave Tack* with the F-111D. [*Pave Tack* comprised a large pod combining an infrared detection set and a laser for night targeting and autonomous delivery of laser-guided 'smart' bombs.[4]] In response, TAC/CC got them a *Pave Tack* pod to play with. It didn't take too long to discover that they had gotten in way over their heads.

Dick Brown reflected that:

I recommended to the Wing Commander at Cannon AFB in 1988 to not get the modification and that it would be a limited enhancement to the F-111D. I told him that more up-to-date systems should be pursued. I am not sure to what extent my advice was in cancelling *Pave Tack* for the 'D' but I do know that shortly after our conversation the upgrade went away. Strangely, being one of the F-111 'experts' I was rarely brought into the modification and upgrade picture. Most of the decisions were made by marginally qualified and inexperienced officers who had minimal time in the aircraft or had a poor understanding of its capability or need!

Jim Rotramel concurred and pointed out that:

Because only 160 *Pave Tack* pods were built, there weren't enough to outfit both the 'D' and 'F' fleets (not to mention the Australian 'C's). Ergo, enter the LANTIRN (Low Altitude Navigation and Targeting Infra-Red for Night) targeting pod. If the F-111D had received the *Pacer Strike* modification, it would have been capable of using the AAQ-14.

Entering service with the F-15E 'Mud Hen' in 1990, the LANTIRN targeting pod was not quite so good as *Pave Tack* in terms of image quality, but was much more compact and reliable and would have been easily carried on a special adapter under the weapons bay. Alas, it was not to be. *Pacer Strike*, which eventually was applied to just a portion of the F-111F force, was a Rockwell Autonetics-run effort which was originally conceived to give both the F-111D and F-111F an AMP class upgrade but packing a bigger computer. However, the 'D' was dropped from the update programme in 1990, preempting the possibility of the aircraft developing further in this arena.[5]

Thus, while the 'smart avionics' of the F-111D bestowed on the model a superb ballistic bombing capability, including the potential to employ the same nuclear gravity bombs used by its *confrères*, the lack of funds to pursue aggressively either LANTIRN or a Precision Guided Munitions (PGM) delivery capability ultimately relegated the type to 'dumb' bomber status. Also, in the absence of such conventional PGM capability it was not deployed to the Gulf in support of *Desert Shield/Storm* and thus became the only one of five tactical USAF models never to see combat duty (although the comparatively primitive F-111Es managed to get a look-in, flying from Turkey, owing to their familiarity in operating from the European Southern Flank).

'D' for Drawdown

When the decision came to axe the F-111D force in 1991, it must have been a blow to many who had seen the aircraft 'come alive' in the 1980s, on the heels of the cockpit avionics upgrades and the wing's proven global mobility. However, the F-111D portion of *Pacer Strike* was never even flight-tested, and 'Deltas' were all gradually flown off to the 'boneyard' as 'F' models arrived from their former home in England to replace them.[6] In the interim, the wing expanded with the creation of the 428th TFTS *Buccaneers*, which became the RTU on 1 April 1990 under Col Peterson after receiving ex-SAC AMP'ed F-111Gs. With the merging of SAC and TAC in October 1991 under the new Air Combat Command, the 27th TFW became the 27th Fighter Wing and the force passed from Twelfth to Eighth Air Force control. It was an ominous prelude. F-111D phase-out began five months later and first to go were those of the 524th *Hounds*, which departed from February 1992 as the squadron traded them for 'F's (and the more exuberant squadron name *Hounds of Heaven*), followed by the 522nd *Fireballs* that August and the 523rd *Crusaders* during December. FWIC's aircraft also gave way to 'F's under the new Detachment 3, and its importance diminished. *Desert Storm* veteran Capt 'Quizmo' Brown, part of the FWIC's last instructor cadre, himself not a graduate, designed and wore several variations on the 'official' grey-silver FWIC shield with its black and yellow target, which emphasized the value of real combat experience that he could teach: 'Graduate: Been There, Done That, a Real F***in' War', and a more laconic version for high-timers without combat hours, 'Non-Graduate: Never Attended, Never Will'. The latter parodied officialdom which had been blunt in making it known to all that the F-111's days were numbered, including those of the F-111D's TF30-P-100-powered, *Pave Tack*-toting F-111F replacements.

In less than ten months the entire F-111D fleet was relegated to 'mothballed' status, never to fly again. In their stead the wing rapidly got to work with its ex-USAFE machines and newfound TDY commitments to the Gulf Region, and with a powerful new model to hand the entire 'Delta' fade-out seemed to have passed by relatively unnoticed. It was further eclipsed by the arrival of the Raven force, which began with the formation of the 430th ECS during 1992 and expanded with the transfer of 429th ECS EF-111As from Mountain Home a year later.

However, the new lease of life was not to endure for long and Cannon's association with the Aardvark ceased in 1996, after twenty-seven years of operations with the attack 'family'. At the time of writing, only the Ravens remain. However, Cannon has forever earned a unique position in the annals of the Aardvark: it was and will remain the only operational base, and wing, to have at one time or another operated every USAF variant of the F-111. Yet it will always remain synonymous with the F-111D, which was on charge for twenty-one of those years. To some it was the most cantankerous variant, but all those who actually flew or maintained it would acknowledge that it was by far the most revolutionary of all the long-snouted Aardvarks.

Over two dozen FB-111As served out their last USAF days flying as RTU trainers with the 428th TFTS Buccaneers at Cannon AFB, whose tower proclaims the base's 4,295ft (1,309m) elevation above sea-level. The F-111G's shallower wheel hubs (accommodating bigger brakes) and unique 'hour-glass' fairing shape (the vent structure between the engine nozzles) is particularly in evidence here. Jim Rotramel

CHAPTER SEVEN

The Sound of Freedom

(Above)
An F-111F 'gasses up' while others lurk below.
via Jim Chamberlain

With the F-111F, the final production variant, the USAF acquired an aircraft which most closely approximated to the original TFX specification. It used a compromise version of the troubled Mk II digital systems of the F-111D known as the Mk IIB, but tailored for tactical operations with gravity weapons, including the full conventional arsenal. Weapons control was through cassettes as in the F-111D/E. The FB-111A's ARS was retained, with an improved AN/APQ-146 TFR and ASG-27 ODS built-in. This set-up remained virtually unchanged throughout the F-111F's service life, although it would have been seriously updated by the Rockwell *Pacer Strike* programme if the F-111F had been allowed to run its full term.

There was also a virtually new engine. Whereas extra power had been found in the F-111D's TF30-P-9 by 'gearing up' the

F-111F 70-2366 served as the Gunfighters' Bicentennial 'flag ship' in 1976, with this patriotic livery. It is seen here thundering over the Grand Tetons in Wyoming. via Jim Chamberlain

F-111F Mk IIB Bomb-navigation Systems

Major James Chamberlain began his USAF career as a Radar Intercept Officer on F-89s and concluded it as a Wizzo flying F-111Fs from both Mountain Home and Lakenheath, by which time he had accumulated some 3,100 hours on fighters. Here, he describes the Mk IIB Navigation systems and procedures used in the 1970s, and the different flying environments in TAC and USAFE in those days:

In my opinion, there is no better place in the world for flying than Mountain Home, Idaho and the great northwest. Situated on the northern edge of the Great Desert, there were few communities to complain about noise and no major air terminals with conflicting traffic. Even at the base itself, we seldom saw anything but other 111s, so there was little concern about mixed traffic. The flying weather was almost always VMC with the occasional high overcast and, although it was cold and windy in the winter, the occasional passing snowfall presented no great difficulty to flying operations. Indeed, if it were not for the AF's own rule about flying IFR whenever possible, there was seldom need to enter the Air Traffic Control system. It was a wide open country with widely separated ranches and vast areas of unpopulated range which meant that civilian light planes, which could be a hazard at low level in other areas, flew well above our low level navigation routes, which we usually had to ourselves, too. The base-controlled Saylor Creek bombing range was seldom used by any other organization, so there was usually no conflict in getting range time, even if one was not scheduled for it. It was truly an aviator's paradise.

The typical training mission profile included an instrument departure, entry into the ATC system, flight at altitude to an established TACAN bearing and distance, where the TFR system operational checks were made, then descent out of controlled airspace for a VFR entry into the low level route, then TFR flight (usually at the 1,000ft (300m) SCP) along the length of the route which terminated either on the bombing range or at an RBS site. Occasionally there would be an air refuelling thrown in for proficiency training before route entry. There were a variety of low level routes which provided training experience in high mountain terrain, the mixed terrain of desert and mountain and a couple of routes that went out over the Pacific Ocean for training in overwater TFR navigation, which is different in that the radar altimeter alone was used to maintain clearance plane since the TFR was virtually inoperable overwater. We used our own Saylor Creek bombing range east of Mountain Home, the Navy's range at Pendleton, Oregon, and the Wendover, Utah, range. The RBS sites we used were Green River, Wyoming, St George, Utah, and one southwest of Boise, Idaho. The few times we didn't enter a range or RBS from a low level route were the trips to Wendover as there were no routes that went that direction or that far. All the bombing ranges were well away from population centers and the low level routes also skirted any built-up area. That was very different from our English experience.

After checking out with the ATC system, the TFR system was coupled to the autopilot and the descent to route entry made automatically, backed up by the crew. When the radar altimeter detected the ground and the pitch angle increased, the crew was really monitoring the system. Approaching the set clearance plane, the aircraft's descent decreased until finally levelling at the selected altitude. All that was required at that point was to set the power for the desired airspeed, monitor the system and keep a watch for birds.

During daylight flights, both crew members monitored the TFR scope, followed the route progress in the route folder, monitored check points, engine instruments and fuel status, made the routine in-the-blind calls of position along the route – and again kept a watch for birds. While the TFR system, through the autopilot, maintained vertical clearance over obstacles along the route, the Bomb-Nav system controlled heading to the next turn point, correcting for drift, turned the aircraft to the required heading for the next turn point in sequence and brought up any offset aim points associated with that turn point for possible update purposes. Approaching the end of the route, the pilot established radio contact with the target control, announcing call sign, location and intentions while the WSO prepared the bombing system for the first pass on target. Radio contact was always a bit dicey, because we were at such low altitude the range of the UHF set was pretty limited. Sometimes it got a little tense because we were not allowed to enter the target area without clearance from the controlling agency and we were trying to meet a specific time-on-target.

The core F-111F Mk IIB Bomb-Nav systems shared much in common with those installed in the FB-111A, including its digital LED counters on the instrument panel, but lacked Astrocompass or a SRAM capability. Instead, the F-111F possessed a broad ballistic bombing capability, including manual reversionary modes, and used a WCP similar to the F-111Es, but mated to a digital Bomb-Nav package. It thus offered the best of all worlds at a time when the F-111D Mk II systems were plagued with systems architecture-induced maintenance problems.

The Bomb-Nav system of the 'F' consisted of the Rockwell Autonetics INS, two virtually identical computers, a General Navigation Computer (GNC) and a Weapons Data Computer (WDC) and a multi-purpose GE AN/APQ-144 ARS which operated in the 16 gigahertz range. The idea was that the INS provided ground speed and drift information to the GNC which directed course turns to the autopilot based on the INS present position and the route of flight which had been either tape-loaded or manually programmed by the WSO. If the INS failed, the GNC was capable of taking up the navigation function so long as some fix could be established, either by use of the attack radar or by overflying a known point and depressing the Enter Visual Fix (EVF) button on the INS control panel. While it usually required a series of updates to the GNC, it could compute all the variables of the INS (ground speed and drift) so that, given a long enough route and good definable fix points for updates, the GNC could do a job equal to that of the INS. Frequent, good fixes were necessary to work out errors as the system would not accept a full update.

The WDC contained the ballistic characteristics of every gravity weapon carryable by the 'F'. Selecting a particular weapon cartridge in the bomb arming sequence meant that no further consideration of weapons release characteristics was necessary. In the bomb release sequence, the WDC decided the correct weapon release point, considering ground speed and drift from the INS, range to the target from the attack radar, and the type of attack from the weapons release panel and the weapons ballistics in the computer.

The control panel of the WDC incorporated windows, each about one by two inches, which showed the type of weapon currently selected. By depressing the windows, the continuous loop tape on which were printed the weapons types, would advance through the entire weapons array and begin again. For range missions, the selections were BDU-33, for the blue practice bombs with the spotting charges, on one cassette, and Mk 106, the practice bomb simulating characteristics of a retarded bomb, on the other. Once on the range, one only had to de-select one type and select the other type to drop whichever type practice bomb was desired in accordance with the checklist and the type of attack being made. The WDC could also provide navigation functions, just as the GNC could solve the bombing problems, but, since each had its own primary function, performance in the alternate computer mode was degraded.

A route of flight could be preloaded into the GNC by a tape loading system located in the nose wheel well. Avionics technicians would load the route data points from a paper tape, very much like the old paper tapes used by Teletype machines, about an inch wide with a series of holes punched in the tape. Somehow, it was all interpreted by the machine which then understood where one wanted to go. Just a word on 'sequence interrupt'; usually the GNC would follow the turn points in the numerical sequence in which they were programmed, but, occasionally, maybe for reasons of time or fuel, one would wish to cut the route short. We could interrupt the normal sequence by manually selecting the desired turn point number and moving it to the head of the list and depressing the insert button and the airplane would immediately take up a heading to that point. One had to be careful about the use of this tool; otherwise, if the new route was not scanned beforehand, one could find oneself flying through some place one did not want to be. Of course, military missions being what they are, one very seldom ended up going on the tape loaded route for one reason or another, so, more often than not, the WSO spent the first twenty minutes after engine start with his head under his right arm, laboriously punching latitude and longitude to the second for each turn point and offset aim points along the route, for the target and the return home. All that information was contained on a table in the route folder which was carried with the crew. A tape load for a training mission at Mountain Home was a rare thing because tape loading took time and men from other jobs, it was not a

> ### F-111F Mk IIB Bomb-navigation Systems (continued)
>
> mission-critical thing and there were a lot of changes in aircraft and the missions they flew so that, even with a tape load, that mission might not be flown.
>
> Navigation procedures, *per se*, changed little in England. However, we quickly realized that this was a much more compact area, with a much higher population density and we had to co-exist with the closer confines and tighter controls. There were also a lot more aircraft competing for training resources than we were accustomed to dealing with. More ranges were available, but they were also thoroughly booked. Suddenly, if one couldn't make a scheduled range time, it was a major loss and we would fly all over the country begging to get on a range and drop at least one bomb. We called it 'bootlegging'. I think we used just about every range in England, Wales and Scotland. Among these were Tain and Rosehearty in Scotland, Jurby on the Isle of Man, Whitby on the east coast and Wainfleet and Holbeach in The Wash. The coast ranges used floating raft targets with radar reflectors which made for easy detection by radar, good visual detection for dive bombing, but sometimes left a lot to be desired in scoring as a splash in the water may not be as easy to see as a good smoke plume rising from the ground.
>
> Dive bombing had been added to the training programme in 1977, as part of the qualification programme for crews *Ready Switching* from Mountain Home to Lakenheath:
>
> It always seemed a dumb idea to me; pulling 'Gs' was not the strong suit of the 111 and it was an awfully big target to hang out over any given target, but since the F-4s [etc] did it, surely the 111 should do it, too? Never mind the suitability or silliness. We did it. We also used ranges on the Continent, which was just an easy jaunt for the long-legged 111. Most of our low-level routes were in Scotland and the lesser populated areas of northern England because of the noise problems to which the 111 was particularly prone. On occasion we also used Continental low-level routes, but that was usually in conjunction with an evaluation. Sometimes there was nothing for it but to make radar bombing passes on some prominent target. Lincoln Cathedral was a favorite; situated on a knoll and being a very big building, it was easy to find on radar. There was also a water works located some distance south of the Cathedral and that was another good radar target.
>
> The biggest adjustment in the lives of aircrew in England was the alert commitment which was very much part of our lives once certified as combat ready. TAC had a mobility requirement, but still one was usually home at night from that. An alert tour was a three-day affair followed by a 'simulated day off' before returning to the flying schedule or a recall for some exercise.

rotational speed of the compressors, the TF30-P-100 pushed that speed further still to 14,870rpm. A new afterburner was designed and overall thrust rose to 25,100lb, (11,380kg) almost 5,000lb (2,270kg) more than in the 'Dash-Nine'. Originally intended for the F-111D, the P-100 began development in 1968 as a means of compensating for the considerable weight increases in later F-111 variants, but delays caused by a number of bench-test failures meant that the F-111D missed the new powerplant completely. When the F-111F entered service it too almost missed out; the first forty-one examples used the TF30-P-9 and were retrofitted with P-100s from 1973. By that time increased costs had ruled out the new engine for all but the 106 production F-111Fs.

A production contract was signed for the F-111F on 1 July 1970, and it entered service with the 347th TFW on 20 September 1971 following a successful first flight by 70-2362 the previous month in the hands of Fort Worth test pilot R.E. Myrann. The wing reached IOC in January 1972 at Mountain Home AFB and by October had survived a number of squadron re-designations, settling down as 389th TFS *Thunderbolts*, 390th TFS *Boars* and 391st TFS *Bold Tigers*. At the end of October, after another name-plate change, the wing became the 366th TFW *Gunfighters* and the 347th TFW re-emerged at Takhli AB in July, 1973, to manage the F-111A operations for *Constant Guard V* in S.E. Asia.

Perspectives

Engine problems recurred during the early years of F-111F flying and they were never fully solved. Whereas the TF30-P-3/9 suffered mainly from compressor stall (most pronounced at lower speeds and high altitude in the F-111D), the P-100 tended to generate afterburner stalls. For several years it was flown with a T-5 thrust limiter fitted, but various failures still occurred. However, pilots found that the new engine gave welcome performance increases, particularly for 'holding G' in a turn. One unforeseen problem was the difficulty with single-engine handling. Maj Dick Brown explained:

> The F-111F was difficult to land single-engine. It was necessary to maintain 85% rpm (because of the hydraulics) on the good engine during landing. At this rpm the aircraft had difficulty in slowing to landing speed. On the other hand the F-111E had thrust problems in single-engine configuration. We nearly lost an F-111E in 1976 when Jim Keisel lost an engine over Jurby range. He could not get the good engine to go into afterburner during configuration for the approach to RAF Valley. Jim turned the aircraft out toward the sea to eject as his airspeed and altitude were ebbing away. At the last minute he got the afterburner alight and flew a successful approach and landing. This is why the procedure to place the slats and flaps down on the downwind leg came about, followed by the landing gear on final descent to landing.

However, the F-111F was on the way to becoming, in Dick's estimation, 'a magnificent aircraft'. In 1972, though, the Mk IIB systems were still young and required considerable attention. After a combat tour on F-100Ds with the 306th TFS at Tuy Hoa AB, Col Tom Barnes checked out on the F-111A at Nellis AFB and was assigned to the still forming 390th TFS (F-111F) at Mountain Home:

> The wing was still building experience in this relatively new aircraft so we flew often to build time on the aircraft, and much of this flying was at night to gain experience in night TFR operations. Part of the lessons learned involving earlier losses of F-111s in Southeast Asia centred on Stateside training in which F-111 pilots did most of their TFR flying training during the daytime, and did TFR by hand-flying the aircraft rather than coupling it to the autopilot, which was more reliable if properly maintained. The 366th TFW had a demanding academic program which drilled its crews thoroughly in systems knowledge (lots of emphasis on TFR) and taught them to accept only a fully operational aircraft (all systems working) and then auto-TFR for night low-level training. In my three years at Mountain Home [1972–75] the wing only lost one aircraft which, I believe, is a testimony to an excellent training program for aircrew who were flying very demanding missions.
>
> Because of the extensive night flying each squadron was open from about 8am to midnight. The work-days were very long, but the workforce didn't complain because we had no weekend flying and because maintenance was

The wintry landscape of Northern Idaho highlights this factory-fresh 391st TFS 'Foxtrot' in November 1972, soon after the squadron received its first aircraft. Col Tom Barnes

excellent and there was a very high probability of having aircraft available to meet the operational flying schedule.

The 366th had a unique maintenance practice consisting of 'Big D' and 'Little D'. 'Big D' was staffed with the sharpest (though not necessarily the most senior) personnel who could come to your aircraft if you had a problem occur after engine start. You called them on the radio and they drove over to your bird, plugged in a ground radio cord and helped diagnose the problem while you had engines running. This procedure, coupled with the most talented people, helped significantly to keep aircraft from aborting.

On return from a mission we radioed our problems ahead to maintenance people who met us when we taxied back. Before shutting down engines they would plug in their headsets and start working to fix your 'write-ups'. Sometimes, you would spend an extra twenty to forty-five minutes sitting in the cockpit while they worked, but you knew that this would help the crews who were flying the next day. Often, these missions lasted up to five hours, taking off late in the afternoon and landing as late as 2am on occasion. A complex night mission might involve doing a low-level navigation route to a bombing range and delivering a 25lb (11kg) practice bomb on six passes at speeds over 500kt (930kph), then rendezvousing with a tanker, followed by high-altitude radar bombing and maybe going to an electronic countermeasures range to make runs against various surface-to-air threats. Sitting strapped in the cockpit after a five-hour mission while they fixed the bird was not pleasant, but it helped.

After about a year at Mountain Home the backlog of new arriving crews waiting to go to Nellis to check out increased to an unacceptable level. I was assigned the task of organizing a ground and flying training program for the F-111F using hand-picked crews at the base. It was a demanding challenge but it worked and the wing ceased sending new crews to Nellis. The crews who worked for me were the most talented group of officers that I ever served with in my Air Force career.

In January-February 1975 I took a contingent of F-111Fs to Alaska for a winter joint training exercise. Temperatures were −20 to −30°F. We decided to leave the aircraft out of doors and get them cold-soaked rather than take them in and out of hangars for maintenance. In this way the various pneumatic and hydraulic seals would not expand in the warm temperatures and shrink when cold. This decision proved correct because once we got the leaks fixed, they remained fixed. In those cold temperatures the F-111F could get airborne in less than 2,000ft (610m). That huge fighter truly leapt off the runway. We had no problems flying TFR over the snow, although everybody was cautious about radar 'energy-absorbing' snow, which might result in misinformation being fed to the TFR.

Col David Reiner, who commanded both the 390th and 389th TFS in succession before becoming Vice-Commander of the 27th TFW on the F-111D, reckoned that:

Most problems with the F-111F were encountered prior to, or immediately after engine start, which maintenance response personnel could usually fix in time to meet the launch requirement. Engine start was approximately one hour prior to launch time which allowed time to fix the glitches in most cases.

I enjoyed flying both the F-111D and the 'F', but in my eyes the F-111F was the Cadillac of the fleet. Mountain Home and Cannon AFB had some of the best maintenance troops I've ever worked with. I don't recall any engine in-flight problems with either model. I was selected to run the TAC F-111 team that entered the annual SAC Bombing Competition for the first time. We selected our flight crews, maintenance and avionics personnel and formed a team that trained for approximately six weeks for the competition. We had a few avionics glitches at first but with the assistance of factory reps and plain hard work from our dedicated maintenance folks we managed to win (beat 'em at their own game!).

Crews came from a variety of backgrounds to Mountain Home. Lt Col Chuck West, who commanded the 391st TFS, noticed that most of the early Mountain Home F-111F pilots were from F-100D units, whereas 'The Navigators/WSOs came from all over'. In all cases the learning curve was a steep one and somewhat pressurized by the 366th TFW's requirement to serve a short-notice, worldwide reinforcement role. Operation *Cape Train* took the Wing's Detachment 1 to Osan, Republic of South Korea, on 22 February 1976 in response to border tension between North and South. *Coronet Patriot* was initiated on 19 August and *Gunfighter* F-111Fs remained at Taegu AB, South Korea, until 16 September. That deployment involved an eleven and a half hour flight with four in-flight refuellings. An alert flight, armed with Mk 82 bombs was ready for action within 31.5 hours of the deployment being ordered. The Wing revisited Taegu for *Coronet Falcon* in March 1978, but by then it had converted to F-111As. Another series of exercises codenamed *Amalgam Arrow* required 366th TFW F-111Fs to fly groups of six or eight aircraft as 'targets' to test NORAD's air defence capability in 1974–75.

Swing and Switch

Mountain Home's ownership of the hot F-111F was curtailed by a USAF policy decision called *Ready Switch* which relocated the equipment of three wings, with side-effects for another. At RAF Lakenheath, the 48th TFW *Statue of Liberty* had been flying the redoubtable F-4D Phantom II when it was decided in November, 1976, to double the UK-based F-111 force. Its

In this rare encounter, a 191st ARS KC-97L cranks up its four piston engines and two jets as it prepares to receive Mountain Home's wing aircraft, 70-2366. Col Tom Barnes

In January 1975 F-111Fs from Mountain Home visited Eielson AFB, Alaska, for Exercise Jack Frost. **In snowy, sub-zero conditions a team of young sled-dogs is substituted for a tow-tractor!**
Col Tom Barnes

three squadrons gradually 'switched' to the F-111F after standing down from *Victor Alert* duty and ceasing F-4D operations by 28 February 1977. Two months later their last Phantoms crossed the Atlantic to equip the 474th TFW *Roadrunners* at Nellis AFB. A vanguard of three ex-Mountain Home F-111Fs, led by Col Messerli, landed at Lakenheath on 1 March 1977, to provide conversion training for the ground troops.[1] Meanwhile, the Nellis-based 474th TFW sent its complement of

---

Ready Switch

Finding enough of the right people to make the switch from Mountain Home (MUO) to Lakenheath (LN, or EGUL) in 1977 was a complex affair involving intricate personnel rules – based on TOS (Time On Station), DOS (Date of Separation), DEROS (Date Eligible for Return Overseas) and ADS (Active Duty Service Commitment), and some major 'scratching around' the F-111 community. Maj Jim Chamberlain, who was part of the 366th DO's (Director of Operations) flying staff at the time, describes the headaches involved:

Fitting together all the pieces of the personnel puzzle was a chore. In-place staff at Lakenheath offered no usefully qualified people except in staff positions and support areas. The then-Wing Commander at LN, Col Robert Messerli and the Assistant DO, Col Bob Baxter, were staying on and checking out in the 'F', but none of the Operations people at LN would be flying – they were kept on to serve out their tours in staff functions. So, the 366th would have only its own flyers and whatever other formerly qualified 'F' people as could be culled from anywhere and requalified on short notice. There were also a few folks from UH [Upper Heyford] who had sufficient time left on their tours to check out in the 'F' and transfer to LN to add some expertise in the European theater. But since the 366th had the only 'F' training sources, anyone coming to the wing for *Ready Switch* had to be checked out at MUO before departure. There weren't very many that could be fitted into the training requirements and still meet the deadline.

Prior to *Ready Switch*, the only overseas assignment for 111 flyers had been Upper Heyford which was replenished with crews from all three 111 models. Most UH returnees went to the 'A' at Nellis because of the similarity of the 'A' and the 'E'; very few UH people had come to MUO. Although their knowledge and experience would have been very valuable, a few who had gone to Nellis were willing and they helped greatly. The transition course from the 'A' to 'F' was considerably shorter than a full ['new guy'] conversion course into the F-111. While, in the end, there would be enough qualified aircrew to take the aircraft across, there would not be the extra margin of crews that one usually looked for in a combat wing. A similar problem existed for the maintenance people. They, too, had to find the right mix of experienced, skilled people with the right mix of dates. Juggling enlistment periods, skill levels, rank structure, type of 111 experience, and so forth. Moving a fighter wing was so much more than simply flying the airplane from point A to point B!

Adding to the aircrew training problem was the fact that the only 'F' simulator in the world was at MUO and it was a vital part of all aspects of crew training. It was essential to training supplementary crews, maintaining crew proficiency and preparing the deployment people. At some point, the simulator had to be dismantled and shipped to LN to be reassembled in preparation for crew training, evaluations and NATO alert preparation. As time wore on, the Operationally Ready (OR) crews received decreasing rations of simulator time as emphasis was shifted to the crews in need of qualification training.

Among the aircrew going to LN, knowledge and understanding of the English and European air space structure and rules was non-existent. Those of us who were going spent a lot of time going over USAFE flying regulations, studying European air space rules, adjusting to filing to European flight plan and understanding the European system of weather reporting. The pilots, too, spent a lot of time flying simulator approaches to LN and many of the surrounding bases as there was a rule that said, in effect, you can't do it until you've done it. Flying instrument approaches to those bases in the simulator filled that square.

An advance party of selected staff people and maintenance crews was sent over about a month before the first deployment, to learn the USAFE and NATO systems, begin the transition and receive the first arrivals. The first deployment was nominally led by Col Messerli, but the 111 experienced leader was Lt Col James C. Sharp who, as 390th Commander, also oversaw the RTU operation.

This wave was a mix of 391st TFS crew dogs and instructors, both pilots (IP) and WSOs (IWSO). There were also a few staff officers, Stan/Eval crews, all essential to set up housekeeping and training. The instructors would be the first to receive the required Theater Checkout (which was accomplished by UH instructors) and they in turn checked out everyone else. The first wave left MUO at the end of May and magically became the 494th TFS upon arrival. Their specific mission was to pass USAFE and NATO evaluations within thirty days to take up the first alert commitment in the Initial Operational Capability (IOC). It would make the 48th an operational, alert-capable wing again, and relieve other USAFE Wings from the 48th's alert requirement.

While those folks were working toward IOC and settling in, the pre-departure training was going on for the two follow-on squadrons. The 390th RTU, now under a new commander, increased the training pace so as to produce as many qualified crews as possible before shifting scenes to LN. They were now working with fewer instructors, which meant a slower pace of training. These trainers and the remainder of the 390th crews were the last to arrive in England.

I was in the second deployment which left on July 30th. On that day we reported about noon so that we could complete whatever needed completion and still have our eight hours of 'uninterrupted crew rest' required before flying a mission. We took care of paperwork, briefed, pre-flighted the aircraft and loaded baggage, then retired to the old SAC alert facility which had enough darkened rooms so that we could get some sleep before the 2300 start engine time. While we were resting, the flight plan for the entire deployment was being filed on our behalf from the paperwork previously completed. I guess we were awakened about 2100, had a steak and eggs breakfast, then suit up, on to the flight line with inflight lunch in hand to climb aboard old '379, strap in, crank up and align the INS. Following an on-time departure and join up in three-ship elements, we headed northeast to join with the tankers taking us all the way to Land's End where we went our separate ways, us to LN, they to Mildenhall. The first refuelling, over Duluth, Minnesota, was to ensure that the refuelling system was operating properly. The three subsequent top-offs were for divert purposes and occurred over St John's, Newfoundland (where the INS inevitably crashed), and two over obscure points over the pond. The idea was to keep enough fuel onboard to make a safe divert if necessary.

There was really nothing to the cross-pond flight – we just hung on the wing of the tanker which did all the navigation. Very junior Captain Jerry Brumby, my crew mate, and I took turns flying the wing in a loose route formation. I'd fly while Jerry ate his peanut butter sandwiches and then we'd switch. That way neither one of us got overly tired and we each had something to look forward to doing. It was a long flight in an aircraft without walk around facilities, no inflight movie, nothing to really look at except a featureless sea and a lot of it. My respect for Lindbergh, always high, increased greatly. The boredom was fierce until we came in sight of Land's End and bid farewell to our friends, the tankers. Once over England, preparation began for the instrument approach to Lakenheath. After ten hours and forty-five minutes of flying time, we were on the ground at our new home, met with a welcoming beer by the guys who had preceded us and some of their wives, but that had to wait for a visit to the loo. There was then time for more beer and visits with guys who were 'old heads' to find out what things were like at the new home and begin the important orientation of where to get a good meal, how to find a place to live and where to get a vehicle that would last the tour.

We were given a day off to adjust and then the work began on the theater check-out, the study of USAFE flying regulations, USAFE drivers school to obtain a license and all the little details of moving to an entirely new place. Following the nagging little housekeeping chores, theater checkout and certification for alert were the orders of business most pressing: the grind had begun!

F-111As to Mountain Home, the first squadron arriving on 6 June, 1977. On 1 June the first major 'switch' of F-111Fs happened. Sixteen *Creek Swing* aircraft, led by 48th TFW Vice Commander Col J.W. Tietge, touched down at Lakenheath after a 4,900 mile (7890km) flight. Another sixteen made the crossing on 1 July, with further batches ensuing to bring the wing up to strength, in stages. One side-effect of *Ready Switch*, which took nearly a year to complete, was the relocation of Nellis's 57th FWW Det 3 Test & Evaluation F-111s to McClellan, California, between 2–15 August 1977.

As the dust settled, Lakenheath's *Statue of Liberty* wing F-111Fs were rearranged initially into the 494th TFS *Panthers* which used the first batch, while later arrivals went successively to the 493rd TFS *Roosters*, 492nd TFS *Bolars* and 495th TFS. The large number of F-111Fs available (given the policy of concentrating each variant at a single base) meant that it was possible to form a fourth squadron and the 495th became a training unit: the *Aardvark University*. As the only RTU in USAFE this unit took over the training of aircrew on F-111F systems, until 'digital Aardvark new guy training' was consolidated at Cannon AFB from 1980, under the 524th TFTS *Hounds*' and 523rd TFS *Crusaders*' F-111Ds.[2] Instructors for the University were drawn from the other three squadrons and retained mission-readiness. It was a unique concentration of expertise, somewhat resembling an RAF Operational Conversion Unit.

Lakenheath's training regime followed a similar pattern to the programme at Upper Heyford. F-111F crews flew range sorties, WDTs to Incirlik and Zaragosa, NATO exercises and occasional *Red Flag* or *Green Flag* detachments just as their 20th TFW counterparts did. Their role would have been to fly deep interdiction missions into Eastern Bloc airspace if necessary, attacking airfields, missile sites, armour concentrations in the rear of the battlefield and transport chokepoints. However, from January, 1981, Lakenheath-based aircraft were given a more specialized role on receipt of a new piece of equipment: *Pave Tack*.

Training for LGB drops took place on 48th TFW WTDs, using inert Mk 82 or Mk 84 bombs with Paveway II/III kits attached. Although it was perfectly possible to practice *Pave Tack* operation without dropping anything, standard BDU-33 practice bombs were usually used for *Pave Tack* range sorties. These were the only occasions on which the laser could be 'squirted' over land, as the powerful lasers could pose an eye hazard for those on the ground and for the crew, who could be affected by reflected laser energy. Potential 'targets' had to be carefully surveyed for these reasons.

(Top) **Another attempt by the 366th TFW's resident humorist to solve traction problems at Eielson AFB!** Col Tom Barnes

(Left) **En route to Alaska, two gun-equipped F-111Fs from the** Gunfighters. Col Tom Barnes

Pave Tack

NIGHT VISION Beginning in 1980 the F-111F fleet began to receive a series of updates which greatly expanded its Mk IIB systems repertoire during the course of the decade. The first of these was the Ford Aerospace (later Loral) AN/AVQ-26 *Pave Tack* laser/Infrared Detection Set (IDS) targeting pod, fitted to the weapons bay in a new rotating cradle, F-101 Voodoo style, in lieu of the old gun. The outer weapons bay doors were retained but incorporated slight cutaways to accommodate the pallet, and would flick open and shut again when the cradle was flipped through 180 degrees to deploy the pod from its more aerodynamic, stowed position.

With the sensor came allied, brand new controls and displays for the WSO. These included a revised multifunction radar control handle, *Pave Tack* mode push-button controls, and a modified ARS redesignated the AN/APQ-169, which featured two displays for radar and *Pave Tack*, collectively known as the VID (Virtual Image Display). These would be viewed simultaneously in the WSO's VID 'feeding trough', and were laced with alphanumerics pertaining to ARS or *Pave Tack* mode, time-to-target and so on.

Rotated into play, with the phallic-shaped pod's turret unstowed, its huge IDS zinc sulphide sensor began 'looking', and feeding its imagery back to the VID display. Wide (12 degrees) and Narrow (3 degrees) Fields of View were available, permitting zooming-in and out, turning night into day and cutting through haze, allowing the WSO to perform incredible feats of target discrimination hitherto well beyond the resolving power of the ARS. It was effective at target- and offset-spotting ranges of up to about 12 miles (19km) slant-range, and at half that distance could discriminate extraordinary details, such as scraped soil (indicating a dug-in tank), the fuel in an oil storage hold or ship, and so on. WSOs would customarily switch from ARS to *Pave Tack* as the primary sensor as range-to-target, or some critical navigation point, closed to within 5nm (9km).

Flight-tested by the McClellan-based 431st TES from 1977, the pod entered production in August 1979. Conversions at SMALC were undertaken at the rate of two F-111Fs a month, with the first example, 72-1441, arriving at RAF Lakenheath in January 1981, to begin re-equipping the 494th TFS *Panthers*. The squadron achieved IOC on the system on 15 September that year, followed by the remainder of the F-111F fleet. The RAAF's F-111Cs adopted *Pave Tack* from September 1986.

METHODOLOGY Boresighted in the *Pave Tack* sensor head with the IDS was a Neodymium Yittrium Allium Garsenide (YAG) laser crystal, described to the authors by Pilot Capt Craig 'Quizmo' Brown as 'probably the single most expensive component of all the thousands that made up the F-111F'. This crystal generated an invisible laser beam which could be used for precise target ranging in lieu of radar, and for 'lasing' targets for LGBs (Laser-Guided Bombs) to home onto. A digital code was entered by the WSO into both the bombs and pod controls, so that multiple aircraft could each guide their own bombs autonomously. Two 'peepholes' adjacent to the IDS window were used for the lasing operation, one to transmit and receive the beam for marking and ranging, and the other to plot the laser 'spot'.

The pod was interfaced with the other Mk IIB nav-and-attack systems, including the ODS gunsight, to provide a number of navigation and targeting modes at a push of a button. The turret could be manually steered all about the F-111's lower hemisphere, looking forward, sideways or aft, by means of the WSO's tracking handle. There were also a number of modes to set it up to look in the 'right vicinity', whereupon the 'Wizzo' would fine-tune tracking with his right-hand controller to keep it on-target.

'Cue' mode automatically slewed the IDS sensor to the target, based on stored coordinates in the navigation computer. 'Snow Plow' provided stabilized tracking at a selected fixed angle in space, for example to follow a highway or river, with the WSO making fine-adjustments to keep the cursor on the object under scrutiny. 'Left/Right Acquire' directed the sensor to look 90 degrees abeam for 'pylon tracking turns' (swinging around an imaginary 'Maypole' in the target vicinity), in a banked aircraft attitude. 'Forward Acquire' was where the sensor was caged at boresight with the pilot's ODS gunsight. The pilot then flew the aircraft to put his 'pipper' on the target, and the WSO would take control of subsequent IDS target tracking. Finally, 'TFR Monitor' pointed the IDS along the aircraft's velocity vector, to assist with TF'ing operations by providing an extra 'eye' to see impending obstacles.

As Maj Jim Rotramel emphasized to the authors, it is important to appreciate that the *Pave Tack* crosshairs, like those for most electro-optic targeting devices and weapons seekers, remained stationary in the middle of the VID display while the infrared imagery was effectively moved about 'underneath' the cursor. The position of a small white square adjacent to the crosshairs also served as a helpful cue to indicate whether the pod was looking fore or aft, left or right. The IDS imagery was also 'auto-rotated' so that it didn't appear 'upside down' when the pod was looking aft, and the display itself could be switched to either 'white hot' or the reverse – the former bearing some resemblance to a monochrome negative image, and the other something akin to a normal, black and white TV-type image. Different WSOs each had their individual preferences.

Learning how to use the system took a lot of practice, and crews were expected to be proficient on radar first. An AVTR (Airborne Video Tape Recorder) recorded *Pave Tack* imagery for the purposes of both BDA (Bomb Damage Assessment), and so that IWSOs (Instructor Wizzos) could gauge the effectiveness of newcomers, and teach them a few tricks by showing them where they might have gone wrong.

Tom Barnes and a laden 366th TFW F-111F. In this case the practice bombs contain concrete rather than high explosive, but duplicate the ballistics of the 'serious' version. Col Tom Barnes

An F-111F in fairly close trail formation, August 1974. Col Tom Barnes

F-111F 70-0396 from the 493rd TFS blasts out 50,000lb (22,680kg) of thrust and leaps from the runway despite the temporary drag of its MLG door-cum-airbrake. Authors

Operation *El Dorado Canyon*

The longest fighter combat mission ever flown was a response to terrorist activities in Europe which Washington increasingly attributed to Libyan origins. An explosion at the *La Belle* disco in Berlin on 5 April 1986 was the latest of a series of attacks on American citizens which had begun with the loss of 200 US Marines in Beirut in 1983. It continued through the June 1985 hijack of a TWA airliner, the death of a civilian on the hijacked liner *Achille Lauro* and the loss of five more Americans in a grenade attack at Rome Airport on 17 December 1985.

Following the Rome incident the 48th TFW *Statue of Liberty* wing at RAF Lakenheath received initial warning of impending military action, code-named *Prime Pump*, on 1 January 1986. The order outlined a long-range attack and requested feasibility studies, without specifying a target. A small group of 48th TFW officers were then called to USAFE HQ at Ramstein to discuss the possibility of strikes against the airfields at Tripoli and Benina. Over the following weeks various options were explored including round-trip flights of over seventeen hours. These were declared unfeasible by Lakenheath's delegation. Apart from the crew fatigue factor it was pointed out that the TF30's oil consumption (only 4 gallons/15l were available for each engine) and the F-111F's avionics were limiting factors. However, it was also clear that USAFE was under pressure to demonstrate its long-range tactical capability in a 'hot spot' where the US Navy had dealt with all Libya's challenges thus far. In any case, the five targets chosen at that point would have required the limited numbers of A-6E TRAM Intruders aboard the two US carriers on station to fly two sorties each.[3] Both the A-6E and F-111F had FLIR and laser-optic night/all weather equipment to enable extremely accurate delivery of ordnance against targets close to civilian areas.

Throughout January and February the 48th TFW planners refined a strategy involving a six-plane night attack on targets selected from up to thirty-six possibilities. Against a background of leaks from Washington and feverish press speculation, all of which focused on Lakenheath as the likely launch-pad, preparations for action commenced. In fact, the training process was impaired by severe problems with the TF30-P-100 at the time, including several concurrently running TCTO mods. Crews were therefore unable to put in the extra training time they needed for the demanding mission which many of them suspected was imminent. A long-range non-stop attack training exercise took elements of the 20th TFW on Operation *Ghost Rider* to Keflavik and Goose Bay, but it was February

Loch Ness, seen through the LCOS of an F-111E at rather higher altitude and slower speed than combat conditions would have required. The F-111F's ODS symbology was virtually the same. Dick Brown

before the 48th TFW began five-hour non-stop flights to Incirlik, Turkey. Instead of the usual WTD routine, elements of six F-111Fs, supported by KC-10 tankers, flew direct to Turkey with inert 2,000lb (900kg) bombs and dropped them on the Konya range before landing at Incirlik. By the time Operation *El Dorado Canyon*, the attacks on Libya, took place, almost all the crews involved had experience of these long-range deployments and several had completed missions of over twelve hours duration a number of times. All projections for the operation presupposed a flight of at least this length because of anticipated political difficulties in overflying France, necessitating a long swing around the coast of Spain before entering Mediterranean airspace.

Lakenheath kept a dozen crews on alert throughout February and March as the possibility of an attack remained high and media attention increased.[4] US Navy action became more pro-active on 24 March, when its ongoing exercise Operation *Prairie Fire* took it into the Gulf of Sidra and over President Ghadaffi's so-called 'Line of Death'.[5] April opened with the loss of three American lives in the bombing of a TWA airliner, and the *La Belle* bomb two days later. A US response seemed inevitable and Prime Minister Margaret Thatcher gave unreserved support for the use of British bases if they were required for this purpose.

In the final stages of planning, less than three days before the operation began, it was decided in Washington that the attack force would be increased from six to eighteen F-111Fs. The purpose may have been to cause maximum visible damage to the targets as a political gesture, but the wisdom of the decision was questioned by Lakenheath's small planning team. With very little time to revise their strategy and organize effectively coordinated individual attacks by all the aircraft, they were also faced with a shortage of aircrew with enough specific training for the mission. Furthermore, another Pentagon decision overturned Lakenheath's detailed mission plans. The original intention was to direct three F-111Fs against the small Sidi Balal terrorist training camp, six at Ghadaffi's Al Azziziyah military barracks and nine on Tripoli airport where light defences and reduced potential for collateral damage made it easier to ensure visible damage for the subsequent reconnaissance flights to record. This plan was polished in Lakenheath's 494th TFS squadron building, but a last minute

White House directive assigned three of the Tripoli airport aircraft (callsigns *Karma 51–53*) to the Al Azziziyah attack instead. Many disadvantages resulted from this, because the F-111Fs had to follow each other along the same approach and attack profile, thirty seconds apart (as required in a night attack). There was no time to arrange deconflicted, coordinated attacks from different headings, a risky business at night, though it had been done in Vietnam where there was rather less emphasis on the risk of collateral damage. The Al Azziziyah attack 'cells' were therefore exposed to Libyan defences for a total of five minutes. Although Ghadaffi's radar-guided missiles were neutralised by the USAF and USN SEAD effort, and the effectiveness of his optical SAMs was reduced by darkness, the F-111F's long exposure gave Libyan gunners plenty of time to adjust to the repeated attack patterns.

Also, the comparatively large number of aircraft attacking in one small area meant that the smoke and debris from the first hits could obscure other adjacent targets and prevent *Pave Tack* seekers in some of the following aircraft from acquiring and holding their aim points. *Pave Tack* can only 'see through' fairly light smoke or dust clouds. The situation was also to be exacerbated by inaccurately forecast winds which blew smoke in unexpected directions.

Take-off

The twenty-four *El Dorado Canyon* crews received their final briefing in the 494th TFS crewroom during the afternoon of Monday 14 April. In a vain attempt to provide 'cover' from the media it was announced that a pre-planned *Salty Nation* mass-launch exercise was in progress. However, TV cameras had already zoomed in on live LGBs being transported to the TAB-Vees.[6] For the majority of the 48th TFW crews the nature of the mission remained unknown until their briefing: Lakenheath had been better at keeping its secrets than some sections of the Washington Administration and only around twenty people at the Suffolk base knew the details. Aircraft began to take-off at 17.36Z on Runway 24, with *Puffy* and *Lujac* cells' eight Aardvarks leading the launch. They were destined for a fourteen-hour flight during which they would attack the military areas of Tripoli airport with Mk 82 AIR bombs. The three cells of four aircraft for the downtown Al Azziziyah complex including Ghadaffi's personal base, followed, each carrying four GBU-10 LGBs.[7] Finally, *Jewel* cell, also with GBU-10s, lifted off, headed for the Sidi Balal training camp. Each cell of four aircraft contained an 'air spare' F-111F and all carried ALQ-119 or ALQ-131 ECM pods which had been pre-programmed for the Libyan threats by CNPA, based on Contingency Sigint data furnished by the Proud Flame San Antonio, Texas-based JEWC (Joint-service Electronic Warfare Center).

Transit and Tanking

Most of the forward planning for the mission had assumed that overflights of NATO countries other than the UK would be politically impossible. When the French refused permission the seven-hour over-sea flight to Tripoli became a certainty.[8] The F-111 had been selected for the task partly because of its superior range capability, though with all its wing pylons occupied by bombs its 5,035 gallon (19,057 litres) internal fuel capacity could not be supplemented by drop tanks. An elaborate aerial tanking schedule therefore had to be put in place.

The introduction of the AN/AVQ-26 Pave Tack **added autonomous delivery of LGBs to the F-111F's repertoire, beginning with the GBU-16B/B. In this view of Bolars 72-1442, with a 2nd BW KC-10A, taken two months after** El Dorado Canyon, **the pod is hanging out.** Jim Rotramel

Ahead of the Lakenheath launch seven KC-135As and ten KC-10As departed RAF Mildenhall from 1800Z to provide a KC-10A for each of the F-111F cells, and top-up facilities for those KC-10As. A substantial proportion of the USAF's KC-10A Extender fleet had been transferred rapidly to the UK and some tanker crews barely had time to recover their breath before briefing for the raid. At RAF Upper Heyford the five 42nd ECS EF-111As (including one air spare) took off for the *El Diablo* radar suppression component of the operation, supported by seven KC-10As and two KC-135s from RAF Fairford. Mildenhall's tankers negotiated their way through the UK's crowded airways to pick up their 'customers' and the whole ensemble headed for the Atlantic. The air spare from each cell was sent home after an initial refuelling. Usually this was the aircraft which was displaying any malfunctions at that stage. There were three more refuellings in radio-silence; the first off Portugal, another south of Spain and the final 'plug' west of Sicily. All aircraft were kept at near-maximum fuel throughout the journey. For most aircrew it was their first experience of tanking from a KC-10A at night but they soon mastered the tricky balancing act of refuelling at the regulation 300–320kt (560–590kph). As the whole show began to run a little late refuelling speeds had to be pushed up by 50kt (90kph) and pilots then had to maintain station on the boom by using one afterburner, with consequent deterioration in the F-111s' handling. In all, 7 million pounds (3 million kg) of JP-8 fuel were consumed en route.

Target

After their final refuelling, timed to allow maximum fuel for afterburners to be used on the attack runs, the F-111Fs turned south towards Libya. On the approach to the 'Line of Death' the 500ft (150m) 'Weather mode' setting was maintained on TFR to reduce unwanted emissions, with the aircraft using inputs from LARA. A few aircraft attempted, without complete success, to correct 'drift' which had crept into their INS during the journey. Later they would become 'target aborts' because they could not update their INS with sufficient accuracy, thereby risking an off-target delivery. Another aircraft had to pull out with a TFR failure. Closer to the coast TFRs were switched to 'primary mode' and the Aardvarks' attack radars were engaged and checked, as were DEWS and weapons release settings. *Pave Tack* pods, also 'set up' at this point, threw up problems in several aircraft too, leading to target aborts or inaccurate weapons deliveries. After the mission it was realised that cooling lines in a number of pods had become clogged over the years, a factor which had not been noticed because the pods had not been 'run' for so long before on a sortie. (One of the few improvements to F-111F systems after *El Dorado Canyon* was that all *Pave Tack* units had these lines cleaned out.) Despite the best efforts of the 48th AMU their jets were developing faults at an uncharacteristically high rate and continued to do so throughout the mission. *El Dorado Canyon* was run to very strict Rules of Engagement, requiring fully operational systems in all aircraft to minimize the chances of collateral damage in civilian areas.

Tripoli

As F-111F 71-0893 led the formation in darkness across the mythical 'Line of Death' the Libyan defences were well-prepared for its arrival. After the mission it was postulated that the Maltese government had passed on to Ghadaffi (with whom it sympathised at the time) NATO radar advice (originating in Italy) of the strike force's presence and heading in the Mediterranean airspace. In any case, the intensive media coverage in the Western world had alerted Libya to the risk. Contrary to expectations Libyan defences were 'working nights' when the F-111s drew near. Radar and SAM indications were picked up on DEWS in '893 and accurate AAA was awaiting F-111F 70-2390, the first to home in on the Al Azziziyah target area. Although it was known that the Libyan Air Force had very little night fighter capability, the possibility of an attempted interception by a MiG-21 or MiG-25 from Benina airfield could not be totally discounted. On the ground, optically guided SAMs were a reduced threat. Radar and radar-guided missiles were virtually neutralized as the three 42nd ECS Ravens began their jamming operation at 2354Z, and USN A-7Es and F/A-18As knocked out the majority of coastal tracking radars with Shrike and HARM missiles. Even so, the Libyan defences had plenty of Russian SA-2, SA-3, SA-6, SA-8 and French Crotale SAMs ready to launch; visually if necessary. At 0001Z the Aardvarks targeted on Ghadaffi's headquarters began their final run-in. They approached at thirty second intervals with a 20–30 degree pull-up for a 'Toss' delivery of their four LGBs. Forty-five seconds after release each slew of bombs should have reached its desired mean point of impact (DMPI) with the aid of *Pave Tack*. The outcome of those cells' efforts is detailed in the panel opposite.

Puffy and *Lujac* cell aircraft used different profiles and weapons for their attacks on the military sections of Tripoli Airport. This was the original, small strike package which Lakenheath had planned four months previously. Avoiding the Libyan defences, it used overland approaches from a variety of headings at 75 seconds separation with offset aimpoints. Here, the element of surprise was attained and there was no opposition, but bomb damage was once again rather less than intended due to minor systems failures.

The third prong of the attack took three aircraft to the Sidi Balal training centre which was thought to be an instruction centre for terrorists with emphasis on underwater sabotage techniques. Some damage was caused, but less than had been intended.

Tracking Back

As the F-111 crews one by one called 'Feet Wet' on re-crossing the coast it was clear that at least one crew had not checked in. An additional radio check, *Tranquil Tiger* for a successful attack and *Frosty Freezer* for the reverse gave an early indication of the effects of the raid. Fuel-hungry crews sought their attendant tankers as they negotiated their way through the USN defensive screen. Initial headings to join up was made by TACAN, but link-ups needed to be made visually, often in cloud. At least one crew resorted to a quick burst of 'torching' to indicate their position to other aircraft. Once the aborts and diversions had been sorted out it was possible to confirm the chilling rumours that *Karma 52* had not made it back to the tankers.[9] Its crew were declared MIA after thirty minutes.

The sixteen remaining F-111Fs (one had diverted to Rota, Spain) landed back at Lakenheath between 0630Z and 0752Z, while their eight ponderous tankers and the Raven components returned safely to their bases. Although they had survived an

El Dorado Canyon 'Cells'

REMIT Al Azziziyah Compound.
All aircraft carried 4x GBU-10C/B LGBs.

Remit 31: 70-2390/495th TFS.
First aircraft to bomb. *Pave Tack* laser 'spot' masked by aircraft's tail when it pulled up from its 'Toss' rather too hard. (Pilot aware that he was being closely tracked by 23mm AAA as he pulled up). Bombs impacted 50ft (15m) short of Col Ghadaffi's house. Aircraft had white bomb mission mark below left canopy after the attack – the only aircraft to be marked this way.

Remit 32: 72-1445/492nd TFS.
Aircraft had to abort 'Toss' manoeuvre because equipment failure meant that Pave Tack was not correctly lined up on aimpoint. Made manual low-level escape over Tripoli and jettisoned bombs at sea. Used afterburner extensively over target to try and make up time, thereby attracting considerable AAA and SAMs.

Remit 33: 74-0178/495th TFS.
Arrived on target 30 sec late with faulty altimeter and *Pave Tack* problems. Laser 'spot' obscured by smoke and debris from *Remit 31's* bombs and *Pave Tack* broke lock, allowing bombs to go ballistic after release. Hit within a few hundred feet of target but no collateral damage.

Remit 34: 70-2382/493rd TFS.
Air spare, returned to LN after first in-flight refuelling.

KARMA Al Azziziyah Compound.
All aircraft carried 4x GBU-10C/B LGBs.

Karma 51: 70-2413/494th TFS.
Had TFR problem near target causing 'fly-up' and flew 'manually'. Pilot avoided using afterburner to deter AAA but had a SAM lock-on near the target. At bomb-release point two bombs 'hung-up' for several seconds while computer found release solution (delay possibly due to incorrectly entered offset coordinates). WSO unable to acquire target on *Pave Tack*. Bombs went ballistic, impacting 1.5 miles (2.4km) from target and causing collateral damage near French Embassy.

Karma 52: 70-2389/494th TFS.
Probably hit by Libyan defences before its attack and caught fire. Crew activated capsule at low-level but main parachutes seem not to have deployed in time. Maj Fernando Ribas-Dominicci (48th TFW Stan/Eval Flight) and Capt Paul F. Lorence appear to have drowned in the capsule. Capt Lorence not recovered. Maj Ribas-Dominicci's body returned by Libyans.

Karma 53: 71-0889/493rd TFS.
Had a systems malfunction before bomb release and aborted, jettisoning bombs at sea.

Karma 54: 70-2415/493rd TFS.
Air spare. Returned to LN.

ELTON Al Azziziyah Compound.
All aircraft carried 4x GBU-10C/B LGBs.

Elton 41: 70-2403/492nd TFS.
Had equipment malfunction and aborted before commencing attack.

Elton 42: 70-2396/492nd TFS.
Equipment failure, air abort before reaching target area.

Elton 43: 70-2363/495th TFS.
Target area abort. On return flight crew had 'wheel well hot' warning due to hot bleed-air venting into wheel-well leading to fire risk (as in loss of RAAF F-111C A8-136 in April 1977). Diverted to Rota, Spain, and returned to LN on 16 April.

Elton 44: 70-0204/493rd TFS.
Air-spare, returned to LN.

JEWEL Sidi Bilal Training Camp.
All aircraft carried 4x GBU-10C/B LGBs.

Jewel 61: 70-2371/495th TFS.
Bombs caused some damage but missed main target. Bombing solutions degraded by inaccurate wind forecast for target area.

Jewel 62: 70-2383/492nd TFS.
Missed main target but caused some damage to surrounding buildings. Aimpoint obscured by debris and smoke from preceding aircraft's bombs.

Jewel 63: 74-0177/492nd TFS.
Pave Tack imagery obscured by smoke from Jewel 61's bombs just before impact and bombs destroyed frogman-training swimming pool 100ft (30m) from original target.

Jewel 64: 70-2386/493rd TFS.
Air-spare, returned to LN.

PUFFY Tripoli Airport.
All aircraft carried 12x Mk 82 AIRs.

Puffy 11: 71-0893/492nd TFS.
Hit an Il-76 Candid transport and damaged several military helicopters. The only completely successful attack on this target.

Puffy 12: 70-2416/494th TFS.
Had minor equipment failure and aborted before target (N.B. this aircraft had an undercarriage collapse on landing at LN, 16 April 1985, with Maj Ribas-Dominicci as pilot, but suffered only minor damage).

Puffy 13: 70-2394/492nd AMU.
Caused some damage to operations building on military side of airport.

Puffy 14: 73-0707/494th TFS.
Became the air-spare after an afterburner malfunction on take-off. Was being flown by one of the wing's most experienced crews whose expertise would have been a great advantage over the target.

LUJAC Tripoli Airport.
All aircraft carried 12x Mk 82 AIRs.

Lujac 21: 72-1449/493rd TFS.
Air abort with equipment malfunction.

Lujac 22: 71-0888/492nd TFS.
Missed main target.

Lujac 23: 70-0387/495th TFS.
Missed main target.

Lujac 24: 70-2405/494th TFS.
Was air-spare, replaced *Lujac 21* and carried out partially successful attack.

OTHER F-111F AIRCRAFT

70-0183/495th TFS.
Aborted 20 mins before take-off with faulty ALQ-119 pod. (Its replacement also had a failed ALQ-119 and an unusable *Pave Tack* pod due to a problem with its environmental control unit, degrading infra-red video presentation. It also had a hard compressor stall on the right engine when the pilot selected afterburner during the 'Toss' release manoeuvre).

EF-111A Ravens.
All aircraft from the 42nd ECS, RAF Upper Heyford.
66-030, 66-033, 66-057, 67-034, 67-041 & 67-052.
This number included one ground-spare. Five took-off, including an air-spare. In the target area three were directly involved in SEAD activity and a fourth was held in reserve in the operational area.

F-111F 71-0893 (492nd TFS) awaits PDM at BAe Filton in the summer of 1988, with PDM-related white square on its fin. As Puffy 11 in the Tripoli Airport element of El Dorado Canyon this aircraft destroyed an Il-76 Candid transport aircraft (of five destroyed or badly damaged) and its Pave Tack imagery of the bombing was seen world-wide ... Authors

... Repeated here, (inset) for posterity. The nine black spots are 500lb (225kg) Mk 82 AIRs falling from F-111F 71-0893 towards Libyan Il-76s parked at Tripoli Airport. Hits by a previous F-111F appear as dark clouds at the top of the frame. At this point in the attack the Pave Tack turret has swung to the rear to generate BDA video of its target as the F-111 flies on beyond its bomb-release point. US DoD

exhausting fourteen-hour flight no flyers had to be carried out of their cockpits, contrary to popular press reports. As the 48th TFW force crossed the English coast an SR-71A *Habu* (17960) passed slightly above them and its crew, Col Walter Watson and Maj Brian Schul noted that two F-111Fs were missing. Their aircraft was the back-up Blackbird for the BDA reconnaissance flights over the Libyan targets, with OBC and TEOC cameras to record the damage in a Mach 3+ 'take' over Tripoli. Despite the tragic demise of *Karma 52*'s crew and the largely unexpected technical problems, the mission was in most respects a success. The aircrew, in most cases flying their first combat mission, had fulfilled the operation's aim of taking aggression back to its instigator. Post-strike analysis of combat video tapes showed some accurate drops but also demonstrated to senior USAF personnel a very high level of aircrew coordination and discipline throughout the mission. Out of eleven F-111Fs which successfully dropped their weapons, four were on or very near their targets. About a third of the total warload of 132,000lb (60,000kg) was not dropped because of systems malfunctions or ROE restrictions. Slightly over a third of the LGBs released found their targets. Arithmetically, the bombing results did not seem particularly impressive, although by the standards of previous conflicts they were very good indeed. On a better day, when things were working more typically, many more hits would probably have been registered.

Predictably, the loss of an F-111, the regrettable civilian casualties near the French Embassy in Tripoli as a result of some 'long' bombs, and the forecasts of immediate terrorist reprisals dominated media coverage of the event in Europe. The authors were told of angry telephone calls to Lakenheath by a prominent Labour MP accompanied by threats to close the base. Aircrew who were involved in the mission 'vanished' into anonymity (where they remain ten years on) for fear of retribution against their families. Undoubtedly the response in Europe initiated a reassessment of America's perception of its role in NATO. There were further terrorist acts in the period following *El Dorado Canyon*, including the appalling loss of Pam Am Flight 103 over Lockerbie in December

On this Panthers F-111F the Pave Tack pallet has swung round through 90 degrees, allowing the sensor head to deploy and enabling the aircraft to target-mark and guide its own Paveway II bombs. 'Buddy lasing' was not liked by 48th TFW crews, who much preferred autonomous tactics – that is, the same aircraft dropping and guiding their own LGBs. USAFE via Lockheed-Martin

Remit 31 (70-2390) of the 495th TFS being prepared for take-off at Lakenheath on 14 April 1986. As the first F-111F to release its GBU-10C/Bs it scored a hit on Col Ghadaffi's HQ. On the first night of Operation Desert Storm this aircraft, flown by Col Tom Lennon, led the first F-111 attack on Iraq. Dale Woodward via Jim Rotramel

1988, although it has been impossible to attribute any of them directly to Libyan retribution. One bizarre threat came from a trainee Libyan pilot at an airfield in Oxfordshire whose phone call describing how he intended to take his training aircraft in a *Kamikaze* attack upon RAF Upper Heyford was fortunately intercepted. Security considerations perhaps motivated the lack of individual awards to the majority of the aircrew involved. Ironically, US Navy Secretary John F. Lehman visited Lakenheath and presented the *Liberty* wing with the Navy Meritorious Unit Citation. However, the 48th TFW decided to make its own 'award' to its aircraft. From June 1986 until the end of their service in the UK its F-111Fs, the only aircraft which could have performed the mission, proudly bore a version of the WWII North African Campaign ribbon on their tails.[10]

Lujac 21 **(72-1449) laden with twelve Mk 82 AIRs, blasts off from Lakenheath on 14 April. Forced to abort near the target with 'down' systems, it was replaced in the attack on Tripoli Airport by air-spare 70-2405.** Dale Woodward via Jim Rotramel

(Below) **In 1989 the 492nd TFS Commander's aircraft wore a winged bowler hat, a visual reminder of the squadron nickname (which was usually spelled 'Bolars').** Robbie Robinson

CHAPTER EIGHT

Desert Pigs: *Desert Shield* and *Desert Storm*

While *El Dorado Canyon* brought the F-111's capability to public prominence at last, some of the aircraft's greatest, but least publicized deeds were performed over the arid expanses of Kuwait and Iraq nearly five years later. By any standards the F-111 was one of the most important aircraft involved in the war. About one third of the active F-111 inventory (some eighty-eight examples) were committed to the conflict, while EF-111A Ravens provided essential SEAD support for the majority of Coalition Forces air operations. The deployed Aardvarks were organized into two Provisional Wings, the larger being the 48th TFW(P) at the modern Taif Air Base in Saudi Arabia and which became the largest USAF wing in the area. By the end of the conflict its sixty-six F-111F aircraft had destroyed half the Iraqi river bridges which were felled, 40 per cent of Hardened Aircraft Shelters (HAS) and 920 Iraqi tanks and AFVs (over 15 per cent of the total, though many more were probably destroyed but unconfirmed by BDA reconnaissance).

At Incirlik in Turkey, to the north of Iraq, elements of the 20th TFW contributed F-111Es to the 7440th Combat Wing (Provisional), the USAF's first Composite Wing. Its twenty-two F-111Es wrought substantial damage to targets in the northern half of Iraq. EF-111A Spark'-Varks were based at both locations.

Neither F-111E/F unit sustained a combat loss; damage was limited to the odd bullet hole or canopy scratch. Of the eighty-seven Coalition aircraft lost to all causes between August 1990 and March 1991, only two were EF/F-111s and both were attributable to crew error. These results were backed up by extremely favourable mission availability rates. *Desert Storm* F-111Fs averaged 85 per cent availability (the same as the F-117A *Nighthawk*) despite their age and somewhat temperamental systems. Even the TF30-P-100 engines held up well with no unscheduled replacements. At Incirlik the even older analogue F-111Es gave their maintainers (predominantly from the 79th TFS) some headaches. However, Col Terry Simpson, commanding the 55th TFS element at the base, reported to the authors that his unit lost 'maybe three or four sorties in the entire period due to maintenance faults'. They flew 1,181 sorties in all.

When President George Bush decided to erect his *Desert Shield* on 6 August 1990, his main purpose was to prevent Iraq from invading Saudi Arabia, as well as liberating Kuwait which had been seized four days previously. At the invitation of King Fahd of Saudi Arabia, the world's largest-ever military airlift began shifting huge numbers of troops and their hardware into his country. The next day, a large proportion of the 1st TFW's F-15C/D Eagles winged non-stop from Langley AFB to Saudi and they were joined by twenty-two more US combat aircraft units in the following weeks. USAFE's first contribution was its premier 48th TFW with F-111Fs. All the plans for liberating Kuwait presupposed the availability of aircraft capable of delivering PGMs, but there was a shortage of these platforms.

In August 1990 a strategy known as *Instant Thunder* was devised by a team led by Col John A. Warden III, principal architect of the air campaign against Iraq. Its name was intended to suggest the antithesis of the agonizing 'gradualism' of *Rolling Thunder* in Vietnam, with its consequent unacceptable casualties. Col Warden established his deputy, Col David A. Deptula in Riyadh as chief planner for targeting in a plan which was intended to deliver a crippling blow to Iraq's offensive might. He described *Instant Thunder* as a 'highly integrated plan like the Bekaa Valley, but more massive than *Linebacker*'. Although the name was subsequently dropped, the philosophy remained in place throughout the next six months of planning, and PGM-capable aircraft such as the F-111F, F-117A, F-15E and the stalwart B-52 were central to this process. One of Deptula's three-man planning team was Lt Col Ron Stanfill, an F-111 pilot. On his advice a decision to send the 27th TFW's F-111Ds into battle was changed in favour of the *Pave Tack*-equipped F-111F.

Desert Nights

RAF Lakenheath's runways began to reverberate to the departing thunder of nineteen 492nd and 494th TFS Aardvarks on 25 August 1990. Each aircraft carried its own initial supply of four 2,000lb (900kg) GBU-24 bombs underwing as these weapons were not in place at their destination; Taif in Western Saudi Arabia.

Eventually, almost 1,200 GBU-24/24As were among the 5,558 bombs dropped from F-111Fs in the campaign. Fourteen jets from the 493rd TFS joined the wing on 2 September, followed by a mixed dozen from the 492nd and 494th TFSs on 29 November, and a group of eleven 495th TFS *Aardvark University* Instructors and their aircraft on 11 December. Further additions put sixty-six aircraft on Taif's spacious base area by the time hostilities began, including most of the GBU-15-capable aircraft. Flying at Lakenheath virtually closed down with only four planes on the base for most of the war. A one-hour alert was established as soon as the 48th TFW(P) arrived and the four squadrons reorganized themselves into teams with names which echoed the *Liberty* Wing's origins: *Justice* (492nd), *Freedom* (493rd), *Liberty* (494th) and *Independence* or '*Indy*' (495th). Each had a well-protected shelter complex. Aircrew then began to train hard, including large scale, radio-silent ('comm's-out') launches and night-tanking sessions which were not often

Paveway Mini-Toss

BACKGROUND Developed during the Vietnam war, the Paveway series of Laser-Guided Bombs (LGBs) comprised passive nose seekers linked to steering canard fins and fixed tail units which were bolted onto unitary 'dumb' bombs to make them 'smart'. Built by Texas Instruments, the series was further matured into the Paveway II extended-range 'family' from 1976, and thence into the low-level launch-capable Paveway III series a decade later. The later, proportionally guided Paveway III bombs flew a more direct path to the target inside the reflected 'laser basket' or cone (instead of bouncing up and down within it, 'bang bang' style). This increased range and kinetic striking power of the weapon, and enabled 'toss' deliveries to be conducted from low altitude if necessary. The chief users in the Aardvark community were the Pave Tack toting F-111Fs of the 48th TFW, and later 27th FW, and the RAAF's similarly equipped F-111Cs of No 82 Strike Wing.

DRY METHODS Deliveries of Paveways were typically high-speed subsonic and originally entailed a manoeuvre known as the '*Pave Tack* toss'. This involved a 3g pull-up from low-level to lob the bomb(s) towards the target, followed by the aircraft 'bellying over' in an arc at 135 degrees of bank to facilitate *Pave Tack* target tracking during the lasing and egress manoeuvre. *Pave Tack* lasers would be 'squirted' at the target during the last few seconds of bomb flight, which was computed as a time to impact and displayed in alphanumerics on the WSO's VID. The LGB would home towards the 'laser spot' in the reflected 'laser basket' to offer a CEP (Circular Error of Probability) of approximately one yard (metre). Deliveries were nearly always autonomous – ie the same aircraft dropping and guiding – though F-111D/Es occasionally practised dropping LGBs against targets 'illuminated' by other aircraft or special operations ground forces.

By the time of the Gulf War, delivery methods had changed to 'mini-Toss' (also known as 'Ramp Level') for medium-altitude drops. Here, the aircraft conducted a gentler pull-up to 'toss' the LGB(s) before rolling 90 degrees onto a wing and making a corner turn, followed by a gradual levelling-out, during which time the WSO tracked the target and 'squirted' the laser as before.

COMBAT AND BOMB CONFIGURATIONS The F-111F was the only Aardvark to employ LGBs in combat. The first occasion was during Operation *El Dorado Canyon* on the night of 14/15 April 1986, where twenty-eight LGBs were actually expended at Al Azziziyah and Sidi Bilal in Libya (sixteen hitting their targets). A further 4,596 LGBs of six varieties were expended by 48th TFW(P) F-111Fs during Operation *Desert Storm* on targets in Kuwait and Iraq, with considerably greater success owing to massively improved aircraft systems reliability.

GBU-10C to F/B.
Mk 84 2,000lb (900kg) general purpose warhead and MXU-651 Paveway II fins. General purpose weapon. 28 GBU-10C/B expended during *El Dorado Canyon*, and 469 GBU-10C to F models during *Desert Storm*.

GBU-10G to J/B
Also known as the GBU-10I. BLU-109/B penetrating warhead and MXU-651 Paveway II fins. HAS or bunker-buster. 389 expended during *Desert Storm*.

GBU-12B to D/B
Mk 82 500lb (225kg) general purpose warhead and MXU-602 Paveway II fins. 'tank-plinker'. 2,542 expended during *Desert Storm*.

GBU-24/B
Mk 84 2,000lb (900kg) general purpose warhead and BSU-84 Paveway III fins. General purpose weapon with low-level LGB capability. 270 used during *Desert Storm*.

GBU-24A/B
BLU-109/B penetrating warhead and BSU-84 Paveway III fins. HAS or bunker-buster with low-Level LGB capability. 924 used during *Desert Storm*.

GBU-28/B
BLU-113/B 4,700lb (2130kg) warhead and WGU-25/36 Paveway III guidance/fins, developed under Project *Deep Throat*. Two expended during *Desert Storm* combat to destroy enemy command & control facilities.

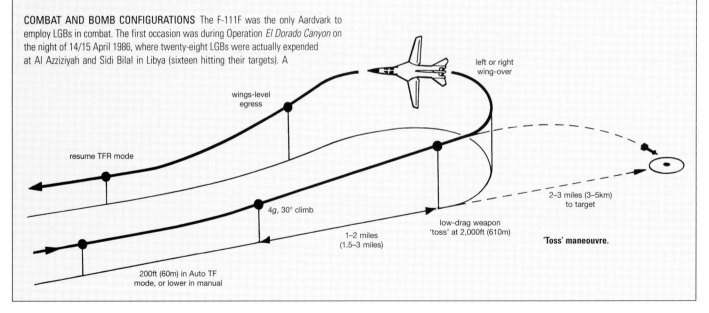

'Toss' manoeuvre.

done in peacetime. TFR sorties began at 400ft (120m) but when hostilities began it was understood that the 200ft (60m) minimum would apply. Low-level training cost the 48th TFW its only casualty on 10 October 1990, when F-111F 74-0183 hit the ground at the Askr Range, killing its crew Capts Thomas R. Caldwell and Frederick A. Reid during a 'mini-Toss' practice sortie. This crash, and others at the time, brought about a safety review which raised the training altitude to an unrealistic 500ft (150m) minimum.

While diplomacy failed to shift Saddam Hussein's forces from Kuwait the planning for a developed version of *Instant Thunder* (*Desert Storm*) proceeded in minute detail. Brig Gen 'Buster' Glosson, a formidable officer in the Norman Schwartzkopf mould, assumed command of all the USAF wings and targeting for the war theatre. He was charged with destroying major strategic targets and a substantial proportion of Iraq's communications and military

Digital Enhancements

DIGITAL COMPUTER UPDATE In the post-*El Dorado Canyon* and immediate pre-*Desert Shield/Storm* era, some six years after the *Pave Tack* update had been completed, the F-111F's Mk IIB DCC complex began to be outfitted with a new 64K digital Weapons-Navigation Computer which could be loaded with the flightplan using a portable flight-line Mission Data-Loader (MDL). In all, the onboard computer could be fed with, and hold up to 1,000 data points and twenty sets of 100 sequence points. In one fell swoop, this replaced the old punched-paper 'tape loader', and similarly bypassed the need for the WSO to enter the coordinates laboriously in the cockpit one at a time before takeoff, in the absence of a suitable 'tape load' (although a complete list of coordinates, including diversionary airfields etc were carried onboard in the 'route folder', so that the WSO could manually enter brand new destinations, if required). Its single apparent drawback was that it employed Jovial computer language 'instead of the harder to program, but more compact Assembly language always used before by the F-111. Using Jovial in our 64K computers resulted in the "20lb of shit into a 5lb bag" routine'.

MISSION SUPPORT SYSTEM Just reaching service during the *Desert Storm* era also was the new Lockheed-Sanders MSS, a portable, giant-suitcase set of computers to aid in mission-planning. MSS offered a staggering new facility for those adept at using it. As maps and computer expert extraordinaire Jim Rotramel noted:

With the advent of computerized planning systems, the primitive [paper map] task was largely eliminated, with crews able to access not only basic navigational charts, but digitized terrain elevation data (DTED) and satellite imagery at the click of a 'mouse'. The imagery could even be 'draped over' the DTED, creating an image of a given area. However, these computerized systems are still extremely cumbersome to use, despite the public relations hoopla.

It took a great deal of practice and cross-checking with others who knew the systems better. However, skilled crews could use the system to determine solar or moonlight grazing angles and shadows and other such factors to help determine the optimum headings to assist with *Pave Tack* and electro-optic 'smart bomb' target acquisition.

Lt (now Capt) 'Quizmo' Brown's F-111F, 70-2364 part of the Liberty Team at Taif on 1 January 1991. On alert status, the Aardvark has two GBU-24/B Paveway III LGBs and a pair of AIM-9P-3 Sidewinders on the inboard pylons. These missiles were not used in combat and were carried by only a few F-111s on the first night of Desert Storm. Craig Brown

facilities before 'preparing the battlefield' by eliminating at least half of the enemy's armour, artillery and troop concentrations ahead of the land war. A former *Gunfighter* F-4 Phantom pilot in Vietnam, Glosson had seen appalling casualties among his fellow airmen there and he was determined to avoid such losses in the Gulf.

Among his more memorable comments was the assertion, 'There's not a damn thing worth dying for in Iraq'.

H-hour, the time for the implementation of those long-gestated plans, was finally set for 7pm Eastern Standard Time in the USA, and around midnight on 17 January 1991 the 415th TFS launched the

F-117A *Nighthawk* 'Stealth' strikers which put the first bomb on Iraqi territory, destroying the air defence centre at Nukayb. It was the first blow in a vast, tightly orchestrated onslaught involving 668 Coalition aircraft that night. Taif's Aardvark Wing put up fifty-four jets against targets in the south and east of

The 13.5ft (4.1m) long Pave Tack pod extended on its weapons-bay cradle, with the gimballed IDS turret looking to starboard, showing the large aperture infra-red window and laser 'peepholes'. Pods were usually painted FS 34087 Olive Drab, as were ECM pods. Jim Rotramel

(Below) **Another** Panthers **F-111F, 70-2387 on alert status at Taif, with a warload of CBU-87 s and AIM-9P-3s. On its fin is the North African Campaign sash worn by 48th TFW Aardvarks after** El Dorado Canyon, **in which this aircraft contributed to the attack on Tripoli Airport. In** Desert Storm **it was one of the pair of F-111Fs involved in the** Deep Throat **attack on Al Taji, scoring a direct hit on an Iraqi High Command underground bunker.** Craig Brown

Iraq. Major airfields and storage bunkers were attacked at Balad and Jalibah in Iraq. Others at Ali al Salem and Al Jabar in southern Kuwait were bombed, as were chemical weapons storage sites at H-3, Salman Pak and Al Divaniyah. The 48th TFW's assertive Commander, Col Thomas J. Lennon led the deepest night-strike to Balad air base, north of Baghdad. He flew F-111F 70-2390 *Miss Liberty II*, the Aardvark which had led the *El Dorado Canyon* raiders over the beach in 1986. Like the other F-111F strike packages of four-to-eight aircraft, Col Lennon's jets were forced down from medium altitude to 200ft (60m) sooner than intended after crossing the border by the unexpectedly vicious defending fire. At 650kt (1,200kph) low-level the Aardvarks burned rather more fuel than planned, causing some anxiety later in the mission. At the target *Miss Liberty II*'s first GBU-15 glide-bomb failed to leave its pylon and the second also remained in place when '390 was forced to break off its attack by extremely heavy barrage Triple-A. Other aircraft managed to take out a hangar and the control tower. GBU-89 Gator area-denial mines were generously distributed across the ends of the runways and among HAS complexes to impede the movement of the resident fighters. It was clear that a return mission would be needed. Some of Iraq's sixty-six major airfields were twice the area of Heathrow Airport with enormous taxiway and HAS provisions.

The mission against Ali al Salem in Kuwait also met walls of AAA. Half the force abandoned their GBU-24A/B attacks leaving three jets to pursue their courses towards the HAS areas. Lt Col Dennis R. Ertler was flying auto-TFR at 200ft (60m) when he saw a SAM launched at him from his left and managed to evade it by 'going manual', missing a barrage of flak in his path at the same time. His WSO, Capt Keith Zeugel got a good *Pave Tack* 'splash' on a HAS and GBU-24s were 'pickled'. Seconds before they hit home Ertler had another SAM on his tail. He broke off and released chaff at the missile which exploded behind his aircraft.

Fortunately, his bombs stayed on target and blew in through the doors of the HAS. Another SAM pursued Ertler's plane as it pulled off target but he managed to escape for the third time. In May 1991, Gen John A. Shaud, Chief of Staff at SHAPE, presented Ertler with the Silver Star, one of five awarded to 48th TFW(P) aircrew after *Desert Storm*.

Some of the four-ship first-night packages flew two GBU-15-toting stand-off aircraft to soften-up the target, and GBU-24s on the other pair to follow through with a penetrating 'hammer blow'. Aircraft attacked singly, in trail formation with about one minute separation. This pattern made a tempting target for the limited number of Iraqi MiG-29s which attempted to interfere with the missions. A MiG tried to drop in behind the second F-111 in a four-ship 'queue', lost him and moved back to the last in line which was chased for 60 miles (95km) down a planned egress route before they lost the *Fulcrum*. Just as it had done in Vietnam, the F-111 once again demonstrated that nothing could catch it flat out on the deck.

The Taif attackers achieved most of their mission objectives without the anticipated losses that night. Col Lennon's 'worst case' estimate was that six Aardvarks might have been downed. In fact, only two suffered very minor damage from small-bore AAA, unnoticed until post-flight inspections. A bigger threat in some ways was the weather. On return to Taif the fuel-hungry aircraft, one with a hung GBU-24, found their base socked in by fog. Tankers kept them airborne until the cloud lifted but over half the force had to divert to Prince Abdul Aziz Airport at Jeddah, home of the local USAF B-52 contingent.

Phase Two of the Aardvark onslaught was delivered on the second night when forty F-111Fs left Taif for a range of targets including Saddam Hussein's palace and command centre at Tikrit. Once again the Iraqi AF made a rare attempt to intervene when a MiG-29 repeatedly tried to jump a line of F-111Fs, but gave up after locking onto the fourth jet, which 'dragged him out' for 70 miles (115km) at low-level. Of the other three Aardvarks, one crew succeeded in putting a 2,000lb (900kg) bomb through the roof windows of the palace. Six aircraft were targeted against Mudaysis airfield, which lay outside the Baghdad SAM ring and was less well defended by AAA. Each aircraft was able to take its time over lobbing GBU-24s singly at HAS targets from 'racetrack' patterns at around 20,000ft (6,100m). Twenty out of twenty-three HAS were collapsed and numerous secondary explosions indicated that the first of around 140 Iraqi aircraft destroyed by the 48th TFW(P) in their 'safe' shelters had been reduced to charred scrap.

One change in the munitions loads for Night Two was the deletion of the AIM-9P Sidewinders which some aircraft had carried the previous night. Iraqi fighters were clearly not going to be a major hazard.

After two nights of carefully executed destruction, John Warden's complex plans were just about worked through. Iraq's defences, airfields and communications were substantially neutralized and it was time to move on to different objectives in response to daily tasking orders from Riyadh. However, airfield attacks continued in the belief that Saddam could be hoarding his air assets for airborne chemical and biological weapons assaults on Coalition troops when they re-entered Kuwait. Revised tactics brought an increase in the size of most F-111 strike packages to around twenty-four aircraft. Crews were then able to plan deconflicted runs at their targets from a variety of different headings and altitudes to dissipate the effect of the defences and to finish off each target with a tremendous weight of precision-guided explosive force.

The *Liberty Wing* earned its second Silver Star on the night of 19/20 January in a concerted attack on Al Habbiniyah airfield near Baghdad. This was one of the smaller packages, with the F-111Fs supported by the usual F-4G *Wild Weasel* SAM suppressers, EF-111A Ravens and F-15C top cover. The leading Aardvark (70-2384) had to abort after a minor mid-air collision with its ANG KC-135E tanker and the No. 2 went home with a mechanical defect before crossing the border. Capt Mike McKelvey and his WSO Capt Mark Chance pushed on, accompanied by Capt James McGovern and Capt Will Ward in ship number four. A timing problem meant that they entered the low-level phase of their sortie before their Eagle top-cover arrived on station, but they chose to rely on speed and low-level to avoid fuel-consuming delays while they waited for the F-15Cs. Just over the border, having completed their 'fence checks' of systems and instruments, they received warning of a MiG-29 lock-on and AAM launch in their direction. Capt McKelvey hauled his

Deep Throat shown here in all its glory before the drop. The 4,700lb (2,130kg) weapon employed rebored artillery howitzer barrels stuffed with Tritonol explosive which were fitted with the GBU-27A/B guidance kit used by Stealth fighter bunker-busting 2,000lb (900kg) bombs. White via Jim Rotramel

aircraft up in a 5g climbing turn as his countermeasures system pushed out clouds of chaff. The missile exploded below him and McKelvey put his plane back on course. Both crews succeeded in cratering the runways at Al Habbiniyah, preventing further MiG take-offs and earning McKelvey and Chance their medals.

A similar situation occurred the following night when twenty F-111Fs snaked along the Tigris River to re-attack Balad Southeast airfield. Coordinated attacks from altitudes between 12,000ft and 20,000ft (3,660m and 6,100m) cratered the runways and taxi-strips with GBU-24s despite severe AAA opposition. Once again the last F-111 in the package picked up a MiG-29 but lost it by using the time-honoured Aardvark tactic of heading for the deck and moving the throttles to the 'speed of heat' setting.

F-111s were also nominated to counter the most potentially appalling weapon in Iraq's armoury: its biological warfare (BW) stocks. After the initial euphoria of the 'opening nights' the first SCUD missile launches against Israel induced a state of near-panic among sections of the Coalition. Retaliatory measures such as the destruction of major dams to flood Baghdad, or the threat of nuclear weapons, were considered in case BW-armed SCUDs were used. Little was known about the actual state of Iraqi BW weapons development but contingency plans had to be laid for the destruction of storage areas which could contain the toxic compounds, even though the attacks might cause the release of these substances into rivers or the air with catastrophic effects on the population. One plan called for F-111s to lay small nuclear warheads or fuel-air explosives among the presumed stores of toxins and bacteria to incinerate them. The ultimate proposal was to use GBU-27 bombs to open up the bunkers, followed by CBU-89 to generate enough heat to destroy the substances. Any spores released into the atmosphere would be killed off by the sun's ultraviolet rays at the rate of 2 per cent per minute, according to this proposal. Eighteen presumed BW sites were given priority in the targeters' lists.

F-111Fs were also put on the SCUD-hunting roster for a while in the frantic attempt to eliminate Iraq's mobile launchers. However, the F-111F's radar was not built with sufficient definition to identify such small targets (the F-111D's may have been capable), and Pave Tack was designed for static targets. The job was given to FLIR-equipped F-15E 'Mud Hens' instead, but they too experienced great difficulty in finding the SCUD vehicles.

Shacks on Shelters

At the outset of the war, Iraq was known to have 594 aircraft shelters, some of them the 'Super HAS' type which was thought to be proof against all forms of attack apart from a direct hit with a 1,000lb (450kg) bomb dropped at a perpendicular angle to the roof. In the first two days of the war F-111 crews were forced to make low-altitude attacks on them, using Pave Tack to try for the very difficult target solution on the shelter's doors. By 23 January the 48th TFW(P) was able to give its full attention to mass destruction of the shelter complexes, as ordered by Lt Gen Chuck Horner, commanding the Coalition air forces. Experiments on similar shelters in New Mexico had yielded inconclusive results regarding their vulnerability, but they did suggest that a medium-altitude attack, imparting more kinetic energy to the bomb, would give the best chance of penetrating the shelters' thick reinforced concrete shells. A reduction in the SAM threat meant that airfield attacks could be made from above the 15,000ft (4,570m) ceiling of Triple-A. At 25,000ft (7,620m) the F-111's handling characteristics became a little 'goosey' with bombs aboard, but accuracy with the GBU-24 was significantly improved. For standard HAS structures it was usually found that a single GBU-24A

493rd TFS Roosters F-111F 72-1450 shows off its PGM package comprising: a pair of GBU-15s, an **ALQ-131** pod under the weapons bay and AN/AXQ-14 data-link pod between the strakes. Note the bulged, closed Pave Tack **cradle, kept in the stowed position in this mission configuration. The F-111Fs of the** Freedom Team **(based on the 493rd AMU) flew 651 of the 48th TFW(P)'s 2,417 sorties, dropping 5,576 bombs.**
Jim Rotramel

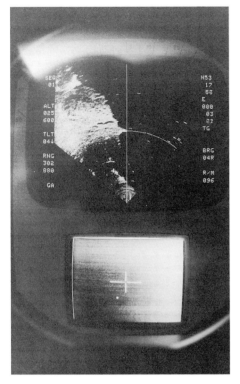

(Right) **An impressive echelon of** Panthers **under the command of Lt Col Ken Coombs at Taif. The 494th Liberty Squadron's bird, 74-0178, chalked-up 56 combat sorties during** Desert Storm. Craig Brown

(Left) **The Kuwait coast, as seen on the WSO's VID, with ARS ground map at top and** Pave Tack **infrared image below. The alphanumerics at top are showing altitude and range amongst other data.** Daughtry via Jim Rotramel

with a delay fuse would make a neat hole in the roof if dropped at the right angle. For 'Super-HAS' roofs a technique was devised using a GBU-24 to crack the roof and another several seconds later to enter the shelter and explode its contents. Given fairly clear weather at night, *Pave Tack* was ideal for this if air superiority could be maintained. On 23 January heavy cloud caused a twenty-aircraft raid to be aborted because *Pave Tack* could not be used. In a medium-altitude drop, the WSO had about a minute from bomb release to guide his LGBs into the laser 'basket' for a precise 'shack' on each shelter. F-117A *Nighthawks* of the 37th TFW were also capable of HAS attacks but they were usually required to hit other specialized targets and the majority of the HAS-busting sorties went to the *Liberty* wing.[1] In all, 245 shelters were shattered by the Aardvarks. In addition to aircraft destroyed in their HAS 'Cocoons' the wing could also be credited indirectly with the removal of another 137 Iraqi combat aircraft from the theatre. Once the Iraqi High Command realised that their airfields were so vulnerable the decision was taken to evacuate a large number of surviving warplanes to Iran rather than watching them being systematically trashed by the 'Fighting Forty-Eighth'. This exodus began on 26 January. Some aircraft were intercepted by the Coalition CAP fighters; others were destroyed by F-111Fs which bombed one of their 'staging' airfields at Tuz Khurmatu, near Kirkup in northeast Iraq. Eight shelters and a transport aircraft were destroyed there.

Bridge Breakers

Having substantially neutralized the Iraqi Air Force, the F-111F wing joined other Coalition strike aircraft in flying several hundred sorties which caused destruction or damage to fifty bridges. Initially this was done because it was thought that fibre-optic cables vital to Baghdad's communications network were routed along them, but disruption to Iraq's road traffic was also intended.[2] 'Buster' Glosson ordered 180 sorties against bridges using unguided weapons in the belief that state-of-the-art weapons aiming systems would ensure good results. As in Vietnam twenty-five years before, the bridges were tougher than the bombs and it was discovered that 'dumb' bombs were nowhere near accurate enough to cause serious damage. On 23 January 416th TFS Stealth fighters began a four-night assault on road bridges. Some rapid research by a civil engineering professor in the USA showed that hits on the bridge stanchions closest to the shore were the most likely way to drop a bridge span. F-111Fs joined the bridge-busting effort on the night of 29/30 January, using GBU-15 and GBU-24 weapons against the five-mile road bridge over the Hawr Al Hammar Lake, north of Basrah. Crews quickly refined their techniques for these targets, often using GBU-15s to blast the spans of the bridge followed by a couple of GBU-24s on the end-stanchions each side. This method usually required four F-111Fs. The BLU-109/B warheads on the GBU-24A/Bs, which had worked so well for penetrating HAS structures, were replaced by standard Mk 84s to spread the explosive effect a little more. When the Iraqis laid replacement pontoon bridges these were bombed too. In total, 160 'shacks' were recorded for the wing's ever-expanding *Pave Tack* Greatest Hits video library.

Twelve bridges were downed and another fifty-two seriously damaged.

As the range of targets widened the 48th TFW(P) devised new techniques to deliver its weapons. 'Wagon Wheel' attacks were used for bombing bunkers and airfields, with aircraft flying a complex radial pattern of individual, elongated race-track orbits, centred on the target at the 'hub'. Very precise timing and altitude-keeping enabled each F-111 to make up to four LGB drops, one from each circuit, saturating the target area with bombs. Large-scale formations continued to be used for targets like the Latifiyah munitions production facility and research centre near Baghdad, and the Tuwaitha nuclear research facility. On the latter mission eighteen F-111Fs with SEAD support attacked one of the most heavily defended targets in Iraq which had previously frustrated raids by F-117As and F-16Cs, costing the loss of one F-16C. An enormous volume of AAA prevented all but three Aardvark crews from reaching the target. One of the jets was flown by Lt Col James F. Slaton and his WSO Capt John 'Bear' Daughtry. Flying below heavy cloud cover they entered a holocaust of gunfire and missiles. The F-4G *Wild Weasels* had expended all their HARM missiles in a couple of minutes against the SAM threats, but there were still active missile sites awaiting Slaton, the Commander of the package. To add to their problems their *Pave Tack* 'went down' just before the target, forcing 'Bear' Daughtry to resort to a series of back-up modes. He persuaded the pod to acquire the target just in time and their GBU-24s took out three of the plant's nuclear reactor buildings and an important part of Saddam's nuclear weapon development programme. Lt Col Slaton and Capt Daughtry each received the Silver Star.

WSO Capt John 'Bear' Daughtry who, with his pilot Lt Col Jim Slaton, was awarded the Silver Star for his attack on the Tuwaitha nuclear research facility near Baghdad. Bomb graffiti ('To the best fighter sqn in the Air Force, the 493rd') was chalked by US Vice President Dan Quayle. Daughtry via Jim Rotramel

F-111E 68-0039 The Baghdad Express, with twenty-one yellow mission marks. Mike Gibson

EF-111A Ravens were an essential component in the Coalition strike packages, so much so that some missions had to be scrubbed because Ravens could not be provided for their protection.
USAF via Northrop-Grumman

(Right) **Raven 66-0050 flew from both Incirlik and Taif, where it acquired the forty 'radar site' mission markings, returning to Dhahran in November 1991 where it was named** Mistress of Deception. **After reassignment to the 366th TFW in 1992 it was back at Dhahran in July of that year.** Mike Gibson

Another major strike on Talil airfield by twenty F-111Fs was aborted by smoke rather than flak. After the bombs fell from the first aircraft, flown by Capt Matt Young and Capt Greg Chapman, the secondary explosion in an ammunition store was so vast that smoke and debris rose to 30,000ft (9,150m), obscuring the target for the rest of the strike force. Coalition ground forces eventually entered the base.

Slick Stoppers

Of all the F-111's varied targets, none demonstrated its unique weapons-delivery capability better than the much-publicized mission to the Al Ahmadi oil pumping stations in Kuwait on 26/27 January. As part of a 'scorched earth' policy to destroy Kuwait when he realized that he could not keep it, Saddam directed his forces to sabotage the huge Burgan oilfield. On 25 January oil tankers containing several million barrels of oil were allowed to empty into the sea off Al Ahmadi and a pipeline leading from the Ahmadi storage terminal to a tanker loading point several miles offshore was opened, venting oil directly into the sea. Preventing the growth of an already-huge oil slick became a matter of extreme urgency as the world contemplated this act of 'environmental terrorism' on its TV screens. After studying the blueprints of the Al Ahmadi

GBU-15 Supersonic Smart Bomb

BACKGROUND This weapon was a passive electro-optically-guided adaptation of a 2,000lb (900kg) unitary 'dumb' Mk 84 warhead fitted with the same TV or Imaging Infra-Red seekers as those developed for the AGM-65 Maverick missile. Unlike Paveway, its forward fins were fixed and bomb steering was accomplished through 'rudders' on the tail fins, which came in both wide-chord and short-chord formats. Built by Rockwell International, the weapon entered service with the Israeli Air Force in 1977 and with the USAF five years later. Within the Aardvark community, it equipped the 493rd TFS *Roosters* at RAF Lakenheath beginning in 1983 and became a speciality of a few select crews, the task being handed over to the 524th FS *Hounds of Heaven* during 1992. The RAAF trialled the weapons but did not acquire them.

DELIVERY METHODS This was a complex task and typically used 'buddy' techniques. To increase accuracy and reduce crew vulnerability, it was customary to perform the attack in pairs or quartets: one or two F-111Fs lobbing the bomb(s) at transonic thru supersonic delivery speeds of up to Mach 1.3 to impart maximum range (preplanned, depending on the threat), and a second crew (or pair) performing the bomb steering via data-link at a suitable standoff distance. This permitted the aircraft to be configured precisely for the attack: one or two lugging bombs, and the 'guiders' AN/AXQ-14 data-link pods.

Following a computed release which lobbed the bomb in the approximate target position, the WSO in the 'guiding' aircraft used a Hughes AN/AXQ-14 data-link pod which relayed the bomb's seeker imagery to the VID display and simultaneously conveyed steering updates back to the bomb. The WSO employed a special toggle switch to 'steer' the seeker precisely on target and would effectively fly it, by remote control, all the way to impact, making adjustments as the target grew bigger in the VID. The seeker image thus remained 'in play' right up until impact. In all, the 493rd TFS launched seventy GBU-15V)2/Bs during the Gulf War, with special attention given to the F-111F crews following the 26/27 January 1991 night strike against the Al Almadi pumping stations. Known as the '*Duck Mission*', it was successfully executed by Capts Brad Seipel and Mike Russell, who guided two GBU-15s lobbed by companions to cut off the oil spill. The first GBU-15 strike of the conflict was executed by Capts Rick Walker and Ken Theurer.

AGM-130 MISSILE Under a contract originating in 1984, and entering service with the F-111Fs of the 524 FS *Hounds of Heaven* at Cannon AFB during 1994, was the follow-on AGM-130 version. This had a Hercules solid-rocket booster strapped to the bomb to nearly triple range to 30nm (55km), along with guidance improvements which included new CCD TV and IIR focal plane array sensor technology, a radar altimeter and new inertial guidance system capable of receiving GPS Navstar inputs, all of them necessary to compensate for the added standoff range. Around the same time a new ZSW-1 data-link was introduced, ostensibly similar to the AXQ-14, also capable of longer-ranged communication with the weapon. The mission and weapons were assigned exclusively to the F-15E upon the 524th FS' disbandment.

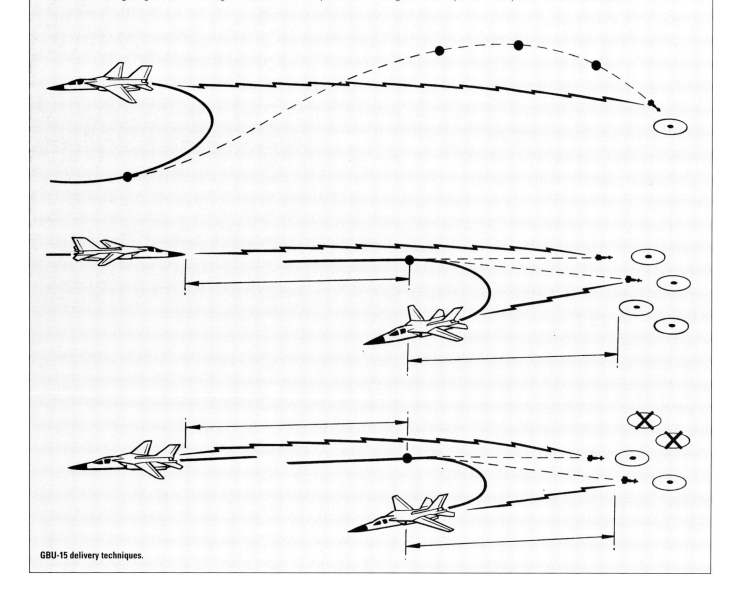

GBU-15 delivery techniques.

GBU-15 Supersonic Smart Bomb *(continued)*	
CONFIGURATIONS GBU-15(V)1/B DSU-27 TV-guided glide version, Mk 84 2,000lb (900kg) general purpose bomb. MXU-724 wide chord wings. GBU-15(V)2/B WGU-10 IIR-guided glide version, Mk 84 2,000lb (900kg) general purpose bomb. MXU-724 wide chord wings. GBU-15(V)3/B Derivative with CBU-75 cluster bomb unit comprising SUU-54 canister containing BLU-63 & -64 fragmentation submunitions for SAM suppression. MXU-724 wide chord wings. Not produced.	GBU-15(V)31/B TV-guided glide version, BLU-109/B 2,000lb (900kg) penetration warhead. MXU-787 short chord wings. GBU-15(V)32/B IIR-guided glide version, BLU-109/B 2,000lb (900kg) penetration warhead. MXU-787 short-chord wings. AGM-130A Derivative short-chord GBU-15(V)1/B with rocket motor. AGM-130B Derivative short-chord GBU-15(V)2/B with rocket motor. AGM-130C Derivative short-chord GBU-15(V)32/B with rocket motor.

complex it was realised that the elimination of two structures housing the valves which controlled the pipeline should cut off the flow. These small targets required extreme accuracy in stand-off bombing. Buster Glosson called the 48th TFW(P).

Five F-111Fs with GBU-15(V)-2/Bs were prepared for the strike, which was postponed for a day because of thick cloud over the target and Kuwaiti doubts about the aircrews' ability to hit such small targets close to oil storage tanks and the town of Al Ahmadi. Finally, the five 493rd TFS aircraft took off at dusk on the night of 26/27 January, shedding one of their number with a mechanical abort soon afterwards. Because the two targets were 3 miles (4.8km) apart the force had to be split into one pair of 'bombers' with the other two acting as 'guides' with the job of steering the GBU-15s to their targets, using the Hughes AN/AXQ-14 data-link pods hung beneath the rear fuselages of the Aardvarks. As the first aircraft, flown by Capt Rick Walker and Capt Ken Theurer, headed in towards the coast at 20,000ft (6,100m) and supersonic speed, its 'guide' orbited 65 miles (105km) offshore ready to 'pick up' the GBU-15 on launch and 'fly' it to the target using the small TV camera in the bomb's nose to provide steering imagery. Walker then turned away to avoid some 100mm AAA. A few seconds after picking up its signal the controller aircraft suffered a break in its data-link with the GBU-15 and transmitted the code word *Goalie* to indicate that it had lost control of the speeding, unpowered missile. Luckily, the second 'guide' F-111F (60-2390, *Miss Liberty II*), following the same offshore racetrack, picked up the signal. WSO Capt Bradley A. Seipel then made out the image of the pump-house target on his cockpit screen and steered the weapon in for a direct hit. His pilot, Capt Mike Russell, swung the Aardvark round for another run down the racetrack enabling Seipel to pick up a second bomb from the aircraft flown by Maj Sammy Samson and Capt Steve Williams (often WSO for Col Lennon). Once again, Brad Seipel 'captured' the bomb and directed it towards the other valve manifold building. Although the subsequent stoppage in the oil-flow may well have been due in part to a little surreptitious valve-closing by Kuwaiti oilfield workers during the attack, the accuracy of the F-111Fs' attack was visible to the world's media via some dramatic cockpit videotape. Some of the worldwide news bulletins correctly attributed the mission to the F-111 too.

Pave Tank

After the main strategic thrust of the air campaign, Gen Norman Schwartzkopf's plan for the war focused on 'preparing the battlefield' before committing ground troops to the liberation of Kuwait. The elimination of about half of Iraq's 5,700 main battle tanks, 5,000 AFVs and 3,700 artillery pieces was a prerequisite. By 23 January it was estimated that less than 3 per cent of the elite Republican Guard's armour had been destroyed. A much faster rate of reduction was required, and the possibility of using large numbers of F-111Fs as instruments in that process was investigated in talks between Col Lennon and Gen Glosson at the beginning of February. The use of CBU-87 CEM, containing BLU-97/B anti-armour submunitions was a logical first suggestion, but it was soon realized that it might have little effect against widely spaced tanks which were 'buried' up to 10ft (3m) in sand dugouts and covered in sandbags. An extremely accurate bomb, dropped from directly above the tank was the only solution, and a speciality of the F-111F.[3]

Although *Pave Tack* could provide the exact aiming solutions needed for a 'through the hatch' tank kill, identifying the targets at night from a safe altitude was another matter. The problem had been recognized during *Desert Shield* when, in exercise *Night Camel*, F-111Fs had found great difficulty in locating US tanks hunkered down in the sand at night. However, with a slight heat differential between the tank and the surrounding terrain *Pave Tack* was able to provide an IR-generated target image on the WSO's scope. Whereas the US tanks in *Night Camel* had been cold for some time, Iraqi tank crews often kept their engines running for a while to provide some heat at night. There was also the phenomenon known as solar loading which caused a metal tank hull to lose heat absorbed from the sun at a different rate from the surrounding sand at night. On the night of 5 February Col Lennon and WSO Steve Williams led a pair of F-111Fs out of Taif to test *Pave Tack* on Iraqi armour. With an array of thermal 'white dots', each one representing a tank, soon appearing in his FLIR display screen, Williams operated his *Pave Tack* tracking handle to place the crosshairs in his VID over tank after tank, releasing his four GBU-12s from 14,000ft (4,270m) on four 'white dots'. A few minutes later the two aircraft, *Charger 07* and *08*, set off for Taif with video footage showing seven targets destroyed by their eight bombs. Each LGB was dropped vertically, an approach which the Iraqis had not expected and one which rendered all their elaborate protection useless.

Having proved the F-111/*Pave Tack* in yet another role, Lennon was able to concentrate his 48th TFW(P) firepower to support Schwarzkopf's plans. Two nights later forty GBU-12-bearing Aardvarks wrought catastrophic destruction on acres of Iraqi tank formations. They kept up the pressure with what became known as 'tank plinking' missions throughout the battlefield preparation period, with a peak night on 13/14 February when 132 tank and AFV targets were knocked out with 184 bombs. By 20 February the total of burned-out tank carcasses had risen to 1,700, with 920 attributed to the 48th TFW(P). WSOs became increasingly skilled at interpreting these small targets on their scopes, discerning 'fresh' targets from bombed-out wrecks rather more accurately than the BDA assessments by reconnaissance platforms. One crew claimed thirty-one tanks by the end of this phase of the battle. For the Iraqis it amounted to the loss of two tank battalions every night.

Deep Throat

At the end of the war the Aardvark's versatility was demonstrated in another role: as a carrier aircraft for the 4,700lb (2,130kg) GBU-28/B bunker-buster bomb. Lacking a suitable weapon to penetrate Saddam Hussein's deeply buried underground command centres the Pentagon instigated Project *Deep Throat*. Eglin AFB-based weapons development engineers were given two months from December 1990 to develop a deep penetration weapon. At the suggestion of a Lockheed engineer a suitable casing was made by reaming out sections of eight-inch howitzer barrels and filling them with 650lb (300kg) of Tritonal explosive. With a reprogrammed GBU-27 guidance kit fitted the weapon had a 14in (36cm) diameter and a length of 18.75ft (5.7m). A test at Tonopah Test Range with the first bomb showed that it could penetrate over 100ft (30m) of earth before exploding. On a rocket-powered sled at Holloman AFB, New Mexico, the second example, at terminal velocity, smashed through 25ft (7.6m) of reinforced concrete slabs, and kept going. The success of these dramatically convincing tests had already been presumed as time was so short. As the Holloman tests took place on 27 February another pair of GBU-28s was on a C-141 transport en route to Taif. In fly-off tests against the F-15E Eagle the F-111F had been judged the preferred 'dropper' aircraft. Within hours of their arrival the two weapons were strapped onto a 'jammer' bomb-loader and hung on the left pylons of F-111F 70-2391 (495th TFS Squadron Commander's aircraft) and 70-2387 of the 493rd TFS. A counterbalancing Mk 84

Capt Craig 'Quizmo' Brown

Craig Brown flew some 26 combat missions with the 494th TFS during the Gulf War. He returned to RAF Lakenheath from Taif and later completed further tours at Cannon AFB with the 524th FS, and 428th FS, before transitioning to F-15Es in North Carolina.

There were usually two waves of F-111Fs each night: the first takeoffs were just after sunset, and a second at 1.30am. A few nights crews raced with the sun! This extract was based on 'Quizmo' Brown's journal to his wife, modified by Craig for publication, which he originally penned during the height of *Desert Storm*.

Al Rose and I usually get up around 4 or 5 in the afternoon so that gives me a couple of hours to wake up, eat over at the mess tent (just like M*A*S*H) and write a quick letter home. They usually run the press conf. on CNN about then so we watch it and get pissed off. Once they open it up to questions we turn it off and try to find out what really happened during the day; did we lose anyone, Eagles get any, and so on? Then around 9 or so we get the flight together and go over to the mission planning center. You get your classified for the night there and do the mission planning. My usual job is to plot out the threats with Intel on our maps. We get the plan there that includes the tanker plan, and what kind of support, if any, we get. The EF-111 guys work there too, so even if they are booked up with other packages to support, a lot of times they will swing through our target area to give a hand. Good bunch of dudes. The Weasels help when they can, but they are spread pretty thin. We get a quick target brief from the flight lead, the rest is standard.

By 11 we are ready to step so we get our blood chit, clean out our pockets and sanitize our flight suits and walk down to life support. We get our pistols, survival vest, extra water and radios on top of the usual stuff. It's quite a load.

Waddle out to the bus and go to the jets. I usually stuff all my garbage in the cockpit while Al checks the weapons and sets the laser codes. Then he stuffs while I do the walk around. BS with the chief for a bit then it's up the ladder, jump in, start up and wait for the INS to align. Get in line to take off while they pull the bomb pins. Get airborne and joined up and head for the tankers up by the border. This is the part I hate. It takes an hour or so to get there and that's a long time on the wing at night with a fully loaded jet. Al's busy keeping the system tight so we don't talk too much. Once we get to the tankers it gets fun trying to hang on and get my gas. It's a real zoo in the tanker track! Six tankers and around 24 jets and who knows what kind of weather. It's a relief to clear the track; all that can happen then is to get shot at!

We split up off the tankers and make our timing good at the border, usually a minute behind lead. He calls AWACS and lets them know we are pressing in. I turn off all the lights, arm up and in we go! Every sense is at 150 per cent. I keep my seat all the way up so I can see over Al's head, which is down in the scope a lot. Going as fast as the jet will go with all the iron on board with my head in a swivel. Usually don't see much until the guys up front get to the target; sure sucks being in the back! Every gunner is wide awake by the time we get there. I usually let the jet fly it IP-to-target so I can concentrate outside. I drop the bombs and he guides 'em in. We joke that I row the boat and he shoots the ducks! As soon as they hit Al always says 'Let's get the f*** out of here!'...and we do.

With the bombs gone we go like a raped ape for the border.

Once we are close to Saudi we get the lights on bright, slow down and scream at AWACS so they don't stick the F-15 BARCAP on us. You always look at each other and smile REAL big once you know you're out. We laugh it up and joke for awhile, but it's over an hour back and I usually end up turning down all the cockpit lights and staring at the stars. Some nights we could see the Southern Cross. After you hear all the buds check out and you know everyone is OK, the adrenalin goes away and I want to sleep. Put it on the ground as soon as I can and taxi back with the canopies open. It's cold but the desert smells better than when I left. Park and climb out and try to stretch after 5 or 6 hours in that thing. Ride back to the MPC and I tell Intel what we saw while Al reviews the tape and they decide if we got a good hit. Lennon always hangs around the machines so we get out of there as soon as we can and go grab some breakfast. Get back to the squadron around 6 to 7 in the morning. By the time I get unwound and in bed it's 8.

'slick' was suspended under their right wings and dropped on Al Taqaddum airfield later in the mission.

Neither crew had any experience of the weapon and only two days' notice of the mission. With only some rushed preliminary performance data from the bomb manufacturers to help them Lt Col Dave White (492nd TFS Ops Officer) and WSO Capt Tom Himes planned a step-climb mission profile to a higher-than-usual drop altitude. With Lt Col Ken Combs and WSO Maj Jerry Hust in the lead aircraft (70-2391) they tanked south of the border and afterburned to gain altitude over the Al Taji airfield complex, north of Baghdad. Beneath the air base lay one of three buried command bunkers which Saddam Hussein's High Command used to oversee the war. White and Himes were delayed forty-five minutes on the ground but caught up with Lt Col Combs at the tanker, which was re-routed to meet them. They then made the first drop on Al Taji rather than their original target. Lt Col White kept the F-111 on course and speed while Tom Himes scored a direct hit on the bunker, producing a large secondary explosion and reducing the numbers of senior Iraqi military staff. The second aircraft also put its GBU-28 on target. Further *Deep Throat* missions against two other bunkers beneath Baghdad were cancelled with the ceasefire, hours after Himes' hit. His was the last F-111 mission of the war and its effect in persuading the Iraqi High Command that they had nowhere to hide seemed decisive.

Back at the 55th FS office at RAF Upper Heyford, Col Terry Simpson catches up on the paperwork and reflects on the Gulf conflict. Authors

Proven Force

While the *Statue of Liberty* Wing was making its vital contributions to the air war, a separate operation known as *Proven Force* occupied the 7440th Wing(P)'s F-111Es at Incirlik. Entering the war a day later than the Lakenheath wing because of delayed Turkish parliamentary approval for the wartime use of the base, the Upper Heyford Aardvarks joined the fight at 0150 hours on the night of 18/19 January. Four radar sites were targeted and seven out of the eight radar installations destroyed, blinding the Iraqi air defence network in the north. The F-111Es used their standard weapon, the Mk 82 AIR bomb and relied on support from 525th TFS Eagles, F-4G *Wild Weasels* from the 52nd TFW, a *Compass Call* EC-130H commjam platform and EF-111A Ravens from the 'home' wing. The following night the Kirkup weapons research facility was their target.

With the 7440th in place, the Coalition planners could add another hundred attack sorties a day to the war effort, with bomb-carrying F-16Cs by day and F-111Es at night, the latter completing 456 combat missions in all plus another 252 for the Spark'Varks. Although it was a smaller operation than the one at Taif it added greatly to the rapid erosion of Iraq's military strength. Formations of between eight and sixteen Aardvarks released up to

On 26 June 1992 the last three Ravens returned to Upper Heyford from Incirlik, ending the Detachment. One was 66-0048 Horse With No Name, **which flew missions from Incirlik throughout** Proven Force. Authors

twelve 500lb (225kg) AIRs each, usually flying straight and level at around 25,000ft (7,620m). While this did not provide the refined accuracy of a solo *Pave Tack* F-111F, or even a solo low-level F-111E attack, it was extremely effective against larger industrial and military targets.

On occasion low-level drops by smaller sections of jets were used too. Capt Greg Stevens and Maj Mike Sweeney (WSO) were given the Al Abbas dam on the Tigris River near Mosul as their target on the first night. At 300ft (90m) Stevens and his wingman headed for the dam from the west while another pair of F-111Es approached on a reciprocal course. Sweeney 'pickled' his twelve AIRs exactly on the hydro-electric power station's transformers adjacent to the dam, later receiving the DFC for his performance under heavy defensive fire. It was one of many weapons launches against electrical power generators, with devastating effects on Iraq's military infrastructure. Over the succeeding weeks airfields, command posts, nuclear and BW weapons sites were added to the target lists for the Upper Heyford crews: a very different daily diet from the routines in leafy Oxfordshire.

The size of Incirlik's Composite Wing was determined by Turkish restrictions on aircraft numbers, and the composition of its F-111 component was largely fortuitous. Col Terry Simpson, in charge of the 55th TFS element at the base, explained the complex sequence of events:

In June 1990 the 55th TFS was in the middle of a three-week WTD at Incirlik, to be followed by the 77th TFS in September. The situation began to get hot and the 55th was kept there another five or six weeks, but the question was how long we could keep people hanging about, flying training sorties. So around Thanksgiving we rotated the *Yellow* Squadron [79th TFS] out there instead. Almost the entire squadron was there when the war started. There weren't enough crews there to make the crew ratio work out the way we wanted in combat so we took four *Blue* [55th TFS] airplanes and ten crews out leaving the *Reds* [77th TFS] as the reserve unit at Upper Heyford. When war broken out most of the 79th was in place with their Squadron Commander and Ops Officer.[4] I was there with half my squadron and my Assistant Ops Officer, leaving my Ops Officer at Heyford to manage the other half. With rotations, *Blue* were in the majority by the end of the war out there. Incirlik had the first USAF Composite Wing and it worked extremely well.

Incirlik became a very busy place, and very overcrowded. Even Colonels had to share a room. There was around-the-clock flying for the whole war. We ran the night show, putting together strike packages, planning deconfliction, altitudes and timing. The entire package had between fifty and seventy aircraft, mostly from Incirlik. Usually they were all launched within thirty minutes. As soon as we crossed the border navigation lights went out. We usually hit three targets per night with four aircraft per target, using varied spacings to avoid getting predictable. The entire strike was usually over in four to five minutes. In the northern part of Iraq missions usually lasted two or two and a half hours, but if we went down as far as

(Right) **A** Desert Storm **souvenir painted on the last EF-111A to leave Upper Heyford, 67-0042** The Old Crow. Authors

The 'Hammer': a Mk 84 AIR bomb on the pylon of F-111E 68-0022. Authors

As the end of the Gulf conflict approached, the Taif bomb inscriptions lost none of their morale-boosting vitriol. US DoD

Baghdad, which we did on many occasions, it was up to four hours. We had a line of demarcation across the country which we operated with the 48th TFW: we kept to the north of it and they kept south, with little cross-over as it caused further deconfliction problems. I personally went to Baghdad on four nights. The first time I was extremely apprehensive because it meant up to two hours over enemy territory both ways. In reality it wasn't nearly as bad as the area around the city of Mosul. I preferred Baghdad; there was a lot more firepower around Mosul.

We saw very few SAMs. A few SA-7s were launched at our first strikes but they went well behind us. The *Wild Weasels* smacked a bunch of them and made them reluctant. But there was plenty of Triple-A and they never even came close to running out of ammunition. It was an amazing experience which I don't want to repeat.

Capt Greg Stevens had similar memories. 'I was basically picking dark spots at night to fly through. Everything else was lit up. Every night we said "When are they going to run out of bullets?".'

No F-111E missions encountered air-to-air threats and AIM-9s were not carried. Unlike their Taif counterparts who used the pivot-pylons' MAU-12s and carried BRUs on only one occasion, the F-111Es usually had them fitted. (Greg remembered that BRUs were decorated with some 'pretty good nose art' too, though this was removed before the trip home.) Standard loads comprised twelve Mk 82 AIRs, or CBU-87 CEM munitions. Col Simpson described one mission where eight F-111Es each carried eight CEM canisters, 'an extremely draggy weapon'. CBU-89 was also used and Mk 84s occasionally. At the end of the war the first two AMP F-111Es arrived at Incirlik and took part in the last combat mission flown by the 7440th CW. Col Simpson noted that the take-off time was 'moved forward so that we could fly it before the ceasefire. The target was billed as an industrial complex but it was more likely one of the nuclear research facilities'. F-111E 68-0050, Upper Heyford's 'working prototype' kit-proofing AMP aircraft carried a bomb silhouette for some time after the mission, which 'involved fourteen F-111Es each dropping four Mk 84s on one target – live on CNN. It would have been helpful to have had more AMP aircraft for the high-altitude bombing, which the analogue F-111E was not so good at, as the AMPs could pass on data to help with ballistics

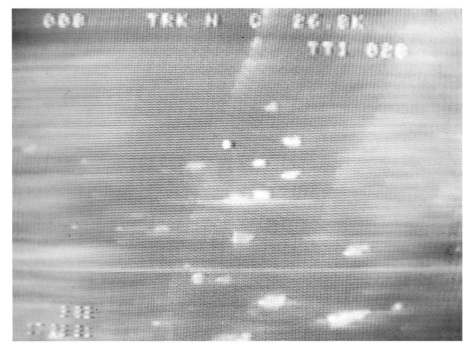

A WSO's-eye-view of an LGB attack during shelter-busting operations. US DoD

A Raven cockpit with its large central navigation panel, plus E-Scope, CRS and ARS scope above (all relocated to the centre of this model), and essential jamming-related digital Data Display Indicator and computer control plinth to right. The individual jammer controls are mounted on the right console. Northrop-Grumman

for non-AMP aircraft. We were working on that on that last mission'. Greg supported that view: 'AMP was the most accurate system for dumb-bombing. Just put the "pipper" on the target and it'll hit'.

Another last-minute initiative was a plan to use 3rd TFW F-4E Phantoms equipped with *Pave Tack* as 'buddy lasers' for the Incirlik F-111Es. The Phantoms were about to be returned to the USA for storage and they were scheduled to fly their only combat sorties with the heavy pod (known as *Pave Drag* to the fighter crews who, unlike the F-111Fs' pallet arrangement, had to carry it on a external fuselage hardpoint). Delays in delivering the pods held up preparations for the missions. Terry Simpson:

> In the last week of the war we were working up some 'buddy-lasing' procedures with the F-4Es on the Konya range [in Turkey], dropping LGBs. Usually it was two *Pave Tack* Phantoms to a four-ship of F-111Es carrying four GBU-24s each. The F-4s would fly to a stand-off position and orbit while the F-111Es did 'Toss' deliveries, with very accurate timing to coincide with the laser beam from the *Pave Tack*. We had scheduled some combat sorties with them against targets in the north of Iraq but the war ended before we could fly them.

Like Taif's F-111s, the Incirlik aircraft racked up large numbers of missions by the war's end. Interestingly, three of Lakenheath's 'top scorers' were *El Dorado Canyon* veterans too. F-111F 74-0178 displayed fifty-six bomb silhouettes on its nose, while Upper Heyford's largest scoreboard appeared on F-111E 68-0036 which returned with thirty-two blue bombs marked-up, though it probably flew more missions.

Homeward Aardvarks

With the cessation of hostilities the majority of the F-111 force returned to the UK. The 48th TFW(P) wound down in March 1991 and reverted to Lakenheath control, although it remained a token presence at Taif until May. The emphasis then shifted to northern Iraq, where the UN Operation *Provide Comfort* to protect the Kurds began on 5 April 1991. Col Tom Lennon and his WSO Capt Williams, on this occasion in *Miss Liberty I* (72-1448), led eighteen aircraft from Taif back to Lakenheath on 11 March, 1991, with another thirty aircraft returning via Sigonella in the following week. *Provide Comfort* demanded the services of the 48th TFW from 25 September, 1991, and a detachment of eleven 494th TFS Aardvarks was kept at Incirlik until October 1992 when the Detachment was switched to 27th TFW control. Upper Heyford's F-111Es returned on 9 March, led in by the 20th TFW DO, Col Ken Peck and his WSO Capt Jeff Zaletel. The base provided a Det of three EF-111As from 6 April to 14 August 1991 at Incirlik. Four Ravens were sent to support the 494th TFS deployment in September, 1991 and the Det was maintained until 26 June 1992. The 42nd ECS also supported a four aircraft Det at Dhahran International Airport until 11 January, 1992, when the job was passed to the 390th ECS.

CHAPTER NINE

Buckshots and Falcons

During the 1990s, national governments have become used to the extended and hugely expensive development cycles for new military aircraft. The Northrop-Grumman B-2A, perhaps an extreme example, had undergone fourteen years of development and six years of flight testing by 1995, yet the US Government's General Accounting Office stated that it was still only a third of the way into its flight testing by mid-1995, with serious problems still to be resolved. In the 1960s things RAAF was expecting to maintain an F-111 fleet until at least 2020. Those who sustained their faith in the concept from the outset can now take just pride in having done so. Celebrating the F-111's first twenty years with the RAAF Air Commodore David Rogers (then Commander of the Strike and Reconnaissance Group, and currently Air Vice-Marshal, Deputy Chief of the Air Staff) said that 'standing by the F-111 was one of the most prudent defence decisions ever made by our nation'.

reconnaissance capability, state-of-the-art ECM, a 1,000nm (1,850km) radius of action, Mach 2.0 at 50,000ft (15,240m), twin engines and two crew. This narrowed the field to the Dassault Mirage IV, McDonnell F-4, BAC TSR-2 and North American A-5 Vigilante. A powerful 'buy British' instinct favoured the promising TSR-2, offered with the interim provision of a couple of squadrons of V-Bombers until the new strike aircraft was ready, but uncertainty about the design's political

Flt Lt 'Tiger' Meadows flies No. 6 Sqn's F-111C A8-129 with Sqn Ldr 'Koz' Osley as Navigator on a deployment to East Sale. W/O Meadows, RAAF

generally happened more quickly and the Australian Government could hardly have anticipated that a decade would elapse between its original F-111 order and the aircraft's RAAF IOC. Equally though, no-one could have forecast that Australian 'Varks would be likely to give up to half a century of reliable service. In 1966 the Australia's order for twenty-four F-111As, placed on 24 October 1963 as the first and only foreign purchase of the Aardvark to be realized, seemed fairly straightforward at the time. The RAAF's Canberra bombers, in service since 1954, needed replacing. Air Staff Requirement 36 called for night, all-weather strike and future (justified in the end) ruled it out.

There was a certain urgency behind the Australian decision in any case. The country was in a confrontation situation with Indonesia, which had displayed open hostility towards the Malaysian Federation since its formation in 1963. Until 1966 the RAAF seemed likely to face a long-range strategic requirement which was beyond the ability of its Canberra fleet. This was probably one reason for Air Marshal Sir Valston Hancock's eight-man evaluation team's initial selection of the formidable, off-the-shelf A-5 Vigilante, which met most of ASR-36's needs. Political pressure soon altered their decision and in October 1963 the F-111 was declared the winner. Although Minister David Fairbairn had stated that 'The RAAF cannot wait for TSR-2' (in response to intense commercial pressure from the UK), he was prepared to await F-111's conversion from a 'paper aeroplane' into viable hardware. As an emollient the Americans offered to match Britain's V-Bomber offer with the free lease of two squadrons of B-47E/RB-47E Stratojets. Three of these Boeing bombers made demonstration flights from a number of Australian bases in November 1963, but the offer was declined, much to the relief of RAAF personnel, who were not impressed by the hard-to-handle swept-wing six-engined jet.

The aircraft which Defence Minister Athol Townley signed for in 1963 was the 'regular' F-111A, then only a year away from its maiden flight. A technical agreement was signed in June 1964, refining the deal to eighteen F-111As and six of the projected RF-111A variant to fulfil the RAAF's reconnaissance needs. A fortuitous sub-clause gave Australia an option on six more F-111As at the same unit price as the original twenty-four.[1] When the RAAF did at last take up exactly that offer, eighteen years later (on four ex-366th TFW F-111As) it had a real bargain.

By April 1966 GD's development F-111As were well into their test programmes and handover of the first production example for USAF service was fourteen months away. GD had begun work on modifying development F-111A No 18 (63-9783) into the first FB-111A, ready for its first flight in July, 1967. Impressed by its projected 4,150nm (7,680km) range, with six drop tanks and a 2,300lb (1,040kg) increase in gross weight, Australia adapted the F-111 contract to include the FB-111A structural modifications to their aircraft. Its 7ft (2.1m) increase in wingspan and FB-111A MLG brakes were both written in, though internally the aircraft remained pure F-111A at the time, including TF30-P-3 engines rather than the SAC model's uprated P-7s. The original F-111A intakes were retained also. At the end of 1966 this hybrid 'Vark had become known as the F-111C. Delays and cost increases, some resulting from these manufacturing changes, others from general cost escalation at source in the USA, meant delivery slipping to the second half of 1968, and overall costs rising from $124.5m to $250m by mid-1967. Rising prices were the first setback for the RAAF. When initial estimates had been given in 1963, GD projected a minimum production run of 1,500 F-111s but there were real hopes that larger numbers for the USAF and USN would drive costs down further; another attraction for the Australian selectors. They were not to know that the final production run would be only 562 new-build aircraft. Sadly, there were worse surprises to come.

Still confident that the US aerospace industry would deliver the goods on time as usual, preparations for the F-111C's arrival were made at Amberley, traditionally the RAAF's bomber base. Its main runways were planned to be extended to a standard 10,000ft (3,050m) length, technical training of RAAF personnel began in the USA and plans were made to develop Wewak airfield in Papua to make it Aardvark-capable if there was renewed tension with Indonesia. There were even moves to select a suitable Aboriginal name for the officially anonymous F-111C. Suggestions such as *Bindana* (Thunder) and

An exciting take-off by Sqn Ldr Geoff Shepherd (later OC No. 82 Wing) and Navigator Terry Delahunty at RAAF East Sale Open Day. RAAF

Bilara (Spear) were advanced, but none was adopted. Instead, an abbreviated version of the usual 'earth pig' appellation has been generally in use: to Australians the F-111 is simply 'The Pig'.

Delays and changes began to influence the entire programme. An early consequence was the loss of the RF-111A option. Despite the expenditure of $118m on developing a very successful RF-111A prototype, using F-111A No 11 (63-9776), US interest waned rapidly as overall programme costs rose, and after a series of structural problems with the F-111A in 1967–68 the USAF's plans for a wing of RF-111D variants had to be scrapped to hold down escalating costs. As early as July 1966, when an RF-111A purchase by the USAF was still in the balance, Australia was considering the return of six F-111Cs to GD for retrofitting with the RF-111A's reconnaissance equipment at a later date.

F-111C production began in 1967 against the background of an increasingly bad press in the USA. Inevitably, this was picked up in Australia too as costs rose and accidents involving the RDT&E fleet were highlighted. When the Australian Government eventually felt obliged to pass a vote of confidence in the aircraft it was prompted by ever-louder calls for cancellation from the F-111's opponents. Such was the RAAF's faith in the reputation of US aerospace products that their contract had been drawn up with little thought of the possibility of cancellation. On 4 September 1968 the first F-111C was handed over to an Australian delegation including Defence Minister Alan Fairhall. It had made a faultless first flight in July, with Fort Worth test pilot Dick Johnson. Mr Fairhall spoke of the F-111's problems having been 'met and overcome'.

Within a month Australia was faced with the prospect of a further, indefinite delay in delivery. In all, to that date, eleven F-111s had crashed, one with an RAAF Navigator aboard, including the three *Combat Lancer* aircraft (at least one with suspected tailplane failure). Even more worryingly, very soon after the handover of the first F-111C, A8-125, a static test Wing Carry-Through Box developed cracks around main bolt-holes, casting doubt upon that most vital part of the F-111's structure. Deliveries of F-111Cs were suspended as trials on the WCTB failure continued and GD sought to rectify the situation by reinforcing pivots and sections of the WCTB with boron-epoxy doubler plates. One failure had occurred in a box which had been fatigue tested to only 8,000 hours. The Australians asked for a 16,000-hour run on a reinforced box and GD responded with tests on F-111A samples to more than twice that figure, or over three times the anticipated fatigue life of the airframe. Modifications to the F-111C fleet began, which had been in storage pending provisional recommencement of deliveries in August 1969. In December of that year Defence Minister (later Prime Minister) Malcom Fraser asked for the twenty-four aircraft to be prepared for delivery once their modifications had been installed and tested. Incredibly, the fifteenth F-111 crash happened a few days later on 22 December, and in that accident a wing came off completely. For the fifth time in eighteen months the entire F-111 fleet was grounded, this time until the end of July 1970. Australia's Aardvarks, already part-disassembled, were placed in long-term storage, while USAF production bottle-necked at the factory. Wings were removed, avionics placed in a temperature controlled store and the de-engined, partially-cocooned fuselages were crammed nose-to-tail in a Carswell AFB hangar at Fort Worth. It seemed likely that they might remain there for several years.

While the Australian Government grappled with their end of the crisis, GD became involved in an FBI investigation of its sub-contractor, Selb Manufacturing Co, which supplied the wing boxes. Improprieties were revealed including a situation reminiscent of Arthur Miller's play *All My Sons*. Inspectors had been effectively bribed to pass illicit welds in the WCTBs before delivery. GD emerged unbesmirched from the legal fracas and proceeded to establish an effective testing and rectification programme, albeit at a cost exceeding $100m.

As the disappointed RAAF aircrew returned from the USA a delegation travelled the other way in May 1970, to find at least a temporary replacement for the long-suffering Canberra squadrons. At first the Australians were offered, in lieu of cancellation, the re-purchase of their unused F-111Cs, at a much-reduced price, for USAF use. There had to be a better offer. Eventually the two-year lease of twenty-four F-4E Phantoms was arranged under Project *Peace Reef*. These arrived at Amberley in Sept–Oct 1970. Although they were not able to fulfil major parts of the RAAF's requirement, the Phantoms were extremely popular and several aircrew had to be reluctantly prised from their cockpits when the time came to return the fighters in the winter of 1973. Australians caught a brief look at some F-111s in March 1971 when a Nellis-based contingent of 430th TFS *Tigers* called in to help mark the RAAF's 50th Anniversary. At the end of 1971, the Australian Defence Ministry announced that it was satisfied with the F-111C rectification work and, rather than purchasing the borrowed Phantoms, moves were made to re-assemble the F-111Cs for delivery to their owners.

Amberley, at Last

Following Defence Minister Lance Barnard's 14 March 1973 announcement that the RAAF would accept its Aardvarks, the first specimen was handed over (again) and the OC (Officer Commanding) of 82 Wing, Gp Capt Jake Newham, in tail number A8-125, led the first six aircraft to Amberley from McClellan AFB, California, via Hickam AFB, Hawaii, and Samoa (Pago-Pago to Americans), arriving on 1 June 1973. Three more *Peace Lamb* sextets arrived on 27 July, 28 September and 4 December, respectively. All had received the new F-111F WCTB and around 240 other smaller modifications resulting from the ongoing evolution of the F-111 programme. Their crews had recommenced training in January 1973, albeit with four crews less than planned owing to the new Labor Government's trimming of the defence budget, and No. 82 Wing immediately set about showing off its new acquisition. In October 1973 it staged an impressive flypast at the opening of the Sydney Opera House (another long-running Australian saga) and in April 1974 No. 6 Sqn's CO, Wg Cdr Ray Funnell commemorated the fiftieth anniversary of the first round-Australia flight. He completed the trip in two days rather than the forty-four days of the 1924 flight. Amberley's two F-111 squadrons, No. 1 (the exclusively 'front line' unit), and No. 6 (also tasked with training), quickly proved the type's suitability for their Air Force. Contrary to the cynics' predictions it established an excellent safety record: 21,000 hours had been flown when the first loss occurred on 28 April, 1977, ironically with a USAF exchange pilot at the

A full load of McDonnell Douglas AGM-84 Harpoons on an F-111C of No. 1 Sqn. RAAF Aardvarks have an important long-range anti-shipping role. RAAF

(Right) Final touches are made to an AGM-84 Harpoon missile before its test launch. RAAF

controls. In 1977 too the wing sent A8-143 to introduce UK airshow audiences to the famous 'torching' routine when it visited the RAF's Jubilee Review at Finningley. Known as 'dump and burn' down under and occasionally performed by two aircraft in line abreast ('double dump'), this popular trick involves the jettisoning of fuel into the aircraft's afterburner efflux via a large vent at the base of the tail. The vent's main function is to reduce aircraft weight quickly so as to assist with emergency recoveries, as four-fifths of the 'Vark's internal fuel capacity is held in its four (two forward, and two aft) built-in fuselage tanks, with relatively little in the sealed wings. It also has limited tactical use as a means of identifying aircraft visually to others at night and in radio silence. Although banned for a time as a pure stunt the 'instant sunshine' gimmick invariably leaves a lasting impression on the crowds.

The two squadrons were integrated into the RAAF's training and exercise plans.

Unlike their counterparts in USAFE and many parts of the USA, crews could 'fly TFR' for the majority of each sortie over Australia's sparsely populated north, using convenient, isolated industrial buildings as targets and radar offsets for realistic low-level attack profiles. 'Bare base' operations were increasingly emphasized from the mid-1980s. Established at three locations around the country's northern coastlands – Curtin, Schergar and Learmouth – these minimal airfields were intended to support quick-reaction detachments of F-111s from Amberley on the east coast, together with their airborne logistics. Their utilization as locations for forces to counter an attack from the north (the most plausible direction) was frequently tested, for example in Exercise *Western Reward*, conducted with the Republic of Singapore Air Force. Frequent exercises in support of the Five Power Defense Arrangements in Malaysia and indigenous serials such as *Pitch Black*, *Coral Sea* and *Kangaroo* have reinforced the F-111's credibility in the role for which it was bought. Multinational exercises often involve USAF squadrons from PACAF, and USN forces at the bi-annual RIMPAC exercise. A 1984 Triad took F-111Cs to RNZAF base Ohakea in New Zealand for simulated combat involving USAF F-15C and F-16C users together with RNZAF Skyhawks and Strikemasters. The RAAF also participated in *Giant Voice* (the SAC Bomb Comp) in 1980, 1982 and 1984, operating out of Mountain Home AFB. *Cope Thunder*, the PACAF exercise which was held seven times a year at Clark AB in the Philippines, often involved RAAF F-111Cs attacking targets in the Crow Valley range area near Clark. RAAF aircrews gained excellent experience against sophisticated AAA/SAM simulations while the training area was still available to them. In another typical excursion ADEX 90-2 took four of No 6 Sqn's aircraft to Butterworth as *Orange* (hostile) forces and they proved to be very elusive targets for the defending RAF Tornado F3s. Nellis AFB *Red Flag* sessions have included Aussie Aardvarks on several occasions, the first being in 1980 on the heels of competing in SAC's *Giant Voice* bombing competition. Quite a schedule.

In all these deployments the F-111's range was always a huge asset. This was demonstrated in 1990 when A8-142 and A8-144 flew from Goose Bay to RAF Upper Heyford, without inflight refuelling, on the last leg of a six-day flight from Amberley. On arrival they still had one and a half hours' fuel aboard. The entire trip was completed with only one minor problem: a faulty VHF radio. The next day the pair hopped over to RAF Boscombe Down and flew two range sorties daily during their brief stay, also making International Air Tattoo 90 Airshow appearances in which Sqn Ldrs Mark Skidmore and Terry Delahunty 'dumped and burned' for the crowds.

When inflight refuelling is needed 82 Wing has to rely on USAF boom-type refuellers. Plans to buy two ex-Qantas Boeing 707-320s and convert them to 'boomers' were considered in the early 1980s and then dropped in 1988. Instead, four Boeing 707s were converted to a probe and drogue refuelling for the RAAF's F/A-18 force. The requirement for F-111-compatible tankers still stands owing to a reduced USAF tanker presence in the region and it is possible that it will still be met in view of the Aardvark's regularly extended future in RAAF service.

Pave Attackers

Pave Tack was one of the main components in a progressive update programme for the F-111C. Under Project Air 65, in July 1980 the RAAF decided to purchase the Ford Aerospace AN/AVQ-26 FLIR/laser acquisition/designation pod as soon as it became practicable. F-111C A8-138 was flown to Fort Worth in December 1983 for conversion and testing. Subsequent modifications were performed by No. 3 Aircraft Depot (3AD) at Amberley, which handled all deep maintenance and engine refurbishment for the fleet.[2] Their first '*Tack*-toting aircraft was rolled out in September 1986. In all, fifteen *Pave Tack* pods have been purchased so far, shared between the F-111C fleet, although the withdrawal of USAF F-111Fs in 1996 may provide a source for additional units.[3] (On some deployment missions, some aircraft are fitted with a big white cylindrical spares and luggage container.) Aircraft modifications included an interface to mate the digital AVQ-26 with the F-111C's analogue avionics, and replacement of the Navigator's (Australian for WSO) attack radar panel with a pair of CRTs for radar and FLIR imagery,

RF-111C cockpit with the ARS hood jutting from the main instrument panel. At top left are the E-Scope, CRS display and the square optical TV video display, and on the right instrument panel can be found the recon controls and large 'organ stops' and knobs associated with the analogue 'A/C Aardvark's WCP. RAAF

including a digital scan converter to 'clean up' the attack radar picture. The *Pave Tack* hand controller and switches were installed, as in the F-111F. Finally, revisions to the stores management system enlarged the potential range of underwing munitions, including AIM-9 Sidewinder, the GBU-10/12 Paveway II LGB. Full GBU-15 'smart' bomb and allied data-link pod capability, including controls, was included, but so far the RAAF have not received any such weapons.[4]

Anti-shipping defence has always been a primary role for Australia's F-111s. Modern naval self-defence techniques have made stand-off, sea-skimming weapons increasingly necessary for this challenging mission and the McDonnell-Douglas AGM-84A Harpoon was the RAAF's choice. Its over-the-horizon, programmable inertial guidance system gives the launch aircraft comparative immunity and a very high chance of hitting its target. The RAAF sent its 'tame' Aardvark, A8-132, to the US Naval Weapons Center at China Lake in 1982 for trials. The F-111C fleet was subsequently adapted to carry up to four Harpoons per aircraft. In view of the stellar cost of each missile, live firings are extremely rare in training and only a few had been 'shot' by the mid-1990s. However, as a Royal Navy Sea Harrier pilot told the authors, firing the very similar Sea Eagle is 'largely a "non-event" from the pilot's point of view, and can now be simulated effectively for instructional purposes'. From time to time one is simply taken out of its storage boxes and fired to verify reliability. Long-range detection of suitable maritime targets would be provided by the P-3C Orions of No. 92 Wing, which can also carry Harpoons. RAAF F-111s are unique among 'Varks with their Harpoon capability.[5] A radar-homing missile capability would also be welcomed. These might be used to knock out radar defences to render them 'blind' to a 'smart' or 'dumb' bomb attack.

New for Old

As the F-111 force faced its third decade of duty 'down under' the question of replacement by a more modern type, or major upgrading, had to be faced. The prospect of replacing the F-111 capability with additional F/A-18s was considered in the late 1980s as a substitute, but soon rejected. The 'Pig' still had much more to offer in several roles than the excellent, but far shorter-legged Hornet. However, retention of the ground-hugging 'swinger' meant replacement of the aircraft's early 1960s-vintage avionics. It was a major commitment which could not be undertaken on a piecemeal basis, a situation summed-up with inimitable Antipodean directness by one RAAF Officer as a case of 'crap, or get off the pot!'. The high costs involved could be justified partly because all the aircraft still had more than half their airframe fatigue lives left to run. As part of the fatigue-management process RAAF F-111s have been put through the McClellan AFB Cold Proof Load Testing facility – where USAF examples were routinely subjected to torture – at regular intervals (approximating to every 2,000 flight hours), starting in 1981. Two wing-pivot fittings failed under the demanding, sub-zero stress tests. At the same time desealing and resealing of internal fuel tanks was carried out. Back at Amberley the big concern was the increasing maintenance loads imposed by ageing electronics, which also seemed slow and cumbersome for the pilots to operate when compared with the slick systems in aircraft like the F/A-18. The RAAF was having to live with MTBF figures of around 3.5 hours for F-111 systems and wanted to increase these to something around the 20 hours MTBF offered by the Hornet.[6]

Early in 1989 the Department of Defence put out Requests for Tender on contracts totalling more than the original cost of the F-111C fleet. Its avionics upgrade programme (AUP) sought to improve upon the USAF's AMP and later

A8-142 with its 'Supersonic Kookaburra' fin design, which marked No. 1 Sqn's 75th Anniversary. It was instigated by the squadron commander, Wg Cdr Peter Criss in time for a visit to TVS 90 at Boscombe Down, England. Authors

Acquisition of the AN/AVQ-26 Pave Tack unit greatly increased the capability of the RAAF's F-111C fleet. On this No. 1 Sqn example the pod's turret is in the 'Forward Acquire' position caged with the pilot's gunsight, although the aircraft's SUU-20 practice bomb container has released its load. RAAF

Although trials with the AGM-88 HARM missile were conducted by a No. 1 Sqn F-111C in the USA, the purchase of a weapon in this category was deferred to the turn of the century. RAAF

aborted *Pacer Strike* efforts. The main thrust of AUP, under a fixed-price contract with Rockwell Autonetics of California, was effectively to gut the aircraft of some 80 per cent of its analogue machinery and install modified or brand new digital avionics systems, centred on the ubiquitous MIL STD 1553B digital databus. Separate contracts totalling $A68m went out to Texas Instruments for a series of kits to modernize the TFR system, upgrading it from the APQ-110 to -171B standard, and to the Ocean, Radar & Sensor Systems Division of Martin Marietta (formerly General Electric) for improvements to the attack radar which equated to the APQ-169 variant. A Honeywell H-423 ring-laser gyro INS, a GPS receiver and new SMS (Stores Management System) similar to the Hornet's were also included. Sqn Ldr John Kearney, resident avionics engineer in the RAAF Project Office at Rockwell Autonetic's Palmdale facility in California, oversaw the development phase and that specifications were adhered to. Central to the revised fit was a 256K weapons computer, far more powerful than the item used in the US AMP effort. The instrumented A8-132 reported to the USA once again as the AUP test and kit-proofing aircraft. This time, '132, ferried by Wg Cdr G. Fitzgerald and Flt Lt N. Meadows, had an attractive overall light grey paint job in place of its usual white undersides and camouflaged upper surfaces. Serving two purposes, the colour scheme provided a better backdrop for photo coverage of weapons separation trials and also tested a fashionably neutral 'maritime strike' finish.

Ground-testing of the new avionics suite began in February 1994 and Flt Lt Cam Morris flew A8-132 once again from Palmdale on 2 December, delayed only by problems with its flight test data recorders. In an adjoining area of Palmdale was another revitalized and irreplaceable classic, the SR-71A, being prepared for its return to service the following year. After intensive three-stage tests culminating in live weapons drops, A8-132 returned to Amberley where companies in the AUP consortium were putting the rest of the fleet through avionics renewal work. Hawker de Havilland (Victoria), the principal subcontractor, along with Honeywell Defence Avionics Systems, and C3 Pty Ltd (a software supplier) were charged with providing new cockpit displays, revised communications and flight control systems as well as installing the updated radar hardware in the remaining twenty-one F-111Cs, which they will deliver through 1998. To complete the package a Harris Govt Systems ATE (Automatic Test Equipment) diagnostic testbed for avionics, plus new support and training equipment were added in. Replacement of Amberley's rather decrepit 1968-vintage GP4B-driven simulator with something more appropriate to the F-111's new and extremely advanced capability was solved when the USAF's 48th FW returned its F-111Fs to the USA. The Lakenheath simulator became available and the RAAF gladly purchased it, then contracted with Wormald (Aust) to modify it to AUP standards until the latest visual systems also can be incorporated.[7]

Other structural modifications have been locally managed by 3AD and Amberley's No. 482 (Maintenance) Squadron, now part of 501 Wing. F-111Cs A8-125 and -126 received laminated ADBIRT windshields to improve resistance to birdstrikes back in 1975, although the other aircraft were not 'birdproofed' until late in 1978. By that time A8-133 and its crew had been lost after three large birds hit the windshield, one of them entering the cockpit. Local remedies were also found for cracked nosewheel assemblies and cracks in the wing-pivot area have been further inhibited by boron-epoxy patches These were developed by Aeronautical Research Labs in Melbourne and fitted to the upper side of the wing pivot fitting. In addition locally produced weapons such as the Karinga CBU have also been produced, adding to the arsenal of the 'Pig'.

Old for New

Another factor in the 'retire or refurbish' debate over the F-111C was the availability of additional ex-USAF F-111s. The RAAF's 1964 option on up to six more new-build F-111As, at 1964 prices, was finally taken up in 1982 when four ex-366th TFW F-111As were ordered as attrition replacements. All were delivered by August 1982, and 3AD proceeded to give them the full Aussie treatment by installing FB-111A-type undercarriages and extended wings, though the original WCTB was retained, a tribute to its basic soundness of design. Since then other updates, including *Pave Tack* cradles and interfaces, have rendered them virtually the same as 82 Wing's other Aardvarks. As at least one RAAF aviator noted, 'The F-111As are now [known as] F-111C and are operated exactly the same as the other F-111Cs.'

When the decision was made in 1992 to extend the 'Vark's unequivocal vitality well into the 21st century the question of long-term attrition replacements became more urgent. Fort Worth's new-build production line had been closed for sixteen years and it seemed that the stockpile of F-111As at AMARC was the obvious best source again. However, late in 1992 the 27th FW at Cannon began to replace its F-111G squadron with ex-20th FW AMP'ed F-111Es for training purposes. The thirty G-models became AMARC candidates too, but were also entirely suitable for RAAF needs. Basically an post-SAC FB-111A gutted of its dedicated nuclear equipment, Astrocompass and AFSATCOM link and modified for tactical weapons employment as a spin-off from AMP, the F-111G was close to F-111C AUP specifications, though not quite as advanced. As the only potential customer for these boneyard-bound birds, Australia was in a good negotiating position and in October 1992 Defence Minister Robert Ray announced the purchase of up to eighteen F-111Gs, later reduced to fifteen plus a dozen spare TF30 engines and numerous other spares, for a mere $110m.[8] The Australian Government outlined to its regional neighbours (in case they were concerned) that the 'Golf' additions were for storage as attrition stock and spares sources. The first pair arrived at Amberley on 28 September 1993 (recoded A8-265 and -270) and had No 6 Sqn's markings applied in 'low viz' on the Gunship Gray paintwork two weeks later. In fact, only one F-111G came from AMARC (68-0272); the rest were straight from use at Cannon AFB.

With the extra aircraft, the fleet will be rotated in and out of storage to spread out hours, enabling 82 Strike Wing to continue operating a two-dozen aircraft force until 2020, if required. As Wg Cdr Frank Atkins, OC No 6 Sqn and himself one of the ferry pilots noted, 'There are no plans to increase the current F-111 operational capability or form an additional squadron. The current flying hours allocation will remain unchanged.' As for commonality, 'Because these avionics are a slightly earlier version of those currently being installed in the RAAF's F-111Cs, the two aircraft will have a great deal in common.

Top Crew award winners at the USAF's RAM 88 reconnaissance competition held at Bergstrom AFB, Texas, were Australians: Sqn Ldr Kym Osley (left) and Flt Lt Mike Sinclair, flying their RF-111C.
RAAF

Because they were made at similar times, they also share a common wing set, undercarriage, and the majority of airframe parts'. All that really differs are the Triple Plow Two inlets of the 'G', and its 'dash 107' engines, offering approximately 11 per cent more power and slightly increased range. Although there are no plans to equip the 'G's with *Pave Tack*, its digital SMS can handle all the weapons in the RAAF inventory and it is a superb radar-aimed ballistic weapons bomber.[9]

'Varks with Vision

While most F-111s sniff their way along low-level routes with TFR there is one unique quartet of 'Pigs' which are far from being 'short-sighted'. In fact, Australia's four RF-111Cs are still among the world's most effective reconnaissance platforms. The untimely termination in 1969 of the RF-111A/D programme (which would also have included an RF-111B for the USN) left Australia with continued faith in the concept but no apparent means of attaining it. Once the F-111C had proved itself in RAAF service the Government approached GD once again in December 1974, paying $280,000 for a project study for converting four aircraft to a 'recon' configuration. A GD/RAAF team headed by J.R. Goodman (including Wg Cdr Errol McCormack of the RAAF) defined a package similar in concept to the RF-111A's, but with the SLAR (Sideways-Looking Airborne Radar) package deleted, and incorporating systems then in vogue on the RF-4 Phantom. This embraced a Fairchild KA-56E low-altitude panoramic, plus CAI Recon-Optical KA-93A4 high-altitude panoramic and KS-87C split-vertical framing cameras to furnish stereo images, plus a Honeywell AAD-5 variable-swath infrared linescanner, all neatly installed on a pallet designed to fit in the space previously occupied by the M61A-1 gun, hinged on the starboard side so that the whole assembly could be swung down to facilitate access to the cameras and linescanner. The inboard port component of the weapons bay door was retained and was simply modified with a window for the rear-mounted framing camera. At a distance, the only external evidence of the 'recon' fit was a boat-shaped protrusion faintly resembling the old 'Gatling gun' fairing, but housing windows for the two 'pan' cameras. Additional modifications included a zoom-capable TV viewfinder to help the crew line-up for the recce run at high altitudes, allied AVTR (Airborne Video Tape Recorder), plus related cockpit TV display centrally located on the forward instrument panel, and reconnaissance controls located just ahead of the right-hand Weapons Control Panel. The film was also to be annotated by a Data Display Set which imprints a host of aircraft variables (altitude, attitude, coordinates, heading and time) fed to it by the aircraft's Central Air Data Computer, to ease with post-mission interpretation of the imagery.

Full Governmental approval for the project was granted in July 1977 and A8-126 flew to Texas in October 1978 for the modifications. Flight testing began at Fort Worth on 18 April 1979, undertaken by Sqn Ldr Jack Lynch (Pilot) and Flt Lt Marty Chalk (Nav) under the watchful guidance of Sqn Ldr Kevin Leo (Project Manager) and Flt Lt Andy Kemble (Project Engineer). Trials then proceeded to RAAF Darwin in Northern Territory for a two-month wringing-out of systems through to the following December. Flight-tests of the all-up system showed the RF-111C to be an extremely stable, fast and long-ranging recce platform with a 1,000nm (1,850km) radius of action, with some 400nm (740km) of it at low-level, for a sortie duration of up to five hours (later ably demonstrated to an international audience during Exercise *Pitch Black 87*). Both 3AD and No. 482 Sqn undertook

RF-111C Reconnaissance Systems

RF-111C reconnaissance systems installed on the pallet. The two vertical CAI KS-87C framing cameras generate 4.5 × 4.5in (11.4 × 11.4cm) frames, offering split-vertical stereo images between them which provide a pseudo 3-D effect to ease with target interpretation after film processing. Different lenses are fitted to suit different altitude/area coverage requirements, varying from 3in (7.6cm) to 12in (30cm) in focal length (generating angular optic coverage ranging between approx 73 degrees and 21 degrees respectively). The Fairchild KA-56E low-altitude panoramic camera generates images each measuring 4.5 × 9.4in (11.4cm × 24cm), and is equipped with a 3in (7.6cm) lens (offering 73 × 180 degree angular optical coverage). The F-111's exceptional 'glassy smooth handling' massively aids with sharp focusing over the preplanned target area, and a specific SCP would be used for the required area coverage. Standoff oblique photography is effected by banking the wings, and simultaneous multiple sensor operation would normally be employed.

The high-altitude KA-93A4 features an 18in (46cm) lens, offering 14 degree angular coverage. A high altitude radar altimeter is used with this as LARA is effective only up to 5,000ft (1,530m) AGL. To assist with line-up for the photo pass during daytime high-altitude reconnaissance, the pallet features a selectable forwards or downwards-looking electro-optic TV viewfinder which can be zoomed in and out, the imagery from which is displayed instantaneously in the cockpit and recorded on the Airborne Video Tape Recorder (AVTR). An additional daytime sensor comprises the KB-18A nose-mounted strike camera, which generates fore-and-aft panoramic images (looking 40 degrees across and 180 degrees along the aircraft's track) on 70mm film, taking frames at intervals of up to 20 sec. This produces frames measuring 2.25 × 9.4in (5.7 × 21cm). As with the chief photo sensors employed on the RF-111C, black and white film is the primary medium because of its superior resolution and reliability in processing, this being available in a number of ISO speeds (40 to 200), though the RF-111C is equally equipped to employ colour film.

Round-the-clock film-based intelligence is collected by the variable-swath AN/AAD-5 infra-red linescanner (which peeps out from behind a shutter in the front centre of the pallet), covering a 60 degree or 120 degree field-of-view. It is especially effective at night, offering thermal 'see-through' images which can help ascertain enemy mission-readiness by distinguishing operational items from decoys or inactive hardware, and can create medium-quality imagery by day too. It is only poor around sunrise and sunset when low solar grazing angles degrade the imagery, and mission-planning would factor this in. IRLS is supplemented by the RF-111C's AN/APQ-113 (or post-AUP APQ-169B) ARS which produces radar PPI ground maps at selectable range sectors varying from 5nm (9km) out to 160nm (296km), from which 35mm Radarscope Photography monochrome snapshots can be garnered. These are taken automatically at preselected intervals of between 1 and 24 seconds or on weapons release, or manually on command, all annotated with a data slate, clock and code lamps (indicating radar range).

Initially assigned to No 6. Sqn, in 1996 the aircraft were reassigned to the No. 1 'Analogue Aardvark' Sqn pending AUP updating.

RAAF RF-111C recce bay.

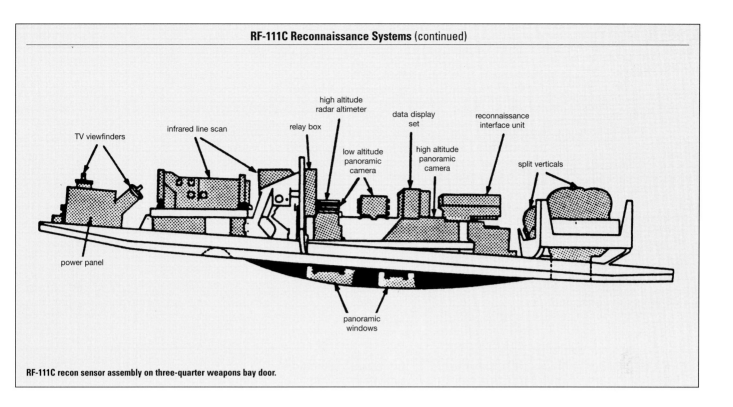

RF-111C recon sensor assembly on three-quarter weapons bay door.

RF-111C A8-146 put in an appearance at RNAS Yeovilton for the 50th Anniversary D-Day flypast in June 1994. Panoramic camera ports can be seen protruding just below the drop tank. The immaculate finish of the RAAF aircraft is always impressive. Authors

conversion of the remaining three 'Photo Pigs' earmarked for the project (A8-134, -143 and -146) using kits supplied by Fort Worth during 1980, with all four aircraft subsequently being issued to No. 6 Sqn. With them came a Hercules-transportable Processing and Interpretation Cabin to handle the mostly film-based intelligence product. All four machines later received the same ongoing updates as the remainder of the fleet, and retained their full offensive capability except for Harpoon.[10]

No. 82 Wing's RF-111Cs are among the hardest-working Aardvarks and they have proved their worth repeatedly. No. 6 Sqn, only 199 points behind the RF-4C Phantoms of USAFE's 26th TRW and the 152nd TRG's *High Rollers*, based on sorties conducted at all hours. However, night sorted out the men from the boys and the Aussie team took the Best Night Team award, including achieving a previously unheard of 'perfect' score on one mission. Flt Lts Mike Sinclair and Kym 'Koz' Osley won the prize for Top Crew overall, against stiff competition from thirty-one other crews from the USAF, USN, USMC, ANG and Luftwaffe. RF-111Cs also appear regularly at RIMPAC and Five Power Defence Agreement exercises in reliability alongside its ever-increasing operational skills, the 'Pig' has long been an essential component in the Australian defence scenario. Longer-term plans include a new electronic warfare suite with MAWS (Missile Approach Warning System) features to detect laser-guided and heat-seeking missiles, with further studies underway designed to provide the recce component with data-linked sensors. The 'Vark's beefy airframe, capacious bay and still hot performance make it almost infinitely adaptable to a host of as-yet unenvisaged tasks too. As Air Vice Marshal David Rogers, who has flown the 'Pig' for

The latest Aussie Aardvark. An F-111G blends with the Snowy Mountains, south of Canberra. In its 'former life' with SAC it was Missouri Miss **with the 380th BW(M).** RAAF

callsign *Falcon*, was particularly pleased with its scores at the USAF's 1988 Reconnaissance Air Meet, RAM-88, held at Bergstrom AFB in the days when the USAF still possessed a considerable tactical reconnaissance capability. The sixty-man RF-111C team, led by Sqn Ldr Noel Furber won 17,457 out of 20,000 points, Malaysia and Singapore airspace. As a do-it-all striker possessing a strategic reconnaissance capability and prodigious range, the RF-111C has for a long time been considered one of Australia's most potent defence assets.

Freed of its 'hot and heavy' analogue avionics and demonstrating considerable over 25 years, summed up, 'The F-111 has defied its critics, proved exceptionally capable in combat… and delighted those who fly it'. The Australians have decided on several occasions that it is literally irreplaceable – a point which has all too sadly been lost upon defence planners in the northern latitudes!

CHAPTER TEN

Last of the Red-hot Porcines

F-111E 67-0120 The Chief **at the height of its powers in 1988 with all of Upper Heyford's four squadrons represented in its fin-cap colours. A sixties-style 20th TFW fin-flash was added in 1992 and remained in place for its delivery to Duxford.** Authors

While the *Desert Storm/Proven Force* F-111s were returning to the UK in the Spring of 1991, plans were already in train to withdraw them to the USA. The rapid thawing of the Cold War and a reluctance to devote dollars to profound Aardvark update programmes made the type vulnerable to the budget trimmers. In the meantime, training resumed at the two USAFE bases. AMP'ed F-111Es were gradually returned to the squadrons from PDM at Filton, most going to the 77th FS.[1] Avionics reliability and nav-attack accuracy improved dramatically. At Lakenheath the experience of *Desert Storm* put 'tank plinking' on the syllabus and increased the emphasis on medium-altitude attacks. For a time it was thought that F-111 numbers would actually increase when the DoD announced the transfer of a squadron of F-111Gs to the UK (probably to Upper Heyford). This proved to be a bargaining chip in the disarmament dialogue and was not implemented.

The 48th FW's F-111F's were poised for another swipe at Saddam Hussein in September 1991, when twelve aircraft with four EF-111As were deployed to Incirlik in response to the Iraqi detention of a UN arms inspection team. Two months after this, Upper Heyford's birds made a final appearance at the Nellis *Gunsmoke* Meet, while in February, 1991, Lakenheath prepared for a new era with the arrival of its first F-15E Strike Eagle. Simultaneously, the F-111Fs began to return to the USA, the 495th FS having already ceased operations on 15 December 1991. The first eight F-111Fs made their way to Cannon AFB on 15 February that year. *Red Flag* and *Green Flag* exercises saw participation by Upper Heyford jets in 1992 while Lakenheath hosted the 27th FW's last F-111D deployment in June, and the Incirlik *Provide Comfort* detachment was passed to the Cannon wing in October.

The slow return of Lakenheath aircraft was paced by the delivery of factory-fresh Eagles to replace them in the two F-15E squadrons, but by 20 April 1992 the 492 FS had ceased F-111F operations and was well into Eagle conversion. The 494th followed shortly afterwards and Aardvark flying ended altogether with the inactivation of the 493rd FS on 14 December.

At Upper Heyford the Ravens were first to go, passing to 366th FW control by July 1992 and enabling the 430th ECS to activate at Cannon in August. On 23 April 1993, the 79th FS *Tigers* disestablished at a ceremony attended by many former squadron personalities including Brad Insley.[2] Two aircraft, including the squadron bird, 68-0079, had previously visited the Czech MiG-29 *Tiger* Squadron to hand over their stuffed tiger mascot. In June 1993, the 77th FS used its AMP aircraft to good effect by winning *Excalibur IX* (which also included 27th FW F-111Fs) but its 'reward', a visit to *Red Flag*, was never received because it inactivated on 9 July. Last to go was the 55th FS whose final activity was the deployment of six aircraft to Incirlik for *Dynamic Guard 93* in September–October. At that point Upper Heyford was already a bleak and empty space. Col Terry Simpson took the authors around the acres of silent bomb-hauling 'jammers', vehicles, starter units and all the paraphernalia of a major USAF combat unit, awaiting transport to the USA. The 55th FS disbanded on 15 October (the same day as the RAF's No. 55 Sqn); but with a flourish. On a breezy but bright 7 December 1993 Heyford's last three Aardvarks waddled out to the runway.[3] Most of the F-111Es went for cocooning at AMARC adding to the 148 present by May 1993. The few AMP models replaced the F-111Gs of the 428th FS *Buccaneers* at Cannon AFB.[4]

At Cannon AFB, conversion to the F-111F began in February 1992, beginning with the 522nd FS, followed by the 524th FS during September and 523rd FS in December, their F-111D complement having been 'AMARC'ed' by then. Techniques refined at Lakenheath were carried over to the more pleasant climate of New Mexico. Frank Rossi described the routine:

> Standard crew showtime was four hours prior to takeoff. Usually the Flight Lead would have done some advanced planning and he would explain the sortie flow and distribute flight planning duties. These would include checking the weather and NOTAMs, planning simulated target attacks from medium and/or low altitude and arranging range attacks and bombing events. For *Pave Tack* missions this planning could become quite involved because of all the factors to consider: sun angle, cloud heights, visibility, winds, infrared detection ranges, simulated threats, etc. Flight briefings would start 2.5 hours before takeoff with crews stepping [to the jets] 1.25 hours prior to takeoff. A typical profile might include takeoff followed by a simulated medium altitude (above 10,000ft/ 3,050m) GBU-10 attack against a building in a city. Then, low altitude navigation with simulated threat reactions to a simulated GBU-24 low-level mini-loft (5 degree) attack against a bridge or building, ending with range work at Melrose. Against cities and other structures we would practise Realistic Target Training (RTT), with all normal release cues and symbology but not actual bomb release – people might get mad if we started bombing their ranches. On the range we would take three or more events; for example radar (level), LGB 30 degree 'loft' and LADD, practising each two or more times. Since everyone was familiar with the range presentations, both visual and radar, rangework was done repetitively to build habit patterns. RTTs were designed to test our first-run attack capability against targets with which we were not so familiar, as in combat.

As Air Combat Command's 'Go-To Wing' the 27th FW worked towards deployments such as NATO's *Salty Hammer/Central Enterprise* exercises each summer, with

Capt Frank Rossi, Desert Storm **veteran and delivery pilot for** The Chief, **seen with his 27th TFW F-111F. It was a delightful opportunity to review the hardware on their penultimate UK deployment, and crowds of enthusiasts gathered around the aircraft to talk to the crews.** Authors

Red/Green Flag at Nellis and occasional *Maple Flags*. It also participated in US Navy exercises off the east coast of the USA called *Joint Task Force*. Within the wing the 522nd FS was the specialist GBU-15 unit, and added the AGM-130 rocket-powered version to its repertoire.

Defence cuts and base closures accelerated in 1994–95. Despite proven cost-savings in maintenance and operations from the AMP and *Pacer Strike* updates these programmes were delayed to the point where only partial implementation was possible. The USAF was already aware of the need to have the dominant voice in defining the crucial Joint Strike Fighter (JSF) which was intended to replace virtually all its existing fighter and attack types. Removing the F-111 from the scene was an easy way of creating a 'requirement'. Its age and misrepresented past meant that few political voices would be raised in its defence when new, work-creating programmes could be generated instead.

The 27th FW's last potentially hostile 'Go-To' operation was Operation *Vigilant* in November 1994, when eighteen F-111Fs were put on standby to counter renewed Iraqi threats to Kuwait. A year later the 428th FS inactivated and F-111F retirement also began. On 11 January 1996 the last three 522nd FS aircraft flew to AMARC, giving way to the F-16C. Shortly before its conversion the 523rd FS made a final visit to the UK.

LAST OF THE RED-HOT PORCINES

Another former 20th TFW Commander's aircraft, 68-0020 basks in the heat of Hill AFB's Museum. It was marked The Chief for its departure from RAF Upper Heyford, having previously carried that name in the absence of 67-0120. Frank Markut

With 'con' beginning to form over its wing-gloves a 48th TFW F-111F reacquaints itself with the Lake District at close quarters, prior to its relocation to **Cannon AFB**. Adrian Walker via Craig Brown

Last Swing of the Hammer

At Cannon the 27th FW maintained a forward deployment capability rather as the 49th TFW had done for *Reforger* exercises to beef up NATO in crises. For the June 1995 NATO *Salty Hammer/Central Enterprise* exercise it was decided to send eight 523rd FS F-111Fs to 'bare base' facilities at RAF Fairford (Lakenheath's runway was under repair). Although it was a shadow of the mass F-111 launches seen in previous *Hammer* exercises the *Crusaders* package took part in strike sorties and acted as threat simulation for missions over the UK, Denmark and Germany. Ten aircraft launched from Cannon with RAAF exchangee Flt Lt Paul Wilmott aboard one. Capt Frank Rossi, in a 'air spare' found himself on the deployment when a mainforce Aardvark's nosewheel steering failed. He had to make the 9.5 hour trip with no food aboard, unlike Keith Gibson whose wife had 'stacked his cockpit with so many home-baked items that they could have survived an Atlantic ditching and rowed their capsule to the UK'. On one of the first sorties 70-2414 blew its left engine and diverted to Leuchars with some severed air lines and, 'half the blades from the rear end of the P-100 engine missing and afterburner spray-bars wedged into its exhaust rings'. It flew again four days later.

When the dark grey aircraft lifted off from Fairford's runway on 26 June they signed off the F-111 attack variant's quarter-century of commitment to NATO. Most were already scheduled for the 'boneyard'. There was an Air Force rumour that the crews would be dehydrated and stored with their aircraft until such time as the politicians realised their mistake and reinstated the F-111 force.

The 'Last Hurrah'

On 27 July 1996 the USAF officially named the F-111 during retirement ceremonies held at the Lockheed Martin Tactical Aircraft Systems facility (formerly General Dynamics Fort Worth), the F-111's birthplace. On hand for the weekend-long bash were over 1,000 people who had designed, built, supported or flown F-111s, including veterans of Vietnam, Libya and Gulf combat and their families. Hosting the 'Last Hurrah' was Col Michael J. Koerner, 27th FW Commander. Before formally announcing the retirement of the aircraft, Maj Gen Lee A. Downer, former 20th TFW CO and Director of Operations at HQ ACC, officially named the aircraft the 'Aardvark'. 'From this day forward it will always be the Aardvark', he proclaimed, inviting the audience to point skywards as the name rang out.

Everyone was delighted with the shindig, though a few voiced reservations about the name. As one crewmen told the authors, 'I would have preferred a more sinister name like *Switchblade* or *Whispering Death*. One just doesn't go to war on a ship named "Lollipop" or in an airplane called Earth Pig. I can call it whatever I wish because I flew it'. It had been in operational service for twenty-nine years with no official name and according to Lee Downer's researches it was the only USAF aircraft to go through its entire service life in that state. In many ways the naming was a symbolic shedding of the 'bastard child' image.

The 'Last Hurrah' was both a joyful and sad reunion for many and a chance to reflect on their youth and the years they had spent dodging the terrain, flak and SAMs, and on lost comrades. In valedictory speeches, commanders emphasized that it was the people, and not the machine which had been crucial to its operational success. The aircraft was simply a tool, but one which would certainly be missed. Conceived by politicians with the aim of eliminating waste through 'commonality', a different generation of politicians and planners did just that by ordering their premature retirement. Most F-111s were barely half-way through their fatigue lives. On a more positive note, LMTAS President Dain Hancock's speech reminded people that the F-111 was the forerunner of today's advanced aircraft programmes: 'This aircraft taught us a lot about integrating sophisticated systems to work as one system. All of these lessons have served us well in the F-16 and F-22 programs, and will surely find an application in the next-generation Joint Strike Fighter program that we are now pursuing.'[5] In many respects, JSF represents exactly what Robert McNamara envisaged back in the early 1960s. By means of modern microelectronics and powerplant technology it may finally be possible to produce 'common' aircraft for different service needs and mission roles.

On Monday 29 July, the last of the 'swing-wing attackers' flew off, bound for

On new 'turf', ex-Lakenheath F-111Fs took on the 27th TFW's markings and its Gunship Gray colour scheme, as contrasted between 71-0890 and its wingmate, both from the 522nd FS Fireballs. Craig Brown

the 'boneyard' in Arizona, marking the end of USAF 'attack' F-111 operations. The 524th FS *Hounds of Heaven* F-111F 74-0187 was one of four 'Foxtrots' present. It bore the sentimental, beautifully airbrushed 'Farewell' nose art bearing the codes or number designations of most of the Aardvark's former operators, the Statue of Liberty and three campaign sashes to represent its combat exploits in S.E. Asia, North Africa and the Persian Gulf. On departure the quartet, led out by Cannon's Vice-Commander Col Gale W. Larson, bore call-signs previously used by three F-111As which were lost in Vietnam, and '187 the F-111F which crashed during *Desert Shield*, mirroring the lost names painted on their nosegear doors.

Pacer Strike-off Charge

Ironically, the aircraft had matured to near-perfection at this point in their careers. The definitive Rockwell F-111F *Pacer Strike* programme had just been applied to twenty-eight of the aircraft, re-equipping the 524th FS and just entering service with the 523rd FS *Crusaders* when the decision

Fort Worth hosted the 'Last Hurrah' in the last weekend of July 1996: these four F-111Fs from the 524th FS Hounds of Heaven, **just beautifully refurbished and** Pacer Strike **modified, flew off to the 'boneyard' on Monday 29 July. What a waste ...** Lockheed-Martin

... among their number was F-111F 74-187 (right), **decorated with combat sashes reflecting its service in Vietnam, North Africa and the Persian Gulf. The name Capt Frederick 'Art' Reid appears in sombre black on the nosegear door in tribute to one of many crewmen who lost their lives during combat deployments. Other aircraft carried similar tributes.** Lockheed-Martin

was made to retire them all as an operations and maintenance cost-cutting exercise. The update included RLG-based INS integrated with GPS Navstar, new computers and the old data entry switches and LEDs replaced by MFDs and CDU displays. Only twenty-six examples saw limited service in this new, trouble-free configuration and, as if to add insult to injury, two of the reworked aircraft (72-1445 and 72-1446) flew directly from the Sacramento rework line to the 'boneyard'. In the words of Frank Rossi:

Pacer Strike can be thought of as the best of AMP and DFCS [a concurrent, fleetwide Digital Flight Control System update]. The intention of the DFCS was to improve maintainability with some enhancement of handling characteristics too, including better roll response. The old flight control system could be pretty temperamental. DFCS also streamlined the amount of internal equipment needed to do the job; it's amazing what twenty years of technology can accomplish! This simplification into fewer and smaller LRUs [Line Replaceable Units] greatly simplified maintaining the aircraft. MTBF rates were improved. The 429th ECS [Ravens] 428th FS [F-111E] were DFCS modified, with just under half the F-111Fs receiving the upgrade. These had gone a long way to solving many of its expensive reliability problems.

Reflecting on the revised right-hand F-111F 'office', retired 'Wizzo Guru' Jim Rotramel reckoned that:

With the advent of AMP and Pacer Strike, most of the avionics reliability problems that had always made the F-111 such a challenge to fly were eliminated. With a reliable INS, especially one being continually 'tweaked' by GPS, the need for offset aimpoints was greatly reduced. By the time it was retired, the *Pacer Strike* F-111F was clearly the most accurate and capable delivery system in the world for 'non visual' deliveries.

With a sense of slight disillusionment, he added:

Not only had the 'F's been modified with DFCS under a separate program prior to their retirement; also, the hardware to replace the weapon panels had been bought, paid for, been delivered to SMALC, and was awaiting installation, but wasn't installed after the decision was made to dispose of the fleet. What a waste...'

Eaglevarks

Capt Dev Basudev, who had flown six F-111 variants including the FB-111A was one of the few to sample the *Pacer Strike* F-111F. After its retirement he transitioned to the jet which replaced it at Lakenheath, the McDonnell-Douglas F-15E Strike Eagle. Combining long-range, deep interdiction with the F-15C's air-to-air capability the F-15E can perform many of the F-111F's missions using LANTIRN in two external pods. It also has a 16,000hr fatigue life and the kind of engines which the F-111 always needed. Dev, well qualified to compare the two, commented that 'the power of the F100-PW-229 engines is incredible. You really feel it every time you plug in the burners'. From the handling viewpoint, 'The F-15E is more of a glass cockpit with very few hard-wired switches. The F-111F *Pacer Strike* still had a lot of those. In handling, the F-15E is superior in all regimes except for low-level ride, where the F-111 was extremely stable and smooth. The Eagle is noticeably more bumpy low down'. Comparing attack systems he observed, 'the *Pacer Strike* F-111F with *Pave Tack* was the ultimate PGM machine. Based on my experience with both LANTIRN and *Pave Tack*, the resolution of *Pave Tack* was much better than the LANTIRN pod. It had a nine-inch collection mirror versus the five-inch LANTIRN type. The USAF didn't fund any improvements on the *Pave Tack* which would have given it the [automatic hold] point tracker/area tracker that LANTIRN has'.

Last of All

Flying in the wake of the USAF Aardvark phase-out are a mere dozen unarmed EF-111A Raven derivatives, which continue to operate at Cannon alongside the diminutive F-16 from the same Fort Worth factory. The Ravens will bow out from service during Fiscal Year 1999, providing a

---

Spark'vark Swansong

The Raven establishment at Cannon was consolidated and contracted to an authorized unit establishment of twenty-four aircraft, all under 430th ECS ownership during 1994 (though numbers remained higher as Congress continued to fund ongoing overseas commitments in Turkey and Saudi Arabia). Cannon's shrunken force reflected those which had or were destined to receive AMP modifications to their navigation systems, virtually identical to the kit evolved by Northrop-Grumman's New York facilities for installation in the F-111E, including GPS Navstar, but optimized purely for precision navigation with the potential to receive expanded jamming capability.

This second major thrust in updating the Raven's capabilities was initiated as the Northrop-Grumman Systems Improvement Program (SIP) in March 1991, under a two-phase project. SIP was designed to upgrade the jammers' exciters (the 'black boxes' which drive the jamming output) to expand and speed-up 'closed-loop lookthrough' waveband coverage to ten bands, including the ability to counter today's and tomorrow's much more frequency-agile radars. The prototype (66-0047) flew successfully from Eglin AFB, Florida with the modifications beginning on 14 March 1995, the start of a two and a half month contractor T&E flight test effort. This later progressed to limited service trials. Funding has been granted to continue work into the late summer of 1997, one year beyond the originally contracted development schedule, as a hedge against the Joint-Service Prowler unit not meeting needs. Two 'stock' AMP'ed Ravens put in a proud appearance at the Fort Worth F-111F Farewell, wearing the new format serials (66-6050 & 66-6028), to remind everyone that the force was still very much active, albeit in much-reduced numbers.

However, with its overseas commitments reduced, the Raven force was scheduled to shrink to just a dozen machines during the course of 1997, and at the time of writing is scheduled for complete retirement before the end of the century.

Although many do not see the US Navy's EA-6B Prowler as a fully viable replacement, the first four USAF aviators to train on the type began conversion with the new joint-service VAQ-134 tactical electronic warfare squadron at NAS Whidbey Island, Washington, during late 1995. Provided the Navy meets its promise and modifies and fields sufficient Prowlers for joint-service operations by June 1997, Raven phase-out will follow and SIP work will cease.

In the interim, the Ravens and their crews have been kept extremely busy. Their most recent call to action was a brief sojourn at Aviano AB, Italy, in August and September 1995, when six aircraft deployed there to provide jamming support for NATO aircraft conducting strikes against Serb positions, the biggest of these taking place on 30 August 1995 as Operation Deliberate Force, following the callous shelling of civilians. This represented the first time that NATO was ever sent into combat as a woven force, and it was a fitting end to an aircraft which had a relatively short but intense career in its guise as the 'Gray Airplane'. On 21 February 1996 the force also celebrated its 2,000th consecutive day of operations from Incirlik, Turkey, latterly in support of Operation *Provide Comfort* which enforces the Northern 'No Fly' zone over Iraq. Deployments to South West Asia will continue until the EA-6Bs take over the duty.

stop-gap until the US Navy reworks sufficient, similarly equipped (but strictly subsonic) Northrop-Grumman EA-6B Prowlers for joint-service use.

The only redeeming feature is that the RAAF envisages continuing operations with its 'Pigs' through to 2015. However, enthusiasts in Europe may have a long wait until they next see them: with the USAFE examples and their massive support infrastructure removed, the RAAF told the authors that, at the time of writing, it has no long-term plans to deploy any to England. The bright light on the horizon is that their Aardvarks are scheduled to make some of their spectacular and highly appropriate 'dump and torch' demonstrations to celebrate Australia hosting the Olympics at the start of the new Millennium. Dedicated followers had best venture 'down under'.

'Farewell my friends': the last four strike Aardvarks in the USAF inventory thunder away to their place of rest. The Sound of Freedom is now a memory, but one which will linger on in the hearts and minds of thousands of crews, engineers and enthusiasts. Lockheed-Martin

Preserved F-111 Aircraft

F-111A
- 63-9766 Edwards AFB Museum, California.
- 63-9767 Rantoul Aviation Complex (formerly Chanute AFB), Illinois.
- 63-9770 McClellan AFB, California.
- 63-9771 Cannon AFB gate, New Mexico, marked 27-234.
- 63-9773 Sheppard AFB, Texas (GF-111A).
- 63-9776 Mountain Home AFB Gate, Idaho, marked 66-022.
- 63-9778 Edwards AFB, California.
- 63-9779 Carswell AFB, Texas.
- 63-9780 Air Force Museum, Wright Patterson AFB, Ohio (capsule only).
- 65-5709 Kirtland AFB, New Mexico.
- 66-0012 Battle Mountain Museum, Nevada.
- 67-0058 Mountain Home AFB, Idaho.
- 67-0067 Air Force Museum, Wright-Patterson AFB, Ohio (marked in 474th TFW markings).
- 67-0100 Nellis AFB, Nevada.

FB-111A
- 67-0159 Preserved at McClellan Aviation Museum, California.
- 68-0245 Preserved at March AFB, California.
- 68-0248 Preserved at Ellsworth AFB Museum, South Dakota.
- 68-0267 SAC Museum, Offutt AFB, Nebraska.
- 68-0275 Kelly AFB, Texas.
- 68-0283 Capsule on display at SAC Museum, Offutt AFB, Nebraska.
- 68-0284 Barksdale AFB, Louisiana.
- 68-0286 Plattsburgh AFB, New York.
- 69-6509 Whiteman AFB, Missouri.

F-111E
- 67-0120 Duxford Museum, Cambridgeshire, England. *The Chief* in 20th TFW markings. One of two former 20th TFW wing 'flagships'.
- 68-0011 RAF Lakenheath Memorial Park, Suffolk, England, marked with 48th FW codes.
- 68-0020 Hill AFB Museum, Utah. 20th TFW *My Lucky Blonde* markings. One of two former 20th TFW Wing 'flagships'.
- 68-0033 Pima County Museum, Arizona. Former 20th TFW Hat Trick flown by Brad Insley.
- 68-0055 Robins AFB Museum, Georgia. Former 55th TFS, 20th TFW squadron 'flagship', named *Heartbreaker*.

F-111F
- 70-2379 Eglin AFB Armament Museum, Florida.

Note: further F-111s are likely to be allocated to museums and bases following deactivation of the F-111F, and some of the EF-111A force. The Air Force Museum will be receiving an F-111F shortly. No details were available at the time of writing.

APPENDIX I

USAF F-111 Operational Variant Main Differences

ITEM	F-111A	EF-111A	FB-111A	F-111D	F-111E	F-111F
Dimensions (ft)						
Length+	75.65	75.65	75.65	75.65	75.65	75.65
Height*	17.04	20.00	17.04	17.04	17.04	17.04
Wingspan (ft)						
@ 16°	63.00	63.00	70.00	63.00	63.00	63.00
@ 72.5°	31.98	31.98	33.98	31.98	31.98	31.98

+ including nose pitot. Length is 73.47ft excluding pitot.
* at normal weights/undercarriage compression.

	F-111A	EF-111A	FB-111A	F-111D	F-111E	F-111F
Weights (lb)						
Empty	46,172	53,418	47,481	46,631	46,172	47,481,
Basic	49,310	54,391	49,090	50,294	49,310	51,190
Max T/O	91,300	87,478	11,4300	100,000	91,300	100,000
Max Land	72,000	80,000	10,9000	72,000	72,000	72,000
Fuel Capacity (US Gal)						
Internal	5,043	5,022	5,623	5,043	5,043	5,035
Tanks	2,400	1,200	3,600	2,400	2,400	2,400
Total	7,443	6,222	9,223	7,443	7,443	7,435
Inlets	TP 1	TP 1	TP 2	TP 2	TP 2	TP 2
Engines and Thrust						
(SL static lb, per engine)						
TF30-P	-3 – 103	-3 – 109	-7 – 107	-9 – 109	-3 – 103	-100
Thrust						
Max A/B	18,500	18,500	20,350	20,840	18,500	25,100
(45mins)		20,840			20,840	
Max	9,800	9,800	10,800	10,600	9,800	13,170
Continuous		10,600			10,600	
Mission Avionics						
Inertial	MkI	MkI Mod	MkIIB	MkII	MkI	MkIIB
Bomb-Nav	AJQ-20A	AJQ-20A	AJN-16	AJN-16	AJQ-20A	AJN-16
		– AMP/SIP	– AMP		– AMP	–Pacer Strike
Optical sights	ASG-23	none	ASG-25	AVA-9	ASG-23	ASG-27

USAF F-111 OPERATIONAL VARIANT MAIN DIFFERENCES

ITEM	F-111A	EF-111A	FB-111A	F-111D	F-111E	F-111F
Radars						
Attack	APQ-113	APQ-160	APQ-114	APQ-130	APQ-113	APQ-144
						APQ-169
TFR	APQ-110	APQ-110	APQ-134	APQ-128	APQ-113	APQ-146
LARA	APN-167	APN-167	APN-167	APN-167	APN-167	APN-167
Doppler	–	–	APN-185	APN-189	–	–
CNI Systems						
Beacon	–	–	URT-33	–	–	–
UHF	ARC-109	ARC-109	ARC-109	ARC-109	ARC-109	ARC-109
HF radio	ARC-112	ARC-112	ARC-123	ARC-123	ARC-112	ARC-123
Intercom	AIC-25	AIC-25	AIC-25	AIC-25	AIC-25	AIC-25
IFF-AIMS	APX-64	APX-64	APX-64	APX-64	APX-64	APX-64
IFF	–	–	APX-78	APX-76	–	–
ILS	ARN-58	ARN-58	ARN-58A	ARN-58A	ARN-58	ARN-58A
TACAN	ARN-52	ARN-52	ARN-52	ARN-52	ARN-52	ARN-52
UHF-DF	ARA-50	ARA-50	–	ARA-50	ARA-50	ARA-50
Unique Equipment	–	ALQ-99E	ASQ-119	AVA-9	–	AVQ-26
				AYN-3*		AXQ-14

* removed mid 1980s.

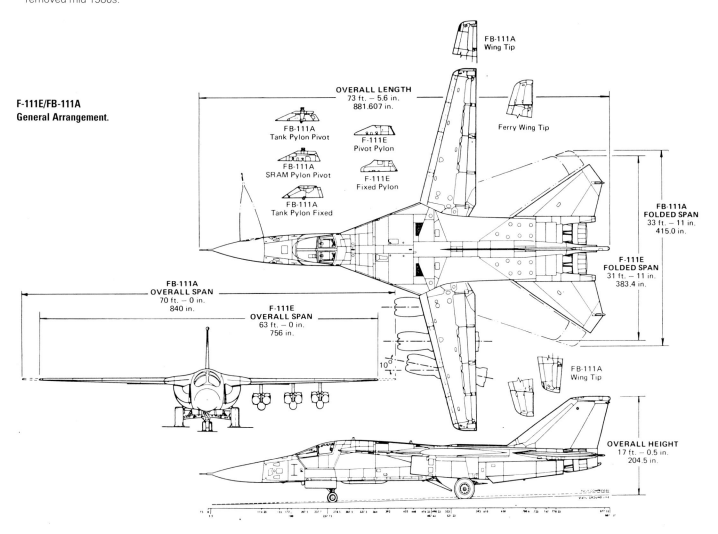

F-111E/FB-111A General Arrangement.

USAF F-111 OPERATIONAL VARIANT MAIN DIFFERENCES

	F-111A	EF-111A	FB-111A	F-111D	F-111E	F-111F
ITEM						
Penetration Aids						
CMRS*	AAR-34	–	AAR-34	AAR-34	AAR-34	AAR-34
CMDS	ALE-28	ALE-28	ALE-28	ALE-28	ALE-28	ALE-28
		ALE-40	ALE-40		ALE-40	ALE-40
RHAWS	APS-109	ALR-62	APS-109	APS-109	APS-109	APS-109
/CRS	ALR-62		ALR-62	ALR-62	ALR-62	ALR-62
Jammer	ALQ-94	ALQ-137	ALQ-94	ALQ-94	ALQ-94	ALQ-94
			ALQ-137			
ECM pods	ALQ-87	–	–	QRC-80	ALQ-101	ALQ-119
	ALQ-119			ALQ-119	ALQ-131	
	ALQ-131			ALQ-131		

* originally known as ALR-23, deleted in mid-1980s.

	F-111A	EF-111A	FB-111A	F-111D	F-111E	F-111F
Unique Weapons	AIM-9	–	AGM-69	–	–	GBU-15
Capability	Trapeze*		Mk/B83			GBU-24
						GBU-28

* deleted from service use in late 1960s.

	F-111A	EF-111A	FB-111A	F-111D	F-111E	F-111F
Service Timeframe	67–91*	82–FY99	69–92*	72–92	69–95	71–96

* with USAF. 19 still serve with RAAF as F-111C/Gs.

Note that RAAF F-111Cs are structurally similar to FB-111As but with TP 1 inlets and TF30-P-3/103 engines, F-111A mission avionics (prior to AUP), and feature AVQ-26 *Pave Tack* and AGM-84 Harpoon capability. Four RF-111Cs carry reconnaissance equipment in lieu of *Pave Tack*.

APPENDIX II

F-111 Production

SUMMARY OF AIRFRAMES

Shop Nos	Model	Function	Nos Built	Contractor Delivery Timeframe
A1	F-111A	RDT&E	18	12.64–12.66
A1	F-111A	Pilot Production	12	04.67–10.67
A1	F-111A	Operational	129	11.67–08.69
A1	F-111E	Operational	94	08.69–05.71
A2	F-111B	RDT&E	7	05.65–02.69
A2	F-111B	Operational	2	scrapped at Bethpage[1]
A3	F-111A	Static Test	1	engineering Article
A4	F-111A/B	Fatigue Test	1	engineering Article
A6	F-111D	Operational	96	06.70–02.73[2]
A7	F-111B	Static/Fatigue	1	engineering Article
A9	F-111-	Airloads Flight Test Wing Article	1	engineering Article
B1	FB-111A	RDT&E	2	08.68 & 10.68
B1	FB-111A	Operational	74	06.69–06.71[3]
B4	FB-111A	Fatigue Test	1	engineering Article
B5	FB-111A	Landing Gear Drop Test Article	1	engineering Article
B6	FB-111A	Landing Gear Fatigue Test Article	1	engineering Article
D1	F-111C	Production	24	09.68–11.69[4]
E1	F-111K	Production	2	scrapped at Fort Worth[5]
E2	F-111F	Production #1-70	70	09.71–06.72
E2	F-111F	Production #71-106	36	02.73–11.76

Total operational airframes	523
Total airworthy airframes	562
Total airframes fabricated	573

[1] Not completed after F-111B production programme terminated 09.07.68 and aircraft subsequently scrapped. RDT&E a/c completed over longer period for Phoenix weapons system trials. 22 incomplete airframe components passed to F-111D production.

[2] A gap of 13 months existed between roll-out of F-111D No 1 and No 2. Aircraft were stored owing to unavailability of Mk II avionics systems. Last 22 F-111D production stretched out to provide a seven-month bridge between fabrication of F-111Fs No 70 and No 71, avoiding lay-offs at Fort Worth.

[3] FB-111A production order reduced on 11.04.69 from 112 to 76 aircraft and 36 subassemblies diverted to F-111D production.

[4] F-111C aircraft placed in storage and refabricated 1973. 23 of the original production flow were completed between Sept and Nov 1969.

[5] Cancelled 17.01.68 and two aircraft scrapped before roll-out. Other incomplete airframes passed to FB-111A production.

RDT&E F-111A

A1-01
63-9766
First ever F-111 to fly, 21.12.64. Was held at Fox Field. To be preserved at Edwards AFB, California.

A1-02
63-9767
Wore bare metal finish for most of the early tests. Was used for engine development trials with Pratt & Whitney's East Hartford Plant in Connecticut, flying from Bradley Field, 1965. Conducted nav-and-attack avionics trials at AFFTC. Later inactive as GF-111A at Chanute TTC, Illinois, as ground instructional airframe, now renamed Rantoul Aviation Complex, where it resides.

A1-03
63-9768
Last reported as inactive as GF-111A ground instructional airframe at Sheppard TTC, Texas.

A1-04
63-9769
Wore bare metal finish for most of the early tests. Performed early aerodynamic and stores compatibility trials (including dummy Phoenix missiles) and was the first to feature pivot-pylons synchronized with the V-G wings. Also conducted spin-recovery trials. Crashed during test flight 08.05.68 while assigned to the AFFTC 6512 TS. Failure of weld in tail-plane control-valve actuator rod.

A1-05
63-9770
Tested M61A-1 20mm gun at Eglin, Florida, 01.67. Later used for ECM trials. Later inactive at Sheppard TTC, Texas, as GF-111A ground instructional airframe, where it remains.

A1-06
63-9771
Last reported as inactive as Gate Guardian at Cannon, New Mexico.

A1-07
63-9772
Conducted weapons separation trials, including weapons bay 'Trapeze' tests with GAR-8/AIM-9 Sidewinder missiles. Last reported as inactive as GF-111A ground instructional airframe at Sheppard TTC, Texas.

A1-08
63-9773
Later inactive as GF-111A ground instructional airframe at Sheppard TTC, Texas, where it remains.

A1-09
63-9774
First F-111 loss 19.01.67, while assigned to the AFFTC 6512 TS. Crashed short of AFFTC runway with 50° wing sweep and no flaps; right-hand crewman died in fire after otherwise safely alighting from a/c.

A1-10
63-9775
Last reported as inactive at Sheppard TTC, Texas, as GF-111A ground instructional airframe.

A1-11
63-9776
RF-111A testbed. Retired to Gate Guard status at MUO marked with the erroneous serial 66-022 in memorium of the first ever F-111A combat loss.

A1-12
63-9777
1st F-111A with McDonnell-Douglas escape module fitted in lieu of Douglas Escapac ejection seats. Also equipped with AAR boom recepticle. Conducted weapons trials. At Davis-Monthan AMARC 'boneyard' as of 03.88.

A1-13
63-9778
Was active with NASA from 1973 as AFTI/MAW testbed at AFFTC. Inactive at Edwards.

A1-14
63-9779
Scrapped and shipped to GDFW as spares in support of 1980s rebuild programme. It now resides at Carswell, Texas.

A1-15
63-9780
First use of escape module, 19.10.67. General Dynamics test flight with contract pilots. Experienced total hydraulic failure nr Bowie, Texas, and ejected at 28,000ft (8,535m) and 280kt (521kph). Capsule now on display at Wright-Patterson AF Museum.

A1-16
63-9781
At AMARC 'boneyard' as of 03.88.

A1-17
63-9782
Conducted weapons trials. Later employed for static ECM trials. Last reported as inactive at Rome Air Development Center, Griffiss, New York.

A1-18
63-9783
Subsequently Cat I/II FB-111A aerodynamic and weapons testbed. Conducted AGM-69 SRAM trials. To AMARC 'boneyard' early 1970s.

PILOT PRODUCTION F-111A

A1-19
65-5701
First of a dozen Pre-Production a/c (A1-19 thru -30). Also the first USAF use of escape module, 02.01.68, while assigned to the AFFTC 6512 TS. Lt Col Joe B Jordan and Col Henry W Brown ejected at AFFTC gunnery range.

A1-20
65-5702
Last reported as inactive at FAA-Atlantic City, New Jersey.

A1-21
65-5703
Crashed in the desert nr Las Vegas during Cat II USAF test flight 09.05.67.

A1-22
65-5704
At Davis-Monthan AMARC as of 03.88.

A1-23
65-5705
At Davis-Monthan AMARC as of 03.88.

A1-24
65-5706
Scrapped and shipped to GDFW as spares in support of 1980s rebuild programme.

A1-25
65-5707
At Davis-Monthan AMARC as of 03.88.

A1-26
65-5708
First F-111A with all-up ECM fit, including ALR-23 CMRS/IRRS. At Davis-Monthan AMARC as of 03.88.

A1-27
65-5709
Scrapped and shipped to GDFW as spares in support of 1980s rebuild programme. Now at Kirtland, New Mexico.

A1-28
65-5710
Scrapped and shipped to GDFW as spares in support of 1980s rebuild programme.

A1-29
66-0011
Was consigned to Davis-Monthan MASDC (later AMARC) by 1970. Reassigned to static electronic warfare tests and last reported at Grumman, Long Island.

A1-30
66-0012
After flight tests it became inactive at Lowry TTC as GF-111A ground instructional airframe. Now at Battle Mountain Museum, Nevada. RDT&E (Research, Development, Test & Evaluation) aircraft flew both Category I (Contractor) and Category II (Initial USAF service) trials primarily at Carswell AFB, Texas and Edwards AFB, California. Pilot-production aircraft flew Category II trials also, plus assisted in Category III early operational service trials at Nellis AFB, Nevada, and Eglin AFB, Florida, 1967–68. Only aircraft A1-31 (66-0013) and on were assigned full-time to operational squadrons.

F-111A PRODUCTION AND EF-111A RAVEN CONVERSIONS

A1-31
66-0013
EF-111A Article A-9, del 30.11.82. Primarily served with the Eglin-based Det 3 TAWC.

A1-32
66-0014
EF-111A Article A-12, del 12.05.83. To MUO. *Desert Storm* veteran.

A1-33
66-0015
EF-111A Article A-13, del 06.06.83. To MUO. *Desert Storm* veteran.

A1-34
66-0016
EF-111A Article A-10, del 14.12.82. To MUO. *Proven Force* veteran.

A1-35
66-0017
W/o 30.03.68 during *Combat Lancer*. Crashed on Thai/Laos border. Loss most probably due to hostile fire resulting in a loss of an engine, then control. Hank McGann and Dennis Graham KIA. A/c was assigned to the 428 TFS, 355 TFW.

A1-36
66-0018
Combat Lancer veteran (commander's aircraft). EF-111A Article A-11, del 24.03.83. To MUO.

A1-37
66-0019
Harvest Reaper a/c. EF-111A Article A-6, del 21.05.82. To MUO.

A1-38
66-0020
Harvest Reaper a/c. *Combat Lancer* veteran. EF-111A Article A-5, del 15.04.82. To MUO.

A1-39
66-002
Harvest Reaper a/c. *Combat Lancer* veteran. EF-111A Article A-7, del 25.06.82. To MUO.

A1-40
66-0022
Harvest Reaper a/c. W/o 28.03.68 during *Combat Lancer*. Hit ground while attacking truck park in N. Vietnam. First ever combat loss. Possible tailplane actuator failure or CFIT during high-speed manual TFR. Ed Palmgren (Ops Officer) and Spade Cooley (USN) KIA. A/c was assigned to the 428 TFS, 355 TFW.

A1-41
66-0023
Harvest Reaper a/c. *Combat Lancer* veteran. EF-111A Article A-17, del 07.10.83. To MUO. W/o during *Desert Storm* 14.02.91 while evading enemy aircraft.

A1-42
66-0024
Harvest Reaper a/c. *Combat Lancer* replacement. W/o 22.04.68 during Combat Lancer due to failed tailplane actuator rod weld. Sandy Marquardt and Joe Hodges ejected and were rescued by helicopter. A/c was assigned to the 428 TFS, 355 TFW.

A1-43
6-0025
Combat Lancer replacement 1968. W/o 20.06.75 during a crash, while assigned to the 474 TFW.

A1-44
66-0026
W/o as A 13.03.84, 2K, while a/c was assigned to the 366 TFW.

A1-45
66-0027
EF-111A Article A-8, del 16.09.82. To MUO.

A1-46
66-0028
EF-111A Article A-28, del 10.09.84. To MUO. AMP update.

A1-47
66-0029
Reported as w/o as A by GDFW by 03.88.

A1-48
66-0030
EF-111A Article A-36, del 02.05.85. To EGUA. *El Diablo* participant. Named *Mild And Bitter* Homebrew 1987–88.

A1-49
66-0031
EF-111A Article A-4, del 28.05.82. To MUO.

A1-50
66-0032
Reported as w/o as A after 1979 and by GDFW before 03.88. A/c was assigned to the 366 TFW.

A1-51
66-0033
EF-111A Article A-24, del 07.05.84. To EGUA. *El Diablo* participant. Named *Excalibur* 1987–88.

A1-52
66-0034
W/o as A 06.06.75 while assigned to the 474 TFW.

A1-53
66-0035
EF-111A Article A-20, del 09.12.83. To MUO. *Proven Force* veteran.

A1-54
66-0036
EF-111A Article A-33, del 30.01.85. To MUO.

A1-55
66-0037
EF-111A Article A-21, del 30.01.84. To EGUA as first USAFE-assigned Raven 03.02.84 named *NATO Raven One*. Named *Prowler* 1987–88. *Desert Storm* veteran.

A1-56
66-0038
EF-111A Article A-27, del 30.08.84. To MUO. Was flown to GDFW 06.11.85 for JSS update tests but project cancelled and Raven returned to MUO 08.04.88.

A1-57
66-0039
EF-111A Article A-25, del 28.06.84. To EGUA. Named *The Sorcerer's Apprentice* 1987–88. *Proven Force* veteran.

A1-58
66-0040
Reported as w/o as A by GDFW by 03.88.

A1-59
66-0041
EF-111A Phase 1B trials a/c at Grumman from 06.75. Subsequently Article M-2, first 'all-up' systems Raven which first flew from Grumman Calverton, New York, 17.05.77. Reworked and delivered 23.05.84. To EGUA. Named *Thumper* 1987–88. *Desert Storm* veteran.

A1-60
66-0042
Reported as w/o as A by GDFW by 03.88.

A1-61
66-0043
W/o as A 04.03.69. A/c was assigned to the 474 TFW.

A1-62
66-0044
EF-111A Article A-14, del 28.07.83. To MUO.

A1-63
66-0045
W/o as A 13.05.82 following loss of control. A/c was assigned to the 366 TFW.

A1-64
66-0046
EF-111A Article A-18, del 28.10.83. To MUO.

A1-65
66-0047
EF-111A Article A-15, del 22.07.83. To MUO. *Proven Force* and *Desert Storm* veteran. AMP update. Subsequently Northrop-Grumman SIP testbed and made 1st SIP flight on 14.03.95 from Eglin, Florida.

A1-66
66-0048
EF-111A Article A-29, del 01.10.84. To MUO. *Proven Force* veteran.

A1-67
66-0049
EF-111A Article M-1, initially an aerodynamic testbed only which first flew on 10.03.77. Reworked and redelivered 20.11.81. To MUO. *Desert Storm* veteran.

A1-68
66-0050
EF-111A Article A-30, del 09.11.84. To MUO. *Desert Storm* veteran. AMP update.

A1-69
66-0051
EF-111A Article A-3, del 04.11.81. To MUO as first TAC delivery, arriving at MUO 05.11.81.

A1-70
66-0052
W/o as A 31.07.79 while assigned to the 366 TFW.

A1-71
66-0053
Was assigned to the AFFTC at Edwards. Not selected for conversion. Served as Grumman/Norden TAWDS Pave Mover testbed 1981–83.

A1-72
66-0054
W/o as A 13.04.83 following engine fire. 2 ejected. A/c was assigned to the 366 TFW.

A1-73
66-0055
EF-111A Article A-37, del 13.09.85. To EGUA. Named *Boomerang* 1987–88. *Proven Force* and *Desert Storm* veteran.

A1-74
66-0056
EF-111A Article A-23, del 03.04.84. To EGUA. Named *Babyjam* 1987–88. *Desert Storm* veteran. Named *Jam Master* when a/c crashed into car park at Barton Hartshorn, 7 miles (11km) from EGUA on 02.04.92 after suffering engine fire. Capts Jeff Coombe (AC) and Dave Genevish (EWO) ejected.

A1-75
66-0057
EF-111A Article A-41, del 08.10.85. To EGUA. *El Diablo* participant. Named *Special Delivery* 1987–88.

A1-76
66-0058
W/o as A 07.10.75.

A1-77
67-0032
EF-111A Article A-40, del 12.09.85. To EGUA. Named *Black Sheep* 1987–88.

A1-78
67-0033
EF-111A Article A-35, del 25.03.85. To MUO.

A1-79
67-0034
EF-111A Article A-38, del 28.06.85. To EGUA. *El Diablo* participant. Named *Let 'Em Eat Crow* 1987–88. *Proven Force* veteran.

A1-80
67-0035
EF-111A Article A-39, del 12.08.85. To EGUA. Fire-damaged at EGUA 16.12.85 and repaired. Named *Ye Olde Crow* 1987–88.

A1-81
67-0036
Reported as w/o as A by GDFW by 03.88. A/c was assigned to the 474 TFW.

A1-82
67-0037
EF-111A Article A-31, del 26.11.84. To MUO.

A1-83
67-0038
EF-111A Article A-19, del 28.11.83. To MUO. *Desert Storm* veteran.

A1-84
67-0039
EF-111A Article A-16, del 17.08.83. To MUO.

A1-85
67-0040
Reported as w/o as A by GDFW (by 03.88) while assigned to the 474 TFW.

A1-86
67-0041
EF-111A Article A-22, del 05.03.84. To EGUA. *El Diablo* participant. Named *Knight Jammer* 1987–88. *Proven Force* veteran.

A1-87
67-0042
EF-111A Article A-26, del 06.07.84. To MUO. Named *Spirit of Idaho* 03.86 as one of two 366 TFW 'flagships' (the other being a stock F-111A). *Desert Storm* veteran.

A1-88
67-0043
Reported as w/o as A by GDFW (by 03.88) while assigned to the 474 TFW.

A1-89
67-0044
EF-111A Article A-42, del 23.12.85 (final delivery). To MUO.

A1-90 67-0045
A1-91 67-0046
A1-92 67-0047
Not selected for Raven conversion. Ended their days with the 366 TFW at MUO.

A1-93
67-0048
EF-111A Article A-34, del 27.02.85. To MUO. Served with Det 3 TAWC late 1980s.

A1-94
67-0049
W/o as A 22.12.69. Catastrophic WCTB failure during the pull-up from a dive-bomb run over the Nellis ranges. A/c was assigned to the 474 TFW. The incident resulted in a fleet-wide ground order which lasted until the end of July 1970.

A1-95
67-0050
Not selected for conversion. Later served as F-111A AMP testbed at Grumman.

A1-96
67-0051
Not selected for conversion.

A1-97
67-0052
EF-111A Article A-32, del 18.12.84. To EGUA. *El Diablo* participant. Named *Cherry Bomb* 1987–88.

All 42 Raven conversions selected from F-111As Nos 31 thru 97, originally delivered from Fort Worth between November 1967 and December 1968 and mostly previously engaged in training duties at Nellis. Grumman Raven delivery dates are formal hand-over dates following FCFs and any resultant fixes. *Combat Lancer* was the March–Oct 1968 F-111A combat deployment to S.E. Asia. Operation *El Diablo* was the Raven's contribution to the Libya raid of the night of 14/15 April 1986, codenamed Operation *El Dorado Canyon* involving six a/c. Operation *Proven Force* comprised nine 42 ECS a/c operating from Incirlik AB, Turkey, as part of the 7440 Combat Wing (Provisional) during the Gulf War, Jan–Feb 1991; those listed as *Desert Storm* veterans prosecuted the jamming campaign from Taif AB, Saudi Arabia, under the 390 ECS, 48 TFW (though 42 ECS elements were present). USAF Official figures list 18 aircraft used during *Desert Storm* and it is likely several aircraft flew missions from both Incirlik and Taif.

FINAL F-111A PRODUCTION

A1-98
67-0053
Ended career 1992 with 366 TFW at MUO.

A1-99
67-0054
Ended career 1992 with 366 TFW at MUO.

A1-100
67-0055
474 TFW. W/o 12.11.74 in mid-air collision with Turbo Commander N40MP over Kingston, Utah.

A1-101
67-0056
Ended career 1992 with 366 TFW at MUO.

A1-102
67-0057
Ended career 1992 with 366 TFW at MUO.

A1-103
67-0058
Replacement combat a/c arr Takhli 21.11.72; *Linebacker II* veteran. Now preserved at MUO.

A1-104
67-0059
430 TFS, 474 TFW *Constant Guard* V veteran. Crashed 05.07.79 while serving with the 366 TFW.

A1-105
67-0060
430 TFS, 474 TFW *Constant Guard* V veteran. Possible SAM hit while attacking Phuc Yen airfield, N. Vietnam, with Mk 84 bombs on night of 16/17.10.72. Crew, Hackridge and Graham, KIA.

A1-106
67-0061
430 TFS, 474 TFW *Constant Guard* V veteran.

A1-107
67-0062
Replacement combat a/c arr Takhli 23.10.72; *Linebacker II* veteran.

A1-108
67-0063
430 TFS, 474 TFW *Constant Guard* V veteran. Combat loss over Laos 08.11.72.

A1-109
67-0064
430 TFS, 474 TFW *Constant Guard* V veteran.

A1-110
67-0065
430 TFS, 474 TFW *Constant Guard* V veteran.

A1-111
67-0066
430 TFS, 474 TFW *Constant Guard* V veteran. Suffered a mid-air collision with 67-0111 over the Plaine des Jarres, 16.06.73, landing at Udorn, Thailand, with wing damage. Subsequently repaired but 'never quite flew straight' again and was nicknamed '*Arnold*'! Subsequently crashed 05.07.79 when assigned to the 366 TFW at MUO.

A1-112
67-0067
Replacement combat a/c arr Takhli 23.10.72. Aircraft now on display at the Air Force Museum at Dayton, Ohio, wearing *Linebacker II* era markings.

A1-113
67-0068
430 TFS, 474 TFW *Constant Guard* V veteran. Lost on the night of 22.12.72. Hit by AAA during *Linebacker II* attack on Hanoi docks; Bill Wilson and Bob Sponeybarger POW.

A1-114
67-0069
430 TFS, 474 TFW *Constant Guard* V veteran.

A1-115
67-0070
430 TFS, 474 TFW *Constant Guard* V veteran.

A1-116
67-0071
430 TFS, 474 TFW *Constant Guard* V veteran. Became 366 TFW 'flagship' at MUO named Spirit of Idaho.

A1-117
67-0072
430 TFS, 474 TFW *Constant Guard* V veteran. Undercarriage failed on take-off 22.02.73 possibly due to exceeding fatigue inspection time. Ran off the runway at Takhli and 24 bombs exploded in subsequent fire. Operational loss.

A1-118
67-0073
429 TFS, 474 TFW *Constant Guard* V veteran. Fuel leak and fire shortly after take-off from MUO, 19.01.82. Crashed 17 miles (27km) NW of the base. A/c was assigned to the 366 TFW.

A1-119
67-0074
430 TFS, 474 TFW *Constant Guard* V veteran.

A1-120
67-0075
430 TFS, 474 TFW *Constant Guard* V veteran.

A1-121
67-0076
429 TFS, 474 TFW *Constant Guard* V veteran. Named *Super Fly*. Later was 474 TFW Bicentennial 'flagship' at Nellis, 1976, named *Spirit of 76*.

A1-122
67-0077
429 TFS, 474 TFW *Constant Guard* V veteran.

A1-123
67-0078
430 TFS, 474 TFW *Constant Guard* V veteran. Number 2 a/c in first strikes by *Constant Guard* V force, 28.09.72. Crew possibly suffered disorientation from setting 'hard ride' TFR. Coltman and Brett MIA. A/c was assigned to the 429 TFS, 474 TFW.

A1-124
67-0079
430 TFS, 474 TFW *Constant Guard* V veteran. Was named *Bionic Annie* for SAC *Giant Voice* Bomb Comp in 1978 when assigned to 366 TFW. Suffered in-flight hydraulic fire in MLG well 21.01.81 while assigned to the 366 TFW. Shipped to Fort Worth 04.06.81 for repairs and returned to duty at MUO on 29.05.82.

A1-125
67-0080
430 TFS, 474 TFW *Constant Guard* V veteran. W/o around 1976 while assigned to the 474 TFW.

A1-126
67-0081
Replacement combat a/c arr Takhli 08.05.73.

A1-127
67-0082
W/o before 03.88. No further details.

A1-128
67-0083
430 TFS, 474 TFW *Constant Guard* V veteran. Crashed at MUO, 30.11.77. A/c was assigned to the 366 TFW.

A1-129
67-0084
430 TFS, 474 TFW *Constant Guard* V veteran.

A1-130
67-0085
429 TFS, 474 TFW *Constant Guard* V veteran.

A1-131
67-0086
430 TFS, 474 TFW *Constant Guard* V veteran.

A1-132
67-0087
430 TFS, 474 TFW *Constant Guard* V veteran.

A1-133
67-0088
430 TFS, 474 TFW *Constant Guard* V veteran. Was named *Streak Bean* for SAC *Giant Voice* Bomb Comp in 1978 when assigned to 366 TFW.

A1-134
67-0089
Replacement combat a/c arr Takhli 25.11.72; *Linebacker II* veteran.

A1-135
67-0090
430 TFS, 474 TFW *Constant Guard* V veteran. Was named *Three Times a Lady* for SAC *Giant Voice* Bomb Comp in 1978 when assigned to 366 TFW.

A1-136
67-0091
429 TFS, 474 TFW *Constant Guard* V veteran.

A1-137
67-0092
429 TFS, 474 TFW *Constant Guard* V veteran. Combat loss over N. Vietnam on night of 20/21.11.72.

A1-138
67-0093
429 TFS, 474 TFW *Constant Guard* V veteran. W/o after explosion while on the ramp at MUO, 09.11.82. A/c was assigned to the 366 TFW.

A1-139
67-0094
429 TFS, 474 TFW *Constant Guard* V veteran.

A1-140
67-0095
429 TFS, 474 TFW *Constant Guard* V veteran.

A1-141
67-0096
429 TFS, 474 TFW *Constant Guard* V veteran.

A1-142
67-0097
429 TFS, 474 TFW *Constant Guard* V veteran. Crashed nr MUO, 26.03.80. A/c was assigned to the 366 TFW.

A1-143
67-0098
429 TFS, 474 TFW *Constant Guard* V veteran. Crashed on take-off at MUO, 08.10.82. A/c was assigned to the 366 TFW.

A1-144
67-0099
429 TFS, 474 TFW *Constant Guard* V veteran. Combat loss over N. Vietnam on 1st day of *Linebacker II*, 18.12.72. Ops Officer Dick Ward KIA.

A1-145
67-0100
429 TFS, 474 TFW *Constant Guard* V veteran. Now on display at Nellis AFB, Nevada.

A1-146
67-0101
429 TFS, 474 TFW *Constant Guard* V veteran. Suffered bird ingestion 02.08.82 while assigned to the 366 TFW, resulting in a major in-flight fire. Repaired at Fort Worth using 4,200 replacement parts and returned to duty at MUO 08.85.

A1-147
67-0102
429 TFS, 474 TFW *Constant Guard* V veteran. Crashed 3 miles West of MUO, 12.01.88. 2K. A/c was assigned to the 389 TFS, 366 TFW.

A1-148
67-0103
429 TFS, 474 TFW *Constant Guard* V veteran.

A1-149
67-0104
429 TFS, 474 TFW *Constant Guard* V veteran.

A1-150
67-0105
429 TFS, 474 TFW *Constant Guard* V veteran. W/o after 1979 and before 03.88. A/c was assigned to the 366 TFW.

A1-151
67-0106
429 TFS, 474 TFW *Constant Guard* V veteran.

A1-152
67-0107
429 TFS, 474 TFW *Constant Guard* V veteran.

A1-153
67-0108
Replacement combat a/c arr Takhli 09.01.73. Was named *Rionto Choice* for SAC *Giant Voice* Bomb Comp in 1978 when assigned to 366 TFW.

A1-154
67-0109
Replacement combat a/c arr Takhli 11.12.72;

Linebacker II veteran. Served with recording cameras for filming other a/c 'TF'ing' over S. E. Asia. Was sold to the RAAF May–June 1982 as an attrition replacement with new serial A8-109.

A1-155
67-0110
429 TFS, 474 TFW *Constant Guard* V veteran.

A1-156
67-0111
Replacement combat a/c arr Takhli 08.05.73. Operational loss over the Plaine des Jarres after a mid-air collision with 67-0066 (which landed at Udorn, Thailand, with wing damage), 16.06.73. A/c was assigned to the 474 TFW.

A1-157
67-0112
429 TFS, 474 TFW *Constant Guard* V veteran. Was sold to the RAAF May–June 1982 as an attrition replacement with new serial A8-112.

A1-158
67-0113
429 TFS, 474 TFW *Constant Guard* V veteran. Was sold to the RAAF May–June 1982 as an attrition replacement with new serial A8-113.

A1-159
67-0114
429 TFS, 474 TFW *Constant Guard* V veteran. Last F-111A to be produced. Was sold to the RAAF May–June 1982 as an attrition replacement with new serial A8-114.

All operational F-111As passed to 366 TFW at MUO during 1977, so all a/c not listed as stricken, reassigned to the RAAF, or assigned as Gate Guards or Museum pieces ended their flying careers under the auspices of the 366 FW and were subsequently put into storage at AMARC.

FB-111A PRODUCTION

B1-01
67-0159
1st airworthy FB-111A produced as such (F-111A A1-18 serving as initial testbed). Featured Triple Plow I inlets and spent most of its active career at SMALC, McClellan AFB, California, on test duties.

B1-02
67-0160
Served with AFFTC. Featured interim 'Superplow' inlet system with two blow-in doors. At the MASDC (AMARC) by 12.74. Subsequently scrapped at GDFW and parts used to help rebuild B1-08/67-7194.

B1-03
67-0161
First all-up FB-111A. To AFFTC for Category II trials. To 380 BW by 08.78 and later named *Liquidator*.

B1-04
67-0162
Cat II trials a/c. Later served with 380 BW Named *Apple 1* for *Giant Voice* 1974 and later named *Nocturnal Mission*. Named *City of Portales* as an F-111G.

B1-05
67-0163
Cat II trials a/c. SRAM test platform. Later served with 380 BW named *Moonlight Maid*. At AMARC by 03.92 coded BF-009.

B1-06
67-7192
Cat II trials a/c. Later served with 380 BW named *Slightly Dangerous*.

B1-07
67-7193
First 'official' delivery to newly created SAC 4007th CCTS, 340 BG, Carswell AFB, Texas, 29.09.69. Later served with 509 BW named *Tiger 'Lil*.

B1-08
67-7194
Severely damaged in fire after heavy landing 02.76. The aircraft was rebuilt using the aft fuselage taken from B1-02 (67-0160). Work started on 01.09.78 and the aircraft was reassigned to the 380 BW in 09.80. Named *Virgin Abroad* but popularly known as 'Frankenvark'!

B1-09
67-7195
Served with 509 BW named *Dave's Dream* and *Big Stink*.

B1-10
67-7196
Served with 509 BW named *Ruptured Duck* and *Sea Coast Cruncher*. Reassigned to 428 TFTS at Cannon AFB.

B1-11
68-0239
Served with 380 BW named Rough Night.

B1-12
68-0240
Served with 380 BW named *Atomic Blonde*. At AMARC by 03.92 coded BF-012.

B1-13
68-0241
Served with 380 BW named *Undecided*.

B1-14
68-0242
W/o after engine fire 08.06.83 while with 509 BW. 2 ejected.

B1-15
68-0243
Crashed nr Johnsburg, Vermont, 02.02.89 while with 509 BW. 2 ejected.

B1-16
68-0244
Served with 380 BW named *Lucky Strike* (also with The Flying Circus/380th Bombardment Group Association artwork on its flanks). Reassigned to 428 TFTS at Cannon AFB.

B1-17
68-0245
Served with 380 BW named *Ready Teddy*. Now preserved at March AFB, California.

B1-18
68-0246
Served with 380 BW named *Royal Flush*. At AMARC by 03.92 coded BF-008.

B1-19
68-0247
Served with 509 BW. Later became one of two FB-111A AMP testbeds (the other being B1-44/68-0272).

B1-20
68-0248
Served with 380 BW named *Free For All*. Now on display at Ellsworth AFB Museum, South Dakota.

B1-21
68-0249
Served with 380 BW named *Gus's Bus* and Little Joe. Last operational FB-111A to leave Plattsburgh AFB, 10.07.91, bound for AMARC. Recoded BF-018.

B1-22
68-0250
Served with 380 BW named *Silver Lady*. At AMARC by 03.92 coded BF-013.

B1-23
68-0251
Served with 380 BW named *Shy Chi Baby*.

B1-24
68-0252
Served with 380 BW named *Six Bitts*.

B1-25
68-0253
W/o at Carswell AFB, Texas, 10.07.70 while with 340 BG.

B1-26
68-0254
Served with 380 BW named *Pappy's Passion*. Subsequently with the 6510th TW, AFFTC 1990–91 in support of F-111 DFCS update tests.

B1-27
68-0255
Served with 509 BW, named *Sleepy Time Gal*.

B1-28
68-0256
Served with 380 BW named *The Screamer*. At AMARC by 03.92 coded BF-017.

B1-29
68-0257
Served with 380 BW named *Maid in the USA*. Reassigned to 428 TFTS at Cannon AFB.

B1-30
68-0258
Served with 380 BW named *Hell's Belles*.

B1-31
68-0259
Suffered major airframe damage on the ramp at Nellis AFB during a *Red Flag* exercise when a BDU-38/B tail chute rod was inadvertently activated and punched through the aft right rear weapons bay and through into the MLG well. Repaired at GDFW from 30.09.81 and reflown on an FCF during 01.83. Returned to SAC service with the 380 BW 04.02.83 and named *Gypsy*. Reassigned to 428 TFTS at Cannon AFB. Reassigned to RAAF as A8-259.

B1-32
68-0260
Served with 380 BW named *SNAFU*. Reassigned to 428 TFTS at Cannon AFB.

B1-33
68-0261
Crashed in Nevada 09.09.79 while with 509 BW.

B1-34
68-0262
Served with 380 BW named *Lady Luck*. At AMARC by 03.92 coded BF-016.

B1-35
68-0263
Crashed into an apartment block at Portsmouth, New Hampshire, 30.01.81, while with 509 BW. 2 ejected.

B1-36
68-0264
Served with 380 BW named *Jezebelle*. Reassigned to 428 TFTS at Cannon AFB. To RAAF as A8-264.

B1-37
68-0265
Served with 380 BW named *Net Results* and *Angel in de Skies*. Reassigned to 428 TFTS at Cannon AFB. To RAAF as A8-265.

B1-38
68-0266
W/o after 1978 but before 03.88 while assigned to the 509 BW.

B1-39
68-0267
Served with 380 BW named *Pom Pom Express*. On display at the SAC Museum at Offutt AFB, Nebraska.

B1-40
68-0268
Crashed on a training sortie on 06.10.80 while assigned to the 380 BW.

B1-41
68-0269
Served with 509 BW named *New Hampshire Special* for *Giant Voice* 1974. Later with 380 BW named *Sad Sack*. At AMARC by 03.92 coded BF-015.

B1-42
68-0270
Served with 509 BW named *Full House*. Reassigned to 428 TFTS at Cannon AFB. To RAAF as A8-270.

B1-43
68-0271
Served with 380 BW named *On De-Fence*. Reassigned to 428 TFTS at Cannon AFB. To RAAF as A8-271.

B1-44
68-0272
Served with 509 BW named *The Wild Hare*. Served as AMP testbed at SMALC 1986–87. To AMARC 1991 and reassigned to RAAF as A8-272.

B1-45
68-0273
Served with 509 BW.

B1-46
68-0274
Served with 380 BW named *Missouri Miss*. Reassigned to Det 3, 431 TES at McClellan AFB. Later to the 428 TFTS at Cannon AFB. To RAAF as A8-274.

B1-47
68-0275
Served with 509 BW. Now at Kelly AFB, Texas.

B1-48
68-0276
Served with 509 BW named *Gruesome Goose*.

B1-49
68-0277
Served with 380 BW named *Double Trouble*. Reassigned to 428 TFTS at Cannon AFB. To RAAF as A8-277.

B1-50
68-0278
Served with 380 BW named *A Wing and Ten Prayers*. Reassigned to 428 TFTS at Cannon AFB. Had 6,630 hours on its clock when transferred to RAAF as A8-278.

B1-51
68-0279
W/o after 1978 but before 03.88 while assigned to the 509 BW.

B1-52
68-0280
W/o after 1979 but before 03.88 while assigned to the 380 BW.

B1-53
68-0281
Served with 509 BW. Reassigned to 428 TFTS at Cannon AFB. To RAAF as A8-281.

B1-54
68-0282
Served with 380 BW named *Old Ironsides*. Later was used to test aborted Mk/B77 nuclear bomb, 1977. Reassigned to 428 TFTS at Cannon AFB. To RAAF as A8-282.

B1-55
68-0283
Crashed at Manderville, Louisiana 08.01.72. Capsule on display at SAC Museum, Offutt AFB, Nebraska.

B1-56
68-0284
Served with 509 BW named *Next Objective* and *Laggin' Dragon*. Finally with 380 BW. Now on display at Barksdale AFB, Louisiana.

B1-57
68-0285
W/o after 1978 but before 03.88 while assigned to the 380 BW.

B1-58
68-0286
Served with 380 BW named *Miss Giving* and *SAC Time*. Now at Plattsburgh AFB, New York.

B1-59
68-0287
Served with 509 BW named *Liberator II*.

B1-60
68-0288
Served with 380 BW named *Peace Offering*. At AMARC by 03.92 coded BF-011.

B1-61
68-0289
Served with 380 BW named *Queen Hi*.

B1-62
68-0290
W/o before 03.88. No further details known.

B1-63
68-0291
Served with 380 BW named *Shady Lady*. Reassigned to 428 TFTS at Cannon AFB. To RAAF as A8-291.

B1-64
68-0292
Served with 380 BW named *Liberty Belle*.

B1-65
69-6503
Served with 509 BW named *Straight Flush*.

B1-66
69-6504
Served with 509 BW.

B1-67
69-6505
W/o before 03.88. No further details known.

B1-68
69-6506
Served with 509 BW. Reassigned to 428 TFTS at Cannon AFB. To RAAF as A8-506.

B1-69
69-6507
Served with 509 BW named *Madame Queen*. Also named *Battle Weary*.

B1-70
69-6508
Served with 509 BW named *Strange Cargo*. Now on display at Whiteman AFB, Missouri (home of the current 509 Wing equipped with B-2A Spirits).

B1-71
69-6509
Served with 509 BW named *Spirit of the Seacoast*.

B1-72
69-6510
Served with 509 BW.

B1-73
69-6511
W/o before 03.88. No further details known.

B1-74
69-6512
Served with 509 BW. Reassigned to 428 TFTS at Cannon AFB, as Squadron commander's aircraft. To RAAF as A8-512.

B1-75
69-6513
Served with both Bomb Wings. At AMARC by 03.92 coded BF-007.

B1-76
69-6514
Last FB-111A built, handed over to the USAF on 30.06.71. Served with 509 BW named *Double Trouble*. Reassigned to 428 TFTS at Cannon AFB. To RAAF as A8-514.

Note that many aircraft have served with both New England Bomb (Medium) Wings, but the chief operators are provided. Most 340 BG aircraft were those later chiefly operated by the 509 BW. All surviving aircraft were modified with AMP in the late 1980s and became known as F-111Gs in 1990, reflecting their new tactical rôle. Twenty-eight of these were transferred to the 428 TFTS at Cannon AFB, New Mexico, beginning in June 1990, which relinquished all its aircraft to the RAAF and AMARC two years later. All FB-111A/F-111Gs not noted as written-off or having been transferred to the RAAF, or assigned to Gate Guard and Museum exhibit status are at AMARC.

F-111B PRODUCTION (GRUMMAN BETHPAGE, NEW YORK)

A2-01
151970
Rolled out 11.05.65. First flight 18.05.65. Scrapped 12.69 after flight test programme completed, at NATF Lakehurst, New Jersey.

A2-02
151971
First flight 24.10.65. Crashed into Pacific Ocean 90 miles (145km) off Californian coast, 20 miles (32km) NW of San Miguel Island, 11.09.68, while on test sortie from NMC Point Mugu, California, with Hughes contractor crew onboard. Barton Warren (pilot) and Anthony A Byland killed. Warren, during radio contact, gave no indication of trouble. Presumed a/c flew into the sea. SS *Mason Lake* reported sighting debris and an oil slick but no sign of survivors.

A2-03
151972
Accepted 29.12.65. Scrapped 12.71 after completion of flight test programme, at NATF Lakehurst, New Jersey.

A2-04
151973
Acceptance records lost. First SWIP model. First F-111B with McDonnell Douglas escape module in lieu of Escapac ejection seats. Crashed at Calverton, New York, 21.04.67.

A2-05
151974
Accepted 15.09.66. Second SWIP a/c. First flight 16.11.68, which also comprised First Article Configuration Inspection (FACI) – an engineering review by Naval Air Systems and USAF Aeronautical Systems to establish the base-line configuration from which all future design changes would be made. Conducted simulated and shipborne carrier trials. Crash-landed Point Mugu, California, 11.10.68, and scrapped as uneconomic to repair.

A2-06
152714
Accepted 17.06.68 and first flew 29.06.68. First with production-standard TF30-P-12 turbofans. Stricken from the inventory 05.71 and last reported inactive at McClellan AFB, California.

A2-07
152715
All-up Phoenix missile testbed. Accepted 28.02.69. First with interim 'Superplow' intakes

with double bloor-in doors. Stricken from the inventory 05.71 and last reported inactive at China Lake, California.

A2-08
152716
Not completed and scrapped *in situ*.

A2-09
152717
Not completed and scrapped *in situ*.

BuNos 153613-153642 and 156971-156978 were also assigned but cancelled before final assembly began. 22 F-111B sub-assemblies were subsequently diverted to F-111D production.

F-111K PRODUCTION GDFW AND RAF NO.

E1-01 67-0149
E1-02 67-0150
Scrapped just before completion.

F-111C PRODUCTION GDFW & RAAF NO.

D1-01
A8-125
1st RAAF F-111C, arriving at Amberley on 17.06.73, flown by Gp Capt Jake Newham and WgCdr Trevor Owen. 1st a/c with new laminated ADBIRT windshield, 1975. Participated in TRIAD 84, a multi-national exercise between Australia, US and New Zealand forces held in NZ in 1984.

D1-02
A8-126
No 6 Sqn. Converted to RF-111C 1979 at GDFW, as 1st RAAF reconnaissance a/c. Flew in RAM 88 at Bergstrom, Texas, 08.88. Participated in an Integrated Air Defence Exercise under the Five Power Defence Agreement (IADE/FPDA) in Malaysia/Singapore/South China Sea 03.90.

D1-03
A8-127
No 1 Sqn. Participated in SAC Bomb Comp 84 (where RAF Tornados made their debut at the Bomb Comp). Flew at RAF 75th Anniversary Airshow at Fairford 07.93. Crashed at Guyra, NSW, 250 mi SW of Brisbane during low-level night sortie 13.09.93. 2K.

D1-04
A8-128
No 6 Sqn. Struck ground during low-level night 'toss' attack sortie on a simulated target nr Tenterfield, NSW, 02.04.87. No attempt to eject. 2K.

D1-05
A8-129
Participated in SAC Bomb Comp 84 and IADE/FPDA 03.90.

D1-06
A8-130
82 SW.

D1-07
A8-131
82 SW.

D1-08
A8-132
Instrumented evaluation a/c. Has conducted numerous trials, including AGM-84 Harpoon missile in 1981, at China Lake, California, HARM missile firings at Woomera in 1988, and AUP from 1991.

D1-09
A8-133
No 1 Sqn. Took three birdstrikes on windshield and crashed nr Evans Head range, NSW, 29.09.77. Ejection attempted outside of envelope. 2K.

D1-10
A8-134
No 6 Sqn. Converted to RF-111C 1979-80.

D1-11
A8-135
Participated in SAC Bomb Comp 84 and IADE/FPDA 03.89.

D1-12
A8-136
No 6 Sqn. Weld failure in 16th-stage bleed-air duct caused fuel-vapour explosion while on sortie over NSW, 28.04.77. 2 ejected.

D1-13
A8-137
No 6 Sqn. Both engines flamed out on t/o after ingesting water from wet runway at RNZAF Ohakea, NZ, 24.08.79. A/c ran off runway and burned out. 2 ejected.

D1-14
A8-138
No 1 Sqn. *Pave Tack* testbed 1983.

D1-15
A8-139
No 1 Sqn. Flew into the sea during a night anti-shipping practice strike nr Montago Island, Bateman's Bay, NSW, 28.01.86. No ejection attempted. 2K.

D1-16
A8-140
82 SW.

D1-17
A8-141
No 6 Sqn. Fire in wheel-well caused by leaking hot bleed-air. Crashed into Hauraki Gulf nr Auckland, NZ, 25.10.78. 2 ejected. Capsule exhibited at RAAF's 75th Anniversary, Sydney, March 1996.

D1-18
A8-142
Participated in SAC Bomb Comp 84. Participated in ALR-62 trials at Eglin AFB, Florida. Deployed to RAF Boscombe Down for IAT 1990.

D1-19
A8-143
Made appearance at RAF Finningley RAF Jubilee Review, 1977. No 6 Sqn, converted to RF-111C 1979–80. RAM 88 08.88 and IADE/FPDA 03.90.

D1-20
A8-144
No 1 Sqn. Participated in SAC Bomb Comp 84. Deployed to RAF Boscombe Down for IAT 1990.

D1-21
A8-145
Participated in TRIAD 84, NZ.

D1-22
A8-146
No 6 Sqn. Converted to RF-111C 1979–80. RAM 88 08.88. To RNAS Yeovilton, England, for June 1994 50th Anniversary of D-Day flypast.

D1-23
A8-147
TRIAD 84 participant.

D1-24
A8-148
82 SW.

F-111C/G ACQUISITIONS FROM FORMER USAF PRODUCTION

A1-154
A8-109
Former USAF F-111A 67-109. Later Known as F-111(A)C by GDFW but as F-111C by RAAF.

A1-157
A8-112
Former USAF F-111A 67-112. Later Known as F-111(A)C by GDFW but as F-111C by RAAF. IADE/FPDA 03.89.

A1-158
A8-113
Former USAF F-111A 67-113. Later known as F-111(A)C by GDFW but as F-111C by RAAF. IADE/FPDA 03.89.

A1-159
A8-114
Former USAF F-111A 67-114. Later known as F-111(A)C by GDFW but as F-111C by RAAF.

B1-31
A8-259
Former USAF F-111G 68-259.

B1-36
A8-264
Former USAF F-111G 68-264.

B1-37
A8-265
Former USAF F-111G 68-265. One of two initial arrivals at RAAF Amberley, 28.09.93.

B1-42
A8-270
Former USAF F-111G 68-270. The first arrival at RAAF Amberley, 28.09.93. By coincidence, the navigator was SqnLdr Richard Owen, the son of WgCdr Trevor Owen, the navigator of the first F-111C to arrive 20 years before!

B1-43
A8-271
Former USAF F-111G 68-271.

B1-44
A8-272
Former USAF F-111G 68-272.

B1-46
A8-274
Former USAF F-111G 68-274.

B1-49
A8-277
Former USAF F-111G 68-277.

B1-50
A8-278
Former USAF F-111G 68-278.

B1-53
A8-281
Former USAF F-111G 68-281.

B1-54
A8-282
Former USAF F-111G 68-282.

B1-63
A8-291
Former USAF F-111G 68-291.

B1-68
A8-506
Former USAF F-111G 69-506.

B1-74
A8-512
Former USAF F-111G 69-512.

B1-76
A8-514
Former USAF F-111G 69-514.

As part of the plans to keep the F-111 fleet operational beyond 2010, aircraft will be rotated in and out of storage to extend flight hours. Thus, not all aircraft listed are currently active.

F-111D PRODUCTION GDFW AND USAF NO.

A6-01
68-0085
AFFTC → Det 2, 57 TTW/431 TES, McClellan 1972 → AFFTC.

A6-02
68-0086
AFFTC → Det 2, 57 TTW, McClellan 1972 → 27 TFW in 10.73.

A6-03
68-0087
27 TFW → AFFTC by 11.78.

A6-04
68-0088
AFFTC → Det 2, 57 TTW/431 TES, McClellan 1972 → 27 TFW.

A6-05
68-0089
AFFTC.

A6-06
68-0090
First of four deliveries to Cannon AFB on 12.11.71, initially to 4427 TFRS, 27 TFW.

A6-07
68-0091
27 TFW.

A6-08
68-0092
27 TFW.

A6-09
68-0093
27 TFW. Crashed into mountain nr Cannon AFB 03.10.77.

A6-10
68-0094
27 TFW.

A6-11
68-0095
27 TFW. Suffered main wheel-well fire and damaged in wheels-up landing 04.76. Stored at MASDC/AMARC (during which time stripped of spares to repair fire-damaged F-111A 67-0089) until 06.84 when transferred to GDFW for restoration. Returned to Cannon 11.88.

A6-12
68-0096
27 TFW.

A6-13
68-0097
27 TFW.

A6-14
68-0098
27 TFW. Lead a/c in three-ship night attack with BDU-33 08.06.88. Hit ground nr Melrose Range on third attack pass. Crew ejected outside of capsule's parameters. Capts Mike Barrett and Glenn Troster killed.

A6-15
68-0099
27 TFW.

A6-16
68-0100
27 TFW.

A6-17
68-0101
27 TFW. Fire in LOX converter severely damaged the airframe. Rebuilt by GDFW over 12 months and returned to Cannon 12.86.

A6-18
68-0102
27 TFW.

A6-19
68-0103
27 TFW.

A6-20
68-0104
27 TFW.

A6-21
68-0105
27 TFW. Crashed after mid-air collision with 68-0158 nr Holbrook, Arizona, 30.03.73.

A6-22
68-0106
27 TFW.

A6-23
68-0107
27 TFW.

A6-24
68-0108
27 TFW.

A6-25
68-0109
27 TFW. W/o prior to 03.88; no further details.

A6-26
68-0110
27 TFW. Crashed nr Woodin, California, with engine fire after takeoff, 27.01.82.

A6-27
68-0111
27 TFW.

A6-28
68-0112
27 TFW.

A6-29
68-0113
27 TFW. W/o nr Melrose, New Mexico, 03.12.73.

A6-30
68-0114
27 TFW.

A6-31
68-0115
27 TFW.

A6-32
68-0116
27 TFW.

A6-33
68-0117
27 TFW.

A6-34
68-0118
27 TFW.

A6-35
68-0119
27 TFW. Crashed nr Clovis, New Mexico, after mid-air collision with Cessna 206 (N7393N), 06.02.80.

A6-36
68-0120
27 TFW.

A6-37
68-0121
27 TFW.

A6-38
68-0122
27 TFW. Served as 522 FS Fireballs 'flagship' nicknamed *Fireball Annie*, 1991.

A6-39
68-0123
27 TFW.

A6-40
68-0124
27 TFW.

A6-41
68-0125
27 TFW. W/o prior to 03.88; no further details.

A6-42
68-0126
27 TFW.

A6-43
68-0127
27 TFW. Electric and hydraulic fire in main wheel-well caused fire damage and gear collapse, 07.07.81. Rebuilt at GDFW over 27 months and signed for by FCF crew on 09.12.83. Subsequently became *City of Clovis* as 27 TFW 'flagship'.

A6-44
68-0128
27 TFW.

A6-45
68-0129
27 TFW.

A6-46
68-0130
27 TFW. Crashed 5 miles (8km) SW of Cannon AFB after engine fire on takeoff, 21.10.88. 2 ejected.

A6-47
68-0131
27 TFW.

A6-48
68-0132
27 TFW. Crashed on landing at Cannon AFB, 17.03.88. 2 ejected.

A6-49
68-0133
27 TFW.

A6-50
68-0134
27 TFW.

A6-51
68-0135
27 TFW.

A6-52
68-0136
27 TFW. Left engine second-stage failure, resulting in in-flight fire which spread to cause major airframe damage after landing, 09.09.79. Into storage at MSADC/AMARC → GDFW rebuild programme by trailer 21.06.81. Rebuilt over 23 months and signed for by FCF crew on 27.05.82.

A6-53
68-0137
27 TFW.

A6-54
68-0138
27 TFW.

A6-55
68-0139
27 TFW. Crashed 9 miles (14km) N of Cannon AFB, 14.07.80. 2 ejected.

A6-56
68-0140
27 TFW.

A6-57
68-0141
27 TFW.

A6-58
68-0142
27 TFW.

A6-59
68-0143
27 TFW.

A6-60
68-0144
27 TFW.

A6-61
68-0145
27 TFW.

A6-62
68-0146
27 TFW. Crashed nr Des Moines, Iowa, 02.09.77.

A6-63
68-0147
27 TFW.

A6-64
68-0148
27 TFW. Left engine fire resulting from failed ninth stage seal caused extensive airframe damage, 17.01.79. Into storage at MSADC/AMARC → GDFW rebuild programme by trailer following rebuild contract dated 05.05.81. Rebuilt over 19 months and signed for by FCF crew on 09.12.83.

A6-65
68-0149
27 TFW.

A6-66
68-0150
27 TFW.

A6-67
68-0151
27 TFW.

A6-68
68-0152
27 TFW.

A6-69
68-0153
27 TFW.

A6-70
68-0154
27 TFW.

A6-71
68-0155
27 TFW.

A6-72
68-0156
27 TFW.

A6-73
68-0157
27 TFW.

A6-74
68-0158
27 TFW. Mid-air collision with 68-0105 nr Hollbrook, Arizona, 30.03.73.

A6-75
68-0159
27 TFW.

A6-76
68-0160
27 TFW. Crashed 15.09.82. No further details.

A6-77
68-0161
27 TFW.

A6-78
68-0162
27 TFW.

A6-79
68-0163
27 TFW.

A6-80
68-0164
27 TFW. W/o 12.09.87. No further details.

A6-81
68-0165
27 TFW.

A6-82
68-0166
27 TFW.

A6-83
68-0167
27 TFW. W/o prior to 03.88; no further details.

A6-84
68-0168
27 TFW.

A6-85
68-0169
27 TFW.

A6-86
68-0170
27 TFW.

A6-87
68-0171
27 TFW.

A6-88
68-0172
27 TFW.

A6-89
68-0173
27 TFW. W/o prior to 03.88; no further details.

A6-90
68-0174
27 TFW. Engine fan blade failure resulted in major fuel fire, 05.76. Into storage at MSADC/AMARC for eight years → GDFW rebuild programme beginning in 07.84. Returned to Cannon 11.87.

A6-91
68-0175
Det 3, 57 TTW → 27 TFW.

A6-92
68-0176
27 TFW.

A6-93
68-0177
27 TFW.

A6-94
68-0178
27 TFW.

A6-95
68-0179
27 TFW.

A6-96
68-0180
27 TFW.

F-111Ds served primarily at Cannon AFB, New Mexico, with the 27th TFW/FW, the only operational Wing to fly this model. Additional examples were operated by Det 2 of the 57 TTW at McClellan AFB, California (becoming part of Det 3 in 08.77, and thence the 431st TES Red Devils in 03.80), most passing back to the AFFTC in the 1980s, where several had begun their flying on Category II trials. Det 1, 57 FWW FWIC flew F-111Ds at Cannon between 06.88 → 06.92 (when it converted to F-111Fs). Note that an additional F-111D was lost on 26.03.90 (serial unknown).

F-111E PRODUCTION

A1-160
67-0115
NASA Edwards, 1975. Reassigned to ADTC and later served as Hughes Pave Mover testbed there during 1983.

A1-161
67-0116
Assigned to ADTC 1973 and crashed on trials 10.76 at Eglin AFB.

A1-162
67-0117
Assigned to AFFTC and crashed in Mojave Desert 23.04.71.

A1-163
67-0118
Reassigned to ADTC 1972 for armament trials. High-pressure bottle related to the module exploded while a/c on the Eglin ramp 06.81. Rebuilt by GDFW over 11 months and reassigned to ADTC 07.82.

A1-164
67-0119
442 TFTS, 474 TFW 1969–72. 57 FWW 1972. Reassigned to 20 TFW. Named *Red Bravo* for TAM 1984. Ret 24.08.93.

A1-165
67-0120
Det 3, 57 FWW 1972. Remained at Nellis until 1978, when reassigned to 20 TFW. One of two 'Es' named *The Chief* from 1987 when assigned to 20 TFW Commanders. Responsibility of Tiger AMU. *Desert Storm* veteran (19 scores). To the Duxford Museum nr Cambridge, 19.10.93.

A1-166
67-0121
442 TFTS, 474 TFW 1969–72. 57 FWW 1972. 20 TFW 1978–92. Named *Night Stalker* 1987–88, Blue. *Desert Storm* veteran (21 scores, incl. one red lorry). Ret 20.10.93.

A1-167
67-0122
57 FWW 1972. Reassigned to 20 TFW and later named *Rowdy Rebel* 1987–88, Tiger. Ret 24.08.93.

A1-168
67-0123
Det 3, 57 FWW 1972. Reassigned to 20 TFW and later named *The Bold One* 1987–88, Tiger. Ret 03.11.93.

A1-169
67-0124
Det 3, 57 FWW 1972. Reassigned to ADTC at Eglin where it served out its days.

A1-170
68-0001
20 TFW. Named *The Stump Jumper* 1987–88, Red. Crashed on Wainfleet Range, The Wash, on a bombing run 05.02.90. Capt Clifford B Massengill (AC) and 1Lt Thomas G Dorsett (WSO) both killed. First 20th TFW loss in nearly six years.

A1-171
68-0002
442 TFTS, 474 TFW initially. To 20 TFW. Named *Imperial Wizard* 1987–88, Tiger. Ret 15.12.92.

A1-172
68-0003
442 TFTS, 474 TFW initially. To 20 TFW. Crashed at Craignaw, Scotland, after range practice at Jurby, Isle of Man, 19.12.79. 2K.

A1-173
68-0004
20 TFW. *Desert Storm* veteran (6 scores, Tiger). Ret 27.10.93.

A1-174
68-0005
20 TFW. Named *Born in the USA*, Blue. *Desert Storm* veteran (29 scores in white, later sand). Ret 20.10.93.

A1-175
68-0006
20 TFW. Named *Free Bird*, Blue. Ret 02.11.93.

A1-176
68-0007
20 TFW. *Desert Storm* veteran (2 scores, Red). Ret 27.10.93.

A1-177
68-0008
20 TFW. Crashed on busy road nr Tarbet, Kintyre, 16.05.73. Tiger. 2 ejected, and rescued by RN Sea King. Wreckage to UPH by C-130 25.05.73.

A1-178
68-0009
20 TFW. Ret 08.05.92. First F-111E to AMARC.

A1-179
68-0010
20 TFW. Ret 10.11.92.

A1-180
68-0011
20 TFW. Now preserved as Gate Guardian at RAF Lakenheath, Suffolk.

A1-181
68-0012
27 TFW, 1969. To 20 TFW 1970. Crashed in woods nr Harlton, Cambridgeshire, during low-level night sortie, 30.10.79. Tiger. 2 ejected.

A1-182
68-0013
20 TFW. Named *Excalibur* 1987–88. Tiger. *Desert Storm* veteran (24 scores).

A1-183
68-0014
20 TFW. *Desert Storm* veteran (24 scores. Tiger). Ret 01.06.92.

A1-184
68-0015
20 TFW. Named *Ozone Ranger* 1982. *Desert Storm* veteran (1 score. Tiger).

A1-185
68-0016
20 TFW. *Desert Storm* veteran (1 score. Tiger).

A1-186
68-0017
20 TFW. *Desert Storm* veteran (6 scores. Tiger). Ret 15.12.92.

A1-187
68-0018
20 TFW. First USAFE loss. Hit hillside at Coupar, Tayside, 18.01.72. Blue. 2 K.

A1-188
68-0019
20 TFW. Took birdstrikes on Tain Range 09.08.84 and crashed on banks of Loch Eye nr Fearn, Scotland. 2 ejected. Tiger.

A1-189
68-0020
20 TFW. Named My Lucky Blonde 1987–88. Second of two 'Es' which were named *The Chief* when assigned to subsequent 20 TFW/FW Wing commanders. Responsibility of Tiger AMU. Ret 07.12.93 and now preserved at Hill AFB Museum, Utah.

A1-190
68-0021
20 TFW. Ret 02.07.93 with grey radome.

A1-191
68-0022
20 TFW. Named *Thundercat* 1987–88, Tiger. AMP Mod, Ret 15.12.92 coded CC. To 428 FS, 27 FW.

A1-192
68-0023
20 TFW. Named *Aces High* 1987–88, Tiger. Ret 12.10.93.

A1-193
68-0024
20 TFW. Fuel leak shortly after t/o from UPH on 11.01.73 caused fire in port engine, melting rudder actuator. Maj Bob Kroos (AC) and Capt Roger A Beck (WSO) attempted recovery with rudder jammed hard right and one engine. Control lost when undercarriage extended and crew ejected. Blue.

A1-194
68-0025
20 TFW. Ret 12.10.93.

A1-195
68-0026
442 TFS, 474 TFW. To 20 TFW. Named *Hawkeye* 1987–88, Blue. *Desert Storm* veteran (23 scores. Tiger). Ret 20.10.93.

A1-196
68-0027
20 TFW AMP Mod. Ret 20.07.93 to become GF-111E ground instructional AMP airframe at Sheppard AFB, Texas.

A1-197
68-0028
20 TFW. Named *Spirit of 76*, 1976. Ret 31.08.93.

A1-198
68-0029
20 TFW. *Desert Storm* veteran (18 scores. Tiger). Ret 16.11.93.

A1-199
68-0030
20 TFW. Named *Top Cat* 1987–88, Tiger. Ret 02.11.93.

A1-200
68-0031
20 TFW. *Desert Storm* veteran (1 score). Ret 10.08.93.

A1-201
68-0032
20 TFW. Named *Kitty* 1982. AMP Mod. Ret 22.04.93. To 428 FS, 27 FW.

A1-202
68-0033
Det 3, 57 TTW 1978. Reassigned to 20 TFW, and named *Hat Trick* 1987. *Desert Storm* veteran (26 scores, white). Tiger. Ret 22.04.93 and now preserved at Pima County Museum, Arizona.

A1-203
68-0034
20 TFW. Named *Drunken Buzzard* 1982. Ret 16.11.93.

A1-204
68-0035
20 TFW. Named *Shamrock Kid*, 1987–88, Blue. Ret 22.04.93.

A1-205
68-0036
20 TFW. Named *Wild Fire* 1982. *Desert Storm* veteran (32 scores, Blue). Ret 15.12.92.

A1-206
68-0037
20 TFW. Ret 03.11.93.

A1-207
68-0038
20 TFW. Ret 01.07.93.

A1-208
68-0039
20 TFW. *Desert Storm* veteran (21 scores. Tiger. Named *The Baghdad Express* 1991). Ret 24.08.92.

A1-209
68-0040
20 TFW. Named *The Other Woman* 1987–88, Tiger. AMP mod; to 2874 TS. Named *Magnificent Marsha* at SMALC, 1988–89. Reassigned to 428 FS, 27 FW. Last F-111E loss, on 16.02.95, on approach to Cannon AFB. 2 ejected.

A1-210
68-0041
20 TFW. AMP Mod. To 428 FS, 27 FW.

A1-211
68-0042
20 TFW. Crashed in sea off Winterden, Yorkshire, after sortie on Cowden Range, 24.07.79. 2 ejected.

A1-212
68-0043
20 TFW. Ret 12.10.93.

A1-213
68-0044
20 TFW. AMP mod. Ret 10.05.93. To 428 FS, 27 FW.

A1-214
68-0045
20 TFW. Crashed into sea off The Wash on range sortie, 12.12.79. 2 K.

A1-215
68-0046
20 TFW. *Desert Storm* veteran (12 scores. Tiger. F-111 silhouette in black). Ret 10.08.93.

A1-216
68-0047
20 TFW, named *'Til We Meet Again* 1987–88, Red. AMP Mod, Ret 10.05.93, to 428 FS, 27 FW.

A1-217
68-0048
20 TFW. AMP Mod. To 428 FS, 27 FW.

A1-218
68-0049
20 TFW. Named *Easy Rider* 1982, and *The Grim Reaper* 1987–88, Red. *Desert Storm* veteran (20 scores). Tiger-tailed scheme for 1991 Tiger Meet. Named *77th Gamblers Last Deal*, 08.93, Red. Ret 12.10.93.

A1-219
68-0050
20 TFW. LOX bottle exploded while a/c on UPH ramp. Rebuilt by GDFW and redelivered to 20 TFW during 11.88. Later was the first AMP delivery to UPH (in short-lived overall grey scheme, replaced by std camouflage for combat duties), and only *Desert Storm* AMP veteran (1 score). Ret 22.04.93. To 428 FS, 27 FW.

A1-220
68-0051
20 TFW. Ret 10.08.93.

A1-221
68-0052
20 TFW. Named *On Guard* 1987–88, Tiger. Crashed short of Upper Heyford runway 09 on 17.09.92, seconds before touchdown after control loss, Blue. Maj David McGuire and Capt Jerry Lindh both killed.

A1-222
68-0053
20 TFW. Ret 25.06.92.

A1-223
68-0054
20 TFW. AMP Mod. To 428 FS, 27 FW.

A1-224
68-0055
20 TFW. Was 55 TFS/FS 'flagship', named *Heartbreaker*, in both 1987–88 and 08.93. Ret 07.12.93 and now preserved at Robins AFB Museum, Georgia.

A1-225
68-0056
20 TFW. Ret 20.10.93.

A1-226
68-0057
20 TFW. Crashed nr Wareham, Dorset, England, 29.04.80. 2 K.

A1-227
68-0058
442 TFTS, 474 TFW initially. 57 FWW, 1975. Reassigned to ADTC 1978.

A1-228
68-0059
20 TFW. Named *The Mad Bomber* 1987–88, Red. Ret 27.10.93.

A1-229
68-0060
20 TFW. Suffered birdstrike during low-level sortie and crashed over The Wash, nr Boston, Lincolnshire, 05.11.75. 2 ejected. Capsule dumped at RAF Benwaters, 1976.

A1-230
68-0061
20 TFW. Named *Big Dealer*, 1987–88, Red. *Desert Storm* veteran. Ret 07.12.93, named *Last Roll of the Dice*. Blue.

A1-231
68-0062
20 TFW. Named *Land Shark* 1987–88, Tiger. Ret 31.08.93.

A1-232
68-0063
20 TFW. Named *A Knight to Remember* 1987–88, Tiger. AMP Mod, Ret 02.07.93. To 428 FS, 27 FW.

A1-233
68-0064
20 TFW. Named *6,000 General Dynamics High Flyer* 04.93. Ret 16.11.93.

A1-234
68-0065
20 TFW. Named *The Armed Citizen* 1987–88. Ret 27.10.93.

A1-235
68-0066
20 TFW. Named *Crazy Horse* 1982. Crashed at Sorgun, 62 miles (100km) from Incirlik, Turkey, during WTD range sortie, 20.07.90. Blue. 2 ejected.

A1-236
68-0067
20 TFW. AMP Mod, Tiger. To 428 FS, 27 FW.

A1-237
68-0068
20 TFW. Named *One Man's Baby*, 1982 and *The Flak Ducker* 1987–88, Red. *Desert Storm* veteran (17 scores. Tiger). AMP Mod, Ret 20.07.93. To 428 FS, 27 FW.

A1-238
68-0069
20 TFW. Named *The Wild Hare* 1987–88, Red. *Desert Storm* veteran (22 scores. Tiger). Named *Love Machine* 1992, Blue. Ret 16.11.93.

A1-239
68-0070
20 TFW. Crashed nr Welshpool, Wales, on low-level sortie, 31.10.77. 2 K.

A1-240
68-0071
20 TFW. AMP Mod. To 428 FS, 27 FW.

A1-241
68-0072
20 TFW. Named *Bad Medicine* 1987–88, Tiger. *Desert Storm* veteran (12 scores. Tiger). AMP Mod, to 428 FS, 27 FW.

A1-242
68-0073
20 TFW. AMP Mod. To 428 FS, 27 FW.

A1-243
68-0074
20 TFW. *Desert Storm* veteran (30 scores. Tiger). AMP Mod, Ret 10.05.93. To 428 FS, 27 FW.

A1-244
68-0075
20 TFW. Named *Galleon* 1987–88, Blue. AMP Mod, Ret 10.05.93. To 428 FS, 27 FW.

A1-245
68-0076
20 TFW. *Desert Storm* veteran (28 scores. Tiger). AMP Mod, Ret 10.05.93. To 428 FS, 27 FW.

A1-246
68-0077
20 TFW. 77 TFS 'flagship' named *June Nite*, then *Red Lady II* 1987–88. AMP Mod, Ret 20.07.93. To 428 FS, 27 FW.

A1-247
68-0078
20 TFW. Named *Whispering Death* 1987–88, Red. AMP Mod. Reassigned to SMALC, McClellan, California, departing UPH with SM codes.

A1-248
68-0079
20 TFW. Named *Tiger Lil* 1987–88, Tiger. Had five Iraqi flags painted under cockpit, 03.91–02.92. AMP Mod, Ret 10.05.93 with *Farewell Tigers* on fin. To 428 FS, 27 FW.

A1-249
68-0080
20 TFW. Named *Strange Brew*, 1987–88, Tiger. *Desert Storm* veteran (10 scores, marked as Iraqi flags). AMP Mod, Ret 10.05.93. To 428 FS, 27 FW.

A1-250
68-0081
20 TFW. Crashed at Shap, Cumbria, 05.03.75. Blue. 2 K.

A1-251
68-0082
20 TFW. Aborted landing 25.03.81 at RAF Fairford resulting in smashed undercarriage and nose. Rebuilt at GDFW over 17 months using parts from F-111A A1-24 (65-5706) and redelivered to UPH on 01.10.82. Named *The Phoenix* 1987–88, Tiger. AMP Mod. To 428 FS, 27 FW.

A1-252
68-0083
20 TFW. Named *Prometheus II*, 1987–88, Tiger. *Desert Storm* veteran (12 scores, marked as Iraqi flags). AMP Mod, Ret 20.07.93. To 428 FS, 27 FW.

A1-253
68-0084
20 TFW. AMP Mod. To 428 FS, 27 FW.

Eighty-eight F-111Es spent the majority of their service careers with the 20 TFW (later FW) at RAF Upper Heyford (ATC code EGUA), Oxfordshire, England, and the squadron colour references/bomb scores used above are Blue for 55 TFS/FS, Red for 77 TFS/FS and Tiger (Yellow) for 79 TFS/FS. Bomb scores acquired during *Desert Storm Proven Force* Gulf War operations from Incirlik, Turkey, were usually repainted in tan after the a/c returned to EGUA and the number of scores displayed was not always an indication of all missions flown. Ret indicates date of return to USA from England, where known. Non-AMP jets went to AMARC unless noted otherwise.

Names in 1982 appeared on nosewheel doors. In 1987–88 they were usually painted on the nose (right, or both sides) with other artwork.

Other operators are listed where known. Refer to the Appendix III dealing with Unit Histories for a fuller explanation of the ins-and-outs of the parent organizations.

F-111F PRODUCTION

E2-01
70-2362
First flew Aug 1971. MUO → EGUL, *Pave Tack* mod → KCVF. *Pacer Strike* mod with 524 FS.

E2-02
70-2363
MUO → EGUL, *Pave Tack* mod → KCVF.

E2-03
70-2364
MUO → EGUL, *Pave Tack* mod → KCVF.

E2-04
70-2365
MUO → EGUL, *Pave Tack* mod → KCVF.

E2-05
70-2366
Bicentennial 366 TFW MUO 'flagship' 1976. MUO → EGUL, *Pave Tack* mod. Flew into sea off Scarborough after control loss, 21.12.83, when a/c was assigned to the 48 TFW. 2 ejected.

E2-06
70-2367
MUO → EGUL.
Suffered mid-air collision with 73-0714 during Tain Range sortie, 20.04.79. Crashed into Donoch Firth. 2 ejected. A/c and crew were assigned to the 48 TFW.

E2-07
70-2368
MUO → EGUL, *Pave Tack* mod. Crashed nr Binham, Norfolk, 02.05.90. 2 ejected. A/c and crew were assigned to the 492 TFS, 48 TFW.

E2-08
70-2369
MUO → EGUL, *Pave Tack* mod → KCVF.

E2-09
70-2370
MUO → EGUL, *Pave Tack* mod → KCVF.

Crashed 22.09.93 while assigned to the 522 FS, 27 FW.

E2-10
70-2371
MUO → EGUL, *Pave Tack* mod → KCVF.

E2-11
70-2372
MUO → EGUL, *Pave Tack* mod → KCVF.

E2-12
70-2373
MUO → EGUL, *Pave Tack* mod → KCVF.

E2-13
70-2374
MUO → EGUL, *Pave Tack* mod → KCVF.

E2-14
70-2375
MUO → EGUL, *Pave Tack* mod. Crashed at Thirlstane Farm, Lauder, Scotland, 28.07.87. Crew and a/c were assigned to the 493 TFS, 48 TFW.

E2-15
70-2376
MUO → EGUL, *Pave Tack* mod → KCVF.

E2-16
70-2377
MUO → EGUL. Crashed into Cuillin Hills, Skye, on low-level night sortie, 07.12.82. Possible TFR failure. 2 K. Crew and a/c were assigned to the 493 TFS, 48 TFW.

E2-17
70-2378
MUO → EGUL, *Pave Tack* mod → KCVF.

E2-18
70-2379
MUO → EGUL, *Pave Tack* mod → KCVF. Now on display at the Eglin AFB Armament Museum, Florida.

E2-19
70-2380
MUO → EGUL. Crashed nr a school at Exning, Newmarket, 15.12.77. 2 ejected. A/c and crew were assigned to the 48 TFW.

E2-20
70-2381
MUO → EGUL, *Pave Tack* mod → KCVF.

E2-21
70-2382
MUO → EGUL, *Pave Tack* mod → KCVF.

E2-22
70-2383
MUO → EGUL, *Pave Tack* mod → KCVF.

E2-23
70-2384
MUO → EGUL, *Pave Tack* mod → KCVF.

E2-24
70-2385
MUO → EGUL, *Pave Tack* mod → KCVF.

E2-25
70-2386
MUO → EGUL, *Pave Tack* mod → KCVF.

E2-26
70-2387
MUO → EGUL, *Pave Tack* mod → KCVF.

E2-27
70-2388
Crashed 10.75 while assigned to 366 TFW at MUO. Wreckage to Mountain Home fire dump. RAAF exchange crew member involved.

E2-28
70-2389
MUO → EGUL, *Pave Tack* mod. Karma 52 in *El Dorado Canyon* attack on Al Azziziyah Barracks, Tripoli, 15.04.86. 495 TFS, 48 TFW crew Maj Fernando Ribas-Dominicci (AC) and Capt Paul F Lorence (WSO) KIA. Possibly hit by a SAM.

E2-29
70-2390
MUO → EGUL, *Pave Tack* mod. First F-111F to drop bombs during both *El Dorado Canyon* and *Desert Storm*. → KCVF.

E2-30
70-2391
MUO → EGUL, *Pave Tack* mod → KCVF.

E2-31
70-2392
MUO → EGUL, *Pave Tack* mod → KCVF.

E2-32
70-2393
Crashed after 1973 while a/c assigned to the 366 TFW at MUO. No further details.

E2-33
70-2394
MUO → EGUL, *Pave Tack* mod → KCVF.

E2-34
70-2395
Crashed after 1973 while a/c assigned to the 366 TFW at MUO. No further details.

E2-35
70-2396
MUO → EGUL, *Pave Tack* mod → KCVF.

E2-36
70-2397
MUO → EGUL, *Pave Tack* mod. Crashed nr Tonopah During *Red Flag* exercise, 05.04.89. 2 K. Crew and a/c were assigned to the 494 TFS, 48 TFW.

E2-37
70-2398
MUO → EGUL, *Pave Tack* mod → KCVF.

E2-38
70-2399
MUO → EGUL, *Pave Tack* mod → KCVF. *Pacer Strike* mod with 524 FS.

E2-39
70-2400
Det 3, 57 FWW, Nellis → Det 3, 57 FWW, McClellan, 08.77. *Pave Tack* mod. Deep Throat trials → KCVF Det 3, 57 FWW, 07.92.

E2-40
70-2401
MUO → EGUL, *Pave Tack* mod → KCVF.

E2-41
70-2402
MUO → EGUL, *Pave Tack* mod → KCVF.

E2-42
70-2403
MUO → EGUL, *Pave Tack* mod → KCVF.

E2-43
70-2404
MUO → EGUL, *Pave Tack* mod → KCVF.

E2-44
70-2405
MUO → EGUL, *Pave Tack* mod → KCVF. First *Pacer Strike* mod, assigned to 524 FS.

E2-45
70-2406
MUO → EGUL, *Pave Tack* mod → KCVF.

E2-46
70-2407
Crashed prior to delivery to 366 TFW, 03.72.

E2-47
70-2408
MUO → EGUL, *Pave Tack* mod → KCVF.

E2-48
70-2409
MUO → EGUL, *Pave Tack* mod → KCVF.

E2-49
70-2410
Crashed before 1973. No further details.

E2-50
70-2411
MUO → EGUL, *Pave Tack* mod → KCVF. *Pacer Strike* mod with 524 FS.

E2-51
70-2412
MUO → EGUL, *Pave Tack* mod → KCVF.

E2-52
70-2413
MUO → EGUL, *Pave Tack* mod → KCVF.

E2-53
70-2414
MUO → EGUL, *Pave Tack* mod → KCVF.

E2-54
70-2415
MUO → EGUL, *Pave Tack* mod → KCVF.

E2-55
70-2416
MUO → EGUL, *Pave Tack* mod → KCVF.

E2-56
70-2417
MUO → EGUL, *Pave Tack* mod → KCVF.

E2-57
70-2418
MUO → EGUL, *Pave Tack* mod. Possibly touched another F-111F on approach, 23.02.87; sustained a fire and explosion, crashing nr Newmarket, Suffolk, and damaging a house. 2 ejected but capsule struck trees causing minor injuries. A/c and crew were assigned to the 492 TFS, 48 TFW. Incident ended 38 accident-free months for the 48 TFW.

E2-58
70-2419
MUO → EGUL, *Pave Tack* mod → KCVF.

E2-59
71-0883
Named *Spirit of Mountain Home* for 366 TFW's participation in *Giant Voice* Bomb Comp 1974. MUO → EGUL, *Pave Tack* mod → KCVF. *Pacer Strike* mod with 524 FS.

E2-60
71-0884
MUO → EGUL, *Pave Tack* mod → KCVF. *Pacer Strike* mod with 524 FS.

E2-61
71-0885
MUO → EGUL, *Pave Tack* mod → KCVF.

E2-62
71-0886
MUO → EGUL, *Pave Tack* mod → KCVF. *Pacer Strike* mod with 524 FS.

E2-63
71-0887
MUO → EGUL, *Pave Tack* mod → KCVF. *Pacer Strike* mod with 524 FS.

E2-64
71-0888
MUO → EGUL, *Pave Tack* mod → KCVF. *Pacer Strike* mod with 524 FS.

E2-65
71-0889
MUO → EGUL, *Pave Tack* mod → KCVF. *Pacer Strike* mod with 524 FS.

E2-66
71-0890
MUO → EGUL, *Pave Tack* mod → KCVF. *Pacer Strike* mod with 524 FS.

E2-67
71-0891
MUO → EGUL, *Pave Tack* mod → KCVF. *Pacer Strike* mod with 524 FS.

E2-68
71-0892
MUO → EGUL, *Pave Tack* mod → KCVF.

E2-69
71-0893
MUO → EGUL, *Pave Tack* mod → KCVF. *Pacer Strike* mod with 524 FS.

E2-70
71-0894
MUO → EGUL, *Pave Tack* mod → KCVF.

E2-71
72-1441
MUO → EGUL. Crashed at East Wretham on approach to Lakenheath, 04.02.81. 2 ejected. A/c and crew were assigned to the 494 TFS, 48 TFW, and a/c had been the first *Pave Tack* delivery to the Wing.

E2-72
72-1442
MUO → EGUL, *Pave Tack* mod → KCVF. *Pacer Strike* mod with 524 FS.

E2-73
72-1443
MUO → EGUL, *Pave Tack* mod → KCVF. *Pacer Strike* mod with 524 FS.

E2-74
72-1444
MUO → EGUL, *Pave Tack* mod → KCVF. *Pacer Strike* mod with 523 FS.

E2-75
72-1445
MUO → Det 3, 57 TTW, *Pave Tack* mod → EGUL → KCVF. *Pacer Strike* mod previously with 524 FS, but sent direct from SMALC to AMARC, post-modification.

E2-76
72-1446
MUO → EGUL, *Pave Tack* mod → KCVF. *Pacer Strike* mod previously with 524 FS, but sent direct from SMALC to AMARC.

E2-77
72-1447
MUO → EGUL. Crew ejected after control loss due to violent pitch-up, 23.06.82. Crashed into hill nr Porin, Rosshire, Scotland. A/c and crew were assigned to the 492 TFS, 48 TFW.

E2-78
72-1448
MUO → EGUL, *Pave Tack* mod → KCVF.

E2-79
72-1449
MUO → EGUL, *Pave Tack* mod → KCVF. *Pacer Strike* mod with 523 FS.

E2-80
72-1450
MUO → EGUL, *Pave Tack* mod → KCVF. *Pacer Strike* mod with 524 FS.

E2-81
72-1451
MUO → EGUL, *Pave Tack* mod → KCVF.

E2-82
72-1452
MUO → Det 3, 57 TTW, *Pave Tack* mod → EGUL → KCVF.

E2-83
73-0707
MUO → EGUL, *Pave Tack* mod → KCVF.

E2-84
73-0708
MUO → EGUL, *Pave Tack* mod → KCVF. *Pacer Strike* mod with 524 FS.

E2-85
73-0709
MUO. Crashed nr China Lake, California, 21.04.77. Crew and a/c were assigned to the 366 TFW.

E2-86
73-0710
MUO → EGUL, *Pave Tack* mod → KCVF. *Pacer Strike* mod with 524 FS.

E2-87
73-0711
MUO → EGUL, *Pave Tack* mod → KCVF.

E2-88
73-0712
MUO → EGUL, *Pave Tack* mod → KCVF.

E2-89
73-0713
MUO → EGUL, *Pave Tack* mod → KCVF.

E2-90
73-0714
MUO → EGUL. Mid-air collision with 70-2367 over Tain Range, touching wings while reforming after 'attack', 20.04.79. 2 ejected, and rescued from Donoch Firth by local fishing boat. (Crew of '367 rescued by RAF helicopter.) A/c and crew assigned to the 48 TFW.

E2-91
73-0715
MUO → EGUL, *Pave Tack* mod → KCVF.

E2-92
73-0716
MUO → EGUL, *Pave Tack* mod. Crashed nr Incirlik, during WTD, 01.11.82. 2 ejected. A/c and crew were assigned to the 48 TFW.

E2-93
73-0717
MUO → EGUL. May have been struck by lightning while entering landing circuit after sortie surge exercise over Jurby Range, 29.03.78. Crashed nr Mundford, Norfolk. Ejection initiated outside capsule's speed and altitude parameters; parachutes did not open. 2 K. Crew and a/c were assigned to the 492 TFS, 48 TFW. Grounding order for module systems safety checks followed.

E2-94
73-0718
MUO → EGUL. Crashed nr Landau, Germany, 04.10.77. 2 K. Crew and a/c were assigned to the 494 TFS, 48 TFW: was the first of the Wing's losses.

E2-95
74-0177
MUO → EGUL, *Pave Tack* mod → KCVF.

E2-96
74-0178
MUO → EGUL, *Pave Tack* mod → KCVF. *Pacer Strike* mod with 524 FS.

E2-97
74-0179
MUO → EGUL. Crashed on approach to RAF Leuchars, Scotland, 16.09.82. Crew and a/c were assigned to the 48 TFW.

E2-98
74-0180
MUO → EGUL, *Pave Tack* mod → KCVF. *Pacer Strike* mod with 524 FS.

E2-99
74-0181
MUO → EGUL, *Pave Tack* mod → KCVF.

E2-100
74-0182
MUO → EGUL, *Pave Tack* mod → KCVF.

E2-101
74-0183
MUO → EGUL, *Pave Tack* mod → KCVF. Crashed in southern Saudi Arabia while practising GBU-24 'mini-toss' at 1.30L, 09.10.90, during *Desert Shield*. Fred 'Art' Reed and Tom 'T C' Caldwell, assigned to the 493 TFS, 48 TFW(P), both killed.

E2-102
74-0184
MUO → EGUL, *Pave Tack* mod → KCVF. *Pacer Strike* mod with 524 FS.

E2-103
74-0185
MUO → EGUL, *Pave Tack* mod → KCVF. *Pacer Strike* mod with 524 FS.

E2-104
74-0186
MUO → Det 3, 57 TTW → KCVF Det 3, 57 FWW 07/92 → *Pacer Strike* mod with 524 FS.

E2-105
74-0187
MUO → Det 3, 57 TTW, *Pave Tack* mod → EGUL → KCVF. Last *Pacer Strike* mod, with 524 FS.

E2-106
74-0188
MUO → EGUL, *Pave Tack* mod. Crashed into North Sea during low-level sortie in bad weather off Germany, 26.04.83. 2 K. Crew and a/c were assigned to the 492 TFS, 48 TFW. Was the 562nd and last airworthy F-111 built.

Ninety-eight F-111Fs saw service with the 48th TFW/FW at RAF Lakenheath (ATC code EGUL) between 1977 and 1992. Sixty-six of these took part in Operation *Desert Storm*, flying from Taif AB, Saudi Arabia, 1990–91. Refer to Chapter 7 for full details of Operation *El Dorado Canyon* participants. All survivors were transferred to 27th FW service at Cannon AFB (ATC code KCVF) during 1992 where *Pacer Strike* was initiated.

APPENDIX III

USAF F-111 Units and Codes

Colour code: red (*r*), yellow (*y*), green (*gn*), blue (*b*), white (*w*), black (*bl*), grey (*gy*), purple (*pr*)

20th TFW, RAF Upper Heyford, UK
Received first aircraft 12 September 1970 for 79th TFS

55th TFS (F-111E) *Fightin' Fifty-Fifth*
US	Not applied due to connotations of unserviceability	
JS *b*		Apr 1971–Aug 1972
UH *b/w*		Aug 1972–Dec 1993

77th TFS (F-111E) *Gamblers*
UT *r*	Some aircraft coded	Dec 1970–Jan 1971
JT *r*	Operational 27 July 1971	Jan 1971–July 1972
UH *r*	On adoption of wing-code	July 1972–Sept 1993

79th TFS (F-111E) *Tigers*
UR *y*		Oct 1970–Jan 1971
JR *y*		Jan 1971–Aug 1972
UH *y*		Aug 1972–June 1993

42nd EC (EF-111A)
UH *gy*	Control passed to 66 ECW from 30 June 1985–25 Jan 1991	Feb 1984–July 1992

(Twenty-two F-111E of 20th TFW assigned to 7440th Wing (P) at Incirlik for Operation *Proven Force*, Jan–Feb 1991. EF-111As of 42nd ECS also deployed)

27th TFW, Cannon AFB, NM

481st TFS (F-111E/D) *Green Knights*
CA *gn*	Few aircraft so marked	Nov 1969–July 1971
CC *gn*	Inactivated 31 Aug 1973	Nov 1972–Aug 1973
CC *gn*	Reactivated 15 Jan 1976	Jan 1976–June 1980

522nd TFS (F-111E/A/D/F) *Fireballs*
CC *r*		Sept–Nov 1969
CC *r*	Aircraft loaned by 474th TFW	Sept 1971–Aug 1972
CC *r*		May 1972–Feb 1992
CC *r*	Ex-48th FW aircraft	Feb 1992–Jan 1996

523rd TFS (F-111D/F) *Crusaders*
CC *b*	Re-numbering of 481st TFS	Aug 1973–Nov 1993
CC *b*	Ex-48th FW aircraft	Nov 1993–mid 1996

524th TFS (F-111A/E/D/F) *Hounds*
CD *y*	Codes probably not used	July 1969
CD *y*	Codes probably not used	July 1969
CC *y*	Became 524th TFTS, 6/80	Aug 1972–mid 1992
CC *y*	Ex-48th FW aircraft	Sept 1992–July 1996

(Few F-111A/E aircraft were actually assigned)

4427th TFRS (F-111D)
CE *pr*		Nov 1971
CC *pr*	Re-numbered 481 TFTS 1/76	Dec 1971–Jan 1976

428th TFTS (F-111G) *Buccaneers*
CC *b*	F-111G withdrawn mid 1993	June 1990–mid 1993

428th FS (F-111E)
CC *b*	Ex-20th TFW AMP F-111Es	March 1993–Oct 1995

430th ECS (EF-111A) *Tigers*
CC *b*		May 1992–mid 1993

429th ECS (EF-111A)
CC *b*	Re-assigned from Mountain Home AFB. Assumed *Tigers* name	mid 1993–current

48th TFW Statue of Liberty Wing, RAF Lakenheath, UK

492nd TFS (F-111F) *Bolars/Bowlers*
LN *b*		July 1977–April 1992

493rd TFS (F-111F) *Roosters*
LN *y, y/bl*	Name seldom used	July 1977–Dec 1992

494th TFS (F-111F) *Panthers*
LN *r*		June 1977–Aug 1992

495th TFS (F-111F) *Aardvark University/Thundervarks*
LN *gn*		July 1977–Dec 1991

(The majority of the 48th TFW deployed to Taif, Saudi Arabia as the 48th TFW (P) from August 1990–March 1991, joined by elements of the 390th ECS (MO) and 42nd ECS (UH) which also retained their normal base codes)

57th FWW /TTW, Nellis AFB, Nev
(Formerly 4525th FWW until 15 October 1968)

4539th CCTS (F-111A)
WF y/bl							July 1968–Oct 1969

422nd FWS (F-111A/D/E/F)
WF y/bl							Oct 1969–Oct 1973

422 FWS (F-111A/D/E/F)
WA y/bl							Oct 1973–Aug 1977

Det 2 (F-111A/D)
CC		Located at Cannon AFB		Oct 1970–Dec 1973

Det 2		At McClellan AFB		May 1972–Aug 1977
(Det 2 (F-111A) became Fighter Weapons School at Mountain Home, July 1977–Dec 1981)

Det 1 USAF Fighter Weapons School (F-111A/D). Redesignation of FWS. Based at Mountain Home and then at Cannon, Jan 1982–May 1988

Det 3 (F-111A/D/E/F)
MO		Based at Mountain Home		Aug 1971–April 1972

Det 3 (F-111A/E)
NA		At Nellis AFB			April 1972–Aug 1977

Det 3 (F-111D/E/F)
WA		At McClellan AFB		Aug 1977–March 1980

Det 3 (F-111F)
CC		At Cannon AFB			July 1992–mid 1996

431st FWS (F-111A/D/E/F) *Red Devils*
WA y/bl							Oct 1980–Dec 1981

431st TES (F-111A/D/E/F) *Red Devils*
WA y/bl	Also used 'visiting' F-111Cs	Dec 1981–June 1992

347th TFW, Mountain Home AFB, Id

4589th TFS (F-111F)
MP y							Sept 1971–Oct 1971

389th TFS (F-111F) *Thunderbolts*
MO		Redesignation of 4589th TFS	Oct 1971–Oct 1972

4590th TFS (F-111F)
MQ r		Code probably not used		Jan 1972–July 1972

390th TFS (F-111F) *Boars*
MO r		Redesignation of 4590th TFS	July 1972–Oct 1972

391st TFS (F-111F) *Bold Tigers*
MO b							June 1971–Oct 1972

428th TFS* (F-111A) *Buccaneers*
HG r		At Takhli / Korat RTAFB		July 1973–June 1975

429th TFS* (F-111A) *Black Falcons*
HG y		At Takhli / Korat RTAFB		July 1973–June 1975
(* From 474th TFW for *Constant Guard V*. Returned to 474th TFW control June 1975)

366th TFW, *Gunfighters*, Mountain Home AFB Id

389th TFS (F-111F) *Thunderbolts*
MO y							Oct 1972–June 1977

390th TFS (F-111F) *Boars*
MO gn							Oct 1972–July 1977

391st TFS (F-111F) *Bold Tigers*
MO b							Oct 1972–July 1977

389th TFS (F-111A) *Thunderbolts*
MO y		Became 389th TFTS, Oct 1979	July 1977–April 1992

390th TFS (F-111A) *Boars*
MO gn							July 1977–March 1982

390th ECS* (EF-111A) *Ravens*
MO							April 1984–Sept 1992

388th TFTS (F-111A)
MO							Aug 1977–March 1984

388th ECS (EF-111A) *Griffins*
MO							Nov 1981–March 1984
(* 390th ECS Dets to 4404th CW, Saudi Arabia from late 1992 to 1995. Unit redesignated 429th ECS, Sept 1992 and transferred to Cannon AFB mid–1993, combining with assets of 430th ECS)

474th TFW *Roadrunners*, Nellis AFB, Nev

428th TFS (F-111A)
NA b		Codes applied July 1968		Jan 1968–Aug 1977

428th TFS Det1 (F-111A)
		Combat Lancer, Takhli RTAFB	March–Nov 1968

429th TFS (F-111A) *Black Falcons*
NB y		Codes applied July 1968		May 1968–Apr 1972

429th TFS (F-111A) *Black Falcons*
NA y							April 1972–Aug 1977

430th TFS (F-111A) *Tigers*
NC r							Sept 1968–April 1972

4527th CCTS (F-111A)
ND							Jan 1968–Oct 1969

442nd TFTS (F-111A)
ND		(NA after Apr 1972).		Oct 1969–Aug 1977
		Renumbered 4527th CCTS.
		Also flew F-111E from Nov
		1969–Sept 1972

(The 429th TFS and 430th TFS deployed to Takhli RTAFB for *Constant Guard V* in Sept 1972. The 430th TFS was relieved by the 428th TFS, March 1973 and, with the 429th TFS it transferred to 347th TFW control 30 July1973 and moved to Korat RTAFB until June 1975 when both squadrons returned to the 474th TFW at Nellis.)

3246th Test Wing (46th TW after Oct 1992)

3247th TS (F-111E)
AD   Coded from Nov 1982   mid 1973–Oct 1989

40th TS (F-111E/F)
ET   Oct 1989–late 1995

4480th TFW (became 474th TFW, Jan1968)

4481st TFS (F-111A)
            Became 428th TFS, Jan 1968   July 1967–Jan 1968
(First operational F-111 unit, prepared *Harvest Reaper* aircraft and aircrew under *Combat Trident*.)

Tactical Air Warfare Center (TAWC), later USAF AWC

4485th TS Det 3 (EF-111A)
OT *bl/w*   At Eglin AFB then Cannon from
              mid–1992

85th TES (EF-111A)
OT   Redesignation of above   Oct 1992

79th TEG Det 7 (EF-111A)
OT   At Cannon AFB,1995

6510th Test Wing

6512TS
ED   Used various F-111A/D/   1982–92
            FB–111A, EF-111A

SM–ALC Engineering Flight Test

2847th TS (later 337th TS)
SM   Used various F-111 Coded from
            June,1992. Test functions moved
            to Eglin, 1994

NB. On 2 October 1991 the designation TFW became FW (Fighter Wing) and TFS became FS (Fighter Squadron).

SAC UNITS, (FB–111A)

340th Bomb Group, Carswell AFB,Tx

4007th CCTS
Training unit; task reassigned to 380th BW   Sept 1969–June 1971

380th Bomb Wing (Medium), Plattsburgh AFB, NY

4007th CCTS
Later redesignated 530th CCTS   June 1971–July 1991

528th BMS
b   July 1971– July 1991

529th BMS
r   Oct 1971– July 1991

(Wing converted to KC–135 as 380th ARW, 1991.)

509th Bomb Wing (Medium), Pease AFB, NH
(First aircraft received Dec 1970)

393rd BMS *Tigers*   Jan 1973–Sept 1990

715th BMS *Eagles*   Jan 1973–Sept 1990

(First FB–111A Wing began operations July 1971. Dates given are for full operational status and deactivation. Both wings moved from 2nd AF to 8th AF control in Jan 1975.)

Notes

CHAPTER ONE

As the embryonic TFX was unlikely to reach the ramps at USAF bases for at least five years from 1961, McNamara began the process of persuading the USAF to accept a variant of the F-4 Phantom, a Navy design, as an interim type, and closed F-105 production. Ironically, the F-4 was destined to remain in service for thirty-four years, retiring in 1996 at much the same time as the F-111.

2. The original FADF selection, the Mach 0.8 Douglas F6D-1 Missileer, had already been cancelled the month before Kennedy took office, though missile and radar development continued and the need for a suitable platform remained. See Chapter 2, Missileers.

3. Variable geometry was considered for a Vickers research aircraft, the Swallow, using research into variable-sweep wing bearings by Sir Barnes Wallis in the mid-1950s. The Swallow was cancelled in 1957 and most of the data passed to NASA and the USAF. The designers of TSR-2, later to be cancelled in favour of the F-111K (also cancelled) considered V-G but rejected it through lack of data on wing-sweep bearings. Apparently they were largely unaware of Wallis's pioneering work. Interestingly, the TSR-2 was reported to be within 2 per cent of its design performance at the time of cancellation, while the F-111A was 20 per cent below its performance targets.

4. For the USN the only consolation was that, by making the CAS requirement purely a secondary function for their aircraft they were allowed to proceed with a separate type specifically for this role. This eventually resulted in the A-7 Corsair II, which was in turn bought in small numbers by the USAF in the name of 'commonality'.

5. Republic's submission had the smallest wing area (a characteristic it shared with its F-105 forbear), with stubby swinging portions.

6. See Chapter 2, Missileers.

7. Report of the McClellan Senate Committee.

8. Curiously, the system appeared to re-emerge in November 1978, with the contract for the Lockheed F-117A. Possibly this was part of the disinformation surrounding the Stealth projects.

9. GD Convair and Stanley Aviation had already used individually encapsulated ejection seats in the supersonic B-58 Hustler bomber. A four-piece visor, with window, clanged down to enclose the crew individually on ejection. Early tests of the system used a chimpanzee and a small bear.

10. A little known fact is that the F-111's GE(USA) Attack Radar Set plus Terrain-Following and Electronic Countermeasures nasal avionics package was also later envisaged for installation in the proposed Lockheed B-12, a purely bomber version of the SR-71 Blackbird which was not proceeded with. This model would have also encompassed Astrocompass and SRAM nuclear missile capability, virtually identical to that evolved for the SAC FB-111A variant.

11. Despite purely monetary inflationary factors, this equated to an approximate doubling of price. In the late 1980s it was estimated that a new-build F-111 would have cost nearly $50m in then-year money.

12. See Chapter 9, Buckshots and Falcons.

CHAPTER TWO

1. Based on their earlier research and development on the FADF radar and that intended for the abandoned USAF/North American ethyl-borane derived zip fuel-powered YF-108 Rapier interceptor, development of which had terminated on 23 September 1959. Lockheed's YF-12 Blackbird interceptor honed development of a similar low-volatility fuel and trialled a very similar Hughes AN/ASG-18 radar package during the early 1960s, just before testing of the F-111B's AN/AWG-9 package began.

2. The chief of Lockheed's 'Skunk Works' design team, Clarence 'Kelly' Johnson, was one of many to voice concerns over US production capacity to meet this need, and companies like North American were experimenting with steel honeycomb structures precisely with costs and availability in mind. It is important to appreciate just how many separate, advanced military aircraft projects were in progress in the late 1950s/early 1960s.

3. The origins of the same team that he later headed every Saturday morning in the Pentagon, beginning on 25 August 1966, and which became known as the Project Icarus Meetings, a phrase originally coined by Col Robin Hansen, USAF (ret) in a lighthearted moment. They involved McNamara, the F-111 System Program Office and General Dynamics and were to continue under the Secretary for Defense's supervision until 'either the meetings are doing no good or the problems are solved'. Icarus spawned all sorts of 'common weapons systems' packages designed to fit in the bay (the Sidewinder trapeze, reconnaissance pallet, among others), some of which were manufactured for use in the F-111A/B but never used operationally for very long.

CHAPTER THREE

1. The TAC F-111 scheme later changed to Federal Standards Colors Gloss Black (17038) undersides, although the official Tech Order specified Matt Black 37038. The standard 'Vietnam' camouflage (TO 1-1-4) of Tan (30219), Medium Green (34102) and Dark Green (34079) was retained on all TAC attack versions, including RAAF examples (although a slightly revised pattern came into vogue with the introduction of the F-111E) long after it was abandoned elsewhere. Even the paint type was an oddity in the 1990s. Unlike other USAF aircraft, which went over to MIL-C-83286 aliphatic polyurethane the F-111 retained a finish of epoxy primer, MIL-P-23377 camouflage and a top-coat of MIL-L-81352 acrylic lacquer.

2. This description of the F-111 was coined by Brig Gen Jay Hubbard, Commander of MAG-12 at Chu Lai.

3. At the first million hours flying time the F-111 had sustained 77 losses compared with 310 for the F-100, 189 for the F-105 and 109 for the F-4.

4. Contemporary US Navy A-6 crews used the similar expression 'Cumulo Rocks'. A-6 Intruders possessed no automatic terrain-following, but did employ terrain-monitoring radar and a radar altimeter to the same end.

5. A fuller account of conventional weapons options available to the F-111 can be found in Chapter 6, High Plains Deltas.

6. Just such an occasion occurred over Buckinghamshire, England, during the 1970s when footage was shot of F-111E 68-024 dumping fuel following an engine fire shortly after takeoff from RAF Upper Heyford on 11 January 1973. Refer to the Appendices dealing with F-111E production.

7. According to Roger Peterson;

> We avoided afterburner at low altitude as it was visible, but given the F-111's bank restriction in TFR this would expand our turn radius significantly. On one mission we crossed into China due to our high speed. You could tell you were in China due to the lack of AAA.

CHAPTER FOUR

1. These have been reported as having been handed over to the USAF as YF-111As, but GDFW records claim they were dismantled. They most closely resembled the RAAF F-111C, described in Chapter 9, Buckshots and Falcons, except that fully fledged production aircraft were to feature the more advanced Mk II system eventually evolved for the USAF F-111D. The Wilson Govt subsequently increased orders for the McDonnell F-4 Phantom II, giving the RAF a great fighter but not the attack machine it really needed, and in 1968 Britain joined up with Italy and Germany to create MRCA (Multi-Role-Combat Aircraft), the 'European mini F-111', produced as the Tornado under the Panavia consortium. Interestingly, RAF Cottesmore, which later was to become the home of the Tri-National Tornado Training Unit, was originally earmarked as both a TSR-2 and, subsequently, F-111K base.

2 67-0159 soldiered on right to the end, as a TCTO verification aircraft with the Sacramento Logistics Center (SMALC) at McClellan, California. 67-0160 was used in a 1978 rebuild programme, and A1-18, the original conversion, was placed in open storage at AMARC in the early 1970s following completion of the SRAM trials effort.

3 Including the wing sweep 'trombone', flat/slat settings, main undercarriage 'lollipop' lever, autopilot coupling panel, and engine shut-down/re-light and fire extinguishers.

4 In addition to ORIs, which examined base preparedness as a whole, crews were monitored on-base by Standardization and Evaluation ('Stan/Eval') crewmen who checked flying proficiency, and by visits by the 1st Combat Evaluation Group (CEVG), which constantly monitored aircrew Radar Bomb Scoring (RBS) performance during practice sorties over RBS Oil Burner (later *Olive Branch*) STRC sites, and ran the annual SAC 'Bomb-Nav Comp'.

5 SPN/GEANS was developed in the late 1970s for the B-52G/H fleet and later became standard equipment on the Lockheed-Martin F-117A.

6 GDFW had long been touting the F-111 as a platform for the Hughes AN/AWG-9 and Phoenix missile system, even after the demise of the mainly GAC F-111B TFX-N. These proposals included the F-111X-7 of the early 1970s, based on the F-111F but with air-to-air avionics and a 100in (2.54m) fuselage stretch for internal missiles and an extra two tons of fuel. That aircraft would have been AIM-7 Sparrow as well as Phoenix missile capable. At the time there existed a requirement for a replacement for the F-106A/B in Aerospace Defense Command service, which was increasingly passed over to TAC F-4 and, later, F-15 units as the 'Century Series' interceptors bowed out.

7 USAF 'high fliers' Brad Insley and Dick Brown flew several TAC variants. As of September 1996, the RAAF 'high fliers' included Pilot Air Commodore Pete Criss, who had logged 3,120 hrs on USAF and RAAF aircraft, and Navigator Wing Commander Al Curr who had flown 2161 hours exclusively in the F/RF-111C.

8 One such previous SAC specialist interviewed by the authors at RAF Upper Heyford reckoned that relatively unskilled Crew Chiefs could turn aircraft around with a good degree of reliability, which speaks volumes for General Dynamics' original claims regarding serviceability.

9 The 428th TFTS, 27th TFW became the 428th FTS, 27th FW after the formation of Air Combat Command in October 1991, when all 'Tactical' designators were dropped. The 'digital RTU' function refers to the role the 428th TFS would subsequently assume at Cannon as nucleus for the entire ACC F-111 combat-capable fleet collocated at the base by then.

10 See Chapter 9, *Buckshots and Falcons*, for a fuller story of the RAAF acquisition.

CHAPTER FIVE

1 Roger Peterson was able to persuade a 'well tuned' F-111A to go supersonic at low level in military power.

2 Refer to Chapter 6, *High Plains Deltas*, for a full account of F-111D systems and operations.

3 Greenham Common housed many of the 20th TFW's aircraft from 1 May to 16 August 1976 while runway resurfacing was done at Upper Heyford and a BAK-12 arresting gear installed.

4 When Upper Heyford was evacuated by the USAF in 1993 the motors for opening and closing the massive shelter doors were evacuated too, leaving them sealed like sarcophagi.

5 Upper Heyford's simulator was flown to Cannon AFB on 18 February 1993 in a C-5 Galaxy.

6 Operation *Ready Switch*, which created the equipment swap-around, is discussed in Chapter 3, *Aces*, and more fully in Chapter 7, *The Sound of Freedom*. Refer to the accompanying box for further details of F-111A and EF-111A Raven training, the latter passing to 388th ECS control in November 1981, leaving just one TFTS at Mountain Home thereafter.

7 Aborts could happen for the smallest reasons. On the occasion of the authors' visit to Upper Heyford in April 1992 an aircraft had to be shut down and abandoned in its TAB-V when a small plastic connector for the intercom fell into the recesses of the cockpit floor; the pilot was concerned that it might have fallen down his oxygen hose, and as nobody could locate the seemingly innocuous device the crew dashed across to another TAB-V and launched in the 'spare': 68-0050, which happened to be the first AMP delivery to Upper Heyford, as described elsewhere in this Chapter.

8 As described in the boxes dealing with analogue and digital navigation methodology and autopilot coupling in Chapters 3, 4 and 6. In a nutshell, completely manual override was possible, but usually pilots would just uncouple roll autopilot to follow the headings provided by the WSO, still leaving the TFR in charge of pitch inputs. This enabled 'snappier' turns to be made.

9 SMALC salvaged many critical parts from the later redundant RDT&E and pilot-production F-111A run, and GDFW's role in refurbishing these components, including WCTBs, tail drive mechanisms and even whole wings (eleven of them), was essential to F-111 availability in the 1980s and early 1990s. Plans to rebuild five salvaged A models to F-111E standards, on the heels of the F-111E 68-0082 *Phoenix* reconstruction, were shelved not only on cost grounds but also to ensure an adequate pool of key spares for the existing fleet.

CHAPTER SIX

1 The definitive F-111F mark is described in the ensuing Chapters, *The Sound of Freedom* and *Desert Pigs*. Individual F-111D airframe through-flow processing at Fort Worth was deliberately stretched further in an effort to provide a 'bridge' between F-111Fs Nos 70 and 71, where there existed a gap of some eight months, owing to political yo-yoing with the order books rather than any developmental problems at that stage. No fewer than sixty-seven F-111Ds were delivered during this time, meaning that only twenty-nine F-111Ds had been completed when seventy F-111Fs were already in service! Production of what eventually amounted to thirty-six extra F-111Fs then followed after the completion of F-111D manufacture. F-111D final assembly at this stage took about fourteen months. Items 8202 and 82 (WCTB primary, forward, centre and aft fuselage and wing structure fabrication) consumed six months, Items 81 and 89 (fuselage mating and inlet installation) plus crew module pre-mate, two months

work, and Items 80 and 30 (primary systems installation) two months more. Item 20 (final assembly) and cold proof-testing added yet another two months, followed by a like amount consumed with painting, systems check-out and flight-testing through acceptance. By contrast, F-111A/E and later F-111F production took only about nine months.

2 The 4427th TFRS was disbanded on 1 January 1976 and the training function passed to the reactivated 481st TFTS. This, in turn, was disbanded on 8 June 1980 when the 524th TFS, now a TFTS, assumed basic 'new guy' basic conversion (F-111D-OOPC/WC), transition (F-111D-TXOPC/WC) and instructor (F-111D-IOOPC/WC) training course duties. These are described in further detail later in this Chapter.

3 Raven crewmen trained under the Transition tracks at Mountain Home, which stipulated that ACs must have already completed a mission-ready tour on an attack type or were previous Raven pilots returning after a lengthy ground assignment. EWOs were usually also 'second F-111 tourists' who attended electronic warfare college and then a further 127hr academics, 30hr simulator time and 20 flying hours before shifting over for Mission Qualification training with the 390th ECS's operational cadre. Newcomers to the right-hand Raven seat became more frequent later in the 'program' and were expected to undergo complete F-111A WSO training with the 389th TFTS before undergoing specialist EWO training.

4 *Pave Tack* is described in Chapter 7 T*he Sound of Freedom* and Chapter 8 *Desert Pigs*.

5 AMP is detailed in Chapter 6 *Echoes at Upper Heyford* and *Pacer Strike* in Chapter 10 *Last of the Red-hot Porcines*.

6 *Ibidem*.

CHAPTER SEVEN

1 Col Messerli was the former F-4D 48th TFW commander. He and the Assistant DO, Col Bob Baxter, were the only two in-place staff to convert to the F-111F.

2 Analogue Aardvark 'new guy' training was similarly consolidated at Mountain Home, preparing F-111A/E aviators for the 366th and 20th TFWs. *See* Chapter 6, *High Plains Deltas*, for more details.

3 USS *America* and USS *Coral Sea*, each with an A-6E TRAM squadron, were on station in the Mediterranean and Vice-Admiral Kelso, on *America*, was effectively in charge of both USN and USAF aspects of the operation. Representatives of the 48th TFW visited the carrier to establish effective IFF procedures so that F-111Fs could safely pass through the carrier force's defensive screen. Several missions were flown in the area by *Liberty Wing* aircraft to practise communication procedures with the ships. In an emergency the carriers were the USAF fliers' only point of contact.

4 A major constraint on US action was the presence of 1,000 US personnel in Libya who could have become hostages if the USA had resorted to something stronger than diplomatic or economic pressure before they could be persuaded to leave.

5 Conducted to assert Freedom of Navigation in international waters, the operation challenged Ghadaffi's threat to destroy any US ship or aircraft which crossed a line drawn from Tripoli across to Benghazi.

The USN ships attracted several SA-5 *Gammon* missiles without damage and 'saw off' Libyan MiG-25 Foxbat-As. USN A-6Es destroyed four Libyan attack vessels which threatened the fleet and A-7Es fired AGM-88A HARMs at a number of radar sites.

[6] The arrival on Sunday 13 April of ten KC-10As at Mildenhall and Fairford, doubling the number of these tankers in the UK, increased the sense of impending action. In all, fifteen KC-10As were in place at Mildenhall by 14 April and another nine at Fairford, with around thirty KC-135s at both bases.

[7] GBU-10 was thought to be less accurate than the 500lb (225kg) GBU-12, but the extra explosive force of the 2,000lb (900kg) weapon was required for the chosen targets. Its successor, the 2,000lb (900kg) GBU-24, which became available for Operation *Desert Storm*, was much more accurate.

[8] In fact, French refusal may well have been the result of internal diplomatic confusion which appeared to rescind the tacit, informal permission for overflights which had previously been assumed.

[9] Unhelpfully, the BBC reported the Libyan claim that five F-111s had been destroyed, much to the consternation of 48th TFW families.

[10] After *El Dorado Canyon* McDonnell-Douglas made a presentation at Lakenheath to demonstrate how their F-15E with its more advanced LANTIRN targeting system could have done the mission better. As one very experienced F-111 flyer commented to the authors, 'True, the F-15E had better avionics but one major problem is that it did not have enough fuel to do the mission. High-speed capability in MIL thrust and a lot of fuel were the best qualities of the F-111F. Next was its all-weather capability'.

CHAPTER EIGHT

[1] The US Navy gave up on shelter attacks early in the war when its AGM-62 Walleye II ER/DL EOGBs merely bounced off the HAS structures.

[2] Gen Colin Powell eventually curtailed bridge attacks because of their predominant effect on civil rather than military activity.

[3] F-111s had shown their tank-killing potential on an earlier occasion too. Brad Insley:

> The crews knew what the airplanes could do and how to do it but the planners had to be convinced. For a few years in the 1970s the NATO commanders had us in a secondary Close Air Support role as a result of an air power demonstration. The weather was bad and only the F-111 could drop bombs. The target was a tank and the F-111 was dropping a BDU-33 from medium altitude through an overcast. The bomb went through the open turret of the tank and gave Army commanders the idea that by carrying 24 bombs we could kill 24 tanks per sortie. Luckily, reason prevailed and we were fragged for low-level attacks against airfields, SAM sites and storage facilities in the 1980s.

CHAPTER NINE

[1] The requirement for additional aircraft to offset attrition, and to provide up to six aircraft for upgrade with a reconnaissance package, was recognized in the early 1960s. Provision was made in the 1963 Townley/McNamara Memorandum Of Understanding for the purchase of attrition aircraft. This option was also included in the 1970 Fraser/Laird Agreement, but was not exploited during the F-111 production run which ended with the F-111F in September 1976.

[2] No. 3 Aircraft Depot and No. 482 (Maintenance) Squadron were combined into No. 501 Wing in December 1991.

[3] Ten *Pave Tack* pods were purchased originally. Five more were acquired in 1991/92 from USAF-surplus ex-F-4E stock.

[4] With AUP 'just around the corner' the RAAF decided instead to opt for the Rafael/Martin Marietta AGM-142 Popeye, rocket-powered electro-optically-guided missile. This works in a similar manner to the AGM-130. The requirement was established under Project Air 5398 proposals, which have since been approved.

[5] In the 1980s a No. 1 Sqn F-111C conducted ground trials with the complementary USN radar-homing AGM-88 high-speed HARM missile. Test firings were conducted from A8-132 at Woomera Range, but the weapon was not purchased. A project to provide some kind of ARM (Anti-Radiation Missile) capability has been approved, with an IOC of 2001.

[6] An MTBF of approx 1 hr is specified for the F-111 Avionics Update equipment, and doubtless this will be exceeded by a wide margin!

[7] The Project Manager for the F-111 Simulator Project (Air 5208) was Sqn Ldr Geoff Northam. Members of the first AUP F-111C conversion course were at the Wormald Plant in Dee Why in August 1996, using the new AUP simulator.

[8] This added up to US$55m for the aircraft and a like amount for the spares. The deal was negotiated in November 1992 with the USAF by an Australian Defence Team led by Air Commodore Errol McCormack, and included the F-111G Project Manager, Sqn Ldr Kym Osley.

[9] 'Buddy bombing' (i.e. one dropping LGBs and another designating the target) with lasers is actually an extremely complex task by night but is possible, as is target designation by special forces on the ground.

[10] Harpoon capability will be available after the aircraft undergo AUP updates. At the time of writing, the RF-111Cs were reassigned to No. 1 Sqn, which currently is acting as the 'analogue F-111' unit while No. 6 Sqn operates a mix of F-111Gs and newly updated AUP F-111Cs. No. 1 Sqn will then follow suit in 1997–98, with the RF-111Cs being some of the last in line for the modifications, this permitting possible incorporation of updated or brand new sensors.

CHAPTER TEN

[1] On 2 October 1991 the designation TFW was changed to FW as part of the USAF's Command reorganization, as noted earlier.

[2] Upper Heyford's first AMARC inmate was F-111E 68-0009 which left on 8 May 1992.

[3] Refer to Chapter 5, *Echoes from Upper Heyford*, for a full account of the final farewell there.

[4] After an initial belief that the 20th TFW nameplate might pass to Spangdahlem AB, part of USAFE's 17th Air Force in Germany, it was finally reallocated to Shaw AFB's F-16 force in South Carolina.

[5] In November 1996 Lockheed-Martin and Boeing were announced as the two 'finalists' in the JSF design competition, and are building two prototypes each. Interestingly, the USAF had refused to host the 'Last Hurrah' at Nellis or Cannon and LMTAS said: 'Come on down'. It gave a select few the opportunity to review LMTAS progress on JSF work at the same time. Their design received a '9/10' score from the Source Selection Board, with Boeing's arguably more revolutionary design '7/10' – though many are placing their money on Boeing's prototypes eventually winning. Could it be the TFX situation in reverse?

Index

aircraft, by type:
   A2F-1 Intruder *see* A-6
   A-3 Skywarrior 32
   A-4 Skyhawk 143
   A-5 Vigilante 19, 141
   A-6 Intruder 19, 27, 118, 186
   A-7 Corsair 2 13, 22, 53, 120, 188
   AC-130 Spectre 88
   AT-33 45
   B-1A 70–1, 73
   B-1B Lancer 73–4
   B-29 Superfortress 66
   B-2A Spirit 72
   B-47 Stratojet 76, 142
   B-52 Stratofortress 53–5, 57, 61, 65, 67–8, 71, 86, 125, 186
   B-58A Hustler 19, 57, 61, 186
   C-130 Hercules 88, 92, 137, 152
   C-141 Starlifter 45, 136, 145
   Canberra, BAC 141, 143
   E-2 Hawkeye 27, 30
   E-4 NEACP 64
   EA-6B Prowler 9, 158–9
   EB-66 Destroyer 54, 86
   EC-130 Compass Call 88, 92, 137,
   EC-135 Looking Glass 64
   F3D Skyknight 27
   F-4 Phantom 2 13–14, 16, 22, 32, 36, 47, 53, 79, 92, 100, 105, 113–14, 127, 129, 137, 140–1, 143, 186–8
   F-14 Tomcat 22, 27, 30, 34, 91
   F-15 Eagle 125, 129–30, 134, 136, 153, 158, 186
   F-16 Fighting Falcon 12, 85, 94, 132, 137, 145, 154, 156, 158, 188
   F-22 Raptor 156
   F-86 Sabre 38
   F-89 Scorpion 110
   F-100 Super Sabre 75–6, 96, 111, 112
   F-101 Voodoo 110, 116
   F-102 Delta Dagger 27
   F-105 Thunderchief 13, 38, 40, 54, 96, 186–7
   F-106 Delta Dart 25, 27, 187
   F-110 Phantom 2 *see* F-4 Phantom
   F-111 Aardvark variants:
      EF-111A Raven 12, 23, 37, 85–9, 92–4, 102, 108, 120–1, 125, 129, 137, 140, 158–62, 165–7, 183–5, 187
      F-111A 9, 15–19, 22–6, 35–60, 64, 73, 75–9, 86–8, 91–4, 96, 98, 102–3, 106, 111, 113, 115, 141–3, 148, 159–69, 172–3, 183–7
      F-111B 23, 27–35, 171–2, 186–7
      F-111C 12, 23, 36–7, 41, 50–1, 59–61, 65, 126, 141–52, 159, 162–3, 169, 172, 186–8
      F-111D 17, 23, 37, 41, 57–61, 71–3, 75, 83, 86, 95–112, 115, 125–6, 130, 153–4, 160–3, 173–5, 183–7
      F-111E 23, 36, 41, 50–1, 58–61, 66–7, 73–94, 96–7, 102, 106, 109–11, 118, 125, 137–40, 153–5, 159–63, 175–8, 183–8
      F-111F 9, 12, 23, 36, 41, 50, 58–61, 64, 67, 73, 77, 79, 84, 86, 88, 92–3, 95–6, 100–3, 105, 106–7, 109–40, 143, 145–6, 153–63, 179–88
      F-111G 37, 54, 74, 108, 148–9, 152–4, 169–71, 173, 183, 188
      F-111K 57, 95, 163, 172, 186
      F-111X-7 187
      FB-111A 23, 36–7, 50, 57–74, 87, 91, 95, 97, 99, 109–10, 142, 148, 159–63, 169–71, 185–8
      FB-111B 69–72
      FB-111C 69–72
      FB-111H 69–72
      RF-111A 24, 26, 142–3, 149
      RF-111B 149
      RF-111C 41, 65, 149–52, 162, 172, 187–8
      RF-111D 94, 96, 149
      YF-111A *see* F-111A
      YF-111K *see* F-111K
   F-117A Nighthawk 72, 79, 88, 125, 127, 131–2, 186
   F/A-18 Hornet 120, 145–6
   Heyford, Handley Page 76
   HH-2 Huskie 43
   HH-3 Jolly Green Giant 40
   KC-10 Extender 63, 101, 118–20, 188
   KC-97 Stratocruiser 113
   KC-135 Stratotanker 42, 44, 47, 53–4, 65, 120, 129, 188
   MiG-21 Fishbed 55, 120
   MiG-25 Foxbat 120, 188
   MiG-29 Fulcrum 129–30, 154
   Mosquito, de Havilland 104
   O-1 Birddog 40
   O-2 Skymaster 40
   P-3 Orion 146
   P-51 Mustang 76
   P-61 Black Widow 104
   P1101, Messerschmitt 13
   RA-5C Vigilante 32
   SR-71 Blackbird 27, 122, 148
   Strikemaster, BAC 145
   Tornado, Panavia 33, 84, 145, 186
   TSR-2, BAC 19, 141–2, 186
   Tu-22 Backfire 71
   W2F-1 Hawkeye *see* E-2 Hawkeye
   X-5, Bell 13
   XF10F-1, Grumman 13
   YF-12 Blackbird 186
aircraft safety, compared 186
Alley, Ken M. 55
Anthony, Jim 44
Armstrong, Mac 39, 44
Arnet, Charlie 39, 44
Atkins, Frank 148
avionics:
   Bomb-navigation System:
      MkI 50–1, 77–8, 91, 160
      MkII 95–9, 103–5, 107, 160
      MkIIB 57, 62, 64, 110–11, 127, 160

avionics *cont.*
  countermeasures 25, 37–8, 48, 51–2, 55, 67–8, 75, 86–7, 90, 152, 162, 164, 172
  data-links:
    aircraft-guiding 30–1
    munitions-guiding 130, 134–5
  dual bombing timer 77, 89
  electro-optics:
    IR search and track 29
    Pave Tack 100, 107, 116, 119, 122–3, 126, 128, 130–1, 145–7, 172, 179–82, 188
  head-up displays 30, 32–3, 36–7, 41, 51, 77, 100, 104, 109, 118
  navigation systems 50–1, 64–5, 68, 98, 100, 127, 160–1
  reconnaissance sensors 149–52
  updates:
    AMP 12, 73, 91, 108, 169, 171, 177
    AUP 12, 148, 162, 188
    Pacer Strike 107–8, 148, 157–8
    Raven SIP 158
  see also radars

Balph, Bob 54
Barnes, Tom 79, 112–13, 116
Barrett, Mike 173
barrier arrestment 33, 55, 187
Bartholemew, Gabriel 36
Basudev, Dev 158
Baughn, Richard 76, 78
Baxter, Bob 114, 187
Beck, Roger A. 177
Bernard, Lance 143
Bikker, David 94
Blesse, Fred 'Boots' 44–5
bombs:
  cluster 46, 52–3, 71, 106–7, 127, 130, 135, 139
  general purpose 18, 40, 44, 46, 48, 52, 56, 71, 78, 89, 106, 115, 120–2, 124, 131, 138–9
  nuclear 19, 67, 77–8, 89, 170
  practice 67, 73, 78–9, 106, 110, 113, 115, 170, 173, 188
  precision-guided:
    imaging 125, 128–9, 131, 134–5, 139, 146, 188
    laser-guided 52, 90, 115–16, 119–23, 125–32, 136, 139–40, 146, 154, 181, 188

rocket-boosted 89, 134
see also missiles
Bradt, D.L. 88
Brandon, Brent 88
Brooks, Roger 88
Brown, Craig 'Quizmo' 108, 136
Brown, Dick 'Downtown' 9–10, 20, 36, 51, 84–5, 97–100, 102–3, 105, 107, 111, 116, 187
Brown, Harold 14
Brown, Henry W. 164
Brumby, Jerry 114
Bush, Bill 33
Bush, George 125
Byland, Anthony 171

Cafarelli 54
Caldwell, Thomas R. 126
camouflage 36, 74, 186
Carter, Jimmy 70–1
Casteel, Larry 92
Chalk, Marty 149
Chamberlain, James 20, 110–11, 114
Chance, Mark 129–30
Chapman, Greg 133
Cheney, Richard B. 73
Coker, Charlie 36–7
Coltman, William C. 39, 44, 47–9
Combs, Ken 131, 137
Cook, David 29
Cooley, Spade 38–9, 165
Coombe, Jeff 88, 166
Criss, Pete 186
Curr, Al 187

Daley, William 94
Daughtry, John 'Bear' 132
Davis, George 35
de Jong, Fred 44
Delahunty, Terry 142, 145,
Denton, James 88
Deptula, David A. 125
Dethman, Ivan 13, 35, 38
Dodd, Lee 36, 45–9, 52, 54
Donahue, Harold M. 62
Donnell, Ralph 'Dixie' 27–9
Dorsett, Thomas G. 176
Downer, Lee A. 156

Eichenlaub, P.R. 88
Eisenhower, Dwight D. 13

Ertler, Dennis R. 128
escape module 14, 17, 40, 164, 171–2, 180
Evans, Don 32
Everest, Frank 14
exercises and deployments:
  ADEX 145
  Amalgam Warrior 113
  Bold Eagle – Surge Delta 100
  Bright Star 101–2
  Brim Frost 101
  Central Enterprise 154, 156
  Cope Thunder 145
  Coral Sea 145
  Coronet Archer 101
  Coronet Beacon 100
  Coronet Comanche 101
  Coronet Diamond 101
  Coronet Falcon 113
  Coronet Hammer 97, 101
  Coronet Kingfisher 100
  Coronet Papago 88
  Coronet Patriot 113
  D-Day Anniversary, 50th 151
  Display Determination 88
  Excalibur 85, 154
  Giant Voice 70, 78, 100, 112, 145, 168, 170, 180
  Green Flag 70, 88, 115, 153
  Gunsmoke 153
  Joint Task Force 154
  Jubilee Review 144
  Kangaroo 145
  Mallet Blow 85
  Maple Flag 101
  Midlink 85
  Night Camel 135
  Northern Wedding 100
  Pitch Black 145, 149
  Proud Shield 68–70, 99, 172
  RAM 149, 152
  Red Flag 70, 84–5, 88, 115, 145, 153–4, 170, 180
  Reforger 85, 156
  Salty Hammer 85, 154, 156
  Salty Nation 119
  TAM 176
  Team Spirit 100
  Tiger Meets 70, 85
  TRIAD 172
  Western Reward 145
  see also operations, ranges

INDEX

Fairbairn, David 142
Fairhall, Alan 143
Ferrero, Jim 27
Fetter, Jerry 54
Fierman, Paul 44
Fighter Weapons School 56, 106–8
Fitzgerald, G. 148
Foster, Chuck 44
Foster, J.S. 26
Francis, C.E. 96
Fraser, Malcom 143, 188
Funnell, Ray 143
Furber, Noel 152

Gawelko, Jack 45
Genevish, David 88, 166
Germscheid, Tom 38, 40, 43–4, 97
Ghadaffi, M. 118, 120–1, 187
Gibson, Keith 156
Giraudo, John C. 38
Glosson, 'Buster' 126–7, 131, 135
Graham, Al 52, 167
Graham, Dennis 13, 39–40, 43, 165
Gun, M61A-1 Vulcan 25, 30, 40–2, 46, 54

Haincock, Dain 156
Hancock, Valston 142
Hansen, Robin 186
Himes, Tom 137
Hockridge, James 52, 167
Hodges, Joseph W. 40, 44, 165
Holder, Ken 94
Holland, Les 39, 44
Horner, Chuck 130
Hubbard, Jay 186
Hussein, Saddam 126, 129, 136–7
Hust, Jerry 137

Insley, Lewis 'Brad' 20, 37, 49, 53–5, 77, 79, 82, 85, 94, 103, 105, 154, 187–8

Johnson, C. 'Kelly' 186
Johnson, Richard L. 22–3, 143
Johnson, Tom 'T J' 69–70 see also colour section
Jordan, Joe B. 164
Jordan, Jon 48, 55

Keene, Joe 39, 44
Keisel, Jim 111

Kelman, George 79, 82–4, 105
Kelso 187
Kemble, Andy 149
Kennedy, John F. 13
Kissinger, Henry 46
Kodak, Doug 49, 54
Koerner, Michael J. 156
Kroos, Bob 177

Laing, Don 45
Laird, Melvyn 57, 188
Lange, Allen 27
Larson, Gale W. 157
Law, Kenneth S. 56
Lehman, John F. 22, 124
Lennon, Thomas J. 123, 128–9, 135–6, 140
Leo, Kevin 149
Lindh, Jerry 177
Livesay, Meade 27
Lorence, Paul F. 121, 179
Lowery, Dudley 'Squid' 84
Lynch, Jack 149

McCance, Doon 35
McCann, Hank 39–40, 43, 165
McCausland, Mark 74
McClellan, John L. 35, 186–7
McConnell, Robert P. 55
McCormack, Errol 149, 188
McGovern, James 129
McGuire, David 177
McIlvane 55
McKelvey, Mike 129–30
McNamara, Robert S. 13–15, 27, 31, 57–8, 76, 156, 186
maintenance 45, 72–3, 87, 91–4, 99, 112, 125, 145–6, 148, 158, 188
Malandrino, J. Paul 74
Mark, Hans 72–3
Marquardt, A. 'Sandy' 39–40, 44, 165
Martin, Eugene 47, 53
Massengill, Clifford B. 176
Mathiasen, Roger J. 35–36, 44–6, 49, 52
Matteis, Richard 13, 36, 38–40, 44, 51, 73, 87
Maul, Paul W. 66
Mead, Bobby J. 35–6
Meadows, N. 'Tiger' 141, 148
Messerli, Robert 114
Miller, Bill 29

missiles:
  air-to-air:
    AAM-N-10 Eagle 13
    AIM-7 Sparrow III 13, 30, 104–5, 187
    AIM-9 Sidewinder 25, 30, 41, 105, 127, 129, 139, 146
    AIM-54 Phoenix 18, 25, 29–30, 33–4, 71, 171, 187
    AIM-120 AMRAAM 105
  air-to-surface:
    AGM-84 Harpoon 144, 146
    AGM-88 HARM 120, 132, 147, 188
    AGM-130 134, 188 see also bombs, imaging
    AGM-142 Popeye 188
  nuclear missiles:
    AGM-69 SRAM 58, 62, 64, 67–8, 74
    AGM-86B 'cruise' 72
Moore, Winston E. 61
Morris, Cam 148
Morrissey 55
Murph, Ben 40, 43–4

Nash, John M. 43
Nelson, William R. 46
Newham, Jake 143, 172
Nitz, Paul H. 27
Nixon, Richard M. 45, 53, 57
Nolte, Patrick 94
Norris, John 29, 31–2
Northam, Geoff 188
Nunemaker, Roger 44
Nuss, Michael 'Pickle' 94

Oldermann, Wade 40
operations:
  Cape Train 113
  Combat Bull's-eye 35
  Combat Lancer 36–40, 43–4, 47, 143, 165
  Combat Trident 35
  Constant Guard V 45–9, 52–6, 167–9
  Creek Swing 115
  Deep Throat 129, 136–7
  Deliberate Force 158
  Desert Shield 84, 108, 125–8, 157, 165–7, 181
  Desert Storm 108, 125–40, 153–4, 165–7, 176–9, 182

191

operations cont.
   El Diablo 88, 120–1, 165–7, 179
   El Dorado Canyon 9, 20, 84, 88,
      118–25, 167, 179, 182
   Ghost Rider 118
   Harvest Reaper 19, 36–8, 165
   Instant Thunder 125
   Linebacker II 53–5, 167–9
   Mayaguez incident 56
   Prairie Fire 118
   Prime Pump 118
   Proven Force 88, 137–40, 153, 165–6,
      176–8
   Provide Comfort 88, 140, 153, 158
   Ready Switch 113–15
   Run Fast 88
   Southern Watch 88
   Vigilant 154
   see also exercises and deployments
Osley, Kym 'Koz' 141, 149, 152, 188
Owen, Richard 173
Owen, Trevor 172–3

Palmgren, Edrin D. 39, 165
Peacock 56
Peck, Ken 140
Perry, Glenn 55
Peterson, Roger E. 36–7, 47–9, 52–6, 186
Phillips, John D. 35
Pickering, Tom 88
Plantikow, John 72–3
Pollock, Neal 43
Powell, Colin 188
Powell, Ken 44
powerplant:
   inlets 22–3, 32, 34, 63, 160
   TF30 turbofans 14–15, 22–3, 32, 34,
      63, 72, 82, 87, 91, 96, 109, 111–12,
      125, 142, 148–9, 160, 171–2, 175–6
Prahl, Val 22, 58
production 14, 19, 33, 57–61, 70–1, 76,
   86–7, 96, 143, 163–81, 187

Quayle, Dan 132

radars:
   air-to-air:
      APQ-130 103–5
      AWG-9 27, 30–1, 34, 186

attack radar sets 19, 49–51, 98, 103–5,
   148, 161
   terrain-following 19–21, 36–7, 48–9,
      54–5, 83–4, 98, 109–10, 120, 148,
      161, 187
ranges:
   CPMs 78–9
   IR/VR routes 69–70
   range terminology 102
   WTDs 84–5, 115
   see also exercises and deployments
Ramsey, Brian 94
Ray, Robert 148
Reagan, Ronald 73
Reed, Charles W. 38
Reid, Frederick A. 126, 157
Reynolds, Douglas 32
Ribas-Dominicci, Fernando 121, 179
Rice, Norm 44
Roberts, Kent 35
Rogers, David 141, 152
Ross, Chris 83
Rossi, Frank 94, 154, 156, 158
Rossman, Ed 23
Rotramel, James E. 51, 84, 99–100, 107,
   116, 127, 158
Runge, Tom G. 96
Russell, Mike 135

Salmeier, Dean E. 38, 44
Samson, Sammy 135
Schemmer, Ben 26
Schmidt, Randall M. 94
Schul, Brian 122
Schuppe, Kenneth A. 43
Schwartzkopf, Norman 126, 135
Shaud, John A. 128
Siepel, Bradley A. 135
Simpson, Terry 77–8, 91, 125, 137–40,
   154
Sinclair, Mike 148, 152
Skakal, David 84
Skeels, Dick 55
Skidmore, Mark 145
Slaton, James F. 132
Smith, Grant A. 76, 78
Sobol, Tony 52–3
Soule, Bill 39, 44
Sponeybarger, Bob 49, 54, 167

Stack, John 13–14
Stafford 54
Stanfill, Ron 125
Stevens, Greg 138–9
structural issues 15, 25, 29, 31, 33, 43–5,
   66, 71–3, 87, 92–4, 143, 146, 148
Sweeney, Mike 138

Tate, Grover 'Ted' 31–2
Thatcher, Margaret 118
Theurer, Ken 135
Tibbetts, Paul 66
Tietge, J.W. 115
torching fuel 53, 144, 186
Tosten, Chuck 44
Townley, Athol 142, 188
Troster, Glenn 173

Van Driel, Charles 43
Van Etten, Chester 38
Veseley, David 88–9
Von Der Heyden, Ralph 27–8
Voorhies, Fred 35

Walker, Rick 135
Wallis, Barnes 188
Ward, Dick 55, 168
Ward, Will 129
Warden, John A. 125, 129
Warren, Barton 171
Watson, Walter 122
Wendrock, Robert F. 49
Wheeler, Tom 35
White, Dave 137
Williams, Steve 135–6, 140
Wilmott, Paul 156
Wilson, Harold 186
Wilson, William F. 54, 167
windshields 89–90, 148, 168, 172
Worth, James N. 88
Wright, Jim 71

Yanni, Tom 107
Young, Matt 133

Zaletel, Jeff 140
Zeitz, Fred 67, 82
Zeugel, Keith 128